LITERA

THE SO

1917–1934

STUDIES OF THE HARRIMAN INSTITUTE

COLUMBIA UNIVERSITY

Founded as the Russian Institute in 1946, the W. Averell Harriman Institute for Advanced Study of the Soviet Union is the oldest research institution of its kind in the United States. The book series *Studies of the Harriman Institute,* begun in 1953, helps bring to a wider audience some of the work conducted under its auspices by professors, degree candidates, and visiting fellows. The faculty of the Institute, without necessarily agreeing with the conclusions reached in these books, believes their publication will contribute to both scholarship and a greater public understanding of the Soviet Union.

LITERARY POLITICS IN

THE SOVIET UKRAINE

1917–1934

Revised and updated edition

GEORGE S. N. LUCKYJ

Duke University Press   Durham and London
1990

Library of Congress Cataloging-in-Publication Data
Luckyj, George Stephen Nestor, 1919–
Literary politics in the Soviet Ukraine, 1917–1934/by George S. N.
Luckyj.—Rev. and updated ed.
Originally published without preface, reappraisal, bibliographical
note, and supplementary index by Columbia University Press,
New York, 1956.
(Studies of the Harriman Institute)
Includes bibliographical references and index.
ISBN 0–8223–1081–3. — ISBN 0–8223–1099–6 (pbk.)
1. Ukrainian literature—20th century—History and criticism.
2. Politics and literature—Ukraine.   3. Ukraine—Politics and
government—1917–   I. Title.   II. Series.
PG3916.2.L8   1990
891.7′909003—DC20   90–3499   CIP

CONTENTS

NOTE ON TRANSLITERATION

The following table shows
the transliteration system for Ukrainian used in this study:

а	a	з	z	о	o	ч	ch
б	b	и	y	п	p	ш	sh
в	v	і	i	р	r	щ	shch
г	h	ї	ï	с	s	ь	'
г	g	й	i	т	t	ю	iu
д	d	к	k	у	u	я	ia
е	e	л	l	ф	f		
є	ie	м	m	х	kh		
ж	zh	н	n	ц	ts		

Ukrainian place names have been given the forms most familiar to English
readers, while their original spelling has been recorded in parentheses
on first mention in the text.
Given names have retained their Ukrainian forms.

PREFACE

This book was first published in 1956 as a volume in the Studies of the Russian Institute series. Columbia University Press advertised its publication as "the first study in English of the fate of a national, non-Russian literature within the Soviet Union." It was, indeed, a pioneering work in Ukrainian studies which at that time occupied an insignificant place at American universities. Even the multinational Soviet Union was then perceived in the popular mind as only Russian. Writing on a Ukrainian topic, I was in the minority among students, but I was fortunate to have the strong encouragement of my professors, the late Ernest Simmons, Philip Mosely, and Clarence Manning. They were on the Ph.D. dissertation committee for my thesis out of which the book eventually developed. In my dissertation I was naturally concerned with providing strong documentation for my statements, and this was sometimes difficult since my topic dealt partly with the imposition of Communist Party controls on literature. I was extremely fortunate, therefore, that the Liubchenko Papers, the personal archive of a Soviet Ukrainian writer, fell into my hands just before publication of the book. I was able to use the archive and corroborate my text with new, unpublished evidence. What began as an investigation of literary politics led me, during the course of the study, to the realization that there had been wholesale liquidation of literary groups and organizations and purges of dozens of prominent writers. The story of what had been a flowering literature in the 1920s ended in tragedy by the time the First Congress of Soviet Writers convened in 1934.

The book was well received in North America and England. Writing in the *American Slavic and East European Review,* Peter Yershov commented:

This excellently documented and reasoned book sets forth thoroughly the tragic fate of Ukrainian literature, squeezed and bled by the Soviet regime. In making use of publications rarely to be found these days (especially outside the Soviet Union) and also of still unpublished material from the collection of the Ukrainian writer Arkadij Ljubchenko who wrote under Soviet domination but fled to the West and died in 1945 (his diary, correspondence with literary personages, copies of the minutes, resolutions and documents of the literary circle *Vaplite*, etc.) the author has given special attention to the stormy Renaissance of Ukrainian culture during the period 1917–1930.[1]

Victor Swoboda, who called the book "extremely well documented," wrote in the London *Slavonic and East European Review:*

Luckyj in his study does not agree with those who ignore Soviet Ukrainian literature as a mere product of the Soviet regime, but he equally disagrees with the current Soviet condemnation of that literature of the years 1917–34 as dangerous opposition to the Soviet regime. While admitting only the partial correctness of both interpretations, he diverges from them, and corroborates his conclusions by an extremely conscientious, scholarly and objective analysis of available facts.[2]

George Shevelov, writing in *Canadian Slavonic Papers,* called the book "an important contribution to the understanding of an almost unknown aspect of Soviet reality":

It offers a most scrupulous scrutiny, based on primary sources, of the evolution of Communist policy towards Ukrainian literature during the first decades after the revolution. The problems discussed are of paramount importance, first of all, for the understanding of cultural processes in the USSR, and secondly, for a better comprehension of what is now happening in the satellite states.[3]

To be sure, these and other reviews were not without some strictures (in particular Shevelov's criticism of chapter II), but on the whole the book's reception in the West was very positive.

A very different response came from the East. The book met with wholesale condemnation by Soviet scholarly journals. The first broadside came from the prestigious Russian *Voprosy literatury* (Problems of Literature), only to be followed by Ukrainian voices. In an article entitled "Under the Mask of Science" T. Tri-

---

1 *American Slavic and East European Review,* XVI (1957), p. 414.
2 *The Slavonic and East European Review,* XXXV (1956–57), pp. 326–29.
3 *Canadian Slavonic Papers,* I (1956), p. 102.

fonova wrote that my claims of Party control over literature were untrue, because literary organizations which were disbanded

died out and became a thing of the past through the will of history, that they ended their existence as a result of the elimination of classes in our country; as a result of the struggle and victories of Marxist-Leninist thought and of Soviet literature vanquishing the survivals of bourgeois ideology—individualism and decadence, formalism and vulgar sociologism, cosmopolitanism and bourgeois nationalism and as a result of mass conversion of the intelligentsia to the position of socialism and the Soviet state.[4]

Apart from the Marxist verbiage and the clear suspicion that my book, financed by a grant from the Rockefeller Foundation, was an instrument of American propaganda "put forward by Dulles and other ideologists of imperialism aimed at undermining the unity of the socialist camp,"[5] the review made only one reference to the purges of writers. "As for violations of socialist legality," it said, "that took place in the past, every unprejudiced person knows that the Soviet government and the Communist Party resolutely condemn them. . . ."[6]

The first Ukrainian response to my book came in 1958 from the Academician Oleksander Bilets'kyi. In several pages of his article he dealt with it, at first in a jocular tone, perhaps wanting to draw the attention of the Soviet reader to the book's existence. Then he claimed that

the fundamental purpose of the book is to uncover the incipient "conflict" between nationalist and communist views of Ukrainian culture and to show how the "centralist" desires of Moscow have, as it were, smothered the growth of the "Ukrainian literary renaissance of the 1920s and early 1930s." It should be pointed out that having concentrated on the external history of literary organizations, the author does not raise questions about the true artistic value of the literary production of those years, avoiding any analysis of literary phenomena, and only touching on this problem in the abstract in the concluding chapter of the book. His task is different—it is to slander the Soviet government and Soviet Ukrainian culture.[7]

---

4 T. Trifonova, "Pod maskoi nauki," *Voprosy literatury,* October 1957; here quoted from *The Current Digest of the Soviet Press,* X, 5 (1957), p. 40.

5 *Voprosy literatury,* October 1957, p. 252.

6 *Ibid.,* p. 254.

7 O. Bilets'kyi, "Zavdannia ta perspektyvy rozvytku ukrains'koho literaturoznavstva, *Zibrannia prats' u piaty tomakh,* III (Kiev, 1966), 76.

Another prominent Soviet Ukrainian literary critic, Leonid Novychenko, chastised the book, but admitted that "as everybody knows, violations of socialist legality have been condemned, their results corrected and everything has been done to prevent anything like that ever happening again."[8]

Today we can say that at the time Bilets'kyi and Novychenko were writing, not all "violations of socialist legality" were condemned and that the rehabilitation of writers started during the so-called "Khrushchevian thaw" was very selective. The era of the 1950s brought with it a new look at the literature of the 1920s and 1930s, and much was done to bring to light historic facts and to republish the works of writers whose disappearance I had made clear in my book. Yet the whole process of rehabilitation of what one émigré critic called a "Garrotted Renaissance" (*rozstriliane vidrodzhennia*) consisted of half-measures. Euphemisms were often used to describe the fate of purged writers ("they were forced to leave the ranks," "became victims of the cult of personality"). The republished works of Mykola Kulish, Hryhorii Kosynka, Dmytro Zahul, Mykola Zerov, and others were incomplete, with tendentious introductions. There was no wide discussion in any journal of the events of the 1930s, and one felt that rehabilitation was being conducted grudgingly.

In the 1960s and early in the 1970s two new waves of repression occurred, this time against dissident writers (Dziuba, Kalynets, Svitlychnyi, Chornovil, Sverstiuk, Osadchyi, Stus) which contradicted the earlier promises not to repeat "violations of socialist legality." The regime of Brezhnev and Suslov, nowadays labeled a period of "stagnation," was cruel and repressive. Such attempts as were made to rehabilitate and reassess the writers of the 1920s and 1930s were incomplete.

In the West, interest in that early period continued. My *Literary Politics* was republished in 1971 and was soon sold out. Several émigré scholars (Kostiuk, Kravtsiv) concentrated on compiling lists of writers who had perished in the 1930s. The list I had compiled in 1956 grew much longer. Evidence for the disappearance of writers was gathered not only on the basis of a sudden break in their publications, but also from accounts of their friends and relatives

---

[8] L. Novychenko, "Na pozvakh z istynoiu," *Vitchyzna*, No. 12, 1959, p. 184.

who had survived. I myself returned to this topic in the publication, in 1987, of *Keeping a Record: Literary Purges in Soviet Ukraine (1930s), A Biobibliography*. Using all the sources available in the West (including the Soviet publications) I came to the conclusion that 254 writers, literary scholars, and critics had been victims of the purges and that only very few survived in the GULAG up to 1956, when they were released and rehabilitated. The iron sweep of Party controls was much greater than I had thought in 1956.

A totally new development in the Soviet Ukraine took place late in 1987 and early 1988. It was a result of the new policy of glasnost proclaimed by Mikhail Gorbachev. An important part of this policy stipulated that "no blank pages be left in Soviet history." This was a signal for Ukrainians to take a closer look at the literary purges of the 1930s. Almost overnight there was a real explosion of articles demanding the truth that festered in the national conscience about the events of the '20s and '30s. The rhetoric of this outcry was heightened when it was openly declared that these literary purges represented Stalin's crimes against the Ukrainian intelligentsia and that there was a connection between these tragic events and the manmade famine in the Ukraine in 1932–33 in which millions of peasants died. Demands were made for a total rehabilitation of the writers, for the complete republication of their works, and for a new, objective history of Soviet Ukrainian literature. Above all, the events of the 1920s and 1930s became a major item on a long list of grievances which the Ukrainians held against the past communist rulers of their country.

This campaign, unprecedented in its frankness and force, was led by Ukrainian writers, members of the Writers' Union. Demands for the instant rehabilitation of the writers were repeatedly made in nearly every journal. They primarily wanted to read the works of the charismatic leader of VAPLITE, Mykola Khvyl'ovyi, who protested against Moscow's policy by shooting himself in 1933. Some of his stories were indeed republished. Another prose writer, hitherto banned, was Valeriian Pidmohyl'nyi, whose novel *Misto (The City)* and short stories were republished in 1989. Gradually, much of the buried literature was restored. A special commission was set up to investigate further the purges of the 1930s. Finally, in September 1989 a National Movement in the Ukraine for Reconstruction, known as *Rukh,* was formed and the restoration of the cultural heritage of the 1920s made part of its program.

All these events in the Ukraine make *Literary Politics* a very topical book. Its main argument remains valid after more than thirty years. In a conversation with the author in 1989, Mykola Zhulyns'kyi, the deputy director of the Shevchenko Institute of Literature of the Ukrainian Academy of Sciences expressed interest in a Ukrainian translation of the book since he believed it had much to tell the Soviet reader. To be sure, in order to make the book more relevant to today's situation, a further chapter (a reappraisal) has been necessary. It sets out the most important developments with regard to the 1917–34 period that have occurred since 1956. It provides material for a study of the latest responses to the traumatic events of the 1930s and of the methods used today to reconquer the past. At the end of the book I wrote:

In their attempt to emancipate themselves as individual artists and to become the bearers of a nascent national literature, the Soviet Ukrainian writers were inspired by their revolutionary national credo, their own brand of Marxism, and their own vision of man. They were halted by the rising demands of the Party to conform to the Soviet cultural policy. Only the future will show whether their failure has had a lasting effect on Ukrainian literature (p. 243).

Today we know the future. The "lasting effect" on literature and culture is evident to all. Yet today, as in 1934, a word of caution is necessary in the total assessment of this story. As I write these words the irreversibility of glasnost seems clear. In the Ukraine it would not be out of place to compare Mykola Khvyl'ovyi and the VAPLITE, to whom I devoted so much space in 1956, to the modern Ukrainian writers who are fighting for similar national and cultural goals. Yet it is, indeed, a continuing struggle. Is it too much to hope that this time it may not end in failure?

One can say, at the present moment, that the consequences of the most recent reappraisal of the literature of the '20s and '30s are indeed far-reaching. The desire to know the truth has pushed the literary establishment to make constant concessions. No name of a writer, not even that of Hryhorii Chuprynka, who was shot as a counterrevolutionary in 1921, may be kept in the dark any longer. Every month new publications bring to light banned works. This wholesale vindication of the past has had a profound effect on the youngest generation of Ukrainian writers. Their poems, in particular, carry echoes of the earlier lyrical harvest. In aesthetics, too, a new type of thinking is clearly evident. Literary criticism is being liberated from the Marxian cliché and a real effort is being undertaken to acquaint the reader with émigré Ukrainian writers (Ievhen Malaniuk, Iurii Klen, Olena Teliha) who had previously been cast out as "nationalists." There is a new excitement in literary circles; one by one, old prejudices from the Brezhnev era are being exploded. This is a time of genuine renewal.

Some material in the postscript has been taken from some of my other publications. I owe thanks to the following scholars for their assistance: George Shevelov, Bohdan Budurowycz, Maxim Tarnawsky, Roman Senkus. My greatest debt is to my wife, Moira.

LITERARY POLITICS IN
THE SOVIET UKRAINE
1917–1934

INTRODUCTION

The present work is a study of Soviet Ukrainian literary life between the years 1917–34. Since this life expressed itself chiefly
through literary organizations, considerable attention is devoted
to them. Their creation, histories, tendencies, and conflicts were
largely determined by the policy of the Communist Party toward
literature. The changes in Party policy and the influence which
this policy had not only on literary life, but also on Soviet Ukrainian literature and culture in general, occupy a central place in the
inquiry. The purpose of the study is, therefore, to determine accurately the course of Party policy toward Ukrainian literature and
also to assess the nature and the extent of the resistance to this
policy.

The conflict between the Communist Party and Ukrainian literature manifested itself both in literature and in the literary life of
the period. Our concern here is with the latter; hence the title of
the present work. Little attempt is made to analyze or to survey the
literary works themselves or to give a sketch of the history of Soviet
Ukrainian literature as a whole, unless this is necessary to illustrate
the main theme. Only one chapter is devoted to a survey of Soviet
Ukrainian literature in the twenties, and even then the emphasis is
placed on the political rather than the esthetic significance of the
works discussed.

In order to deal with the subject adequately, it has been found
necessary to relate the changes in the Soviet regime in the Ukraine
to the Bolshevik theories of national self-determination and cultural efflorescence on the one hand and to the strivings of the
Ukrainians on the other. As a result, the conclusions reached in this
study may be of interest to the literary historian, to the student of
Soviet history, or to the sociologist. The central theme of the study

—the unfolding and, later, the stifling of a national literature through Party controls—is germane to all these fields. Moreover, the conflict between Ukrainian writers and the Party, the acceptance of controls by some and their rejection by others, and the influence which this period of Soviet Ukrainian literary history exerted on future events offer new explanations of the cultural framework of the USSR and of the Soviet satellites.

Two primary sources were used in the present study. The first was supplied by Soviet publications which appeared in the period under investigation. Later Soviet sources were found to be of little use. Another important source was the Liubchenko Papers, containing unpublished material, correspondence, and notebooks from the period 1924–39. While the first source made possible the restoration of the literary history from the contemporary official point of view, the second supplied a valuable corrective and a personal and uncensored commentary on the literary developments of the time.

It is inevitable, however, that omissions should occur in this field of investigation; these will have to be filled in by future research. For this reason, the present work does not claim to be complete or authoritative. All it hopes to achieve is to lay the foundation for a study of Soviet Ukrainian literary history and to illuminate the conflict between national aspirations and Soviet cultural policy.

[I]

REVOLUTION OF 1917

IN THE UKRAINE

The seventeen years of Soviet Ukrainian literary history (1917–34) which are here the subject of research belong to those periods of Soviet history which recent Soviet (Stalinist) historiography most blatantly distorts. If the agelong Russian-Ukrainian relations are regarded as a stream in which the Ukrainian and Russian currents intermingled and often vehemently opposed each other, then this period marks a strong upsurge of the Ukrainian tide, a flood stemmed only by force. In the Ukraine, the spontaneity and energy of the cultural processes released by the Revolution produced a literary revival which, for different reasons, has been little explored by either Soviet or émigré Ukrainian scholars. While the former condemn it as dangerous opposition to the Soviet regime, the latter often ignore it as a product of that regime, which they dismiss as a period of Russian Communist occupation of the Ukraine. Paradoxically, both are partially correct, although a student following only one of these interpretations would gain a very incomplete picture of the submerged period of Ukrainian history from 1917 to 1934. The present study departs from both these interpretations.

Developments in Soviet Ukrainian literature can be properly understood only when they are seen against the background of history. There is wide measure of agreement as to the nature of the revolution in the Ukraine. While in Russia the Revolution of 1917 had a social and political character, in the Ukraine it was fought primarily as a war for national liberation. The revolutionary forces in the Ukraine were not Communist but primarily national. Early

Soviet Ukrainian historians usually acknowledged two revolutions in the Ukraine: the national and the proletarian, which, although slightly overlapping, followed each other in time.[1]

In March, 1917, simultaneously with the downfall of the Romanov dynasty and the institution of the Provisional Government in Russia, the Central Rada, a council representing various Ukrainian organizations, was set up in Kiev (Kyïv) under the chairmanship of Professor Mykhailo Hrushevs'kyi. It was soon to become the nucleus of a Ukrainian government. In April, 1917, the All-Ukrainian Congress summoned by the Rada demanded autonomy for the Ukraine, and when the Russian Provisional Government refused either to recognize the Rada or to acknowledge its claim, on June 23, 1917, the Rada issued the so-called First Universal in which it stated its determination "that the Ukrainian people receive on their own territory the right to organize their own life." It was then (July 16) that the Provisional Government recognized the Rada, which also became more truly representative of the Ukraine by including Jewish, Polish, and Russian delegates in its secretariat. The General Secretariat of the Rada, consisting mainly of Ukrainian socialists with the writer Volodymyr Vynnychenko [2] at its head, became in fact the first Ukrainian government with real powers. After the fall of the Provisional Government in November, 1917, all power in the Ukraine passed into the hands of the Rada, which on November 20, 1917, proclaimed the Ukraine a separate Ukrainian People's Republic (Ukraïns'ka Narodnia Respublika) in federation with Russia and other nationalities of the former Empire (Third Universal).

In this way the Ukraine set herself apart from Russia, now controlled by the Bolshevik government. The Third Universal with its provisions for the redistribution of land, the establishment of an eight-hour day in industry, a political amnesty, abolition of capi-

---

[1] Cf. Ivan Kulyk, *Ohliad revoliutsiï na Ukraïni, passim;* M. Iavors'kyi, *Korotka istoriia Ukraïny,* pp. 122–40.

A most useful source for the history of the Soviet Ukraine is Jurij Lawrynenko, *Ukrainian Communism and Soviet Russian Policy toward the Ukraine: An Annotated Bibliography, 1917–1953.* The best accounts of the revolution in the Ukraine available in English are: John S. Reshetar, *The Ukrainian Revolution,* and Richard Pipes, *The Formation of the Soviet Union: Communism and Nationalism, 1917–1923.*

[2] Vynnychenko (1880–1951) was a very prominent novelist and playwright, combining realism with keen psychological insight and social interest.

tal punishment, the safeguarding of minority rights in the Ukraine, and election of a Ukrainian Constituent Assembly proved a powerful antidote to Bolshevik propaganda in the Ukraine. The Soviet government in Moscow denounced the Rada as reactionary and sent it an ultimatum demanding that the Red Army be allowed to cross Ukrainian territory in its offensive against General Kaledin's troops in the Don region. The Rada's decision to reject the ultimatum and to continue to disarm Red Army units in the Ukraine led to an open declaration of war by the Soviet government. At the same time the All-Ukrainian Congress of Soviets was held in Kiev on December 17, 1917. Planned as a meeting of protest against the Rada, it turned into a patriotic Ukrainian demonstration by nearly two thousand delegates. A small minority of about a hundred and fifty Bolsheviks and their sympathizers left the Congress and moved to Kharkov (Kharkiv). There they formed the Central Committee of Ukrainian Communists, which became the nucleus of the Ukrainian Communist Government and proclaimed the Ukraine a Soviet Republic.

That the Rada enjoyed the wide support of the Ukrainian population can be seen from the results of the elections to the Constituent Assembly, in which only 10 percent of the votes were cast for the Bolsheviks (in the *gubernias* of Volhynia—4 percent, Kiev—8 percent, Poltava—6 percent, Kharkov—11 percent, Kherson—11 percent, Chernigov (Chernihiv)—20 percent), while in Russia the average vote cast for the Bolsheviks was 40 percent.[3]

Faced with the invasion of the Ukraine by the Red Army following the declaration of war, the Rada proclaimed, on January 22, 1918, the complete independence of the Ukraine (Fourth Universal). The successful advance of the Red Army on Kiev in February, 1918, came to a halt when in the same month the Soviet government was forced to sign the treaty of Brest Litovsk in which Germany and the Central Powers recognized the Ukraine as a separate state under German occupation. The Germans soon controlled the whole Ukraine, abetted the abolition of the Rada, and set up the puppet government of Hetman Skoropads'kyi, who in turn was deposed by the national uprising led by Petliura. In December,

[3] M. Popov, *Narys istoriï KP(b)U*, 2d ed., p. 121. Cf. Oliver H. Radkey, *The Election to the Russian Constituent Assembly of 1917*, pp. 18–19.

1918, power was again restored to the Ukrainian national government, which, under the name of the Direktoriia, continued to oppose the Red Army that once more invaded the Ukraine after the withdrawal of German troops in January, 1919. In February, 1919, the Petliura government left Kiev and after more than a year of bitter civil war the Bolsheviks finally became the masters of the country.

Any account of the Revolution in the Ukraine would be incomplete without some reference to the role played by the Ukrainian Communist movement during those years. Again, for reasons of space, only the most significant aspects may be mentioned here.

The Theory of Self-Determination

There is no doubt that Lenin's theory of self-determination of nations, as well as his early pronouncements on the role of the nationalities of the Russian Empire, played a considerable part in forming the views of the Bolshevik political leaders in the Ukraine. Long before the Revolution, Lenin was a staunch believer in the self-determination of nations as a means of consolidating the power and influence of the Communist movement among the non-Russian nationalities. The basic tenet of Lenin's theory of state was clearly international. To paraphrase his own words, Marxism could never be reconciled with nationalism. Yet the idea of national self-determination advanced by Lenin later became an important tactical weapon of the Bolsheviks.

During the Second Congress of the Russian Social Democratic Workers' Party, held in 1903, Lenin defended this idea against the so-called Polish section of the Party, led by Rosa Luxemburg, and the Jewish Bund.[4] Later, in August, 1912, Lenin reiterated his belief in self-determination during the conference in Vienna, and it was in that year that Stalin, under Lenin's direct guidance and inspiration, wrote his *Marxism and the National Question,* which is perhaps the best exposition of Leninist principles in the sphere of the nationality policy. Yet in spite of the professed belief in self-determination, there was an obvious ambivalence in the Bolshevik

[4] Cf. Stanley Page, "Lenin and Self-Determination," *Slavonic and East European Review,* XXVIII, No. 71 (April, 1950), 342-58.

formulation of it which was manifest as early as 1913, during the Party conference in Poronin.[5]

Thus far, Lenin's doctrine on the national problem existed in the realm of theory; its practical application was still to be tested by history, for as yet no opportunity offered itself to present it as a plan of action for European nations; but the doctrine had a tactical and political purpose. When possibilities for the separation of nations did not exist, Lenin granted these nations the right to self-determination and in this way won the support of some, though not all, national groups within the Party. In 1917, when the time for action had at last come, Lenin proclaimed the slogan of the self-determination of nations as a revolutionary weapon. During the April conference (April 24–29, 1917) Lenin's resolution on granting the nationalities the right to self-determination was carried by fifty-six votes to sixteen, with eighteen abstentions.[6] His April "Theses"[7] which made public this policy were, however, sharply criticized by some members of the Party who, like Bukharin and Piatakov earlier,[8] saw a contradiction between Lenin's plea for an international socialist society and his principle of national self-determination. It is clear from Lenin's writings[9] that in propound-

[5] The resolution on the nationality policy stated, among other things, that "the question of the right of a nation to self-determination . . . must not be confused with the question of the advisability of separation of this or that nation. The latter question must be decided by the SD Party independently in every single case from the viewpoint of the interests of the general development and of the class struggle of the proletariat in the cause of socialism" (*Vsesoiuznaia kommunisticheskaia partiia (b) v rezoliutsiiakh eë s"ezdov i konferentsii*, 3d ed., p. 160).

[6] *Ibid.*, p. 183.

[7] Lenin, "Sotsialisticheskaia revoliutsiia i pravo natsii na samoopredelenie, Tezisy," *Sochineniia*, 3d ed., XIX, 37–48. The third edition of the collected works of Lenin is cited, unless otherwise stated.

[8] Page, "Lenin and Self-Determination," *Slavonic and East European Review*, XXVIII, No. 71 (April, 1950), 352.

[9] Cf. V. I. Lenin, "K peresmotru partiinoi programmy," *Sochineniia*, XXI, 295–318, especially pp. 316–17. Perhaps the best evidence of Lenin's hope that the Ukraine would not wish to secede from Russia can be found in his (unsigned) article in *Pravda* (No. 82, June 15, 1917; see also "Ukraina," *Sochineniia*, XX, 534–35; or, Lenin, *Natsional'ne pytannia*, pp. 28–29). Commenting on the Central Rada's First Universal, Lenin wrote: "These words are perfectly clear. They declare very distinctly that today the Ukrainian people does not wish to separate itself from Russia. It demands autonomy. . . . No democrat, not to mention a socialist, will dare to contradict the complete justice of Ukrainian demands. No democrat, also, can deny the *right* of the Ukraine freely to separate herself from Russia. It is the unconditional recognition of this right which alone provides the opportunity to agitate for a free union of Ukrainians and Great Russians, for a voluntary union of two peoples in one state. . . . We are not in

ing the slogan of self-determination, he always assumed that even if granted the right to secede from Russia, the non-Russian nationalities would voluntarily stay in union with Russia.

The events of the second half of the year 1917, however, brought a great disappointment to Lenin. He was taken at his word. The Finns, the Georgians, the Ukrainians, and other non-Russian nationalities of the former Empire demanded complete autonomy, even independence. It was then, after finding themselves in this awkward predicament, that the Bolsheviks thought of a modification of their slogan of self-determination, and it was Stalin who, in January, 1918,[10] reiterated a very important qualification of Lenin's original theory of self-determination. He proclaimed that only the "toiling masses of a nation" could legitimately exercise the right to self-determination. The claims of the national bourgeoisie must be disregarded. This shrewd and well-timed reminder provided the Central Committee of the Russian Communist Party with an excuse to give full support to those Ukrainian Communists who, in the Committee's view, represented the interests of the Ukrainian toiling masses.

The Communists in the Ukraine

It must be remembered that in 1917 the Communists had few followers in the Ukraine and no organization of their own. Their local groups, directly dependent on the Russian party, were not united in a single Ukrainian territorial organization, but formed three distinct centers, mostly Russian in composition: the Kharkov-Katerynoslav group, led by Kviring and Sergeev, who relied almost entirely on the guidance of their Russian colleagues and were later referred to as "Rightists"; the "Left" group of Piatakov and Bosh, centered in Kiev; and Skrypnyk's group (the Center), which believed in the possibility of a genuinely Ukrainian Communist

favor of the system of small states. We stand for the closest union of workers of all countries. . . . But because of that, in order that this union may be voluntary, the Russian worker, distrusting the Russian and the Ukrainian bourgeoisie, now supports the right of the Ukrainians to separate and does not burden them with his friendship, but wins them by treating them as equals, partners, and brothers in the struggle for socialism. . . . Long live the voluntary union of free peasants and workers of the free Ukraine with the workers and peasants of revolutionary Russia."

10 J. Stalin, *Sochineniia*, IV, 31, 32, 33.

movement. After a very brief period of power during the spring of 1918, which lasted only as long as the Russian Red Guards occupied the Ukraine, the Ukrainian Communists were compelled to retreat from the Ukraine before the advancing Germans. In an attempt to rally their scattered forces and also to iron out their internal differences, they convened the Second Congress of the Soviets in Katerynoslav (now Dniepropetrovsk) in March, 1918. The leading figure in the debates of the Congress was Skrypnyk. The Ukraine was proclaimed a Soviet Republic in union [11] with Russia. To escape from the Germans the leaders of the Congress moved to Taganrog, where they continued their sessions during April, 1918. It was there that the decision was taken to form a Communist Party of the Ukraine.

The discussion preceding the choice of name for the Party was indicative of the great uncertainty which many delegates had shown as to the Ukrainian character of the Party. Thus, for instance, the delegates from Katerynoslav proposed that the Party be called "The Russian Communist Party of Bolsheviks in the Ukraine." Finally, however, Skrypnyk's suggestion to name it the "Communist Party of Bolsheviks in the Ukraine" was accepted. It was also owing to the increasing strength of the "Center" that the CP(B)U was created as an independent Party. The leader of the "Right Wing," Kviring, wrote later that

The issue which was at stake here was whether the Ukrainian organization would create its own independent policy toward the revolutionary struggle in the Ukraine, only "coordinating" its activity with the Russian Communist Party through the Comintern (as was decided at the Taganrog conference), or whether the Ukrainian revolution would be regarded as a part of the Russian revolution and the Ukrainian organization would be under the direct supervision of the Russian Communist Party.[12]

With their government ousted from the Ukraine, the Ukrainian Communists were ready to proclaim their own "independence" in the Party organization in order to secure the future support of the Ukrainian population, while at the same time they agreed to accept the political strategy of the Russian Communist Party. For this reason, the newly created CP(B)U voted, against some opposition,

[11] The term used was *soiuz*, which can mean both "alliance" and "union." The ambiguity resulting from this terminology persisted for a long time.
[12] *Pervyi s"ezd KP(b)U, Statyi i protokoly s"ezda*, p. 7.

to accept the Brest Litovsk treaty so as not to provoke the Germans to a new war with Russia.

The first period of Communist government in the Ukraine was brief (February–April, 1918). The Soviet regime, established by the bayonets of the Red Army, led by ex-tsarist officer Muravëv, was extremely unpopular largely because of its complete disregard for the rights of Ukrainian language and culture. "The [Ukrainian] press," writes Vynnychenko in his reminiscences of those days, "was banned, Ukrainian printing houses were confiscated, the book-stores and libraries shut down, schools closed, and people were seized on the streets for speaking Ukrainian and, if not condemned to be executed, were suspected of counterrevolution." [13]

At the end of April, 1918, the Central Committee of the CP(B)U left the Ukraine for Moscow. It was in Moscow, too, that the CP(B)U held its first Party Congress from July 5–12, 1918. The most important issue under debate was how to further the Communist revolution in the Ukraine. The Congress voted in favor of the resolution put forward by the "Left" faction which was based on the assumption that "there is a chance for a victorious uprising in the near future." [14] At the same time all delegates agreed on the need for stronger ties with the Russian Communist Party. A resolution to that effect was passed by fifty votes with seven abstentions. Another resolution outlined the future policy of the Party with regard to Russian-Ukrainian relations. It was based on four assumptions: (1) there was an economic unity between the Ukraine and Russia; (2) separation of the Ukraine from Russia would in the present circumstances invite occupation of the former by a hostile power; (3) the idea of an independent Ukraine had no support among the Ukrainian toiling masses; (4) the unity of the Ukraine with Russia was in accordance with the aims of the Revolution. [15]

The logic of the above premises appeared doubtful even to some delegates who were present. Skrypnyk, for instance, felt uneasy about the disregard of the principle of self-determination and found it necessary to explain that

the slogan of the right of a nation to self-determination even to the point of separation was only justified before the October Revolution.

[13] V. Vynnychenko, *Vidrodzhennia natsiï*, II, 271.
[14] *Pervyi s"ezd KP(b)U*, p. 72.   [15] *Ibid.*, p. 136.

In the course of the class struggle it is possible to assume various attitudes to this problem. Particularly in the case of the Ukraine, a dialectical change of our attitude to this question is characteristic. Before October, our line was quite right, but as soon as the proletariat came to power, the situation changed radically. . . . We are now opposed to separation, since independence is now a disguise for an anti-Soviet struggle. However, our slogan [of self-determination] had at one time its purpose and will still be of use, if only in the first phase of the revolution in Austria-Hungary. It is too early yet to bury it.[16]

Skrypnyk's argument illustrates very clearly the use of theories as tactical weapons to achieve Communist ends.

The date for a Communist uprising in the Ukraine was set for August 5, 1918, but the attempted revolt ended in complete failure. As a result of it the policy of the "Left" within the CP(B)U was condemned during the Second Party Congress, held also in Moscow in October, 1918, and the "Rightists" came to the fore. They felt now even more justified in advocating their policy of entire dependence on Soviet Russia. This new attitude was best expressed in the resolution proposed by Epstein (Iakovlev), on Russian-Ukrainian relations, which was unanimously passed by the Congress:

The main task of the CP(B)U is the union of the Ukraine with Russia, the strengthening of the Party apparatus, the transfer of the main activity of the Party to the Ukraine, the concentration of all forces first in industrial centers, and the creation of a good fighting force. While using mass terror as a weapon against the enemy, and especially against the hostile White Armies, the Party decidedly condemns the use of partisan warfare, which could involve the workers of the Ukraine in a premature rising. In all its preparatory work the Party should seek the support of proletarian Russia; it should coordinate all its steps with the Central Committee of the Russian Communist Party and only with its consent choose the moment for open action.[17]

Following this line, the Congress, in the words of a Soviet historian, "prepared the movement of the Red Army into the Ukraine." [18] It is also significant that, for the first time, Stalin was elected to the Central Committee of the CP(B)U and was put in

16 *Ibid.*, p. 138.
17 Quotation taken from M. Iavors'kyi, "K istorii KP(b)U," in *Oktiabr'skaia revoliutsiia*, p. 73.
18 Popov, *Narys istoriï KP(b)U*, p. 168.

charge of the special bureau to assist liaison between the Russian
Communist Party and the CP(B)U.

The situation in the Ukraine did not look very hopeful for the
Communists. The rising against the Germans was successfully undertaken not by the Communists but by the nationalists (National
Union), who overthrew the regime of Hetman Skoropads'kyi and
reinstated the Ukrainian People's Republic (December, 1918)
under the government of the Direktoriia.

When a few months later the Red Army, commanded by An-
tonov-Ovseenko, began its second invasion of the Ukraine, the
national and cultural policy of the Bolsheviks was unchanged in
practice. It evinced no sympathy for the development of Ukrainian
culture, and the head of the Soviet Ukrainian government, Rakovskii, declared that "authorizing Ukrainian as a language of state
administration would be a reactionary measure. It is quite unnecessary." [19] The Soviet bureaucracy in the Ukraine, chiefly composed of Russians, was openly hostile to Ukrainian culture and
ideas.

The Borot'bists

The political developments in the Ukraine were even less favorable to the Bolsheviks than the military events. The most powerful
Ukrainian political party, the Ukrainian Socialist Revolutionary
Party, which formerly had a majority in the Rada, split in May,
1918, into two groups. The Left SR's, who commanded a numerical
majority, formed a new party which later accepted the name of its
party journal, Borot'ba (The Struggle). The Right wing of the old
SR Party formed what was called a "Centralist" group.

The formation of the new SR Party (Borot'ba) was of crucial
significance for the further development of Ukrainian-Russian
relations, since the political platform of the Borot'bists was not very
far removed from that of the Bolsheviks. Although it advocated
revolutionary struggle and establishment of a socialist state, the
policy of the Borot'bists was motivated by strong national sentiments. It might be said that they were not unlike the Yugoslav
Communist Party in and after 1948. The Borot'bists enjoyed stead-
ily increasing support among many of those Ukrainians who

[19] Vynnychenko, *Vidrodzhennia natsiï*, III, 310.

wanted to combine a Soviet system with national autonomy, and they became therefore the rivals of the CP(B)U.

A similar split developed within the Ukrainian Social Democratic Party in January, 1919. Its Left wing ("Left Independents"), led by M. Tkachenko, advocated a Soviet form of government, and in August, 1919, merged with the Left SR's (Borot'ba) under a new name: Ukraïns'ka Komunistychna Partiia (borot'bystiv).[20] On August 28, 1919, the Central Committee of this party applied for membership in the Third International, claiming that it alone represented the Communist movement in the Ukraine.[21] In January, 1920, the Left SD's formed a Ukrainian Communist Party (Ukraïns'ka Komunistychna Partiia) commonly known as the "Ukapisty."

At the end of 1918, after the collapse of the German occupation of the Ukraine and the establishment of the Direktoriia in Kiev, the Russian Communist Party, in conformity with the decisions of the Second Congress of the CP(B)U, decided to promote the proletarian revolution by letting the Red Army invade the Ukraine. The Ukrainian National Army, led by Petliura, was defeated, and in February, 1919, the government of the Ukrainian People's Republic was forced to abandon Kiev. Many Communists admitted at that time that, as Kviring put it, "Soviet power was established in the Ukraine not by internal forces, but only with the help of the mightier Soviet Russia, at the time of the collapse of the German army." [22] The second period of Communist government in the Ukraine came to an end in August, 1919, when the country was partly invaded by the forces of General Denikin and partly reoccupied by the army of the Ukrainian People's Republic. Not until December, 1919, did the Bolsheviks, in their third armed assault against the Ukraine, succeed in occupying most of the country.

It must not be assumed, however, that the Bolsheviks hoped to gain control of the Ukraine by force alone. Having learned from their past experiences that the national reawakening was a very powerful element in the Ukraine and that the Ukrainians were unwilling to take orders from the Russians, the Bolsheviks in their third invasion of the Ukraine, which started in December, 1919, resorted to an entirely new policy.

The chief engineer of this policy was Lenin himself, who at that

[20] M. Ravich-Cherkasskii, *Istoriia kommunisticheskoi partii Ukrainy*, p. 143.
[21] *Ibid.*, p. 144.　　　　[22] Preface to *Pervyi s"ezd KP(b)U*, p. 13.

time devoted much attention to the Ukrainian problem. The two main premises were: a return to the self-determination principle and promises of national autonomy; and secondly, institution of a Bolshevik regime in the Ukraine by all available means (including alliances with the Borot'bists). Perhaps the first point was only a tactical consideration resulting from the second. This radical change in Bolshevik policy was dictated by the experiences gained during the two previous periods of Soviet power in the Ukraine. The Ukrainians had to be reckoned with. Any further disregard of the principle of self-determination might have exposed the character of the Civil War in the Ukraine which was fought rather along national than along class lines. Therefore the Party's decision to set a new course in the Ukraine was an attempt to preserve the Soviet order at all costs, even at the cost of making concessions to the Ukrainians and thereby alienating the Russian public which still refused to recognize them as a nation.

In November and December, 1919, a conference was held in Moscow on the initiative of the Central Committee of the Russian Communist Party at the time of the Eighth Congress of the RCP(B).[23] The following were the most important resolutions in the field of Ukrainian-Russian relations which implemented Lenin's new policy:

(1) The Russian Communist Party emphasized once more the principle of self-determination of nations and acknowledged "full independence" of the Soviet Ukraine.

(2) The Communist regime guaranteed full development of Ukrainian culture and language.

(3) From now on, the mainstay of the Communist Revolution in the Ukraine was to be not the poor peasant but the "middle peasant"—*seredniak*.[24]

A resolution "On the Soviet Government in the Ukraine," approved by the Central Committee of the RCP(B) and passed by the Party conference on December 2, 1919, read as follows:

1. Inflexibly applying the principle of self-determination of nations, the Central Committee deems it necessary to stress once more the fact that the RCP(B) stands for the recognition of the independence of the Ukrainian SSR.

[23] Iavors'kyi, "K istorii KP(b)U," in *Oktiabr'skaia revoliutsiia*, pp. 114, 117.
[24] *Ibid.*, p. 114.

2. Regarding the need for closest union of all Soviet republics in the struggle against the threatening forces of world capitalism as obvious to any Communist and any enlightened worker, the RCP(B) considers that the establishment of the exact form of this union will be definitely decided by the Ukrainian workers and toiling peasants themselves.

3. At the present time the relation between the Ukrainian SSR and the Russian SFSR is that of federal union, according to the resolutions of the RSFSR of June 1, 1919, and of the Central Executive of the Ukraine of May 18, 1919.

4. In view of the fact that Ukrainian culture (language, schools, etc.) has been suppressed for centuries by tsardom and by the exploiter classes of Russia, the Central Committee of the RCP(B) calls upon all members of the Party to facilitate in every way the removal of obstacles to the free development of the Ukrainian language and culture. Since, among the backward sections of the Ukrainian masses, nationalist tendencies may be observed as a result of a century-long oppression, the members of the RCP(B) should treat them with the utmost patience and tact, counteracting these tendencies with a friendly explanation of the identity of interests of the toiling masses of the Ukraine and Russia. The members of the RCP(B) should foil any attempts to reduce the Ukrainian language to a secondary place and they should strive, on the contrary, to transform the Ukrainian language into the weapon of Communist education of the masses. It is essential that there should be enough officials in the Soviet administration who know Ukrainian, and in future all officials should be familiar with the use of Ukrainian . . .[25]

To mark the change of policy toward the Ukraine, Lenin issued in December, 1919, a special letter "To the Workers and Peasants of the Ukraine," the second paragraph of which started with the words "the Central Committee of the Russian Communist Party has accepted as a fact the full independence of the Ukraine." Lenin went on to assure the Ukrainians that only on the basis of full equality could the two nations collaborate in the creation of a Soviet society.[26] The new policy reflected the realization on the part of the Bolsheviks that if Communism was to spread in the Ukraine, it must do so under the guise of a national movement of liberation. This was all the more necessary since the Borot'bists were gaining an ever greater measure of popular support.

At the same time that the Russian Red Army marched into Kiev, the Borot'bists, who were then beginning to call themselves "Borot'bists—Communists," denounced the move of the Red Army

[25] B. Borev, *Natsional'ne pytannia*, p. 88.
[26] Lenin and Stalin, *O bor'be za ustanovlenie sovetskoi vlasti na Ukraine*, p. 59.

as an army of occupation. It is no wonder, therefore, that Lenin
and the Russian Bolsheviks faced a grave danger in deciding to
follow a more pro-Ukrainian policy, since it could easily lead to
bolstering the National-Communist forces in the Ukraine which
were reluctant to take orders from Moscow.

That the policy which the Russian Communists adopted was
purely a matter of necessity and political maneuver is obvious since
at no time did the Bolsheviks abandon the ideal of a highly central-
ized Party. The meaning of Lenin's concession to the Ukraine in
Party terms was that in the regional Party organization in the
Ukraine the Ukrainians were to be given wider scope. This did not,
however, give them the opportunity to influence or to change the
policy of the central organs of the Party.

The recent publication by Mr. Bertram D. Wolfe [27] of correspondence between Lenin and Russian Red Army commanders
about the Ukrainian problem has brought to light an important
piece of documentary evidence which illustrates developments in
Ukrainian-Russian relations during late 1919 and early 1920. One
document in particular which, according to Mr. Wolfe, "gives
every appearance of having been drafted by Lenin," is so illuminat-
ing of the concern with which the indigenous Ukrainian Communists were regarded by Lenin and the Russian Bolsheviks that it
deserves to be quoted extensively. It bears the date May, 1919:

  1. The bloc of our Party with the *Borotbisty* had as its aim to attract
to a sustained Communist policy a young political party in the socialist
structure of the Ukraine, still so poor in experience.
  2. In making this experiment, our Party had clearly in mind the fact
that it might have directly opposite results, namely that it might hasten
the degeneration of the *Borotbisty* into a militant party of counter-revo-
lution, with the splitting off from it of its most honest and conscious
socialist elements. . . .
  4. At the present time it can be confirmed with full conviction that
the Party of the *Borotbisty* has evolved to the right, i.e., to the side of
degeneration into an intellectual political group basing itself mainly
on kulak elements of the villages and on swindler-scoundrelly elements
of the city, including also the greater part of the working class . . .

    [27] Bertram D. Wolfe, "The Influence of Early Military Decisions upon the National
Structure of the Soviet Union," *American Slavic and East European Review,* IX, No. 3
(October, 1950), 169–79. The article is based on material in the Trotsky Papers at
Harvard.

7. Under the guise of a struggle for Ukrainian independence, which found its expression in the Ukrainian Soviet Government, the *Borotbisty* have carried on a disorganizing struggle against the necessary union and unification of the economic apparatuses serving the interests of both countries. By this they help economic chaos and threaten to undermine all the work for economic construction in the Ukraine and in Russia.

8. Especially criminal, however, is the work of the *Borotbisty* in the military field. In the guise of the struggle for an independent Ukrainian army, the *Borotbisty* support the partisan bands, by word and deed opposing them to the Red Army, and are multiplying thereby the elements of bandit chaos which are leading the Ukraine to the brink of chaos. . . .

11. It is incumbent upon the leading elements of our Party and of the Soviet Power in the Ukraine to open a most serious, attentive and energetic campaign against the Party of the *Borotbisty,* exposing its intelligentsia-careerist, chauvinist and exploiter-kulakist character. . . .

14. . . . It is necessary to reckon with the fact that a certain number of the pure socialist elements have so far stayed in the ranks of the *Borotbisty* because of the official communist banner of this Party and its external revolutionary phraseology.

15. By means of all the measures indicated above . . . our Party must in a short time prepare the conditions for driving the *Borotbisty* out of the ranks of the government, and for the complete liquidation of the *Borotbisty* as a recognized Soviet Party. . . .[28]

Lenin's tactics were successful. After being refused admission to the Comintern (Communist International), the party of the Borot'-bists, under strong pressure from the Bolsheviks, who were advocating its merger (or, more accurately, its absorption) with the CP(B)U, dissolved itself in March, 1920. In April of the same year a large group of 4,000 Borot'bists was admitted to the CP(B)U.[29] "It is true," wrote Iavors'kyi, "that this party has not cut all ties with nationalism and that it has not yet accepted the platform of the dictatorship of the proletariat; however, its program was symptomatic of the new currents among the Ukrainian intelligentsia after the fall of Denikin and Petliura." [30]

28 *Ibid.,* pp. 177–78.
29 M. Skrypnyk, "Za zdiisnennia teorii na praktytsi," in *Statti i promovy,* II, 12.
30 Iavors'kyi, "K istorii KP(b)U," in *Oktiabr'skaia revoliutsiia,* p. 116.

A Temporary Compromise

It was in this atmosphere of compromise between the Borot'bists and the CP(B)U that the Fourth Congress of the CP(B)U was held in Kharkov, in March, 1920. Stalin represented the Central Committee of the Russian Communist Party. After bitter debates in which the Borot'bists and their sympathizers proved to be no less astute than the Bolsheviks, a series of important resolutions was approved. In all of them Russia and the Ukraine were referred to as two separate and almost sovereign states. A special resolution guaranteed the "independence" of the Soviet Ukraine, and confirmation was given to the fusion of the Borot'bists with the CP(B)U.[31] Two prominent leaders of the Borot'bists, Blakytnyi and Shums'kyi, were elected to the new Central Committee. The stormy debates during the Congress made it necessary for the Central Committee of the Russian Communist Party to dissolve, on April 7, the newly elected Ukrainian Central Committee and to reorganize it.[32] This action alone showed most clearly the fictitious character of the "Independent Soviet Ukraine."

In the reorganized Central Committee of the CP(B)U, most of the Ukrainian Communists (Blakytnyi, Shums'kyi, Chubar, Petrovs'kyi, and Zatons'kyi) were to be found, while the leaders of the old Left and Right wings (Piatakov and Kviring) were excluded. The composition of the new Central Committee revealed the policy which Lenin pursued toward the Ukraine in 1920. For a moment it seemed that after years of struggling for power, the divergent views would merge and some semblance of unity would be given to the CP(B)U. For a moment it seemed that Lenin's desire was to leave the fate of the Soviet Ukraine in the hands of Ukrainian Communists. But it could have seemed so only to political leaders in the Soviet Ukraine at that time. Today, after the study of all available sources and secret documents like the one brought to light by Bertram Wolfe, it is impossible to arrive at such a conclusion. It is not justified since the Bolshevik policy toward the Ukraine remained for the Russian Communists a tactical weapon with which they hoped to achieve their ends. Lenin's own explanation of these tactics, given in March, 1920, was most candid:

[31] Popov, *Narys istoriï KP(b)U*, pp. 222, 225.   [32] *Ibid.*, p. 226.

[Comrade Bubnov] said that the Central Committee is guilty of strengthening the Borot'bists. This is a complex and important question and I am of the opinion that in this important problem, where very careful maneuvering was needed, we are the victors. When in the Central Committee we spoke of maximum concessions to the Borot'bists, we were laughed at and told that we are not straight in our dealing with them. But one can attack one's enemy directly only when he is in a straight line; once he decides to dodge, we must pursue him at every turn. We promised the Borot'bists maximum concessions but on condition that they should pursue our policy. . . . The victory lies with us.[33]

The political successes which the Borot'bists gained in 1920 and the following years were limited. After the alliance with the CP(B)U, their hope of playing a decisive role in the self-styled socialist construction of the Ukraine could never be fulfilled. Although they enjoyed some support among the Ukrainian population and strongly influenced the policy of the Soviet Ukrainian government, the Borot'bists lacked the power necessary to achieve a synthesis of national rebirth and world revolution. However, they remained a vital force in Ukrainian politics until 1937, when the last prominent ex-Borot'bist, Panas Liubchenko, at that time the Chairman of the Council of People's Commissars in the Ukraine, committed suicide.

The Ukrainian Bolsheviks came to share the Borot'bists' tragic role of intermediaries between national self-assertion and the centralizing tendencies of Moscow. The struggle between the Ukrainian and the Russian Communists, brought about by these irreconcilable forces, continued to be waged after the end of the Civil War. The progress of this battle is particularly dramatic in the records of the Tenth, Eleventh, and Twelfth Congresses of the Russian Communist Party, held in 1921 and 1922. On all three occasions the Ukrainian Communists spoke with courage in defense of their country's rights and privileges. No less remarkable was the survival of the UKP (Ukapists) as a legally tolerated opposition group in the Soviet Ukraine until 1924, the last exception to the rule of a "one-party system" in the entire Soviet Union.

It is easier for us today to see who was destined to gain ultimate victory in this contest. Yet in 1920 the issue was far from being decided.

[33] *Deviatyi s"ezd RKP(b): Protokoly*, pp. 96–97.

It was necessary to dwell at some length on the history of the Communist movement in the Ukraine during the Revolution and the Civil War for two reasons. Many personalities of the Ukrainian Communist movement were very closely connected with literature. Several Ukrainian writers were active Borot'bists and Ukapists. The names of Skrypnyk, Shums'kyi, Blakytnyi, and others we shall meet again in the ensuing chapters.

It was also imperative to sketch the way in which Communism came to the Ukraine and how it acquired the character of a Ukrainian movement for political and cultural self-expression within the Soviet state and Communist ideology. There is no denying that the Ukrainian Communists enjoyed a spell of triumph. This was particularly true of the cultural field, where the Ukrainian Communists in the 1920s became the spearhead of a movement which, in its own way, aimed at the further emancipation of Ukrainian literature and its closer integration into European tradition.[34] The ground conquered by Skrypnyk, the Borot'bists,[35] and the Ukapists was firmly held by those who believed in these ideals. They saw no reason why Soviet Ukrainian culture and literature could not follow their own course.

The leading representatives of Soviet Ukrainian literature symbolized not only the new and buoyant energies of the Ukrainian revolution but also much older traditions of Ukrainian history. Before them was the attractive prospect of cultural pioneering in a new socialist style, but behind them was the heritage of the Ukrainian cultural renaissance of the nineteenth century, which was not fully revealed until 1917. For the first time in Ukrainian history the complete works of Ukrainian classics and literary criticism were published. For the first time it was possible to assess the full meaning of the Ukrainian National Revival of the nineteenth century, the fruits of which Soviet Ukrainian literature had inherited.

[34] The most trenchant statement of Borot'bist cultural policy is contained in the "Draft of a Decree" supporting Ukrainian culture, prepared in 1919 by Shums'kyi, the Commissar of Education during the second period of Soviet government in the Ukraine. The full text is printed in Appendix A.

[35] I am indebted for the information on the Borot'bists to Iwan Majstrenko, *Borot'bism; a Chapter in the History of Ukrainian Communism*, New York, Research Program on the USSR, 1954.

[I I]

TRADITIONS OF UKRAINIAN

LITERATURE

The Road from Oppression to Freedom

The sources of the Ukrainian National Revival were many and various, and a complete analysis of them would require a separate study. However, whether we consider the spread of freemasonry, the Ukrainian Decembrists, the interest in ethnography and folklore, the secret Brotherhood of Sts. Cyril and Methodius, the sentimentalism and romanticism in literature, or the socialism of Drahomanov, all of them fused into one outstanding product—modern Ukrainian literature, which in turn became the mainspring of further national and cultural enlightenment. Throughout the nineteenth and early twentieth centuries literature played such an important part in the Ukraine because it was the only means of expression for the new national spirit. In spite of severe controls imposed upon it by the tsarist regime, it fulfilled many functions because, together with the theater, and in the absence of any Ukrainian political life, it was not only a vehicle for ideas but also a potent instrument of education in history, language, and political theory among both the broad masses of the people and the intellectual elite.

The characteristic bi-polarity of Ukrainian cultural life in the late nineteenth and the early twentieth centuries was due to the increasingly closer contact between the Dnieper Ukraine, which was part of the Russian Empire, and Galicia, the Ukrainian province under Austro-Hungarian rule. Beginning with the 1860s, many Ukrainian writers, unable to print their works in Kiev or Kharkov, published them in L'vov (L'viv). Some Ukrainians from the east (Drahomanov, for example) found a following in Galicia, and in 1894 Mykhailo Hrushevs'kyi was appointed to the chair of Ukrainian history in L'vov. Relations between L'vov and Kiev were reciprocal. Western Ukraine not only offered a haven to some young Ukrainian intellectuals from the east and helped in the publication of Ukrainian literature; in due course it came to be regarded with admiration by eastern Ukrainians as a place where, in spite of the pro-Polish policy of the Austro-Hungarian government, Ukrainian culture was developing much more freely than in Russia. In the early twentieth century these mutual ties were reinforced. Scholars, writers, and politicians from both sides of the border paid prolonged visits to each other's territory. L'vov and Galicia were rightly regarded as the Piedmont of the Ukrainian *risorgimento*.

In the field of Ukrainian literature and literary theory this east-west relationship was of the greatest significance. For the east it opened the door to Western Europe, while the Galicians were made aware of the heritage and aims they held in common with other Ukrainians. On the eve of World War I, Ukrainian literary schools and tendencies, by virtue of their Galician contacts with the West (Poland, Germany), had ceased to be dependent on Russian influences.

One other aspect of the Ukrainian literary revival deserves to be mentioned because of its direct bearing on the revolutionary and post-revolutionary periods. It concerns the repeated attempts by the tsarist administration to hinder, suppress, and ban the growth and use of the Ukrainian language and literature. The arrest of Shevchenko in 1847 with the explicit order that he should be prevented from writing or painting, the notorious pronouncement of the tsarist minister of the interior, Valuev, in 1863 that "there never has been, is not, and never can be a separate Little Russian language," and the consequent ban on practically all Ukrainian books except belles-lettres culminated in the 1876 prohibition of all Ukrainian publications, except historical documents and censored belles-lettres,[1] and the simultaneous ban on the importa-

---

1 The following is the text of the so-called ukaz of Ems of 1876:

"(1) The importation into the Russian Empire, without special permission of the Central Censorship over Printing, of all books and pamphlets in the Little Russian dialect, published abroad, is forbidden,

tion of all Ukrainian books from abroad. These harsh measures of a despotic regime seriously hindered the development of literature.[2] A period after 1905 of greater leniency in the matter of Ukrainian publications was followed once more in 1914 by the strictest censorship, which again forbade all Ukrainian books and newspapers and affected also Russian-occupied Galicia, the foremost bulwark of the Ukrainian revival.

Thus the relief which the 1917 Revolution brought to literature was tantamount to liberation. It is important to note, however, that the Soviet claims to the effect that it was the Bolshevik Revolution which was responsible for the abolition of the tsarist censorship in the Ukraine are not true. The forces which brought freedom to the Ukraine were those of Ukrainian nationalism, which, as we saw, was the first power in the Ukraine after the fall of tsardom. The great enthusiasm for the printed Ukrainian word which swept the Ukraine in 1917 was the fulfillment and the culmination of the Ukrainian National Revival. The Ukrainian Communist Koriak wrote in 1921 that "the 1917 Revolution liberated all Ukrainian forces, but not all of them were the bearers of revolution; most were counterrevolutionary and only single individuals threw in their lot with the revolution." [3]

Literature and scholarship were well represented in the Ukrainian government of the Rada by such men as Volodymyr Vynny-

---

(2) The printing and publishing in the Empire of original works and translations in this dialect is forbidden with the exception of (a) historical documents and monuments; (b) works of belles-lettres but with the provision that in the documents the orthography of the originals be retained; in works of belles-lettres no deviations from the accepted Russian orthography are permitted and permission for their printing may be given only by the Central Censorship over Printing.

(3) All theatrical performances and lectures in the Little Russian dialect, as well as printing of texts to musical notes, are forbidden." I.R., "Ne dozvoliaiu," *Radians'kyi knyhar*, No. 8 (April, 1930), p. 8. For a complete discussion of the 1876 ban see Fedir Savchenko, *Zaborona ukraïnstva 1876 r.*

[2] The figures on publication of Ukrainian books in the period of most severe repression (1847–1905) are as follows: 1847—0; 1848—3; 1849—2; 1850—1; 1851—2; 1852—1; 1854—3; 1855—4; 1856—5; 1857—12; 1860—24; 1861—33; 1862—41; 1863—15; 1864—11; 1865—5; 1870—5; 1875—30; 1877—2; 1880—0; 1881–83—75; 1894—23 ("Vydavnytstva," *Entsyklopediia ukraïnoznavstva*, III, 974). The great majority of Ukrainian books published at that time appeared in Galicia.

[3] V. Koriak, "Etapy," *Zhovten'*, 1921; see also A. Leites and M. Iashek, *Desiat' rokiv ukraïns'koï literatury (1917–1927)*, II, 58. The first volume of Leites and Iashek contains very detailed biographical and bibliographical data on Ukrainian writers. Together with the second volume, which consists of excerpts from source material concerning literary life, it represents a most valuable work of reference.

chenko and Mykhailo Hrushevs'kyi, but the undercurrent of social thought was weak in comparison with the deluge of what Iavors'kyi described as an "awakened national romanticism." [4] Moreover, the struggle which led to this victory over tsarist tyranny had a distinct anti-Russian character; now, at last, the Ukrainian language and literature were to be given their natural right to develop in the country where they had been suppressed by the Russian government and displaced by Russian literature and culture. Thus, in one of the earliest manifestoes on art, issued in September, 1917, by the outstanding Ukrainian producer and director of the Molodyi Teatr, Les' Kurbas, we find the following pronouncement:

After a long epoch of Ukrainophilism, romantic admiration for the Cossacks, ethnographism, and modernism based on Russian patterns, we see in our literature, which has hitherto reflected all social moods, a vital and most important turning point. It is directed straight toward Europe . . . without any intermediaries or authoritative models. This is the only true path for our art.[5]

Yet this uncompromising attitude was not chauvinistic. This was because even before 1917 Ukrainian literature, in spite of all the external persecutions, had achieved a difficult but definite maturity. Even at a time of complete upheaval of values, it could not but remain true to its heritage. This heritage is the second important influence on Soviet Ukrainian literature to be considered here.

Perhaps the herald of modern Ukrainian literature, Ivan Kotliarevs'kyi, was not fully aware of the importance which the appearance of his travesty of the *Aeneid* in 1798 would have for the succeeding generations of writers. Determined to show that the Ukrainian language was suitable for literature apart from burlesque, Kotliarevs'kyi, a poet of genius, stirred the imagination of his fellow countrymen by his vivid pictures of the past glories of the Cossack Ukraine. On the other hand, the classicism of the first Ukrainian novelists (Hryhorii Kvitka-Osnovianenko, for example) and the interest in folklore and social problems of writers like Marko Vovchok, Oleksa Storozhenko, or Osyp Iurii Fed'kovych were the results of European trends toward romanticism and senti-

[4] M. Iavors'kyi, "K istorii KP(b)U," in *Oktiabr'skaia revoliutsiia*, p. 94.
[5] *Robitnycha hazeta*, September 23, 1917.

mentality. Taras Shevchenko was also much more than a "national bard." Sprung from the people, he clothed Ukrainian thought with garments of poetic beauty. His poetry is as much historical as it is lyrical, philosophical as much as political. He is the finest symbol of the Ukrainian National Revival with his deep concern for the future of the Ukraine, his sharp criticism of national weaknesses, his condemnation of social and political injustice in government, and his quest for a moral code which all men could accept.

Shevchenko's followers in the Dnieper Ukraine (Stepan Rudans'kyi, Ivan Nechui-Levyts'kyi, Panas Myrnyi, Mykhailo Kotsiubyns'kyi, Lesia Ukraïnka) and in Galicia (Ivan Franko) enlarged the literary horizons and wrote in the best traditions of European literature. By the time of the Revolution, Ukrainian literature was mistress in her own right, no adolescent or nursling. The bright path which lay ahead was but an extension of the rough road trodden in the past.

The Impact of the Revolution on Literature

The impact of the Revolution, exerting both national and Communist pressure on a literature fully developed in all its genres, could not but act as a potent and invigorating stimulus. When literature is discussed in connection with the 1917 Revolution, the term includes not only books, publications, and printing presses but also, and perhaps chiefly, the writers. On them the events of 1917 had a most profound influence. But what is of far greater importance for us is the fact that in the Ukraine the writers suddenly emerged from what was often social obscurity into a prominent position of intellectual leadership. For the first time in Ukrainian history, the Ukrainian intelligentsia and literary elite felt no need to follow either the Russian or the Pole. In the past this often meant Russification or Polonization of the Ukrainian intellectual elite and the Ukrainian upper classes. Now the whole social as well as political structure of the country was shaken and fundamentally altered. Ukrainian writers not only became respected members of the community; they "dined in the same cafe as the ministers and officials of the Central Rada," [6] and were regarded as important supporters of the new state.

Cultural and literary activities continued during the years of bitter fighting in 1917–19, despite the many changes of government. Moreover, each new government placed special emphasis on cultural policy, vying with its opponents for the title of most "culture-minded." Thus the Rada as well as its antagonists, the Borot'bists, tried to advance Ukrainian literature to the best of their abilities and tastes. The period of the Hetmanate also witnessed a singular revival of Ukrainian arts and letters which was in striking contrast to the Hetman's reactionary social and economic policy. It was during the Hetmanate that the Ukrainian Academy of Sciences, the state university in Kiev, the National Museum, the Ukrainian State Theater, and the State Drama School were founded. Book production for 1918 was 1,084 titles, in comparison with 747 for 1917 and 665 for 1919.[7] The collapse of the Ukrainian People's Republic in 1919 led to the mass emigration of Ukrainian intellectuals, and thus had a serious effect on literary life. The Communists found themselves in control of the field, but the field was almost deserted.

In the sphere of literary theory and esthetics the 1917 Revolution also aided new developments. Once more, it is important to bear in mind the general picture of the literary scene in 1914–19 in order to realize the complexity of these radical changes.

Perhaps the greatest single contribution to literary theory in prerevolutionary Russia was made by Oleksander Potebnia (1835–91), a great Ukrainian scholar who wrote in Russian and in Ukrainian. His ideas of "the identity of the linguistic and poetic processes, of image as the basis of poetry, of criticism as the creative transformation of a work of art," writes Hordyns'kyi, "even now provide stimulus for lively controversies in Ukrainian poetics." [8] To claim, however, as Hordyns'kyi does, that Ukrainian poetics follow Potebnia is to do injustice to that great thinker, whose theories were

[6] Leites and Iashek, *Desiat' rokiv,* II, 58.

[7] V. Doroshenko and P. Zlenko, "Vydavnytstva," *Entsyklopediia ukraïnoznavstva,* III, 976.

[8] Iaroslav Hordyns'kyi, *Literaturna krytyka pidsoviets'koï Ukraïny,* pp. 18–19. This scholarly work offers the fullest and most objective treatment of the development of Ukrainian literary theory and criticism from 1917 to 1938.

well ahead of his time. Their influence was most noticeable not so much in revolutionary Ukraine as in Russia, where they provided some stimulus for the so-called Formalist movement which "developed as a specific reaction against the Imagism of Potebnia." [9]

Formalism, however, came to the Ukraine only after the Revolution. Owing to the ban on Ukrainian publications, the years 1914–15 were marked by a virtual silence. In May, 1915, after the retreat of the Russian armies from Western Ukraine (Galicia), Ukrainian literary life was somewhat rekindled. However, Ukrainian literary theory was still relying for the most part on the old, outworn ethnographic and romantic theories, although from time to time it was swayed by Western European trends chiefly of the "art for art's sake" school. Of special importance were the so-called Khatians (a group of writers, contributors to *Ukraïns'ka khata* [Ukrainian Home]). They were sharply opposed to the national and populist approach to literature, and propagated the ideal of an art, pure and undirected. "Art comes from inspiration," wrote their leading theorist, Ievshan, "from a divine spark. It may not contain any lofty ideal, or humanitarian aim, but only one thing: its inspired, uplifted language, its new and pure melody. . . . Let art be just art." [10] The early Marxian theory of literature failed to penetrate the Ukraine, and the esthetic views of such writers as Plekhanov were practically unknown.

In the absence of theoretical literature it is all the more noteworthy that two distinct schools of poetry developed in the Ukraine before 1917. Both arose under Western European and Russian influences, and left very deep impressions on the post-revolutionary literature.

Ukrainian Schools of Poetry

That discerning Soviet Ukrainian literary critic, M. Zerov, believes that "the diarchy of neo-realism and neo-romanticism has been characteristic of literature up to the present day." [11] The off-

[9] W. E. Harkins, "Slavic Formalist Theories in Literary Scholarship," *Word*, VII, No. 2 (August, 1951), 178–79.

[10] M. Ievshan, "Suspil'nyi i artystychnyi element u tvorchosti," *Literaturno-naukovyi vistnyk*, III (1911); here quoted from V. Koriak, *Narys istoriï ukraïns'koï literatury; Burzhuazne pys'menstvo*, p. 588.

[11] M. Zerov, *Nove ukraïns'ke pys'menstvo*, p. 20.

shoot of neo-romanticism which became the dominant "modernist" literary trend in Russia and the Ukraine at the very beginning of the twentieth century and which reached its zenith in the early work of the greatest Soviet Ukrainian poet, Pavlo Tychyna, was Symbolism. Originating in France, it soon became a European literary movement of great significance assuming different, specific forms in various European countries. In 1901 the young Ukrainian poet Mykola Voronyi published what might be described as a "modernist manifesto," in which he called on his fellow poets to devote themselves to pure art and to reject "social themes and the feeling of duty" as "realist." [12]

The Symbolist school in the Ukraine was related to the modernist literary groups of Ukraïns'ka khata (Ukrainian Home, Kiev, 1909–14), and "Moloda muza" (The Young Muse, L'vov, 1906–14) which preceded it. Unlike Western European Symbolists, Ukrainian Symbolists were not concerned with protests against materialism. They reacted against the narrow ethnographism of nineteenth-century Ukrainian literature and represented a literary trend toward "Europeanization," while trying to preserve their national identity.

At first, in 1918, the Symbolists (P. Tychyna, D. Zahul, K. Polishchuk, M. Tereshchenko, P. Fylypovych, O. Slisarenko, and V. Kobylians'kyi) grouped themselves about the *Literaturno-krytychnyi al'manakh* (Literary and Critical Almanac) and after 1919 around *Muzahet* (Musagete, a name borrowed from A. Belyi's Symbolist group Muzaget). They proclaimed their belief in "art for art's sake," but this did not lead them to "ivory towers." On the contrary, having among them such talented critics as Iurii Ivaniv-Mezhenko, Iakiv Savchenko, and Dmytro Zahul, they were the first to formulate the basic postulates of a new theory of literature. The influence of the Symbolists spread to the Ukrainian theater. In writing "Teatral'nyi lyst" (A Letter from the Theater) in *Literaturno-krytychnyi al'manakh* (No. 1, 1918), Les' Kurbas strongly attacked "realism—the greatest enemy of art." He visualized the art of the future as coming from the "homeland of symbolism."

The Symbolist credo was expressed with great force and clarity by Iurii Ivaniv-Mezhenko in the article "Tvorchist' individuuma i kolektyv" (The Creative Art of the Individual and the Mass).[13]

---

[12] Khronika, *Literaturno-naukovyi vistnyk*, No. 9, 1901, p. 14.
[13] *Muzahet*, 1918.

Mezhenko's basic premise is that "a creative individual [artist] can create only when he holds himself higher than the mass, and if, independent of it, he still feels nationally a sense of identity with it." The two, in his opinion, are indispensable to each other, and although a true artist transcends the mass, his art must have its roots in a national soil. "Nationality dictates its conditions to the individual [artist] and that is why we know of no nonnational or international artists. It is a different question as to how this or that work of art will be used by other nationalities; the important thing is that the creative moment was achieved on the foundation of a national and a popular spirit." [14]

Mezhenko viewed with grave apprehension the efforts of the "proletarian" hack writers to impose the will of the mass on the artist. "In this," he wrote, "I see the victory of a material culture over a spiritual, or rather not a victory but the first determined and obstinately warlike thrusts." [15] He attempted, therefore, to sustain the national art, which for him was the only true art. "Let us turn to the people; our people still do not know the machine; even if they do, the machine will never be able to befoul their imagination and psyche and dominate them. I shall only say one more thing: that material culture cannot destroy the national character of a people and therefore I advance the principle of nationality as something permanent and unchangeable." [16]

In another article in *Muzahet,* I. Maidan (pseudonym of Zahul) wrote that the "national revival was brought about by poetic romanticism. . . . It is no wonder that the ideologists of the proletarian movement put all their hopes in the future of proletarian culture and proletarian art, and endeavor by all means to create such a culture. It is still a gamble as to whether they will succeed, or whether they will be forced to admit that there can only be a national culture." [17]

How daring such statements were we can judge from the fact that after their publication the journal *Muzahet* was banned by the Soviet authorities in the Ukraine, and some of its contributors were threatened with arrest.[18]

This interference of the Party in literary affairs may be regarded

---

[14] Leites and Iashek, *Desiat' rokiv,* II, 16–17.
[15] *Ibid.,* p. 18.
[16] *Ibid.*
[17] *Ibid.,* p. 61.
[18] Hordyns'kyi, *Literaturna krytyka,* p. 12.

as one of the first acts of political control, although it was merely
a ban on what was thought to be something "nationalist and bourgeois." The Symbolists were forced to take up a defensive position. The Muzahet group ceased to exist and some of its members
joined the new association Grono (Cluster), which issued a manifesto more palatable to the Party,[19] while others joined forces with
the Neoclassicist group ASPIS (Asotsiiatsiia pys'mennykiv) or remained individual "fellow travelers." [20] The magazine *Grono* soon
ceased publication, but the *Muzahet* tradition was given a new,
almost "proletarian" twist in the publication *Vyr revoliutsii*
(Whirlpool of the Revolution, 1921, edited by Valeriian Polishchuk). However, individual Symbolists continued to play an important part in literary life up to the late twenties. The breadth
of their vision and their knowledge of European literary criticism
had helped them to remain a vital force in Soviet Ukrainian literature.

It is, of course, extremely dangerous to fix any definite lines of
descent of literary organizations or groups. Such generalizations as
are offered here are made in order to clarify somewhat the complex
literary scene.

If, for the sake of simplification, we agreed to regard the Symbolists as a product of "neo-romanticism," then it would be per-
missible to regard the Futurists, the literary school second in importance in prerevolutionary Ukraine, as having evolved from
"neo-realism." In fact the Futurists were not hostile to the Symbolists, and on many occasions M. Semenko, the most talented Ukrainian Futurist, published his works in *Literaturno-krytychnyi al'manakh*. The Futurists were also in the stream of "Europeanization."

The Futurists were organized as a literary group in Kiev in 1913
under the leadership of M. Semenko. A product of Western Europe, Futurism came to Russia before 1910, and emerged as a distinct literary movement in 1911–12. Directed partly against Symbolism and Acmeism, and armed with revolutionary theories and
apocalyptic visions of the new art, Futurism soon gathered a con-

19 For the full text see Leites and Iashek, *Desiat' rokiv,* II, 29–30.

20 The use of the term "fellow travelers" (*poputnyky*) had even less justification in
the Ukraine than in Russia. Those Ukrainian writers who did not support the Soviet
regime in the Ukraine were generally outright opponents of it and could not be described as Communist sympathizers.

siderable following among the Russian poets, who later formed several separate groups. The two most renowed among the Russian Futurist poets were V. Khlebnikov and V. Maiakovskii. Another well-known Russian Futurist, Igor Severianin, exercised strong influence on Semenko.

The Futurist credo, as expounded by Marinetti in 1909, was in general accepted by both Russian and Ukrainian Futurists. All of them preached with excessive zeal the necessity of the abolition of literary traditions, showed boundless enthusiasm for the future society liberated from all prejudices, and, rejecting all known poetic conventions, wrote their poems in exuberant *vers libre*. Like the Russian Futurists, Semenko and his followers not only showed a passion for the destruction of accepted standards but also left a considerable body of highly original poetry of lasting interest. Their influence on the development of poetic form was very stimulating. Semenko published his first two volumes of Futurist poetry in 1914, *Derzannia* (Audacity) and *Kvero-Futuryzm* (Quero-Futurism), but it was not until after the Revolution that his talent was fully revealed.

In 1919 Semenko organized a Futurist group in Kiev under the name of "Flamingo," and in June, 1921, the Kharkov Futurists (Slisarenko and Shkurupii) formed the group "Komkosmos." [21]

Some Futurists in Russia and in the Ukraine welcomed the Revolution as the beginning of a new era in history. They regrouped their forces, partly adapting them to the demands of the time by creating in 1922 the new "Pan-Futurist" literary organizations, which will be more fully treated in the next chapter.

While the Symbolists (Muzahet) came under fire from the Bolsheviks, the Futurists met with their conditional approval. Neither group, however, could be classed as "proletarian," since both viewed Soviet rule with reserve.

A third important "nonproletarian" group of writers which came into being in 1917–18 was that of the Neoclassicists. It consisted of poets and critics having close ties with the Ukrainian Academy of Sciences in Kiev (founded in 1918), among whom the most talented were Mykola Zerov, Maksym Ryl's'kyi, Mykhailo Drai-

[21] See M. Kachaniuk, "Materialy do istoriï futuryzmu na radians'kii Ukraïni," *Literaturnyi arkhiv*, I–II (1930); III–IV (1931).

Khmara, Pavlo Fylypovych, and O. Burkhardt (known under the pseudonym of Iurii Klen). The name given to them was not very appropriate. The poets in this group, apart from Zerov, wrote neither in the tradition of the Greek and Roman masters nor of the French Parnassians of the nineteenth century, but rather in that of Romanticism and Symbolism. In literary theory and criticism, their *maître*, Zerov, opposed the chaotic impressionism of most of the contemporary "revolutionary" poets. "With very few exceptions," he wrote, "our poets learn very little, and do not try to improve their command over words. They seize on *vers libre* like savages on glass jewellery . . . cutting off the roots of any further growth of a poetic style." [22] To this common practice Zerov opposed his ideal of classical detachment and perfection. An interesting feature of this group which a few years later gained great prominence was that they rejected the commonly held belief that organization in literature was necessary. Zerov, who in 1918 was the editor of *Knyhar* (Bookman) and later became a professor of literature, wrote that "we must protest against group-mindedness, group-patriotism, and group-exclusiveness. We must protest against the belief that in a literary group we have the sole criteria of truth." [23]

Thus the Neoclassicists, who even disliked the label given them (they were also referred to as Academists), preferred to exist as a small group unaffiliated to any particular journal. Although the Neoclassicists maintained close contact with the Academy of Sciences, they strongly opposed the "populist" (*narodnyts'ka*) theory of literature of the Academician Serhii Iefremov. After 1921, the Neoclassicists were referred to as a definite literary organization with their own ideology, which will be treated more fully later.

Early Nonproletarian and Proletarian Literary Groups and Organizations

The establishment of Soviet rule in the Ukraine in 1919 had brought with it the gospel of Marxian literary theory. This theory, although not yet hardened into dogma, incorporated nevertheless

[22] From a preface to *Kamena;* here quoted from V. P., "Mykola Zerov: Kamena, Poeziï," *Ukraïns'kyi zasiv,* No. 4, 1943, p. 146.
[23] Quoted in Iurii Klen, *Spohady pro neokliasykiv,* p. 22.

some fundamental assumptions about the nature and purpose of literature. Perhaps the most significant article of the new doctrine as expounded by Lenin was the belief that literature must be subordinated to the government and the Party and must serve as their weapon in the creation of the socialist state.

In 1905 Lenin had stated the principle of "Party literature" in the following terms:

In what, then, does this principle of party literature consist? Apart from the fact that for a socialist, proletarian literature cannot be a means of profit for persons or groups, it cannot altogether be the concern of an individual, independent of the proletarian cause. Down with the nonparty littérateurs; down with littérateurs-supermen. Literature should become a part of the all-proletarian cause.[24]

This concept of Lenin's was rooted in the belief that

One cannot live in a society and be free from that society. The independence of the bourgeois author, artist, and actress is merely a pretended independence from the money-bag, from the bribe, from being kept.[25]

Hence only a socialist revolution can promote free creativeness, "since not profit or career, but the idea of socialism and interest in the workers will attract new forces into its ranks." [26]

It should be borne in mind that Lenin's article of 1905 referred to a particular historical event. As Viacheslav Polonskii pointed out in 1928, "our party had for the first time come out of the underground. It was confronted with the task of gathering the genuine revolutionary forces. . . . Up to 1905 the entire legal social democratic activity was non-party. That is, it did not enter into the party organization but stood outside." [27] Apart from Polonskii, however, very few Soviet critics were conscious of the qualifications which this statement of Lenin's included.

On the other hand, it was common knowledge among both Soviet literary critics and politicians that Lenin believed in making use of the bourgeois culture of the past,[28] so that proletarian culture

---

[24] Lenin, *Sochineniia*, VIII, 387.   [25] *Ibid.*, p. 389.
[26] *Ibid.*, p. 390.
[27] Quoted from Max Eastman, *Artists in Uniform*, pp. 248–49.
[28] Lenin, *Sochineniia*, XXV, 357; also V. I. Lenin, "The Tasks of the Youth Leagues" (speech delivered at the Third All-Russian Congress of the Russian Young Communist League, October 2, 1920), *Selected Works*, II, 664.

might be developed from the store of knowledge accumulated by mankind. From Lenin's words it was clear that in the Soviet state literature was to be guided, although its growth might be fostered by the literary heritage, properly selected and utilized, of the past.

The implementation of the Communist theory of literature confronted the Party with many difficulties which could not be satisfactorily solved during the period of War Communism (1917–20). The pragmatic theory of literature which it preached sanctioned all means toward the fulfillment of the goal. This goal, of course, was the creation of a truly "proletarian literature." In so far as the destruction of the old bourgeois literary conventions was held to be imperative, the Futurists, although themselves of undeniably bourgeois origin, were encouraged to carry on their debunking campaigns. At the same time, the training of new proletarian writers became urgently necessary, especially since many prominent Russian and Ukrainian writers found themselves outside the boundaries of the Soviet state.

The opportunity to provide literary education on a mass scale was seized by A. Bogdanov and his Proletcult. Conceived primarily as a chain of training centers in art and literature, the Proletcult was, as its name conveyed, an attempt to foster "proletarian culture." However, although the Proletcult clearly postulated the creation of a literature which would satisfy the needs of the proletariat through the collective effort of proletarian writers, it made an important reservation: there must be no interference in its activities by the Party. It was this claim to autonomy which later made the Proletcult the target of Party attacks.

In the Ukraine, Proletcultism exhibited all the features which it displayed in Russia. It existed as a large, well-organized network of literary workshops until 1923, when it finally disintegrated following the sharp attacks which Lenin made against it in 1920, and then in 1921 and 1922.[29] The first Ukrainian Proletcult groups were organized in 1919, after the Russian pattern, in the larger cities of the Ukraine. They never became very popular and were strongly

[29] For Lenin's opposition to the Proletcult, see *Literaturnaia entsiklopediia,* VI, 212–16.

Apparently the Central Committee of the CP(B)U, on the occasion of the Proletcult's condemnation by the Party, issued a special resolution on literature ("Tezisy o khudozhestvennoi politike," *Komunist,* September 1, 1921). This document, mentioned in *Ocherk istorii ukrainskoi sovetskoi literatury* (pp. 55, 57) could not be obtained.

criticized in the Symbolist (Muzahet) and other quarters. In 1922 an Organizational Bureau was formed in Kharkov which undertook to unite all the Proletcults in the Ukraine into one organization.[30] This attempt ended in failure, partly because the Proletcult "anti-Leninist approach to the nationality problem stirred opposition from Ukrainian writers." [31]

Although one cannot, of course, regard the Proletcult movement in the Ukraine as an instrument of the Party's policy, it cannot be denied that Proletcultists were the first to create a new literary organization which was proletarian in spirit. Their suppression in 1923 marked the first major act of Party control within Soviet literary life. Yet during the period of the Proletcult's activities, the Party's attitude to literature was rather ambivalent. Relative freedom was allowed, so long as it did not endanger the "interests of the proletariat," and it was hoped that under the gentle guidance of government agencies a new "proletarian literature" would somehow arise.

A Literary Committee was created in the Ukraine in 1919 as a branch of a government agency in charge of the arts. In March, 1919, this All-Ukrainian Literary Committee (Vseukrlitkom) published in the literary supplement to the government newspaper *Izvestiia vremennogo raboche-krestianskogo pravitel'stva i kharkovskogo soveta rabochykh deputatov* (later known as *Visti VUTsVK*) an announcement about the proposed publication of a literary journal, *Siiach* (Sower). It is interesting to note that this announcement was printed in Ukrainian in contrast to the rest of the paper which was in Russian.

The Literary Committee had under it small sections of writers who were assigned special tasks. The section of "proletarian writers" which partly absorbed the small group "Gild Kameniariv" (The Guild of Quarrymen), created in Kharkov in 1918, was responsible for the publication of two issues of the journal *Zori griadushchego* (The Stars of Tomorrow),[32] printed partly in Ukrainian and partly in Russian. Their contributors included Khvyl'ovyi, Sosiura, Senchenko, Dolengo, Korzh, and Mykhailychenko.

The CP(B)U could not exercise any effective control over litera-

[30] *Visti VUTsVK*, May 1, 1922 (cited hereafter as *Visti*).
[31] O. Vedmits'kyi, "Literaturnyi front: 1919–1931," *Literaturnyi arkhiv*, IV–V (1931), 111.
[32] In 1921 this journal was taken over by the Proletcult.

ture in 1919–20 because its rivals, the Borot'bists, also had their literary movement headed by such talented writers as Vasyl' Chumak and Hnat Mykhailychenko (both executed by the Denikin troops in 1919), Andrii Zalyvchyi (shot in 1918), and Vasyl' Ellan Blakytnyi.[33] In 1918 these writers formed the literary group "Borot'ba," led by Blakytnyi and Mykhailychenko, which in 1919 published the symposium *Zshytky borot'by* (Chapbooks of Struggle) and *Chervonyi vinok* (The Red Wreath). In 1919–20 they published, on behalf of Vseukrlitkom, the journal *Mystetstvo* (Art) with contributions by Semenko, Mykhailychenko, Chumak, Zahul, Savchenko, Tereshchenko, and Tychyna.

It was in this latter journal (*Art*) that Hnat Mykhailychenko published his "Theses on the New Proletarian Art," which in their appeal to the masses competed with the Proletcult, with one important distinction, namely, the emphasis laid on the national aspect of art. "Proletarian art," wrote Mykhailychenko, "can reach its international goal only through channels national both in content and form." [34]

Although chiefly concerned with problems of the present and the future, literary critics occasionally attempted to cast a glance into the past. After some hesitation as to whether Shevchenko, under the new regime, deserved the prominent place which he held in the consciousness of most Ukrainians, the Communist critics decided to accept him as "one of us." Accordingly, Koriak attempted what was one of the first interpretations of Shevchenko's work in a Communist spirit.[35] He refused to regard Shevchenko as a "poet of the people," and saw in him "one of the first prophets of the proletariat and the future socialist revolution." [36] Subsequently, the Soviet view of Shevchenko underwent frequent revision, and often the current interpretation of the work of that poet is a touchstone of the literary policy of the Party.[37]

The difficulties which beset the Soviet authorities in what Koriak aptly called "the organization of the October literature" were not made easier by the absence of several prominent writers and critics

[33] See M. Tarnovs'kyi, "Pionery ukraïns'koï zhovtnevoï literatury," *Vpered, Kalendar.*
[34] Leites and Iashek, *Desiat' rokiv,* II, 27–28.
[35] V. Koriak, *Borot'ba za Shevchenka.*   [36] *Ibid.,* p. 58.
[37] Cf. P. Odarchenko, "Soviet Interpretation of Shevchenko," manuscript in the Research Program on the USSR.

(Oles', Nikovs'kyi) who after the Revolution left the Soviet Ukraine. Others, who stayed behind, had made themselves unpopular with the new regime. In 1921, the well-known poet Hryts'ko Chuprynka was executed on charges of counterrevolution.

In 1920 Kharkov became *de facto* the capital of the Soviet Ukraine. In this city where, in comparison with Kiev, Ukrainian cultural life was stagnant, the Literary Committee made a supreme effort to gather all the writers around its new publication *Shliakhy mystetstva* (The Paths of Art, 1920–22). Aided by some Borot'bist writers, this journal expressed the hope that it would become the platform "where in free discussion there will crystallize a single trend and a single school . . . the school of Communist art." [38]

However, all attempts to create a more permanent organization of writers who declared themselves to be on the side of the Soviet government ended in failure. After the *Shliakhy mystetstva,* the group "Zhovten' " (October, 1921; comprising Khvyl'ovyi, Sosiura, Iohansen, Koriak) and the "Federation of Proletarian Writers and Artists" (1922) both failed to last longer than a year. In 1921, Blakytnyi became the editor of the official daily of the government, the *Visti VUTsVK,* which began to be an important factor in literary life. Another able editor, Serhii Pylypenko, was publishing *Selians'ka hazeta* (The Peasant News), a successor to *Bil'shovyk,* which became a platform for peasant writers.

This period of searching and probing most clearly manifested itself in the ideological meandering of Iurii Ivaniv-Mezhenko, who, as we saw, was a staunch defender of national art and individualism in 1918, but who one year later joined Grono and subscribed to its formula of compromise between individual and collective art. In 1921 Mezhenko wrote an article in *Proletars'ka os'vita,* proclaiming that "we do not understand and do not want to understand your feeble literary 'I,' because we are striving toward a spontaneous and creative 'We.' " [39] V. Koriak, commenting on these swift changes, expressed the belief that the Ukrainian intelligentsia, "formerly in the clutches of the petit-bourgeois, nationalist ideology, has become *déclassé* and proletarized and therefore must accept the rule of the victors and faithfully serve them." [40]

Koriak's hope was premature. The struggle between the Com-

[38] Hordyns'kyi, *Literaturna krytyka,* p. 36.
[39] Leites and Iashek, *Desiat' rokiv,* II, 62.   [40] *Ibid.,* pp. 63–64.

munist and national forces which arose during the 1917 Revolution continued during the subsequent years. As far as literary tendencies were concerned, this contest produced one important result. It proved that while some prerevolutionary literary schools had lost their appeal, and others (the Symbolists) were in decline, the new Communist attempts to create a formula of "proletarian literature" had ended in failure. Although there could be no return to the old values, new ones were not easy to create. The very concept of "proletarian literature," which came to play an important role in literary politics, was not clearly defined. By 1922 it was obvious that the Party did not support the interpretation which the Proletcult had given to it earlier, implying that "proletarian literature" could be created by artists of proletarian (that is, Communist) orientation, working collectively for the education of the masses through literature. On the other hand, some of the principles of the Proletcult (art must serve the interests of the proletarian class) were taken over by the Russian "proletarian" literary groups. These groups were chiefly concerned with the task of "organizing" [41] the efforts of proletarian writers to create a literature which would reflect the interests of the proletariat. Utilization of bourgeois art for that purpose was grudgingly approved, but the main emphasis of the "proletarian writers" (who did not have to be workers themselves) was laid on the subordination of literature to the interests of the proletariat and hence to the Party.

At the same time, however, it became abundantly clear that politics could not successfully invade the field of literary theory. The introduction of the NEP (New Economic Policy) in the Ukraine in 1923 brought further compromises between the outlook of the Communists and that of the fellow travelers, leading to a synthesis of their literary beliefs.

[41] In Soviet parlance literature became a matter of "organization." Cf. V. Koriak, *Orhanizatsiia zhovtnevoï literatury.*

[I I I]

LITERARY ORGANIZATIONS AND

LITERARY POLITICS, 1922–1925

Literature and the Cultural Policy of the Party

The very fact that as a result of the Revolution literary life in the Ukraine as well as in Russia manifested itself almost exclusively through literary organizations is of great significance. The importance of doctrine impressed itself upon the revolutionary elite with singular force. In the vacuum created by the complete destruction of the old order, there was a deeply felt need for new clear-cut systems and theories of literary creation. Nourished by a truly revolutionary fervor, these new literary groups, schools of poetry, and magazine coteries attempted to interpret Marxism in many different ways in the hope of distilling from it the precious essence of proletarian literature. The search for such a formula at once united and divided them, for though they often agreed upon the ultimate goal, they differed sharply as to the means of reaching it.

Preoccupation with the theory of literature and with literary organization nevertheless betrayed a certain sterility and decay within the literature itself. Through the verbal barrage of various manifestoes and literary doctrines, one could often glimpse the withered wellsprings of creative art after the upheaval of the Revolution.

Those few contemporaries who were aware of this pleaded for a concentrated endeavor by individual writers. Zerov complained that "there is very little literary education, and therefore very little possibility of learning from literary models, of testing various styles, of emancipating oneself from the strong influence of a master in order to crystallize one's own literary personality." [1] The reasons for this condition, according to Zerov, lay in the provincialism of the large Ukrainian cities, in the ignorance, arrogance, and graphomania of many writers. What was needed was "less patronage and soft soap, and more refinement and criticism." [2]

Literary life in the early twenties was viewed with obvious alarm by Iefremov, a scholar of the old school. Yet his appraisal of the situation cannot be disregarded. "On the surface," wrote Iefremov, "literary publications give the illusion of a turbulent life, but in reality it is something ephemeral, a froth, carried idly by the stormy wave." [3] Noticing the shift of interest from the country to the city, he caustically observed that "the glorification of the city began at the time of its greatest ruin and decay; hymns to the machine were sung when no machines were left intact, and the factories became heroic when they ceased working." [4] Iefremov felt confident, however, that the new literary tendencies did not portend great changes. "Fortunately," he wrote, "over the abyss of chaos there hovers already a divine spirit—the spirit of real creativeness. In the last resort talent alone is decisive; and it grows ever larger than the frames made for it." [5]

Iefremov's skeptical view of post-revolutionary literary tendencies represented the beliefs of a great many Ukrainian intellectuals who were classed as "inner emigrants." In the twenties they occupied a prominent place in the cultural life of the country (Iefremov, Nikovs'kyi, Chuprynka, Mohylians'kyi, Kapel'horods'kyi), and their conviction that art and literature should be independent of current politics was shared by many older Ukrainian writers and scholars. The "inner emigration" was particularly influential in the publishing world (publishers like Rukh, Slovo, and others). Soviet sources grossly minimize the part played by this group in the cultural life of the Ukraine. Its influence was felt by some young writers, by the village intelligentsia, and by the peasantry. The small space in this study devoted to the representatives of the "inner emigration" has been dictated by the fact that the latter took no active part in literary politics but merely formed a

[1] M. Zerov, Do dzherel, p. 40.   [2] Ibid., p. 41.
[3] S. Iefremov, Istoriia ukraïns'koho pys'menstva, II, 342.
[4] Ibid., p. 344.   [5] Ibid., p. 347.

passive opposition to the Soviet regime. Labeled as the remnants of the "dying order," they were allowed to vegetate, but were unable to offer any leadership to the young generation.

The Symbolists were scattered and had no journal of their own, while the Neoclassicists held themselves aloof. Whatever other passive resistance to the "proletarian" literary groups existed found its expression in the creation of the Ukrainian fellow-traveler group "Lanka" (The Link), in Kiev. Formed in 1924 from a small group of ASPIS (Asotsiiatsiia pys'mennykiv—Association of Writers), Lanka consisted of B. Antonenko-Davydovych, V. Pidmohyl'nyi, H. Kosynka, Ie. Pluzhnyk, T. Os'machka, and M. Halych. Like the Neoclassicists they remained active until the late twenties.

The Ukrainian Futurists continued for some time their habit of sitting on the fence. In 1922 they formed a Pan-Futurist (ASPAN-FUT) organization which offered its services to the regime but claimed at the same time that Pan-Futurism alone had a "practical system of proletarian art," and that it intended to be "organizational ideologically." [6] The subsequent history of Ukrainian Futurism is a process of continuous division and discord, most of it hardly worth the attention of a literary historian. In 1924 the ASPANFUT split into the AsKK (Asotsiiatsiia komunistychnoï kul'tury—Association of Communist Culture) and an independent group, Zhovten' (October). In April, 1925, AsKK merged with the disintegrating "Hart." However, while Ialovyi, Slisarenko, Shkurupii, and Bazhan were ready to accept Hart's platform,[7] the noisiest Futurist poet, Semenko, was determined to follow a solitary path only to reappear with a new organization at a later date.

The reason for the weakness of the fellow travelers was to be found, not in their general acquiescence to Soviet rule, but rather in the privileged position of the Ukrainian Communists of Borot'bist orientation within the cultural life of the Ukraine. With the Commissariat of Education in the hands of Hryn'ko and then of Shums'kyi, Ellan Blakytnyi established as the editor of *Visti*, and Shums'kyi in charge of the newly established (1923) "thick" magazine *Chervonyi shliakh*, the Borot'bists were able to exert a strong

[6] Verbatim from "What Panfuturism Wants" (in English), *Semafor u maibutnie*, 1922; full text in A. Leites and M. Iashek, *Desiat' rokiv ukraïns'koï literatury (1917–1927)*, II, 113.

[7] "Uhody mizh orhanizatsiiamy 'Hart' i AsKK (Komunkul't)," *Visti*, April 5, 1925.

influence on cultural and literary activities. It must not be assumed, however, that these Ukrainian Communists were the sole masters of the literary Ukraine or that they always agreed on matters of national policy. This is clearly indicated by the attitude of the secretary of the Central Committee of the CP(B)U, D. Lebid',[8] which took as its starting point the existence in the Ukraine of a "struggle of two cultures." [9] According to Lebid's theory, the Russian culture which still prevailed in Ukrainian cities must inevitably clash with the culture of the Ukrainian villages, and there was no certainty as to which of them would be victorious. However, all these fears were dispelled by Moscow's decision to allow the "Ukrainization" of the Ukraine.

This may be regarded as the last victory of the Borot'bist elements within the Party. At the Sixth Party Conference, in November, 1921, when neither Blakytnyi nor Shums'kyi was elected to the Central Committee of the CP(B)U, their political influence declined considerably, but their role in cultural and literary affairs was undiminished. The Ukrainization, strongly advocated by the Borot'bists, was initiated by the following decree of the CP(B)U, issued on August 1, 1923:

The workers' and peasants' government deems it necessary . . . to center the efforts of the state on the widest diffusion of the Ukrainian language. The formal equality of the two most widely spread languages in the Ukraine, Ukrainian and Russian, which has been recognized up to now, is not sufficient. The slow development of Ukrainian culture in general, the shortage of suitable textbooks, and the lack of well-trained personnel have brought about a situation in which the Russian language enjoys, in fact, supremacy. In order to abolish this inequality, the government will initiate a series of measures which, while respecting the equal rights of all languages on Ukrainian territory, will safeguard the position of Ukrainian; a position to which the numerical and other preponderances of the Ukrainian people entitle it.[10]

The policy of Ukrainization, of encouraging the widest possible cultural and linguistic freedom, was, in point of fact, the last concession made to Ukrainian nationalism by the Soviet rulers. The theory behind this policy was that of Lenin and his chief expert

[8] *Kommunist*, March 23, 1923.
[9] *Biuleten' piatoi vseukrainskoi konferentsii KP(b)U* (1920).
[10] S. Nykolyshyn, *Kul'turna polityka bol'shevykiv i ukraïns'kyi kul'turnyi protses*, p. 15.

on national problems, Stalin. In 1921, Stalin, addressing the Tenth Congress of the RCP(B), declared that "even if the Russian elements still dominate Ukrainian cities, there is no doubt that in the course of time these cities will be Ukrainized." [11] However, it was decided to adopt this theory as a policy only after the Twelfth Congress of the RCP(B), when Lebid's theory of the inevitable struggle of two cultures (Russian and Ukrainian) was definitely discarded.[12] The actual implementation of the Ukrainization policy came still later, in 1924–25.

It is interesting to note that even during the debates on Ukrainization in the Central Executive Committee of the USSR,[13] Ienukidze, the secretary of the Committee, expressed the sincere hope that other non-Russian republics would not be as impatient as the Ukraine to introduce their native languages into official use, and was persuaded in favor of Ukrainization by the argument that such a policy was good not intrinsically but for the purposes of propaganda aimed primarily at Ukrainians living in Poland, Czechoslovakia, and Rumania.

The Party's decision to adopt the policy of Ukrainization had no less significance for the development of Ukrainian literature than for the Ukrainian language. Indeed, in spite of the official recognition of Ukrainian language and literature as legitimate expressions of the people, there was, until 1923, some doubt as to their exact position in the Soviet state. The Ukrainians must have remembered the article in *Izvestiia* by their Chairman of the Council of the People's Commissars, Khristian Rakovskii, pleading that Ukrainian should not be allowed to become the language of administration in the Ukraine.[14] They must have had their doubts as to the actual equality and freedom promised to Ukrainian culture and language by Lenin, when, during the period of War Communism (1917–21), they saw the heavy preponderance of Russian books and newspapers in the Ukraine. The Soviet Ukrainian press of that period is full of complaints about discrimination against the use of Ukrainian. In 1923 it looked as if the Party was seriously

[11] *Stenograficheskii otchët X s"ezdu RKP(b)*, p. 93.
[12] Leites and Iashek, *Desiat' rokiv*, II, 388.
[13] *Tsentral'nii ispolnitel'nii komitet, 3 sozyva, 2 sessiia, stenograficheskii otchët*, pp. 458 ff.
[14] Kh. Rakovskii, "Beznadezhnoe delo," *Izvestiia VTsIKS*, January 3, 1919.

introducing a change. The Rumanian Rakovskii was replaced by the Ukrainian Chubar, and Shums'kyi, an ardent believer in home rule, was appointed Chief of the Agitation and Propaganda Section of the Central Committee of the CP(B)U. To the average Ukrainian, or even to the average Ukrainian writer, this probably did not appear at the time as a move in the Communist strategy to win the support of the people and of the Ukrainian intelligentsia. The latter welcomed this opportunity to propagate Ukrainian language and culture, forgetful of that part of the bargain in which they were required to pay the devil his due.

Literary Organizations Pluh and Hart

The official declaration on Ukrainization very nearly coincided with the creation of the mass organization of peasant writers, "Pluh" (Plough), founded in 1922. Led by the fable writer Serhii Pylypenko, Pluh aimed at "uniting the dispersed peasant writers who, supporting the idea of a close union of the revolutionary peasantry with the proletariat, will advance with the latter toward the creation of a new socialist culture and will disseminate these ideas among the peasant masses in the Ukraine regardless of their nationality." [15]

In their literary program members of Pluh had as their primary aim the "creation of broad pictures, works with universal themes, dealing primarily with the life of the revolutionary peasantry." [16] Acknowledging the importance of content rather than form, the Pluzhians pledged themselves to exercise "the greatest simplicity and economy in artistic methods." Their credo was rooted in the conviction that

our epoch is a period of transition from the capitalist to the Communist system, from the class to the classless society, a period of revolutions and wars which began here with the October Revolution. The struggle is between the bourgeoisie on the one side and the proletariat on the other. Other classes can choose between these two; there is no third camp. In this process of class struggle the peasantry shows its lack of unity and is divided between partial support of the bourgeoisie (the "kulaks" and the well-to-do peasants) and partial support of the proletariat (poor

---

[15] Leites and Iashek, *Desiat' rokiv*, II, 75.
[16] *Ibid.*, p. 76.

peasantry, agricultural laborers, and the "middle "peasant). The latter groups we regard as revolutionary peasantry. . . . Hence the peasantry is potentially the proletariat and its place is on the anti-bourgeois front.[17]

In order to create conditions suitable for mass production of peasant writers, Pluh developed a wide network of study groups, branches, and circles throughout the country. It published a journal, *Pluzhanyn* (Ploughman), later a monthly, *Pluh,* and *Pluh— Literaturnyi al'manakh,* all of which were widely read. With such aids it was hoped to realize the new concept of literature as a "process in which masses of literary workers, from those with the highest qualifications and the greatest talent down to village correspondents and contributors to wall newspapers and circulars," would collaborate.[18]

This attempt to form a mass literary organization in the Ukraine (the second after the termination of the Proletcult) met with success. Pluh had hundreds of disciplined members; it formed its own Central Committee with special sections for the Komsomol (Communist Youth League), for women, for children, for drama, and also a group—"Western Ukraine"—representing Western Ukrainian (Galician) writers living as political immigrants in the Soviet Ukraine. Among Pluh's members were some well-known writers (Holovko, Panch, Paniv, Epik, Kopylenko, Usenko). Its rapid growth revealed, however, those internal weaknesses which were shortly to be attacked by another literary organization with an ideological and esthetic platform different from that of Pluh.

In January, 1923, the so-called proletarian writers, some of whom had previously belonged to the Borot'bist literary group or to Zhovten', founded a new organization of proletarian writers called "Hart" (Tempering). Its aim, as the first paragraph of its constitution stated, was "to unite the proletarian writers of the Ukraine, including the artists active in the field of the theater, art, and music, who, using Ukrainian language as a means of artistic expression, aim at the creation of one international, Communist culture, and who spread Communist ideology and fight against the petit-bourgeois propertied ideology." [19]

[17] *Ibid.,* p. 73.   [18] S. Pylypenko, "Nashi hrikhy," *Pluzhanyn,* No. 4–5, 1925.
[19] Leites and Iashek, *Desiat' rokiv,* II, 374.

Hart is rightly regarded as the progenitor of Ukrainian proletarian literature; its members were destined to play a crucial part in
the literary politics of the period covered by this study. The most
prominent among them were: Ellan Blakytnyi, Volodymyr Sosiura,
Mykola Khvyl'ovyi, Maik Iohansen, Ivan Kulyk, Pavlo Tychyna,
Valeriian Polishchuk, Ivan Dniprovs'kyi, and Volodymyr Koriak.

The leader, Blakytnyi, was a veteran ex-Borot'bist politician and
a brilliant organizer. Educated at a theological seminary and a com-
mercial institute, he was ready to become a revolutionary youth
leader. During the Revolution he edited *Borot'ba,* was the literary
expert of the Borot'bist party, and in his spare time wrote revolutionary verses and some parodies. Despite his delicate health, he was
a tireless worker, an excellent orator, and a first-rate editor of the
organ of the Ukrainian Central Executive Committee, *Visti.*

Volodymyr Sosiura was a poet whose revolutionary verses, well
spiced with purely Ukrainian romanticism, made him very popular
with readers.

Mykola Khvyl'ovyi was a young man with a future. A writer of
romantic and impressionist short stories on contemporary topics,
he described himself in these words:

I passionately love the sky, the grass, the stars, pensive evenings, and
soft autumn mornings . . . all that perfumes the sadly gay land of our
motley life. I madly love gentle women with good, wise eyes and bitterly
regret that I was not destined to be born shapely as a leopard. I also love
our Ukrainian steppes swept by the blue storm of the civil war. I love
our cherry orchards. . . . I believe in the distant Commune, I believe
in it so fiercely that I am ready to die for it. I am a dreamer, and from
the height of my incomparable insolence I spit on the skeptics of our
age.[20]

Maik Iohansen, of German origin, was an accomplished linguist
and a master of intellectual poetry. Ivan Kulyk spent much of his
time in Canada where he organized the first proletarian literary
groups among Ukrainian settlers. He is the author of an anthology
of American poetry in Ukrainian translation. Pavlo Tychyna, the
greatest talent of them all, was a Symbolist who welcomed the
Revolution with vivid poetic images which ring true even now, despite the author's later career as Stalin's court poet. Valeriian Po-

---

[20] Mykola Khvyl'ovyi, "Vstupna novela," *Etiudy, Tvory,* I, 11.

lishchuk, a prolific and rhetorical writer, was often castigated for his "unhealthy eroticism." The list ends with Ivan Dniprovs'kyi (pseudonym of Ivan Shevchenko), a promising young playwright, and the ex-Borot'bist Volodymyr Koriak, a literary critic and historian.

These writers declared themselves to be an "organization of Communists and Communist sympathizers whose aim is to facilitate the work of the Communist Party by gathering all the creative forces and organizing the production of art." They based "their works on Marxian ideology and the program postulated by the Communist Party, the members of which were given priority in enrollment . . . without regard to their artistic qualifications." [21]

In view of this purely pragmatic conception of literature and the declared subservience to the Communist Party, the Hartians seemed at first to be content with an immediate program of work without much regard to esthetics or literary theory:

Art [wrote Blakytnyi] differs from science, sport, and technology in that it deals with human emotions. . . . We do not know whether, during Communism, emotions will disappear, whether the human being will change to such an extent that he will become a luminous globe consisting of the head and brain only, or whether new and transformed emotions will come into being. Therefore we do not know precisely what form art will assume under Communism. . . . However, the fact that we do not project our ideas into the field of the indefinite future we regard as an advantage, not a drawback. For it is better to feel firm ground under our feet and see the tasks dictated by today and tomorrow without attempting to leap over to the day after tomorrow. . . . This situation gives rise to one logical line along which we can create literary values; they must be created not for the use of the artists, or small ruling circles of society, but for the benefit of the wide masses of workers and peasants.[22]

This emphasis on the masses which characterized the programs of both Hart and Pluh betrayed the determination of each to exploit the cultural policy pursued by the Party at that time.

In Russia and the Ukraine the cultivation of literature was urged as a means of Communist indoctrination of the masses. The tradition of the Proletcult was still very much alive, and Lenin himself

21 Blakytnyi, "Bez manifestu," full text in Leites and Iashek, *Desiat' rokiv*, II, 84–85.
22 *Ibid.*, p. 88.

declared in 1920 that "art belongs to the people. It should let its deep roots go into the very core of the working masses. It must be understood by these masses. . . . It must comprehend and elevate the feelings, thoughts, and desires of the masses. . . . So that art can come to the people and the people to art, we must first of all raise the general level of culture." [23]

From the four records of Hart's meetings (November 1 and 18, December 28, 1923; January 10, 1924) preserved among Liubchenko's papers, it is evident that this organization placed great emphasis on drama and the theater. At the first meeting Blakytnyi spoke of the "urgent necessity of creating a drama workshop of the workers' theater affiliated with Hart," in order "to unite in one organization those active adherents (in the widest sense) in the workers' (again in the widest sense) theater, permeated with a Communist ideology." At the meeting held on December 28, 1923, membership in Hart was extended to a director of the drama workshop in the School of Red Army Officers, and on January 10, 1924, "Experimental Workshop No. 1," consisting of the former "Lesia Ukraïnka Drama Studio," was set up under Hart's management.

It soon became clear that both Pluh and Hart vied with each other for the favors of the Party by attempting to lead the masses to literature and literature to the masses. The author of the leading article in the literary supplement to *Visti* recalled that it was necessary to

bear in mind the resolutions of the Thirteenth Party Congress in the field of literature:
The basic task of the Party in the field of literature should be to take cognizance of the creative work of workers and peasants who in the process of the cultural growth of the wide masses of the Soviet Union become proletarian and peasant writers. . . . The Congress stresses the necessity for the creation of mass literature for the workers, peasants, and the soldiers of the Red Army.
A glance through the reports on the later activities of Hart and similar groups indicates that they give an account of just such work; work among the village and factory correspondents, in workers' literary circles, publication of literature for the masses, and education of the reader and the large cadres of the workers in literature alike. This work has only begun. Therefore let us not be dismayed that we still have no "great

23 K. Zetkin, *O Lenine,* pp. 34–35.

names." They will come. There will come a time of flowering, not of sugary, tinsel, or genteel, but of real, strong, iron, and earthy literature.[24]

To gain a free hand in the creation of mass literature both Pluh and Hart sought to insinuate themselves into the good graces of the Party by subordinating literature to its command, as long, of course, as they too had a voice in it. This is clearly evident from the inspection report which a special commission made on the activities of Pluh and Hart:

The workers' and peasants' inspection has in the last days completed its examination of Hart and Pluh. The inspection was conducted with the aim of surveying the material situation and resources of these organizations as well as clarifying the methods of guidance and supervision of these two groups by the Party organizations. The following are the results of our investigation: Pluh and Hart are literary organizations which provide village and city with suitable Ukrainian literature which is also in accord with the Party's policy of Ukrainization.

After praising the work of these organizations, the report goes on:

Having taken into account the fact that up to the present day the wide masses of the people are poorly informed about the activities of Pluh and Hart and that there is, as yet, no clear understanding by Party organizations of the work of these bodies, that no constructive criticism exists, and that finally no adequate material support has been offered, the inspection commission considers all these matters worthy of general attention. Furthermore it is thought necessary to suggest that Pluh's activities in the villages be conducted with caution. The heads of their branches should be Communists. . . . The Central Committee has expressed its agreement with the conclusions reached by the administrative and social inspection commission.[25]

The task of channeling those forces eager to organize literature for the masses could not be left in the hands of writers and poets alone. Both in Russia and in the Ukraine the literary organizations of proletarian writers gathered momentum in 1924 and used aggressive propaganda techniques, based no doubt on Communist practices, but used without the sanction of the Party. In Russia in

24 "Na pidhotovlenomu grunti," *Literatura, nauka, mystetstvo,* August 10, 1924.
25 "Otsinka roboty 'Hartu' i 'Pluha,'" *Literatura, nauka, mystetstvo,* September 14, 1924.

1923 the more radical group of writers and critics belonging to the literary organization of proletarian writers "Oktiabr'" (October) began to publish vitriolic attacks in the journal *Na Postu* (On Guard) with the aim of annihilating the fellow travelers and thus uniting all proletarian writers under its leadership. This group (the "Octobrists" and the "On Guardists") also dominated VAPP (All-Russian Association of Proletarian Writers) and, as we shall see later, were gaining pan-Union influence.

Blakytnyi's reference to the resolutions of the Thirteenth Party Congress shows that decisions arrived at in Moscow were of the utmost practical importance for the Ukraine. It is therefore most vital to review briefly the All-Union Party policy as it manifested itself in the resolutions on literature between 1924 and 1925.

The 1925 Party Resolution on Literature

Four months after Lenin's death, on May 19, 1924, a conference was held in Moscow in the Press Department of the Central Committee. It was convened to discuss the Bolshevik attitude to literature and is usually regarded by literary historians as the first public interference of the Party in literary life. Writers from all the Russian literary organizations took part in this conference which, guided mainly by the counsels of Bukharin and Lunacharskii, adopted a series of resolutions, later incorporated in the resolution on the press passed by the Thirteenth Party Congress (held May 23–31).[26] After referring to the "creative work of the workers and peasants," the May resolution went on to declare that "it is imperative to continue to support the most talented writers belonging to the so-called fellow travelers," and, what is perhaps most important, that "no single literary trend must come forward in the name of the Party."[27]

This pronouncement was in fact a vote of censure on the Oktiabr' –Na Postu group which was trying to do just that, and an endorsement of freedom for fellow travelers. A special committee was then appointed to study this directive further and on July 1, 1924, it issued an extended version of the directive[28] which reaffirmed the

---

[26] *Rezoliutsii i postanovleniia XIII s"ezda RKP(b)*, pp. 59–60.   [27] *Ibid.*
[28] See Joseph Freeman, Joshua Kunitz, and Louis Lozovick, *Voices of October*, pp. 59–65.

Party's decision to "declare itself in favor of the free competition of various groups and tendencies in the field of literature," [29] and proclaimed that "it is necessary to pay more attention to the development of the literatures of the national minorities in the various republics of the Soviet Union." [30]

Yet it was not until another year had elapsed that, on June 18, 1925, the final version of the Party resolution on literature was adopted by the Central Committee of the Communist Party.[31] This verbose document expressed the Party's ambivalent attitude to literature and reflected the ideological heterogeneity of the Party leadership at that time. While insisting that the Party stood firm in its decision to curb the "On Guard" radicals, the resolution promised qualified support for the proletarian writers. Therefore, both the On Guardists [32] and the fellow travelers regarded it as a victory for their cause, although, for a moment at least, the latter were the real victors. However, the proletarian writers and their organization VAPP continued to play a prominent part in Russian literary life.

The repercussions which the decisions of the Party, taken at the meeting of the Central Committee in Moscow, had on the Ukraine were far-reaching. On the surface the rivalry between Pluh and Hart in 1923–25 seemed to be concentrated on the problem of how to bring literature to the people. Pluh was accused, among other things, of lowering literary standards and of promoting *pros'vitianstvo*, [33] while Hart was blamed for an attempt to impose proletarian ideology on the peasants. The real source of conflict, apart from these theoretical and individual differences, lay elsewhere.

These two organizations, which had both developed under the eyes of the CP(B)U and were in fact more concerned with ideology and cultural politics than with literature, showed different reactions to the decisions and events in Russia and came to hold opposite views on the nature and purpose of a national literature within the Soviet Union. They clashed violently over the basic problem: How should Union literature be organized?

[29] *Ibid.*, p. 63. [30] *Ibid.*, p. 65.
[31] Published in *Pravda* on July 1, 1925.
[32] See "Slovo partii skazano," *Oktiabr'*, July 7, 1925.
[33] *Pros'vitianstvo*, from *Pros'vita* (the name of an influential prerevolutionary organization for the education of the peasants), a term originally applied to peasant enlightenment; here used derogatively and synonymous with "cultural provincialism."

In Moscow during 1924–25 the main issues of this problem became crystallized. It must have been clear to the leading literary politicians in the Ukraine that in the Soviet state, which was incompatible with complete individual freedom of artistic creation, the organization of literature was not only a social necessity but also a political game. As long as the Party was still too weak, or believed that the time was not yet ripe to create its own literary union of writers, literary politicians of all proletarian brands took their chance and formed with their followers strong ideological bastions which they hoped would force the Party to a compromise. The history of the Russian Octobrists and On Guardists is most instructive in this respect.

In the Ukraine, Pluh and Hart represented, literary manifestoes apart, two different political concepts. As was pointed out, Hart continued to develop in the tradition of the Borot'bists and stood for independent Ukrainian National-Communism.

The conduct of Hart's leader, Blakytnyi, epitomized the inflexibility and intellectual courage of the Borot'bist writers. As early as 1920 Blakytnyi was violently attacked by Iakovlev during the session of the Fifth Congress of the CP(B)U for an article he had written for *Kommunist* in 1920.[34] In it, according to Iakovlev, he "approached the question of the Party organization exclusively from the nationalist point of view."[35] In 1924, at the height of the literary conflict between proletarian and fellow traveler writers, Blakytnyi did not hesitate to defend the Neoclassicist Zerov against the "hooligan attacks" of Iakiv Savchenko, a critic who enjoyed the Party's confidence.[36]

Ever since its foundation in 1923, Hart had shown great interest in establishing contacts with other national literary groups inside and outside the USSR. In 1923 it established close liaison with the Belorussian literary group "Maladniak," and in 1925 Hart's Congress passed a resolution in favor of "contacts with the proletarian literary organizations of other Soviet republics (Belorussia, RSFSR), Western Europe, France—group 'Clarté,' Germany—'Rote Fahne,'

[34] V. Blakytnyi, "Komunistychna partiia Ukraïny i ïï zmitsnennia," *Kommunist*, No. 258, November 17, and No. 260, November 19, 1920.
[35] *Biuleten' V-oi vseukrainskoi konferentsii KP(b)U*, No. 4, November 22, 1920, pp. 36–37.
[36] V. Blakytnyi, "Pytannia shcho stoït' na poriadku dennomu," *Literatura, nauka, mystetstvo*, September 21, 1924.

and Czechoslovakia—'Rude Pravo.' " [37] In 1923 a delegation from Hart traveled to Western Europe, and in 1924 an American and a Canadian branch of Hart were founded. Both of these played a significant part in the Communist movement among the Slavs in the United States and Canada.

Yet in its contacts Hart was not indiscriminate. For instance, it refused to collaborate with VUAPP (Vseukrainskaia assotsiatsia proletarskikh pisatelei—The All-Ukrainian Association of Proletarian Writers), which was branded by Blakytnyi as a splinter of the "stillborn Proletcult," [38] and was later (1925) openly accused by him of "Russophilism." [39] VUAPP was organized in 1924 by the Russian writers living in the Ukraine and officially stood for "underscoring the proletarian line in the struggle for the domination of culture." [40] It was the first literary organization in the Ukraine with a Muscovite orientation. Claiming direct descent from the Proletcult, VUAPP was fulfilling the functions of the Ukrainian section of VAPP (All-Russian Association of Proletarian Writers) which in 1923–24 was dominated by the October–On Guard groups. It is significant that this attempt to attract writers in the Ukraine to a Russian sponsored organization ended in failure.

However, this failure was not immediate or complete. While Hart rejected VUAPP's offer of merger, Pluh was ready to accept almost any invitation to federate. It had laid itself open to outside influences by allowing its members to participate in other literary organizations. At the time when Hart was busy building up its own network in Canada and in the United States, as well as organizing Ukrainian painters, musicians, and a special theater section (1924), Pluh assumed the role of a trade union for adaptable and spiritless littérateurs of all nationalities. But what brought about an open war was the relation of Pluh and Hart to VAPP, of which both were members. The pot came to the boil during the First All-Union Conference of Proletarian Writers, sponsored by VAPP and held from the 6th to the 12th of January, 1925.

37 H., "Pidsumky zïzdu obiednanykh hartovans'kykh orhanizatsii," *Kul'tura i pobut*, March 20, 1925, p. 6.
38 Vasyl' Ellan (Blakytnyi), "Pered orhanizatsiinoiu kryzoiu v ukraïns'kii revoliutsiinii literaturi," in Leites and Iashek, *Desiat' rokiv*, II, 154.
39 *Ibid.*, p. 159.
40 "Platforma vseukrainskoi assotsiatsii proletarskikh pisatelei," *Kommunist*, February 28, 1924; reprinted in Leites and Iashek, *Desiat' rokiv*, II, 147–49.

The dominant views during the conference were those of the Russian Octobrists–On Guardists and their supporters. Summing up the results of the congress, S. Rodov pointed out that "the most serious disagreements and deviations showed themselves in the national problem. However, here also the conference ended in agreement, with the delegates of Hart [who, as Rodov mentioned previously, attempted to protest against the creation of a central executive] voting together with the rest of the conference." [41] Yet it appeared that the Hartians, seven of whom were present at the conference, had certain misgivings about the organization of VAPP. They made their representation dependent on "confirmation by the All-Ukrainian Congress of Proletarian Writers." [42]

On March 11, the Congress of Hart was held in the presence of three delegates from VAPP. The following account of it appeared in VAPP's journal *Oktiabr'*:

A hot debate arose during the discussion of Hart's platform, which deviates from the specific class tasks of proletarian literature. Many wrangles were caused by the problem of relationship with the All-Union and with the All-Ukrainian Association of Proletarian Writers (VUAPP). . . .

Many serious observations and unanimous criticisms by worker correspondents, by the delegates of VUAPP, Pluh, Zaboi, and other organizations, did not change in the slightest the basis of the organization of Hart, and it bypassed the problem of VAPP's platform . . . side-stepping also the question of union on a Pan-Union scale, while defending the system of liaison through the Commissariat of Education. Needless to say such measures, foreign to Bolshevik organizational principles, have alienated from Hart many proletarian writers.[43]

Hart's refusal to accept VAPP's policy intensified the contest. Having had the courage to disagree with VAPP, the Hartians now attacked Pluh, whose delegate, Pylypenko, showed no opposition to VAPP, and whom, therefore, Blakytnyi openly accused of "attempting to ignore the principle of representation by National Republics and of forming instead an executive according to the representation from large industrial centers." [44]

[41] S. Rodov, "Pos'le vsesoiuznoi konferentsii proletarskikh pisatelei," *Oktiabr'*, No. 2, February, 1925, p. 130.
[42] "Khronika," *Oktiabr'*, No. 2, February, 1925, p. 158.
[43] "Khronika," *Oktiabr'*, No. 3–4, March–April, 1925, pp. 255–56.
[44] Leites and Iashek, *Desiat' rokiv*, II, 161.

Faced with Hart's stubbornness, VAPP made strenuous endeavors to win Ukrainian proletarian writers away from Hart. On April 6, 1925, two conferences of Ukrainian proletarian writers were held in Kharkov on the initiative of the Central Bureau of VAPP.[45] Hart was deprived of formal representation in the VAPP executive and replaced by other delegates showing greater willingness to cooperate with VAPP. Pluh, oblivious of the fact that it was an organization of peasant, not proletarian, writers, remained loyal to VAPP. Yet another controversy which made the whole literary situation even more explosive was that arising out of the creation of an All-Ukrainian Center of Revolutionary Literature.

In order to avert an even wider rift between the warring groups, the CP(B)U decided to intervene. On May 10, 1925, two months before the publication of the famous July 1 resolution on literature by the All-Union Communist Party, it issued the "Resolution of the Politbureau of the Central Committee of the CP(B)U concerning Ukrainian Literary Groupings." [46]

The first part of the resolution

reaffirms that no one existing literary organization, including Hart, can claim that it alone represents the Party in the field of literature, or holds a monopoly in applying the Party line in this field. At the same time the Politbureau of the Central Committee regards as harmful the agitation against Hart, alleging that it is a nationalist organization, hostile to the Party, etc. Notwithstanding some errors . . . the Politbureau of the Central Committee recognizes that Hart, during the entire period of its existence, has accomplished a great deal in uniting around the Party and Soviet government the most active and talented representatives of contemporary Ukrainian literature and poetry. To a certain extent Hart has unified the Ukrainian front of proletarian writers against the bourgeois nationalist ideology.[47]

It went on to say that "the existing organization of peasant writers, Pluh, is carrying on a great and responsible work which the Party must support on condition that the local groups of Pluh do not assume a mass character and do not merge with the organizations of village correspondents. . . . Pluh should remain an organization of peasant writers. Local centers of Pluh must be created

45 "Khronika," Oktiabr', No. 3–4, March–April, 1925, pp. 255–56.
46 For the full text see Appendix C.
47 Leites and Iashek, Desiat' rokiv, II, 304.

only where there are Party organizations to direct their work." [48] As for the fellow travelers, the resolution declared that the "fellow traveler organization Lanka, a group of writers centered around the journal *Zhyttia i revoliutsiia* (Life and Revolution) and accepting the platform of the Soviet government, should be treated according to the directive on fellow travelers issued by the All-Union Party." [49] It stressed further that "the organization of a single All-Ukrainian Center of Proletarian Writers is premature, since certain conditions necessary for it do not yet exist." [50]

The May resolution had a decisive effect on the ideological warfare in Soviet Ukrainian literature. While following the general lines of the All-Union decree on literature (July 1, 1924), the Ukrainian resolution rejected in no uncertain manner VAPP's encroachment on the Ukraine's literary life and rehabilitated Hart and Pluh, reminding them, however, of their own fields of activity and denying their claims to literary hegemony.

The fact that the CP(B)U sided with the Ukrainian, rather than the Russian, conception in Pan-Union literary affairs did not necessarily show its power. The Ukrainian Communists merely followed the general Party line which at that time favored a compromise between the cultural policies of the radical proletarian writers and of the fellow travelers. In 1925, the "Party line" was still, in fact, a compromise between several conflicting views within the Party. In this situation it was possible for the Ukrainian Communists to take sides and, occasionally, to follow their own "line."

Temporarily, at least, the CP(B)U resolution meant a definite setback for VAPP. In the leading article in *Oktiabr'* [51] the Vappists lamented that "in some literatures (Ukrainian, Belorussian, Kirghiz) a slogan of all-national literature enjoys a partial success. Under these un-Marxian, un-Leninist, and in fact reactionary circumstances opportunism and intolerance are hidden." The resolution also gave a breathing space to the fellow travelers and created a new atmosphere in which old disputes assumed larger and more manifold proportions.

---

[48] *Ibid.*   [49] *Ibid.*, p. 305.   [50] *Ibid.*
[51] "O literature narodov SSSR," *Oktiabr'*, No. 10, October, 1925.

[IV]

FIRST MAJOR CONFLICTS AND

DEVIATIONS

The Emergence of VAPLITE

The most significant event in Ukrainian literary life at the end of 1925 was the disintegration of Hart. Foiled in a bid for hegemony, this organization could not survive a serious crisis, especially after the death of its leader, Ellan Blakytnyi, on December 4, 1925. Early in 1926 Hart dissolved itself (some of its branches, among them the one in the United States, continued to exist), and about the same time the existence of its rival VUAPP also came to an end.

Many of Hart's members were tired of politics and were eager to develop as writers. Ideologically, most of them remained faithful to Blakytnyi's national-plus-Communist doctrine. However, some Hartians (e.g., Koriak) came to distrust this policy and hewed to the political path of the Kremlin rather than that of Kharkov. One aspect of this divergence of views was later mirrored in two rival interpretations of Blakytnyi's ideas. Old Borot'bists like Koriak and Khvylia attempted to "rescue" him from those Ukrainian writers and intellectuals who formed a new literary group and were inspired by his ideals of a vigorous cultural revival in the Ukraine.

As early as 1924 a draft constitution of a new literary organization was worked out by Blakytnyi, a copy of which has been preserved among the Liubchenko papers.[1] Entitled "Manifesto of the All-Ukrainian Literary Academy" and "The Position of the All-Ukrainian Literary Academy," it began with the following statement:

[1] For the full text see Appendix B.

The national rebirth of the Ukraine coincided with her social liberation. On the historical and cultural stage there have appeared at the same time a young nation and a young advanced social class at its head. This is why the flowering of Ukrainian letters at the present time inevitably shows itself in proletarian literature. This is why contemporary October Ukrainian literature should and does enter the arena of world culture as one of the first proletarian cultures of the world, marking the way which sooner or later will be taken by literatures of other nationalities.

Claiming that in the interests of the Revolution Ukrainian literature should be led out "into the broad, all-Union, and European arena," Blakytnyi demanded further that the Literary Academy should "strictly adhere to the class principle in the field of culture," should organize a network of cells of Ukrainian proletarian literature in Western Europe and America, and should "take the initiative in organizing similar literary academies in the federal Soviet republics."

Many sections of the statute of this Literary Academy were, in 1925, incorporated into the statute of the Free Academy of Proletarian Literature (VAPLITE). This document, dating from 1924, is important because it establishes beyond doubt the line of descent from Borot'bist literary groups through Hart to VAPLITE.

On October 14, 1925, a meeting of seventeen writers was held in Kharkov. Among them were members of a small circle called "Urbino," [2] headed by Khvyl'ovyi, who outlined "the structure of the future organization of proletarian writers." [3] The meeting passed the following resolution:

The [future] literary organization should unite qualified writers: former members of Hart, Pluh, and others. The management of the organization should be in the hands of a council elected from the representatives of various schools and tendencies. The Council should designate one of its members as a chairman (or president) and another as secretary. The organization should consist of several literary schools, forming one organization with a [common] ideological basis, while retaining wide autonomy as far as their literary work is concerned as well as in purely formal matters of publishing, the recruitment of young

[2] Raphael's birthplace. This group, according to Liubchenko, met at Khvyl'ovyi's home (A. Liubchenko, "Ioho taiemnytsia," *Nashi dni*, No. 5, May, 1943, p. 12).

[3] "Protokol narady pys'mennykiv m. Kharkova, vid 14 zhovtnia 1925 roku," Liubchenko Papers.

literary forces, and the accomplishment of cultural work outside the organization.

The organization must be united, although consisting of separate units and schools which, however, should not have a separate legal existence.

The new organization, VAPLITE (Vil'na Akademiia Proletars'-koï Literatury—Free Academy of Proletarian Literature), was finally formed in November, 1925.[4] Among its members were the following leading Ukrainian writers of the day: Bazhan, Dniprovs'kyi, Dos'vitnyi, Epik, Ialovyi, Ianovs'kyi, Iohansen, Khvyl'ovyi, Kopylenko, Kotsiuba, Kulish, Liubchenko, Panch, Senchenko, Shkurupii, Slisarenko, Smolych, Sosiura, and Tychyna.

The composition of VAPLITE showed that, apart from the old Hartian guard, the new organization included several young writers who had previously belonged to rather esoteric literary circles or to Pluh. Thus, although formed in a distinctly Borot'bist tradition, VAPLITE became representative of a wider sector of Ukrainian Communist literature.

VAPLITE's constitution[5] coincided on many points with Blakytnyi's "Manifesto" and "Position." Among its objectives were: establishment of close relations with proletarian literary groups in other countries, organization of lectures and literary enterprises of all kinds, and promotion of Ukrainian proletarian literature both at home and abroad.

Behind this blueprint for a socialized literature there lay a deep concern for quality and artistic integrity. Although not as exclusive as Blakytnyi's demand that the Literary Academy should be limited to nine members, and should hold its general meetings only twice a year (on the anniversary of Shevchenko's birth and that of the October Revolution), VAPLITE's platform appeared too restrictive and incompatible with the Party's prescription of "culture for the masses."

Yet the main object of the organization was precisely to aim at quality not quantity, and to elevate the cultural life of the Ukraine,

[4] The minutes of the meeting were recorded in "Protokol orhanizatsiinoho zasidannia hrupy pys'mennykiv proletars'koï literatury, 20 lystop[ada], 1925," Liubchenko Papers.

[5] "Statut Vil'noï Akademiï Proletars'koï Literatury VAPLITE," Vaplite, zoshyt pershyi, 1926.

a country which, in Khvyl'ovyi's words, was inclined to imitate her masters.[6]

Anticipating the charges of splendid isolation, Oles' Dos'vitnyi wrote on behalf of the VAPLITE:

An Academy imposes responsibilities. It binds its members as academicians to take a serious attitude toward the creation of proletarian literature, to be cultured writers with definite ideological class principles as opposed to the recently created tradition that a writer should be bound to nothing and literary organizations could spring up like mushrooms after rain, without an obvious need. We have undertaken great cultural regeneration. We realize that a writer must understand his duties and responsibilities. . . . We are very young . . . therefore let us learn, let us learn, let us learn.[7]

The imposing seriousness of such a pronouncement might have seemed affected were it not supported by a bold and new theory of Ukrainian proletarian literature and culture formulated by VAPLITE's leader, Mykola Khvyl'ovyi.

In the history of Soviet Ukrainian literature the figure of Khvyl'ovyi is perhaps the most striking and the role he played the most dramatic of all. A member of the Communist Party, Khvyl'ovyi came to the forefront of Ukrainian literature in 1921 through his reputation as a poet and short story writer. At the same time he was a master of biting invective and satirical criticism, and a brilliant pamphleteer. In 1925 and 1926 Khvyl'ovyi published a series of pamphlets and articles in which he expounded his views on the tasks of Ukrainian literature. They were sufficiently revolutionary and explosive to stir at first a great debate, the so-called Literary Discussion, and then to draw down the rage and retribution of the Communist Party. A more detailed analysis of Khvyl'ovyi's literary ideology will follow in the next chapter. At this stage it is important to become acquainted with Khvyl'ovyi's program for VAPLITE, which was best expressed in his *Dumky proty techii* (Thoughts against the Current):

A writer's contribution to organizational and social activities lies first of all in his works, then in the part he plays in his trade union, and lastly in his conduct with the masses. If a writer drifts along with a score of other writers who have been artificially drawn into literature

---

[6] M. Khvyl'ovyi, "Dumky proty techii," *Kul'tura i pobut,* November 29, 1926.

[7] O. Dos'vitnyi, "Do rozvytku pys'mennyts'kykh syl," *Vaplite, zoshyt pershyi,* p. 9.

and with whom he has nothing much in common, he is by no means engaged in a useful social work. On the contrary, he obstructs it. If, however, he meddles in social life on his own initiative, he does what we really want. Therefore we say: it is time to end the half-dead group mentality as an anti-social phenomenon. . . .

Let us no longer imitate the "Pope." All these All-Ukrainian Central Committees are quite unnecessary for a Ukrainian writer. What is important is not a Central Committee—but literature. . . .

Hart and Pluh took upon themselves not so much constructive as destructive tasks. This was the role assigned to them by history: they were intended not so much to create the art of a fledgling class as to demoralize the camp of bourgeois writers and thus extricate the masses from the influence of the old art's ideology. . . . If we survey the past work of Hart and Pluh we must say that they have carried out this task. . . .

The Revolution has now entered upon a new period of peaceful construction—the period of the NEP. The struggle goes on; it has only assumed other and more concealed forms. . . . Who is to lead this struggle in that tenuous ideological superstructure which is called art? Hart and Pluh have attracted a wide mass membership . . . but they have hindered the development of their writers. . . . This has led to a situation in which many of those who received their membership cards regarded themselves as finished writers. . . .

From today the slogan is not "give us quantity—who can give more?" but "give us quality!" It is necessary to reinstate the destroyed artistic criteria.[8]

This manifesto, mild as it was in comparison with some of Khvyl'ovyi's later declarations, expressed in plain words not only a direct criticism of all attempts to regiment writers in large, centrally controlled organizations, but also a new belief in the value of literature with the emphasis on quality and artistic criteria. That VAPLITE's stand evoked a favorable response from many eminent writers and intellectuals was a testimony of its popularity. The publication of *Vaplite* (journal, 1927) as well as of *Vaplite, zoshyt pershyi* and *Vaplite Al'manakh* stirred wide interest and discussion. In less than a year (1926) VAPLITE succeeded in rallying all the free forces, including the Neoclassicists and the theatrical company Berezil', still left in the cultural life of the Ukraine to do battle against the controls of the Party.

The enthusiasm and the creative atmosphere which were charac-

[8] M. Khvyl'ovyi, *Dumky proty techii*, pp. 70–76.

teristic of the early period of VAPLITE's activity are revealed in the "Literaturnyi shchodennyk" (Literary Diary) of VAPLITE, preserved in the Liubchenko papers. In it are recorded spontaneous and spirited observations on life and literature by various members of the organization. Those of them who have since accepted controls and have turned into Soviet panegyrists might recognize in what they wrote in 1926 a lost zest for beauty and a distant youth. "A writer," wrote one of them, "must never be given advice; this only confuses him." Another wrote: "Khvyl'ovyi encouraged Liubchenko to continue working on the tale, which resembles a French short story, remarking that it was something new in Ukrainian literature and should be cultivated." Or: "Serbian epos fills my soul; what else can I write? There is no time, and the opportunities, devil knows, how many."

Having made high artistic quality the prerequisite of literature, the Vaplitians found their natural allies in the Neoclassicists, although their ideology was generally labeled "petit-bourgeois." The *Vaplite, zoshyt pershyi* contained two articles concerned with the Neoclassicists. One of them, written by the former Futurist Slisarenko, was unfavorable to the Neoclassicists, although it found that "in practice, any replacement of esthetic ideas by ideological maxims brings about a complete and hopeless failure on the cultural front." [9] In the second article, O. Dos'vitnyi attempted to show that in terms of "the only Marxian theory of art which was worked out in detail by Plekhanov," the Neoclassicists "are trying to understand the class struggle . . . and are beginning to comprehend it through the prism of revolutionary Marxism." [10] Hence they cannot be regarded "as our enemies." [11]

The Party and its literary spokesmen viewed these developments with alarm.[12] VAPLITE's preference for quality and artistic form and its own brand of literary ideology were sufficient in themselves to put the Party on guard. But what made matters even worse was

[9] O. Slisarenko, "V borot'bi za proletars'ku estetyku," *Vaplite, zoshyt pershyi,* 1926, p. 19.

[10] O. Dos'vitnyi, "Do rozvytku pys'mennyts'kykh syl," *Vaplite, zoshyt pershyi,* p. 16; also Leites and Iashek, *Desiat' rokiv,* II, 203.

[11] Leites and Iashek, *Desiat' rokiv,* II, 203.

[12] For the official Party view, see Chubar's article in *Kommunist,* No. 22, 1926; also, Panas Liubchenko, "Stari teoriï i novi pomylky," *Zhyttia i revoliutsiia,* No. 12, December, 1926.

the political role which VAPLITE's ideologist, Khvyl'ovyi, came
to play within the CP(B)U. As a result of it, the CP(B)U was, in
fact, battling all through 1926 with its first serious crisis. Fortunately some documentary accounts of this internecine conflict are
at hand, and so the extent of the Party's internal disagreements
over Ukrainian culture can be assessed with some accuracy.

The Rise and Decline of Shums'kyi and Khvyl'ovyi

In a series of pamphlets and articles written in 1925 and 1926,
Khvyl'ovyi put forward several ideas which boldly expressed a new
conception of Ukrainian Communist culture.[13] The most revolutionary of them were the following: (1) Ukrainian writers should
orient themselves toward Europe, "this experience of many centuries . . . not the one that is rotting . . . but the Europe of a
mighty civilization, the Europe of Goethe, Darwin, Byron, New-
ton, Marx, and others." [14] (2) Ukrainian literature must develop independently of Russian influence. "We must not borrow anything
from Russia; we must formulate that which is our own." [15] With
particular severity Khvyl'ovyi attacked the Ukrainian intelligentsia
who were always ready to follow Russia. Theirs is "a slave mentality," he declared, and if "Stalin tells them that the development of a
national culture depends on the nation which is creating this culture, our epigones understand it in this way: come and rule over
us." [16]

The motives which prompted Khvyl'ovyi to pose the question of
Ukrainian culture and literature in such terms have been iden-
tically explained by both Soviet historians and Ukrainian émigrés.
Both interpretations hold that Khvyl'ovyi somehow became a nationalist, a chauvinist, and a fascist. A study of his own life and
writings, as well as of the milieu of the Ukrainian Communists and
ex-Borot'bists in which he lived, does not warrant such an explanation. When Khvyl'ovyi wrote that his "attitude is the logical conclusion drawn from the policy of our Party in regard to the national
problem," [17] he was probably both sincere and correct. He was cer-

---

13 *Kamo hriadeshy*, (1925); *Dumky proty techiï*, (1926); *Apolohety pysaryzmu* (1926).
14 *Kamo hriadeshy*, p. 42.
15 "Apolohety pysaryzmu," *Kul'tura i pobut*, March 28, 1926.
16 *Dumky proty techiï*, p. 50.   17 *Ibid.*, p. 49.

tainly not the only Ukrainian Communist who thought that the growth of Ukrainian proletarian culture should not be impeded by any Russian centralist restrictions. But Khvyl'ovyi was one of the first to pluck up the courage to speak and write about it.

There are strong indications that in the struggle which was raging at that time between Stalin and Trotsky, Khvyl'ovyi sided with the latter. Trotsky's ideas of permanent revolution and his esthetic theories coincided in certain respects with those of Khvyl'ovyi. Yet, in sharp contrast to Trotsky, Khvyl'ovyi's ideology was rooted in his national soil. Therefore to label Khvyl'ovyi a "Trotskyite" is to be guilty of the same kind of oversimplification as those who consider him merely a "nationalist."

Khvyl'ovyi had a powerful ally in the person of the Ukrainian Commissar for Education, O. Shums'kyi, a former Borot'bist. Both were on the editorial board of *Chervonyi shliakh* of which Shums'kyi was the chief editor, and at least on one occasion Khvyl'ovyi openly named Shums'kyi as the one "who has placed on the agenda the great task of cultural revolution." [18] At the beginning of 1926 Shums'kyi voiced his disagreement with the cultural policy of the Party, demanding a quicker pace in the application of Ukrainization and less dependence on Russian directives in the cultural life of the Ukraine. His views were debated by the Party and transmitted through the proper channels to Moscow. On April 26, 1926, Stalin wrote the following letter to Lazar Kaganovich, who was then the Secretary of the CP(B)U:

It is true that a wide movement toward [the development of] Ukrainian culture and Ukrainian social life has started and is gaining strength in the Ukraine. It is true that on no account should it be allowed to fall into the hands of elements that are hostile to us. It is true that many Communists in the Ukraine do not understand the meaning and importance of this movement and therefore do not take steps to dominate it. It is true that it is necessary to make a radical change in the [training of] our cadres of Party members and Soviet workers, who are still pervaded by the spirit of skepticism in the questions of Ukrainian culture and social life. It is true that one must carefully select and create cadres of people who would be capable of mastering this new movement in the Ukraine. However, comrade Shums'kyi has committed in this instance at least two serious errors.

18 *Kamo hriadeshy,* p. 58.

First of all he confuses the Ukrainization of the Party and other apparatus with the Ukrainization of the proletariat. It is right and it is necessary to Ukrainize at a certain rate our state and other administrative organs which serve the population, but it is wrong to Ukrainize the proletariat from above; it is wrong to force the Russian working masses to renounce their Russian language and culture and to accept as their own the Ukrainian language and culture. This contradicts the principle of the free development of nationalities. It would be equivalent not to national freedom but to a particular form of national oppression. There is no doubt that the Ukrainian proletariat will gain in numbers and strength in proportion to the industrial development of the Ukraine and to the influx of Ukrainian workers into industry from the nearby villages.

There is no doubt that in its composition the Ukrainian proletariat will be more Ukrainized, just as for instance the proletariat in Latvia and Hungary which had a German character later began to Latvinize and Magyarize. But this is a long, spontaneous, and natural process. Any attempt to replace this spontaneous process by a forced Ukrainization of the proletariat from above means to apply a harmful Utopian policy which may well provoke an outbreak of anti-Ukrainian chauvinism among the non-Ukrainian proletariat in the Ukraine. It seems to me that comrade Shums'kyi does not correctly understand the problem of Ukrainization and does not take into account this last danger.

Comrade Shums'kyi does not realize that in the Ukraine, where the Communist cadres are weak, such a movement, led everywhere by the non-Communist intelligentsia, may assume in places the character of a struggle for the alienation of Ukrainian culture from the All-Soviet culture, a struggle against "Moscow," against the Russians, against the Russian culture and its greatest achievement, Leninism, altogether. I need not point out that such a danger grows more and more real in the Ukraine. I should only like to mention that even some Ukrainian Communists are not free from such defects. I have in mind that well known article by the noted Communist, Khvyl'ovyi, in the Ukrainian press. Khvyl'ovyi's demands that the proletariat in the Ukraine be immediately de-Russified, his belief that "Ukrainian poetry should keep as far away as possible from Russian literature and style," his pronouncement that "proletarian ideas are familiar to us without the help of Russian art," his passionate belief in some messianic role for the young Ukrainian intelligentsia, his ridiculous and non-Marxist attempt to divorce culture from politics—all this and much more in the mouth of this Ukrainian Communist sounds (and cannot sound otherwise) more than strange. At a time when the Western European proletarian classes and their Communist Parties are full of affection for Moscow, this citadel of the international revolutionary movement, at a time when Western European proletarians look with enthusiasm to the flag that flies over Moscow, this Ukrainian Communist Khvyl'ovyi has nothing to say in favor of Moscow except to call on Ukrainian leaders to run away from Moscow as fast as possible. And this is called internationalism. What can we say about other members of the Ukrainian intelligentsia from the non-Communist camp when the Communists begin to talk and not only to talk but indeed to write in our Soviet press with Khvyl'ovyi's words. Comrade Shums'kyi does not understand that in order to dominate the new movement for Ukrainian culture in the Ukraine the extreme views of Khvyl'ovyi within the Communist ranks must be combated; comrade Shums'kyi does not understand that only by combating such extremisms is it possible to transform the rising Ukrainian culture and Ukrainian social life into a Soviet culture and Soviet social life.[19]

[19] In 1948, the full text of this letter was published for the first time (I. V. Stalin, *Sochineniia*, VIII, 149–54). It reveals that before he wrote this letter Stalin had a long conversation with Shums'kyi.

"He thinks," Stalin writes, "that Ukrainization is slow, that it is regarded as an unpleasant duty and therefore is carried out with great delay. He thinks that the growth of a Ukrainian culture and of the Ukrainian intelligentsia are proceeding at a rapid pace and that if we do not take this movement into our hands, it may pass us by. He thinks that at the head of this movement should be placed those people who believe in the cause of Ukrainian culture, who know and desire to know this culture. He is particularly dissatisfied with the behavior of the Party and trade union elite in the Ukraine who, in his opinion, have put the brakes on Ukrainization. He thinks that one of the greatest sins of this elite is the fact that it does not attract to the leadership of the Party and Trade Union work those Communists who are directly connected with Ukrainian culture. He thinks that Ukrainization should be carried out first of all within the ranks of the Party and among the proletariat. . . . He proposes to raise Hryn'ko to the post of the Chairman of the Council of the People's Commissars, to make Chubar the Secretary of the CP(B)U. . . . He is especially dissatisfied with the work of Kaganovich. He thinks that Kaganovich has succeeded in regulating the organization of the Party, but that the organizational methods employed by Kaganovich make normal work impossible."

In his reply, Stalin stated that "Shums'kyi is right in maintaining that the Party and other elite in the Ukraine should become Ukrainian. However, he is wrong as to the pace of it, which is now the most important thing. He forgets that purely Ukrainian Marxist cadres are at present insufficient for that purpose. He forgets that these cadres cannot be created artificially. . . . What would it mean if Hryn'ko were now elevated to the post of Chairman of the Council of the People's Commissars? How should such a move be judged by the Party as a whole, and by the cadres of the Party in particular? Would it not appear that we are trying to lower the standard of the Council of the People's Commissars? Because it is impossible to hide from the Party the fact that the Party and revolutionary standing of Hryn'ko is much lower than that of Chubar. . . . I am in favor of reinforcing the composition of the Secretariat and the Politbureau of the Central Committee of the CP(B)U with Ukrainian elements. However, one cannot consider the case as if there were no Ukrainians in the leading organs of the Party and the Soviets. What about Skrypnyk, Zatons'kyi, Chubar, Petrovs'kyi, Hryn'ko, and Shums'kyi—aren't they Ukrainians?

Shums'kyi's error consists in this that, while having a correct objective, he does not reckon with the pace. And the pace is most important now."

It is interesting to note that by 1938 all the Ukrainian Communist leaders named above fell victim to one or another of the purges.

Stalin's letter amounted to an official criticism of Shums'kyi's deviation and was taken as a basis for discussion at the June plenary session of the CP(B)U which convened on May 12, 1926. Here Shums'kyi was asked to admit his error and to declare his disagreement with Khvyl'ovyi's ideas.[20] Yet Shums'kyi refused to yield and announced that he "did not intend to repudiate his past," and that "from the first days of the revolution" he "had been a Ukrainian Bolshevik," and he "is one now." As for Khvyl'ovyi, all he (Shums'kyi) would say was that he regarded him as a "cultured young proletarian who feels it his duty to carry on a cultural revolution." [21]

Shums'kyi's attitude put the CP(B)U in an awkward predicament. A joint letter from Kaganovich and Chubar to the Politbureau, dated June 4, 1926, described the situation as follows:

Shums'kyi's declaration illustrates to a certain degree the complexities and difficulties which we face in solving our problems. . . . It is necessary to analyze the nourishing soil which makes it possible for this question to germinate at this time. . . . How to rid ourselves of such incidents is our basic concern. First of all, through the correct application of the nationality policy, and a further strict adherence to Ukrainization. . . . One must reckon with the danger that as a result of the irresponsible behavior of comrade Shums'kyi a reaction can set in causing a departure, at first psychological and then practical, from the national policy of the Party, which is that of Ukrainization. This would bring about a threat of greatest danger to the Party.[22]

The June Plenum of the CP(B)U also issued *Theses on the Results of Ukrainization*.[23] They affirmed that

the Party stands for an independent development of Ukrainian culture, for an expression of all creative forces displayed by the Ukrainian people. The Party supports the wide use by the Ukrainian socialist culture of all the treasures of world culture. It is in favor of a definite break with the traditions of provincial narrowness, in favor of the creation of new cultural values worthy of a great class. However, in the Party's view, this cannot be done by contrasting Ukrainian culture with the cultures of other nations, but through brotherly cooperation between the working and toiling masses of all nationalities in the raising of an

20 Mykola Skrypnyk, *Dzherela ta prychyny rozlamu v KPZU*, p. 18.
21 *Ibid.*, pp. 13–14.   22 *Ibid.*, pp. 21, 22, 23.
23 *Komunist* (since June, 1926, it appeared in Ukrainian, hence only one "m"), No. 134, June 15, 1926; the full text may be found in Leites and Iashek, *Desiat' rokiv*, II, 293–303; a translation of the more important passages may be found in Appendix E. See also N. Skrypnik, "Itogi literaturnoi diskussii," *Bol'shevik Ukrainy*, I, 1926.

international culture to which the Ukrainian working class will be able to contribute its share.[24]

At the same time strong pressure put on Shums'kyi to force him to an anti-Khvyl'ovyi declaration proved of little avail. Although at a meeting in the Commissariat of Education Shums'kyi repudiated Khvyl'ovyi, he refused to allow this lecture to be published as an article.[25] The defiant ex-Borot'bist continued to be the source of major conflict within the CP(B)U in 1927, when he found ideological followers in some members of the Central Committee of the CPWU (the Communist Party of the Western Ukraine). In the end, however, Shums'kyi was silenced. First, he was ousted from his post as the chief editor of *Chervonyi shliakh* (in 1927) and relieved of his duties as Commissar for Education. Then his attitude was condemned by the Declaration of the Central Committee of the CP(B)U before the Executive Committee of the Comintern (June, 1927),[26] and finally he was removed to Leningrad, expelled from the Party, and then arrested and deported in 1933.

Simultaneously with the elimination of Shums'kyi and "Shumskism," the CP(B)U took steps to discipline the VAPLITE. Under pressure from the Party, three of its members who headed the *Vaplite* (O. Dos'vitnyi, M. Khvyl'ovyi, and M. Ialovyi) published in 1926 in *Visti* a long open letter in which they admitted their "mistakes":

> We acknowledge that the watchword of orientation toward "psychological Europe," no matter whether past or present, proletarian or bourgeois, coupled with an attempt to sever relations with Russian culture and to ignore Moscow (which is the center of world revolution) as a center of world philistinism, were definite deviations from the proletarian line of internationalism. . . .
>
> We fully share the opinion of the Central Committee of the CP(B)U about literary groups like the Neoclassicists . . . We regard, therefore, comrade Khvyl'ovyi's definition of such groups . . . erroneous. . . .
>
> We recognize our ideological and political errors and we openly repudiate them. We do not in any way dissent from the Party line and

---

[24] Leites and Iashek, *Desiat' rokiv,* II, 301.   [25] Skrypnyk, *Dzherela,* pp. 18, 20.

[26] For the study of "Shumskism," a primary source, containing reports of the plenary sessions of the Central Committee of the Party and of the Comintern, is *Budivnytstvo radians'koï Ukraïny: Zbirnyk,* 2 parts.

recognize its policy and work, directed by the Central Committee of the CP(B)U, in the field of cultural reconstruction as entirely correct.[27]

In order to satisfy the appetite of the Party for national deviationists and also in order to enable the organization to continue its work, the general meeting of VAPLITE expelled, on January 28, 1927, Khvyl'ovyi, Ialovyi, and Dos'vitnyi from its ranks.

However, one document in the Liubchenko papers reveals that the Central Committee of the CP(B)U was displeased with the timing and the manner in which the three writers were expelled. A top secret "Excerpt from the 69th Meeting of the Secretariat of the Central Committee of the CP(B)U on March 14, 1927," signed by the secretary Klimenko, pointed out the "incorrect action of the Communist faction VAPLITE in the matter of the expulsion of comrades Khvyl'ovyi, Ialovyi, and Dos'vitnyi from the ranks of VAPLITE without submitting the matter for approval and receiving the sanction of the Central Committee for their expulsion." [28]

The reprimand by the Central Committee is highly significant because it discloses the intensity of the conflict between the Party and VAPLITE. The solidarity of fellow writers, devoted to the idea of keeping alive their literary organization, clashed violently with the Party discipline to which those Vaplitians who were its members were subject. The Central Committee of the Party was deeply perturbed by this act of insubordination. A letter to VAPLITE from Andrii Khvylia, who was in charge of the Press Section of the Central Committee of the CP(B)U, complained that the reasons for the expulsion of the three were not made clear and that he feared that with only six Communists left in VAPLITE, this organization would be seriously weakened.[29] But one wonders if the real reason for the Party's annoyance was not so much its concern for VAPLITE's ideological purity as the latter's defiant and peremptory decision to expel Khvyl'ovyi, Ialovyi, and Dos'vitnyi, thus making the task of fighting a dispersed opposition to the Party doubly difficult.

---

[27] *Visti*, No. 280, 1926; also, Leites and Iashek, *Desiat' rokiv*, II, 205–6.

[28] "Komunistychna partiia (b–v) Ukraïny: Tsentral'nyi Komitet; tsilkom taiemno; vytiah 69 zasidannia S-tu TsK KP(b)U vid 14, III, 1927 r.," Liubchenko Papers.

[29] "Do komfraktsiï 'Vaplite'" (a letter from Khvylia, dated February 4, 1927), Liubchenko Papers.

The new president, Kulish, sent the following explanation of this move to the Press Section of the CP(B)U in reply to repeated requests to clarify the situation (one of the requests sent on February 9, 1927, demanded that those members of VAPLITE who were Party members should send in their reaction to events within the organization within twenty-four hours). Kulish explained that the expulsion of Khvyl'ovyi, Ialovyi, and Dos'vitnyi was carried out since

these comrades made a mistake, tried to repair it, but will not be believed and will be distrusted in the future. Thus the situation of the organization is getting worse every day and assumes a tragic character (there are hints that the entire organization is untrustworthy, and an almost continuous smear campaign by other organizations).

Apart from this, we are not sure whether comrades Khvyl'ovyi, Ialovyi, and Dos'vitnyi, if they were allowed to stay in VAPLITE, would not again produce some ideas and statements which would once more assume a definite political significance.[30]

It was true that in the atmosphere of the nationalist witch hunt in the Soviet Ukraine one could never be sure whether one had committed a "political error." On the other hand, the public recantation of the expelled members of VAPLITE did not mean that the Vaplitians had undergone a sudden change of heart. On the contrary, they intensified their activities with the same purpose of challenging the centralist and increasingly totalitarian practices of the Party in literary and cultural affairs.

There is no better source for an intimate study of the conflict between VAPLITE and their opponents than the already mentioned "Literary Diary" in the Liubchenko papers. Although, of necessity, it views the struggle from one particular angle, it gives an authentic version of uncensored individual reactions to a major problem of the day. This part of the diary was written by Liubchenko himself, the secretary of VAPLITE. Here are some of the entries:

December 11, 1926. Koriak's lecture in Artemivka [The Artem Communist Institute in Kharkov] on the subject "The Three Musketeers" (Khvyl'ovyi, Ialovyi, Dos'vitnyi). The lecturer held his breath. He was obviously frightened by the appearance at the lecture of Khvyl'ovyi and other Vaplitians. The lecture came to nothing. "Three Musketeers" re-

30 "Do viddilu presy TsK KP(b)U," Liubchenko Papers.

mained an empty phrase. Khvyl'ovyi demanded the right to speak. Then why bother?

December 12. At the Institute of People's Education [University] appearances by Kovalenko and Le who arrived from Kiev. Kovalenko railed against VAPLITE, especially against Tychyna and Khvyl'ovyi. The students sent in many written questions which remained unanswered. When they protested to the presidium, Koriak, who was in it, declared that Kovalenko was right. . . .

December 14. . . . The journal *Vaplite* has been held up by the Holovlit [Chief Administration of Literary and Publishing Affairs] for almost two weeks. Promise to pass it tomorrow. The material has been read by the publication section of the Central Committee. Koriak's lecture in Artemivka was conditioned by the fact that he had already read Khvyl'ovyi's article about himself which is included in the first issue of the journal. The subsidy for the journal has suddenly been cut off. We are short 666 rubles. We shall take the matter up with Zatons'kyi. . . .[31]

Yesterday Usenko did not greet us; others also refused. Are they writers or schoolboys, or simply unfortunate and hopeless people? Where is literature, where the seriousness and sincerity in creation?

December 22. On Monday the 20th, Kulish went to the Central Committee to see Zatons'kyi. Had a long and interesting talk. As far as VAPLITE is concerned, things begin to clear up a little. Such was his impression. Khvylia was present during the conversation. Among the subjects discussed were the need for a declaration on the part of VAPLITE; the difficult atmosphere; and even the subsidy from the Central Committee for the travels of writers in the USSR and abroad.

The first issue of *Vaplite Al'manakh* appeared on December 21. Kulish saw Khvylia about the reorganization of the editorial board of *Chervonyi shliakh*. Today Kulish became virtual editor of *Chervonyi shliakh*. Conversation with Khvyl'ovyi about the All-Ukrainian Congress of Proletarian Writers. Dniprovs'kyi asked if VAPLITE would take part in *Chervonyi shliakh*. My answer: yes.

December 20. An evening devoted to the memory of Blakytnyi, held in the Public Library. . . . Taran's lecture aimed at the defense of Blakytnyi before Khvyl'ovyi. . . .

January 13, 1927. Today the *Kharkivs'kyi proletarii* printed the speech by comrade Chubar, delivered at the district Party conference criticizing Tychyna's "The Mother Peeled," and scolding VAPLITE. In *Visti* there appeared today a speech by comrade Petrovs'kyi at the congress of national minorities. Scolds VAPLITE for nationalist(!) deviations.

In January, 1927, the first issue of the journal *Vaplite* was on sale. Instead of the customary manifesto of aims, the first article con-

---

[31] For the list of the leading Ukrainian Communist Party officials see Appendix I.

sisted of a fragment from a satirical biographical story of the obsequious Kholui (Toady) by I. Senchenko.[32] Kholui does not belong to "philosophers, to people with ideas (and empty pockets), or to those who criticize everything and finally end up under the hedges on the roadside." His most striking natural quality is his "flexible spine," his greatest virtues—obedience, humility, and silence. He is an excellent crawler and his advice to others is to "let your spine bend, don't spare it; if you let it bend once it will save you from a thousand dangers." Kholui is proud of his spineless constitution. He realizes that before his time there were

thousands of prophets who wished to lead men on to a new path. They all inevitably went bankrupt. . . . All was madness and nonsense. Everything went along its course because no one understood, no one sensed what the incomparable Pius desires. Pius is the only truth for us. . . . Everybody wanted to be a Prometheus . . . but who told you that you are a Prometheus? This is a misunderstanding. Prometheus is a dream, you are a reality. . . . Avoid the bloody shadow of Prometheus. . . . Every superfluous thought creates more trouble in life. Avoid thoughts. . . . Look into Pius's eyes—there is an ocean of inspiration for you. . . . I tell you: keep your mouths shut, or better still, ask that they be shut for you. . . . Look into Pius's eyes: let his words be your words. Thus unanimity dawns, and unanimity brings peace.[33]

It is indeed difficult to believe that such a transparent satire in the Orwellian vein could have been published in the Soviet Union. One of the reasons was perhaps the fact that the "almighty Pius" was at that time still in the making. However, even if such ridicule was written, it was certainly not tolerated. "Proletarian literature," commented *Literaturna hazeta*, "appears here under the juicy synonym 'Kholui'—and the Party which steers this literature is represented by Pius. This is a dirty attack upon the Party itself." [34]

The Party Sponsors a New Literary Organization—VUSPP

In order to defeat Khvyl'ovyi and VAPLITE it was necessary to take subtler and more devious measures than those described above. At the end of 1926 a new literary organization of proletarian writers was established, enjoying the full support and confidence of the

32 I. Senchenko, "Iz zapysok," *Vaplite*, No. 1, 1927, pp. 3–11.
33 *Ibid.*, pp. 3, 4, 5, 6, 10, 11.
34 *Literaturna hazeta*, No. 12, 1927.

Party. It was the Vseukraïns'ka Spilka Proletars'kykh Pys'mennykiv (VUSPP)—the All-Ukrainian Union of Proletarian Writers, which held its first congress on January 25–28, 1927. There is ample evidence in the Liubchenko papers that VAPLITE was not invited to participate in the new venture of VUSPP lest it might prove stronger than the new body of proletarian writers. In any case, Mykytenko, on behalf of the Organizing Committee of VUSPP, issued what was virtually an ultimatum to VAPLITE. It was a request, sent to members of VAPLITE on January 25, to appoint one delegate to the proposed congress by 6 P.M.[35] This was rejected by the general meeting of VAPLITE, held on January 25, 1927.[36]

The well-publicized gathering of VUSPP was addressed by the representative of the Central Committee of the CP(B)U, Zatons'kyi. The Russians were represented by no less a dignitary than Lunacharskii, VAPP's delegate, the Russian writer Serafimovich, and the literary critic Selivanovskii. Among its Ukrainian organizers were Koriak, Khvylia, Mykytenko, and Kovalenko. Held in an atmosphere of joyous consolidation,[37] the Congress had two main objectives: first, to create an organization which could compete with VAPLITE, and secondly, to woo some writers away from Pluh, and thus weaken its second rival. Pluh was represented at the Congress by several writers, including its leader, Pylypenko.

In 1926 and 1927 Pluh managed to survive a grave internal crisis and outside attacks. In the autumn of 1925 it had been reorganized with a more selective membership, and a year later many of its provincial branches were abolished.[38] Yet in spite, or perhaps because, of it, Pluh continued to play an important part in Ukrainian literary life.

During the VUSPP Congress Pylypenko delivered one of the best speeches; in it he pleaded for clarification of the terminology

[35] "Do chleniv Vaplite," Letter from Mykytenko in the Liubchenko Papers.

[36] A translation of the "Resolutions of VAPLITE," found among the Liubchenko Papers and dealing with the VUSPP Congress as well as with other problems, is printed in Appendix F.

[37] The following comment on the VUSPP Congress was made by M. Semenko, G. Shkurupii, and M. Bazhan in their booklet *Zustrich na perekhresnii stantsii* (On the Crossroads): "When all enemies were laid out . . . the speaker cast his eye around the dead tired audience and said: 'I have finished, are there any questions?' A hand was raised: 'How soon will they issue us uniforms?'"

[38] O. Vedmits'kyi, "Literaturnyi front: 1919–1931," *Literaturnyi arkhiv*, IV–V (1931), 121.

used by literary politicians of that day, and defended literature (which he regarded as a free growth) against attempts to regiment it.[39] Similarly, when accused by A. Khvylia of trying to make Pluh a "political" organization, Pylypenko was not afraid to interrupt and point out the political character of VUSPP.[40] In the end, disgusted with the belligerent attitude of the Vusppists, Pylypenko left the Congress, after eight of his Pluzhians went over to VUSPP.

To make admission easier, VUSPP accepted a semi-federative principle of organization, and apart from Koriak, Kovalenko, and Mykytenko, P. Usenko, representing the organization "Molodniak" (Youth), and B. Gorbatov, chief delegate of the Donbas literary group "Zaboi," were elected to the Secretariat of VUSPP. The First VUSPP Congress was characterized by unusually vitriolic attacks on VAPLITE and Ukrainian nationalism. In this respect the general tone of the debates and speeches was exactly opposite to the mild plea made at the opening by Lunacharskii: "Show an honest writer the way," he said, "guide him properly, let him write as well as he can, and I am sure that he won't do any harm." [41] After bitter harangues by Khvylia and Koriak, the Congress issued a manifesto in which it declared that "the main danger lies in the poisonous work of moderate bourgeois ideologists who often pretend to be sympathizers with the Soviet system. Having on the surface accepted the Soviet platform, they unobtrusively but systematically inject into literature elements of their ideology and world outlook, thus contaminating a part of the intelligentsia already weak in its proletarian ideology, and imbuing it with a nationalist outlook, discouraging it from the creative paths of the revolution, and [inducing] ideological skepticism, and a passive inertness which do not at all harmonize with the volitional and joyous psychology of the victorious class to which the future belongs." [42] Moreover, these evil ideologists "understand very well that by antagonizing different nationalities of the USSR, they will prepare the ground for an internal ideological and later political intervention of capital, especially after they have created a chasm between the proletarian cultures of Soviet Ukraine and Soviet Russia." [43]

[39] *Pershyi vseukraïns'kyi zïzd proletars'kykh pys'mennykiv*, Stenohrafichnyi zvit, pp. 93–99; subsequently referred to as VUSPP Congress.
[40] *Ibid.*, p. 30.   [41] *Ibid.*, p. 15.   [42] *Ibid.*, p. 114.   [43] *Ibid.*

In the attempt to unite the proletarian forces "in the ideological war against all those who wish to exploit literature in the interests of a hostile camp," VUSPP had to lean heavily on the support of its Russian colleagues. A. Selivanovskii, in his speech at the Congress, informed the Ukrainian writers about the literary situation in Russia and the successes which the reorganized VAPP was achieving in helping to build a pan-Union federation of writers (later known as VOAPP—All-Union Association of Proletarian Writers). "VAPP works solely," he declared, "under the guidance of the Party and the Party relies on VAPP in its attempts to create a federation of proletarian writers." [44]

VUSPP, therefore, accepted "the principle not of national, but of international union of proletarian writers of the Ukraine, irrespective of the language in which they write." [45] It pledged itself to maintain close contact with men who were organizing VOAPP, of which it later became a member.[46] It is important to remember that VAPP (the parent organization of VOAPP) was then under strong pressure from the radical elements within its organization, and that in 1928 it became, under the new name of RAPP, the most influential literary group in Russia. The Rappists advocated direct control by the Party over literature and rejected all compromise with the fellow travelers. They came to the top at the end of the NEP period and were strongly supported by the Party which, at the end of 1927, was preparing to launch the First Five-Year Plan and therefore came out openly in favor of an organization which subordinated literature to the great tasks of socialist reconstruction. The year 1927 was therefore auspicious for both Ukrainian and Russian centralists.

The CP(B)U also came to the aid of VUSPP by issuing in May, 1927, a resolution on the *Policy of the Party concerning Ukrainian Literature*.[47] Although the resolution asserted that it accepted fundamentally the Party decree of 1925 and restated that "no single literary group existing in the Ukraine can claim a monopoly or priority," it went on to say that "anti-proletarian tendencies are reflected in the work of Ukrainian bourgeois writers like the Neo-

[44] *Ibid.*, pp. 50–51.   [45] *Ibid.*, pp. 83–84.   [46] *Ibid.*, p. 85.
[47] Mentioned in *Visti*, May 17, 1927, printed in full in *Komunist*, June 15, 1927; also in Leites and Iashek, *Desiat' rokiv*, II, 306–10; for a translation see Appendix D.

classicists," and are finding support from "some fellow travelers as well as in VAPLITE headed by Khvyl'ovyi and his group." [48]

It specified further that these anti-proletarian tendencies were welcomed by the Western Ukrainian nationalist writers in Poland who "together with fascist Poland prepared a literary campaign against the socialist Ukraine." [49] "All this demands from the Ukrainian proletarian writers that they . . . most definitely rid themselves of all bourgeois influences." Point ten of the resolution marked a clear departure from previous directives on literature. It enunciated that

ideological differences as to literary forms among groups which continue to sustain the tasks of socialist culture must not assume the form of enmity: they should be manifested on the unifying ground of proletarian solidarity, which sets before all literary groups the task of their union in an All-Ukrainian Federation of Associations of Proletarian Writers which should also embrace the literary groups of the national minorities in the Ukraine.[50]

Moreover, the Party envisaged the creation in the Ukraine of an organization for Western Ukrainian writers which would also become a member of the proposed All-Ukrainian Federation, and which, it was hoped, would in turn unite with the similar federations of other Soviet nationalities into "an All-Union Alliance of Literary Federations of All Peoples of the USSR on the principles of proletarian internationalism." [51] At the end of the resolution definite instructions were given to the Commissariat of Education and the Press Department to "take concrete steps toward the implementation of the above resolutions and to take prompt action to see that they are carried out." [52]

Though the oracle had spoken, the words had still to be interpreted by the prophets. The Vusppists saw in the new Party directive a veiled go-ahead signal for their own program. After all, why should not they, now the most powerful proletarian group in the Ukraine (apart from the persecuted VAPLITE), be given the task of organizing such an All-Ukrainian Federation? In December, 1927, VUSPP issued a declaration in which it gave its wholehearted

[48] Leites and Iashek, *Desiat' rokiv*, II, 308.   [49] *Ibid.*
[50] *Ibid.*, p. 309.   [51] *Ibid.*, pp. 309–10.   [52] *Ibid.*, p. 310.

support "to the creation of one literary revolutionary Soviet front in an All-Ukrainian Federation of Soviet Writers." [53]

The Literary Policy of Mykola Skrypnyk

VUSPP's bid for hegemony was, however, a little premature. For the time being no one except the Party itself could be entrusted with such a task. The CP(B)U's policy in literature after 1927 was dictated to a very large extent by Mykola Skrypnyk, who in that year replaced Shums'kyi as the Ukrainian Commissar for Education. A man of real integrity and great intellectual gifts, Skrypnyk was put in charge of Ukrainian cultural affairs at a most critical time. While the RCP(B) in Moscow was winning the battle against the Left Opposition (Trotsky, Zinov'ev, Kamenev), the CP(B)U had its own serious troubles. The Ukrainization policy had led to nationalist deviation ("Shumskism" and "Khvyl'ovism"), the CPWU (Communist Party of the Western Ukraine) had suffered a serious split after Maksymovych and others were condemned as nationalists, while the Literary Discussion was creating a stir among writers and intellectuals. To suppress Ukrainian nationalism at home and at the same time to attract Western Ukrainians to the Soviet way of life, to soft-pedal Ukrainization without wiping out what were generally regarded as the achievements of Soviet Ukrainian culture, was a difficult task even for a man with Skrypnyk's abilities. An old Bolshevik and a personal friend of Lenin, he was destined to undertake the role of the last Ukrainian National-Bolshevik.

The Tenth Congress of the CP(B)U held in November and December, 1927, thus assumed unusual importance. In a speech before the Congress, Lazar Kaganovich once more made a bitter attack on Khvyl'ovyi and Shums'kyi, accusing them of "putting their hopes in the restoration of a bourgeois government in the Ukraine with the help of the armed forces of foreign imperialism." [54]

Kaganovich used such strong language because Shums'kyi's "nationalist deviation" had in the meantime most serious repercus-

---

[53] Iaroslav Hordyns'kyi, *Literaturna krytyka pidsoviets'koï Ukraïny*, p. 50.
[54] "Ukraïnizatsiia Partiï i borot'ba z ukhylamy," *Visti*, November 27, 1927.

sions on the Communist Party of the Western Ukraine (Ukrainian territory under Polish rule). The delegate of this party, Maksymovych, declared his sympathy for Shums'kyi and described Khvyl'ovyi's utterances as a "voice of despair, complaining that conditions for Ukrainian proletarian creative work are not quite so favorable, . . . that Ukrainian literature and Ukrainian culture still have to fight for recognition." [55] This led to a deep split in the CPWU and the matter was referred to the Comintern which in 1926 appointed a special commission to investigate "Shumskism" in the CPWU. For three years the Comintern and its Russian sponsors made a determined effort to force Shums'kyi and Maksymovych to their knees and, by admitting their mistakes, disappoint those malcontents in the Party who did not agree with its nationality policy.[56] However, the defiant stand of these Ukrainian National-Bolsheviks led to increasing deviations. In February, 1928, the Comintern expelled a large faction of the CPWU led by Maksymovych's supporters, Vasyl'kiv and Turians'kyi, and in 1929 (in spite of the statement allegedly made by Shums'kyi and Maksymovych to the effect that they did not question the policies of the CP(B)U) the CPWU's influence in Western Ukraine showed a rapid decline.

At the Tenth Congress of the CP(B)U Skrypnyk delivered a lengthy speech on the "Tasks of Cultural Construction in the Ukraine." [57] In response to it the resolution of the Tenth Congress announced "a complete reshaping of the educational system, all science and culture for the purpose of strengthening the proletarian dictatorship and consolidating the union of workers and peasants for the socialist reconstruction of society." [58]

In the field of literature this new vigilance did not mean conceding Vusppist demands. Skrypnyk declared himself in favor of a real federation of literary organizations, not the merger suggested by VUAPP. "I am in favor of an All-Ukrainian Federation of Literary Organizations. Let us first however, develop such organizations.

[55] *Stenohrafichnyi zvit plenumu TsK i TsKK KP(b)U*, June 1–6, 1926, p. 49.
[56] For a full account see Ie. Hirchak, *Shums'kizm i rozlam v KPZU*.
[57] "Tezy do dokladu tov. Skrypnyka na X-mu zïzdi KP(b)U 'Pro zavdannia kul'turnoho budivnytstva,'" *Visti*, November 1, 1927.
[58] "Rezoliutsiia po dokladu t. Skrypnyka 'Pro zavdannia kul'turnoho budivnytstva na Ukraïni,'" *Visti*, December 4, 1927.

Then we shall form the federation. If, however, it is proposed that we set up only one organization which, in the opinion of comrade Koriak, should bind together all proletarian writers and be called a federation, then I must protest against such claims." [59]

The Commissariat of Education was therefore fully empowered to take an active part in literary life. Its Council of Political Education (Upravlinnia Politos'vity Narodn'oho Komisariatu Os'vity Uk.SSR), headed in 1927 by Ozers'kyi, became an influential factor in the lives of writers, artists, and scholars. It could, for example, subsidize publications, encourage or discourage literary plans, and hold literary and musical competitions, with awards for the best works celebrating the October Revolution.[60]

The Commissariat of Education viewed the literary scene with interest and not without some concern. Toward the end of 1926 still another literary group was formed by some former members of Pluh and Hart. It was the organization of young writers, Molodniak, which served primarily as a literary center for the members of the Komsomol. Beginning with 1927, it published a monthly, *Molodniak* (edited by O. Korniichuk, O. Donchenko, P. Usenko, and others). Ideologically this group was very close to VUSPP; like VUSPP, Molodniak became a member of VOAPP.

On the other hand, VUSPP's opponents also showed signs of life. In 1926, Valeriian Polishchuk with the help of some former Futurists formed a new group of "dynamists," or "spiralists"— called "Avant-garde"—which in 1928–29 published three *Bulletins of Avant-garde,* and survived until 1929. In 1927, another restless spirit, Mykhailo Semenko, founded from Futurist remnants a new organization called "Nova Generatsiia" (New Generation) which published a monthly magazine with the same name. The journal, while paying lip service to the Party, was an important mouthpiece of independent literary criticism.

As the Party-inspired opposition to VAPLITE increased in strength, so did its sympathizers. The Kiev group Lanka transformed itself in 1926 into MARS (Maisternia revoliutsiinoho slova —The Workshop of the Revolutionary Word), which shared not

[59] M. Skrypnyk, *Nasha literaturna diisnist',* p. 37.
[60] "Mystets'ki konkursy do X rokovyn zhovtnevoï revoliutsiï," *Visti,* March 18, 1927.

only VAPLITE's platform but also its fate in 1928. A document among the Liubchenko papers testifies that on February 14, 1927, a group of eight Russian writers in Odessa informed VAPLITE of its desire to form a Russian section of VAPLITE in Odessa. In all the branches of artistic and intellectual life of the Ukraine, especially in the fine arts, the theater, and film, many of the foremost representatives were fired with the enthusiasm emanating from Khvyl'ovyi and VAPLITE, an enthusiasm for a new and revolutionary Ukrainian art and literature.

VAPLITE's Opposition to the Party Policy

The only organization which still refused to accept the Party line and which continued to develop in spite of the abuse with which it was vilified was VAPLITE. The campaign waged by VUSPP against VAPLITE was fierce and indiscriminate, often ending in mere insults and name-calling, a favorite device of the official Soviet smear technique which makes retaliation very difficult. In one of his articles, for instance, Koriak accused VAPLITE of reviving the bourgeois ideology of the prerevolutionary literary group Ukraïns'ka khata.[61] In this way he helped to implant in the public mind the notion that Khvyl'ovyi's group had nothing new to offer but merely represented a new aspect of the old "Ukrainian bourgeois nationalism"; hence it had to be destroyed as a malign vestige of the past. On January 8 and 9, 1927, the Party organ Komunist published a bitter denunciation of Vaplite, No. 1, by F. Taran.

Khvyl'ovyi, although no longer a member, was a frequent contributor to the journal Vaplite, five issues of which were published in 1927. In an editorial in the third issue of Vaplite,[62] VUSPP was accused of carrying on indiscriminate and slanderous warfare against the Vaplitians. A reply appeared in VUSPP's journal Hart,[63] in which VAPLITE was reproached for "violating and breaking the most recent directive of the Party."

To this the president of VAPLITE, Mykola Kulish, retorted with a blistering article [64] in which he vigorously defended the

[61] V. Koriak, "Z literaturnoho zhyttia," Kul'tura, No. 3–4, March–April, 1927, p. 107.
[62] "Nashe siohodni," Vaplite, No. 3, 1927, pp. 131–40.
[63] "Retsydyvy vchorashn'oho," Hart, No. 2–3, 1927, pp. 74–84.
[64] "Krytyka chy prokurors'kyi dopyt," Vaplite, No. 5, 1927, pp. 146–57.

principle expressed in the Party resolution of denying to any literary group the right to speak in the name of the Party. "One should be on guard," he wrote, "over Ukrainian proletarian literature, VAPLITE should be watched, but literature cannot be subjected to a garrison rule as a result of which the Vusppist guards would be inviolable." [65]

Printed just after the Tenth Congress of the CP(B)U, the fifth issue of *Vaplite,* which carried Kulish's reply, also contained contributions by two other intrepid writers. Khvyl'ovyi wrote an "Open Letter to Comrade Koriak," reminding this ex-Borot'bist of his earlier beliefs in the uniqueness of the Revolution in the Ukraine, this "purgatory in which the revolution from the East will be transformed into a Western revolution." [66] The author of the second article, Pavlo Khrystiuk,[67] not a member of VAPLITE, analyzed a short story by Hryhorii Epik.

However, a real furor was created by the publication in the same issue of the journal of the first part of Khvyl'ovyi's novel *Val'dshnepy* (The Woodsnipes).[68] According to Khvylia, the author wrote this novel "in order to show that the Soviet Ukraine is not Soviet, that the dictatorship of the proletariat is not real, that the nationality policy is a sham, that the Ukrainian people are backward and will-less, that a great rebirth is still to come, and finally, that the Party itself is an organization of hypocrites." [69] The heroine of *The Woodsnipes,* Ahlaia, was, for Khvylia, a "Ukrainian nationalist and a fascist." Through her Khvyl'ovyi "cast a slogan of struggle against our society; he acknowledged that the Revolution . . . has found herself in a blind alley, that the Party has become a group of Pharisees, that there is no hope, and therefore the only watchword should be to educate, in the spirit of Ukrainian nationalism, young men who will lead the Ukraine to her national regeneration." [70]

Khvylia's appraisal of *The Woodsnipes,* amounting to an official censure of the novel, was based on an incomplete portion of the

[65] *Ibid.,* p. 149.
[66] M. Khvyl'ovyi, "Odvertyi lyst do Volodymyra Koriaka," *Vaplite,* No. 5, 1927, p. 162.
[67] P. Khrystiuk, "Rozpechenym perom," *Vaplite,* No. 5, 1927, pp. 194–203.
[68] M. Khvyl'ovyi, "Val'dshnepy," *Vaplite,* No. 5, 1927, pp. 5–69.
[69] A. Khvylia, *Vid ukhylu u prirvu,* p. 3.
[70] *Ibid.,* p. 25.

work (only 64 pages were printed in *Vaplite*, No. 5) and on the second instalment (which never appeared in print but which was read by Khvylia). This fact alone makes the condemnation of *The Woodsnipes* highly suspect. To be sure, the plot of the early part of the novel suggested the conquest of the disillusioned Communist Karamazov by the strong-willed Ahlaia who was ready to lead him and all those who "are lacking in individual initiative . . . to create a program for a new world outlook." [71] Yet, although Ahlaia made no secret of her admiration for Ukrainian nationalism (she herself came from Russia but found her spiritual home in the Ukraine, where the Revolution had not been compromised as deeply as in Russia), there is no knowing what ultimate fate was prepared for her by Khvyl'ovyi. Regardless of the final outcome of the story, the novel was condemned for its outspoken criticism of the Communist Party and for the romantic aura it lent to Ukrainian nationalism.

Kulish tried to pour oil on troubled waters by sending a letter to the *Komunist*,[72] explaining that Khrystiuk's article was published on his (Kulish's) own responsibility and admitting that in doing so he had committed a political error. Kulish also admitted that VAPLITE, having expelled Khvyl'ovyi, Dos'vitnyi, and Ialovyi, "made an error in not barring them from the journal *Vaplite.*"

However, this time recantation was of no avail. The editor's postscript to Kulish's letter clearly stated that "this is not an answer to questions which were put to it [VAPLITE]." It wanted to know whether other members of VAPLITE felt equally guilty, and finally it declared that the Party could not trust VAPLITE any longer, since the latter could not get rid of dangerous political tendencies.

The full story of the Party's acrimony toward VAPLITE, which culminated in the dissolution, by intimidation, of this literary organization, may be gathered from the unpublished papers of VAPLITE's secretary, Liubchenko. Most revealing in this respect are the minutes of the last meeting of VAPLITE, held on January 12, 1928.[73]

---

[71] M. Khvyl'ovyi, "Val'dshnepy," *Vaplite*, No. 5, 1927, p. 67.
[72] *Komunist*, January 12, 1928.
[73] "Protokol zahal'nykh zboriv 'Vaplite' 12.I.28," Liubchenko Papers.

When the president of the organization, Kulish, laid before the members the agenda of the meeting, they were filled with dismay and resignation mingled with indignation. One of the more forthright speakers, Slisarenko, described the situation in these words:

> The Literary Discussion began before VAPLITE was formed. Later there arose a separate political discussion. These two were unjustly connected and associated with each other. Some "writers" began to exploit this situation; having failed to gain glory with their poor verses they took to writing articles, which although they were even worse, were accepted as valuable simply because they were directed against VAPLITE. These merchants are profiting by the Literary Discussion, while we, the writers, must neglect our work in order to reply to their lies and slander. In this way, the literary work, for which VAPLITE was founded, has been seriously hampered.
>
> On the other hand, we are branded as deviators, the Literary Discussion is tied up with politics, and we are regarded almost as counter-revolutionaries. The result is that the libraries fear to give our publications to the readers. To maintain our organization in such conditions means to bring harm to literature. And yet we feel responsible to the Party, to the Soviet citizens, and to the proletariat since we bear the honorable name of proletarian writers.
>
> Apart from this, in this atmosphere it may look as if we were a purely political organization. There is only one way out—to dissolve.
>
> [Interjection by Dniprovs'kyi]: And what is the outlook for the future?
>
> [Slisarenko]: Our present state offers us even less. After the dissolution each one of us will be responsible for himself. If he does do anything wrong—let him be responsible for it.
>
> [Another interjection]: What if our dissolution should be interpreted as a demonstration?
>
> [Slisarenko]: Everything can be termed a demonstration, even if we should decide not to dissolve and continued to exist. Why, in Taran's official article the hint at dissolution was expressed quite plainly.

The next speaker, Liubchenko, remarked bitterly that "we cannot take one step without being accused of something." He agreed with the majority that because of the constant attacks from the Party, VAPLITE should dissolve. After some discussion as to whether self-dissolution might not be interpreted as a demonstration, the members voted 14 to 2 (with one abstention) in favor of dissolution. One of the two votes against this decision was cast by Kulish, who was aware that "on no account should we create the impression that we have been 'smothered' (*prydushyly*)." Forced to disband the organization, the Vaplitians, however, did not intend to lay down their arms, but, as Iohansen expressed it, to continue their work "singly."

What was going on in the mind of Kulish during this meeting? Clearly, he was motivated, as he himself said, by personal concern for, and loyalty toward, VAPLITE, and partly by a purely tactical consideration to find a way out which, as he put it, "could not bring harm to Soviet people," as well as by the last flicker of hope that things might turn out well for his organization.

Two days after their final general meeting, the Vaplitians gathered once more and issued their last proclamation. They admitted that in the past they had made mistakes, but they left no doubt as to who was to blame for the dissolution of their organization. Their declaration read:

Until the very end, our errors, which we confessed, were used by several organs of literary groups in order to badger us as writers. This has created an atmosphere which is too oppressive for our literary work and which prevents each one of us from working productively as *members of this organization* for the benefit of Ukrainian proletarian literature. Therefore, we, the members of VAPLITE, think it better that our organization should be dissolved in order to enable writers who are members of VAPLITE to work more productively for the benefit of Soviet proletarian culture as it is guided by the Communist Party.[74]

The mental anguish of VAPLITE's president in those critical days has been recorded by him in daily jottings, preserved among Liubchenko's papers. This document, two pages of which are translated here intact, is at the same time a unique reflection of a Soviet writer's mind in crisis.

January 12, 1928. Letter to the editorial board of *Komunist*. The meeting of VAPLITE. Resolution to dissolve (in principle).

13. At Khvylia's. "A heart-to heart talk." He said: "The fourteen voters were right." Draft of the letter to the editorial board. Signatures.

14. Went to Khvylia to show him the draft of the resolution [about VAPLITE's dissolution]. Change in his mood and ideas. General meeting of VAPLITE at night, in the Building of Scholars. Decision to formulate a new collective resolution about dissolution. Election of the liquidating committee.

---

[74] "Rezoliutsiia zahal'nykh zboriv Vil'noï Akademiï Proletars'koï Literatury 'Vaplite' 14 sichnia 1928 roku; m. Kharkiv," Liubchenko Papers.

15. A day of despondency and low spirits.

16. Announcement about dissolution to the People's Commissariat of Education, the Press Section [of the CP(B)U], and to the editorial board of *Komunist*.

18. At Skrypnyk's. Discussion with commentaries. Shorthand.

20. I have been called to appear before the Secretary-General, Kaganovich. A frank conversation.

23. Unexpected blast from the Press Section, with an order to call the "former ones [members of VAPLITE]." Meeting and waiting in the literary club.

29. A dream. First letter to H-ch [Khvyl'ovyi].

31. A dream: meeting with H-ch in Oleshky. Dusk. He is going away (across the sand and the steppe). We bid each other farewell. I am crying.

February 1. A dream: someone carried someone else to the grave pit, which is all ready. They say that he is dead, but I see how D's legs bend up. Frightened.

2. A dream-nightmare: a house, myself, someone enters. I defend myself with a bottle of oil.

4. Second letter to H-ch.

6. Received a letter from H-ch.

9. Third letter to H-ch.

18. Fourth letter to H-ch. Dreams (a teacher throws himself down from a tall building).

28. A letter from H-ch. The end of Khvyl'ovism. A dream (I, L-ko in Chaplyn).

March 1. Fifth letter to H-ch.

2. Civic inspection of the *Malakhii* [Kulish's play].

8. A dream (that there are errors in the *Commune in the Steppes*).

9. Sixth letter to H-ch.

16. Seventh letter to H-ch.

20. At the ballet—Joseph the Most Beautiful (art. Dulenko).

21. Eighth letter to H-ch. I have a drink in the literary club. Behind the doors—shots of billiard cues.

27. Ninth letter to H-ch.

31. The premiere of the *People's Malakhii*.

The fact that within eight weeks Kulish wrote nine letters to Khvyl'ovyi shows that the latter was still regarded by him as the spiritual leader of VAPLITE.

Curiously enough, Khvyl'ovyi was at that time abroad. Although it has not been possible to establish the exact date when he left the USSR, on December 16, 1927, he wrote a postcard to Liubchenko from Berlin. "Tell them [the Vaplitians]," he wrote, "that Europe invites them to visit her for two or three months. There is a lot to be seen."

From Berlin Khvyl'ovyi went to Vienna, where he stayed until March, 1928. None of the letters he wrote at that time to Kulish has been preserved, and therefore we do not know precisely what advice he might have given to VAPLITE's president in the moment of its most serious crisis. One thing, however, is certain. While abroad Khvyl'ovyi could make a choice of two possible alternatives: he could refuse to return home and make an open break with the Soviet regime; or he could recant and return as a penitent sinner. The first would mean personal safety and international notoriety, the second humiliation and possibly further accusations. Yet the second choice also offered a possibility of continuing the resistance on a more limited scale, in a different form. It would mean that in the hour of dire need Khvyl'ovyi did not forsake his friends and followers. He chose the second alternative. From Vienna he wrote a letter to the *Komunist*. In it he admitted his errors in *The Woodsnipes*, asked his literary colleagues to forsake the polemical paths along which he had attempted to lead them, and announced that he had destroyed the second part of *The Woodsnipes*. Finally, he threw himself upon the mercy of the Party whose erring but repentant member he was. In a closing paragraph Khvyl'ovyi begged that no one regard his declaration as insincere. It was a "product of the psychological conversion which has been developing in me for several years and which has finally restored me here, in Western Europe." [75]

This was his return visa to the USSR. From a postcard and a letter which Khvyl'ovyi wrote from Vienna to Liubchenko it is clear that the fate of the Vaplitians and the future of Soviet Ukrainian literature were very much in his mind and heart. In a postcard, written in February, 1928, he begged Liubchenko "as the secretary of VAPLITE, to take great care over the dear president, comrade Hurovych [Kulish]. I also ask all the Vaplitians to do the same. So that he may come to no harm. The beauty of life, as a champion motorcyclist has said, is in the solitary struggle." [76]

In a letter, dated March 2, 1928, Khvyl'ovyi wrote:

[75] Dated February 22, 1928; for the full text, see Leites and Iashek, *Desiat' rokiv*, II, 209–11.

[76] George S. N. Luckyj (ed.), *Holubi dylizhansy: lystuvannia vaplitian*, p. 12.

The enthusiasm of the "former ones" is a great joy for me. I wonder what you are writing? I have just started to write a novel (this is really the first one, since the fate of *The Woodsnipes* you know, and *Iraïda's* was similar). I don't know how it will turn out. In any case, as I have already written to somebody, I am not my old self. How are the translations into German going? At all costs, we must lead our literature onto the broad European arena. In a word, let us take courage; what lies ahead is ours. Greetings to all "former ones." The Free Academy of Proletarian Literature is dead—long live the State Academy of Literature! [77]

The dissolution of VAPLITE and the return of Khvyl'ovyi from abroad ended a chapter in the history of Ukrainian literature. Although the future looked forbidding and dark, the vitality of this literature, after a decade of comparative freedom, was far from exhausted.

VAPLITE's Nationalism Reexamined

In the conflict between the Party and VAPLITE a new term of denunciation was coined. It was "bourgeois nationalism," which came to be used ever more frequently to stigmatize all types of Ukrainian literature which did not conform with the Party line. The evidence collected in this chapter supports the conclusion that this new charge, brought against Ukrainian writers, was yet another weapon in the Soviet semantic armory. It became a club to strike down all opponents and had little relation to the actual literary situation in the Ukraine. VAPLITE's struggle was waged just as much for individual as for national freedom of thought and expression. Indeed, in the entire discussion of nationalism in Ukrainian literature it must be borne in mind that the "nationalist deviation" within the Soviet Union is but one aspect of the more fundamental issue of individual freedom.

VAPLITE was not, as was charged, a clique of literary highbrows and nationalist chauvinists bent on destroying the Soviet system; it was a group of talented writers and idealistically-minded Ukrainian Communists, of whom only a handful belonged to the Party, who attempted to preserve what they believed was the true heritage of the Revolution. They claimed for the Ukraine equal rights with

[77] *Ibid.*, p. 13.

Russia, and wanted full self-government in the literary and cultural
life of their country. This was strictly in accordance with the letter
if not with the spirit of the Soviet constitution.

The Ukrainians were well aware of the fact that the anti-Ukrainian feelings of the Russians were not dead. In spite of the official
"brotherly" atmosphere, occasional expressions of anti-Ukrainian
sentiments in the Russian press and literary periodicals aroused old
fears in the Ukraine. What dismayed the Ukrainians even more was
that such public statements went unnoticed and unpunished by the
Party. There was no outcry about Russian nationalism as there was
about Ukrainian nationalism.

The Russian theatrical magazine *Zhizn' iskusstva,* published in
Leningrad, in 1926 printed several articles on the Ukraine full of
ill-disguised scorn and harsh admonition. One of them, entitled
"Self-Determination or Chauvinism?," derided the idea of putting
on operas in Ukrainian. "Even if *Aida* should be performed in
Little Russian," it read, "it will not become a Ukrainian opera."
The article ended with these words of caution: "Comrade adherents of the national culture [*tt. natskul'turniki*], slow down a little
on the bends, lest the national self-determination lead you to the
blind alley of chauvinism. It is necessary once in a while to read
the A B C of Communism. This will save you from committing
many errors." [78]

In the spring of 1928, a group of five Ukrainian writers living in
Moscow, not one of them belonging to VAPLITE, wrote an open
letter to Gorky, asking him if Slisarenko's charge "that Gorky refused to have his works translated into the Ukrainian dialect" was
true.[79]

Their letter stated very succintly the Ukrainian point of view on
Russian-Ukrainian cultural relations. It read:

During the past 350 years we were being exterminated as a nation;
our writers were jailed solely on the ground that they wrote in their
native language. Ukrainian children languished in the foreign-language
school which was compared by the well-known pedagogue Ushinskii to
a tavern, while in the Ukrainian village only the tapster and the teacher
spoke the "common-Russian" language which was invented for the pur-

---

[78] "Samoopredelenie ili shovinizm?" *Zhizn' iskusstva,* No. 14, April 6, 1926. See also
Islamei, "Ieshchë ob ukrainskom shovinizme," *Zhizn' iskusstva,* No. 24, June 15, 1926.
[79] For a discussion of this controversy see below, pp. 225–26.

pose of Russification. Our musical language became the language of slaves, our people became the object of jibes, and, having lost their name, turned simply into *khakhly*.[80] Yet now, after the great revolution which brought us social and national liberation, we begin to exchange our cultural treasures with representatives of other nations. Is it any wonder that we are rejoicing?

Our culture is not so poor as it appears from the side. We are convinced that great Russian writers will any moment learn of Ukrainian literature and will proclaim to the whole world with authority that the Ukrainian people have a cultural life of their own. . . .

Whether they say so or not, we are convinced that the moment is near when Ukrainian literature, as happened with Scandinavian literature, will be "discovered" and united with the international culture. This is guaranteed by the fact of the existence of the Ukrainian Socialist Soviet Republic and the tremendous development of cultural activities shown in the last years by Ukrainian society. . . .

[However,] the representatives of Russian literature have failed in the last decade of the Revolution to respond to the call for cooperation between two cultures which in the years of the Civil War was sounded by our poet Pavlo Tychyna. The years went by, yet our literature was passed over in silence. The problem of the mutual relationship between Russian and Ukrainian culture was debated in the Ukraine for three years in the bitterest polemics. Yet none of the representatives of Russian culture noticed it. Ukrainian literature continued and continues to be ignored. Only from time to time the Ukrainian cultural workers who, at that time, fought for the idea of cooperation between the two cultures were subjected to such "pleasant surprises" as the ridicule of the Ukrainian language by Bulgakov, the attacks on Ukrainization by Shklovskii, and the resurrected *khakhol* in the works of Maiakovskii. . . .[81]

It was primarily because VAPLITE defended views such as these that it enjoyed great popularity among the Ukrainian intelligentsia, and on the other hand drew upon itself the wrath of the Kremlin. The blow administered to it by the Party was severe. It might have been a death blow to all Ukrainian independent spirit as represented by VAPLITE were it not for the wide influence which this organization exerted on contemporary literary and cultural life and which was manifested most of all in the Literary Discussion lasting from 1925 to 1928.

[80] *Khakhly*—a derogatory Russian appellation given to Ukrainians.
[81] K. Burevii, A. Chuzhyi, H. Koliada, P. Opanasenko, and M. Chyrykov, "Otkrytoe pis'mo M. Gorkomu," Moscow, March 27, 1928, Liubchenko Papers.

[V]

THE LITERARY DISCUSSION

1925–1928

The Last Free Debate

On April 30, 1925, Khvyl'ovyi, replying to an article by Iako-venko,[1] threw down the gauntlet to the Party literary notables. He directed his attack ostensibly against the "graphomaniacs, speculators, and other 'enlighteners.' "[2] In this "first letter to literary youth" he wrote that "as long as we are entangled in proclamations, platforms, and manifestoes, everyone of us feels like a god; as soon, however, as some 'literary facts' have to be produced, he becomes perplexed. Why? Simply because we have not been armed with the technique a qualified artist must have."[3] Yet, after severe censure of the "Red graphomania which floods our book market," Khvyl'ovyi drew a startling conclusion: "To the most pressing question 'Europe or Pros'vita?'[4] we must at once answer: 'Europe.' "[5] If young writers, that is, are to learn their craft properly, they must learn it from European sources, not from local "enlighteners" endorsed by the Party.

This challenge by Khvyl'ovyi dominated the whole Literary Discussion which it provoked. Beginning as the Russian *literaturnaia diskussiia* was drawing to a close, the great controversy in Soviet Ukrainian literature was more concerned with ideology than with

[1] H. Iakovenko, "Pro krytykiv i krytyku v literaturi," *Kul'tura i pobut*, No. 17, April 30, 1925.
[2] M. Khvyl'ovyi, "Pro satanu v bochtsi abo pro grafomaniv, spekuliantiv, ta inshykh Pros'vitian," reprinted in *Kamo hriadeshy.*
[3] *Ibid.*, p. 8.   [4] For an explanation of "Pros'vita" see above, p. 53.
[5] Khvyl'ovyi, "Pro satanu v bochtsi abo pro grafomaniv, spekuliantiv, ta inshykh Pros'vitian," in *Kamo hriadeshy*, p. 17.

literary techniques. It was the direct outcome of the profound ideological crisis within the political and cultural life of the Soviet Ukraine which has been outlined in the preceding chapters.

The Literary Discussion was not only conducted through articles, pamphlets, and books (over a thousand were produced on this topic), but it was also carried on in verbal exchanges, debates, and lectures. Thus in May, 1926, a great debate on Europe took place before an audience of eight hundred,[6] and the closing session of the Discussion, in February, 1928, was held before several hundred participants and listeners in the Blakytnyi Home of Literature in Kharkov.

The Literary Discussion is usually divided into three stages, corresponding to the course of Party policy in literature:[7] I. April, 1925—September, 1926; II. October, 1926—December, 1927; III. January, 1928—February 21, 1928.[8]

The focal points of the discussion became evident during the first phase, largely due to the provocative pamphlets of Khvyl'ovyi and the replies by the spokesmen for the Party. The second phase was the climax of the controversy, which led to the most striking expression of "Khvyl'ovism" in the publication of *Vaplite,* and ended in the disbandment of the literary organization VAPLITE. The final phase was an aftermath of the main debate and concerned itself with the official termination of the discussion.

An attempt will be made here simply to illuminate the main issues and theories in this debate and to assess their influence on the politics and literature of the period.

This purpose might best be served by outlining the views of the four main participants in the Literary Discussion whose contributions to it both demonstrated originality and had a lasting appeal. They are Mykola Khvyl'ovyi, Mykola Zerov, Andrii Khvylia, and Mykola Skrypnyk. The first two were avowed protagonists of the independent development of a national Ukrainian culture, while the latter two represented the attitude of the Party.

6 Iaroslav Hordyns'kyi, *Literaturna krytyka pidsoviets'koï Ukraïny,* pp. 65–66.
7 See: A. Leites and M. Iashek, *Desiat' rokiv ukraïns'koï literatury (1917–1927),* II, 316; Hordyns'kyi, *Literaturna krytyka,* pp. 58–59.
8 For a fairly complete bibliography of the Literary Discussion, listing over 600 items, see Leites and Iashek, *Desiat' rokiv,* II, 323–56.

The Issues and Their Exponents

The radical Mykola Khvyl'ovyi, who in 1926 had been branded a nationalist, wrote in the preface to his first collection of essays, *Kamo hriadeshy* (Whither Are You Going? 1925), this curious declaration of his literary faith:

> Most of all I have been tantalized by the idea of an Asiatic renaissance and the clarification of two psychological categories: Europe and *Pros'vita*. . . . Let us hope, therefore, that these pamphlets will be the opening paragraphs of the primer to a theory of new art. The theoretician himself must come later; we are waiting for him. He will be a romantic of *vitaism*, the agitator and propagator of our major principles.[9]

The call to follow Europe rather than the local folk culture (Pros'vita), as we have seen, drew upon Khvyl'ovyi the wrath of the Party. The reason for this was clear. Unlike the call "to the West," issued in 1922 by the Russian fellow traveler Lunts, Khvyl'ovyi's watchword, coming from a Communist, was a dangerous heresy in the eyes of the Kremlin, the citadel of Russian Communist centralism. Yet Khvyl'ovyi never abandoned his belief in Europe and explained what he meant by it with that characteristic verve which quickens the style but so often blurs his thought:

> You ask which Europe? Take whichever you like: past or present, bourgeois or proletarian, the ever changing one. For indeed, Hamlets, Don Juans, or Tartuffes were in the past, but they exist also now, they were bourgeois, but they are also proletarian; you may think they are immortal, but they will also be capable of change. Such is the wayward path of dialectics when it is lost in the labyrinthine superstructure.
>
> Here at last we come across the ideal social man, who has developed his biological or rather his psychophysiological constitution through the course of many centuries and is therefore common to all classes.
>
> In this sense we have nothing against comparing Lenin with Peter the Great: both belonged to the same ideal type of man given to us by Europe. . . .
>
> This type is the European intellectual in the highest sense of this word. He is, if you like, the wizard from Wittenberg so well known to us, who revealed to us a magnificent civilization and opened before us boundless perspectives. He is Doctor Faust, if we mean by him the questioning spirit of humanity. . . .

[9] *Kamo hriadeshy*, p. 4.

This type of man is the product of a great force—psychological Europe—toward which we must orient ourselves. This force will lead our young art onto the broad and happy path to the world goal.[10]

Khvyl'ovyi's admiration for Europe did not prevent him from believing in an imminent "Asiatic renaissance":

There cometh a mighty Asiatic renaissance in art, and we, the "Olympians," are its precursors. As at one time Petrarch, Michelangelo, Raphael, and others from their Italian nook set Europe afire with the flame of Renaissance, so new artists from the once oppressed Asiastic lands, new artists-communists who will follow us, shall climb the Helicon and place there the beacon of a Renaissance which, amid the distant cries of barricade fighting, will flare up in a purple-and-blue pentagram over the dark European night.[11]

Further on, in the same pamphlet, Khvyl'ovyi explains that

speaking of the Asiatic renaissance, we mean a future undreamt flowering of art among such nations as the Chinese, the Indians, and others. By this we mean a great spiritual regeneration of the backward Asiatic areas. This Asiatic renaissance must come because the ideas of Communism appear as a nightmare not so much to Europe as to Asia. Asia, which realizes that only Communism will liberate it from economic slavery, will use art as a weapon.[12]

It may be rather difficult at first to understand how the head of a Ukrainian Communist could generate such uncommon ideas expressed in such paradoxical terms. His ideas were not original; they were borrowed from Spengler and Marx. It is their formulation and their unique appeal to the Ukrainian intelligentsia which make them interesting. Today Khvyl'ovyi's opinion on Asia sounds prophetic. The fact that the great awakening in Asia has so far produced no startling developments in art Khvyl'ovyi might have explained by the regimenting influence on Asia of Soviet literature and its present high priests, whose powers in 1925 were small indeed.

Khvyl'ovyi not only envisaged a new era of Asiatic art but clearly conceived the stages of development between that and the "proletarian" literature which, in his opinion, "is determined by the same laws of evolution as those of bourgeois art":

All the chatter about the "absolute" realism of proletarian art is quite unfounded. . . . Proletarian art will pass through periods: romanti-

---

[10] *Dumky proty techiï*, pp. 44–46.   [11] *Kamo hriadeshy*, pp. 31–32.
[12] *Ibid.*, pp. 33–34.

cism, realism, and so on. This is a closed circle of laws governing the development of art.[13]

While regarding proletarian art as that of a period of transition, Khvyl'ovyi was deeply dissatisfied with its theory and content in his own day. That is why after Hart, "potentially the only association within the territory of the Union which could take upon itself the organization of real proletarian art," [14] had failed in its task, Khvyl'ovyi organized his VAPLITE. His purpose was to swing the creative forces of the Soviet Ukraine away from the Party models—toward what he held to be the true literary theory of proletarian art.

When we now ask ourselves what trend must characterize our period of transition, we answer: a romantic *vitaism* (vita—life). . . .

We repeat again. The real destroyers of proletarian art are the Octobrist simplifiers and vulgarizers. In Russia this has degenerated under the influence of "mother Kaluga" into "factory whistles and sirens," while in our country it is turning to "tractors and ploughs." The enlighteners are resting on their laurels; they are "creating a new life," they do not feel or wish to feel the world catastrophe—the epoch of civil wars.

The proletarian art of our VAPLITE's time is a Marseillaise which will lead the avant-garde of the world proletariat on to barricades. Only Communists can create the romantic *vitaism*. It is like all art, for those with developed intellects. It is the sum total of a new outlook on life, new and complex vibrations. This [romantic *vitaism*] will be the art of the first period of the Asiatic renaissance. From the Ukraine it must spread to all parts of the world and play there not a domestic role but a universally human one.[15]

Under this welter of words Khvyl'ovyi's main conception conceals itself. It is that while Russia is unable to lead proletarian art in its true direction—toward the era of the Asiatic renaissance—the Ukraine can do it. Khvyl'ovyi's ideas may be regarded as Ukrainian messianism, but it must be borne in mind that this messianism was tempered by self-criticism and nonviolence. He was extremely critical of his own people; he took every opportunity to castigate Soviet Ukrainian literature. But while doing all this he felt that the Ukraine could pass to other countries what seemed to him the true heritage of Communism, better and more liberally than Russia. The clue to this problem lay in Khvyl'ovyi's formulation of his

[13] *Ibid.*, p. 35.   [14] *Ibid.*, p. 36.   [15] *Ibid.*, pp. 36–37.

ideal Ukrainian proletarian art—or as he called it, the "romantic *vitaism.*"

Our watchword is: strike yourself and others, set someone against society; prevent it from falling asleep. Our watchword is: reveal the duality of the man in our time, show one's true self. . . . If you are a revolutionary, you will often split your "I." But if you are a citizen or a servant, let us say, in one of the departments, you are in fact a Gogolian hero even if you feel like the king of all creation. The question is whether to be an Akakii Akakievich or a *derzhymorda*.[16] Here is your choice.

This, then, as you see, is the complex situation now facing proletarian art.[17]

To preserve the purity and spontaneity of revolution, to cast aside all authorities, to trust in people since "history is made not only by economics but by people," and to regard art not as a means to political ends but, like Plekhanov, as a "method of knowledge of life," [18] were, for Khvyl'ovyi, not mere theories. An intense interest in politics and practical cultural problems fed by what was described by Iurynets' as "disappointment in our [Soviet] construction after the great epoch of the civil war," [19] and "the love for irrepressible and strong human spontaneity," [20] forced Khvyl'ovyi to consider seriously Russian-Ukrainian relations and the future of the Ukraine.

Khvyl'ovyi's demand to "run away from Moscow as fast as possible," which irked Stalin and stirred serious trouble within the CP(B)U, was the inevitable conclusion dictated by the logic of his esthetic rather than his political outlook. This outlook was not that of a frustrated romantic or a Trotskyite (although many regard it as such), but of a Ukrainian National-Bolshevik. If Communism and proletarian art were to be saved from the Russian strait jacket, Ukrainian culture and literature would have to emancipate themselves from Russian influences and serve as a spearhead of the "Asiatic renaissance."

[16] Akakii Akakievich, hero of Gogol's *The Overcoat,* is the epitome of servility and meekness, while a *derzhymorda* is a bully. Derzhymorda is a character in Gogol's *The Inspector General.*

[17] *Kamo hriadeshy,* pp. 37–38.

[18] *Dumky proty techii,* p. 42.

[19] Hordyns'kyi, *Literaturna krytyka,* p. 60.

[20] *Ibid.*

Khvyl'ovyi gave the clearest formulation of his anti-Moscow views in a series of articles, "Apolohety pysaryzmu" (The Apologians of Scribbling): [21]

Since our literature at last can follow its own path of development, we are faced with the following question: "Toward which of the world's literatures should it orient itself?"
On no account toward the Russian. This is unconditional. One must not confuse our political union with literature. Our poetry must run away as fast as possible from Russian literature and its styles. The Poles would never have produced Mickiewicz if they had followed Muscovite art. The point is that Russian literature has been burdening us for ages; it has been the master of the situation, who has trained us to imitate him slavishly. Thus if we try to feed our young art with it, we shall impede its development. Proletarian ideas did not reach us through Muscovite art; on the contrary, we, a young nation, can better apprehend these ideas and recreate them in proper images. Our orientation is toward Western European art, its style and its techniques.[22]

Even bolder sounds Khvyl'ovyi's voice in "Ukraïna chy Malorosiia" (Ukraine or Little Russia), a pamphlet which was never published, but parts of which appeared in Ie. F. Hirchak's *Na dva fronta v borbe s natsionalizmom* (Moscow–Leningrad, 1930):

We are truly an independent state which is one of the republics of the Soviet Union. The Ukraine is independent not because we, the Communists, so desire, but because it is made imperative by the iron and unwavering power of the laws of history, because only in this way shall we hasten class differentiation in the Ukraine. If any one nation (much has been written about it before) shows throughout many centuries a will to express itself as an entity in the form of a state, then all attempts to arrest in one way or another this essential process on the one hand hinder the formation of class forces, and on the other bring an element of chaos into the general historical development of the world. To attempt to rub out independence by empty pseudo-Marxism means a failure to understand that the Ukraine will continue to be an armory of counterrevolution as long as it does not pass through that essential stage which Western Europe underwent at the time of the formation of national states.[23]

Against Russian literature Khvyl'ovyi speaks in terms stronger than those used by Chaadaev in his survey of Russian history:

21 First published in *Kul'tura i pobut*, February–March, 1926.
22 M. Khvyl'ovyi, "Apolohety pysaryzmu," *Kul'tura i pobut*, March 28, 1926.
23 Ie. F. Hirchak, *Na dva fronta v borbe s natsionalizmom*, p. 62.

In his article on Fonvizin, V. Belinskii writes that "the Russians are the inheritors of all the world, not only of European life," that "they have a right to be so, and that they should not and will not be like the French, the Germans, or the English, but they must be Russians." So think the contemporary members of the Russian imperialist intelligentsia, and no matter how much we shout that such a view is obsolete and does not answer the needs of the present day, the Muscovite messianism will live on in the heads of the Russian intelligentsia, since even today that intelligentsia is brought up on the same Belinskii. . . .

To crush Russian messianism means not only to raise the semaphore signal for the express of joyful creativeness, which with the onrush of its passage will start a real Spring among the peoples, but also to liberate Russian youth from the agelong prejudices of imperialism. . . .

The great Russian literature is above all the literature of pessimism or rather passive pessimism. . . . Russian passive pessimism brings forth cadres of "superfluous men," or to put it simply, parasites, dreamers, and "people without definite occupations." In modern Russian ethnographic romanticism we can see the same idealization of Razins and Pugachëvs, mixed with a feeling of Russian patriotism and vague dreams about the future. We cannot go further along that road. Great Russian literature has reached its limits and has found itself at the crossroads.[24]

Like a good Marxist, Khvyl'ovyi sought a historical and economic foundation for his cultural theory:

It is true enough that the development of a culture is dictated by economic conditions. However, the point is that these conditions are not the same in both countries [Russia and the Ukraine]. They are the same only as far as world economy is concerned and also for the purpose of a united front against the bourgeoisie. But the Ukrainian national economy is not that of Russian and cannot be one were it only[25] for the fact that the Ukrainian culture which grows out of our economy has a reciprocal influence on it and imparts to it special characteristics. In a word, the [Soviet] Union remains a union, and the Ukraine is an independent unit. . . . Under the influence of our economy we apply to our literature not a "Slavophile theory of originality" but a theory of Communist independence.[26]

24 Hirchak, *Na dva fronta,* pp. 55–56.
25 Khvyl'ovyi's ideas influenced the Soviet Ukrainian economist Volobuiev, who in a series of articles in *Bil'shovyk Ukraïny* (1928) sharply attacked the Soviet economic policy in the Ukraine. "Just as Khvyl'ovyi and Shums'kyi," writes Hirchak (*Shumskizm i rozlam v KPZU,* p. 195), "raised the slogan 'Away from Moscow and her culture,' so Volobuiev's watchword is 'Away from Moscow's economy!' "
26 "Apolohety pysaryzmu," *Kul'tura i pobut,* March 28, 1926.

Passionately convinced that equality within the Union was not a mere formality and that Ukrainian culture had every right to rid itself of Russian protection, Khvyl'ovyi wrote:

Because for centuries the Ukrainian nation strove for its liberation, we must regard this urge as an expression of its strongest desire to manifest and expend its national (not nationalistic) traits. These national traits show themselves in a freely developed culture. . . . This national craving must spend itself in art.[27]

A far less belligerent participant in the Literary Discussion was Mykola Zerov. The spiritual leader and chief theoretician of the Ukrainian Neoclassicists was a striking contrast to the others, not only in his behavior, which was that of a self-possessed professor of literature, but also in his literary views. When in 1925 he entered the wide literary arena, it was only to reaffirm and amplify his old beliefs. His direct contribution to the Literary Discussion was very small in volume [28] yet most germane to the central issues of the debates.

The Neoclassicist stand may best be summed up by Zerov's watchword *Ad Fontes* (To the Sources), the title also of his collection of essays.[29] In it he wrote that

we must not avoid ancient or even feudal Europe. Let us not fear that it will contaminate us (who knows, perhaps it is better for a proletarian to become infected with the class determinants of a Western European bourgeois, than with the lukewarmness of a repentant Russian patrician). We must get to know the sources of European culture and we must make them our own. We must know them, or else we shall always be provincials. To Khvyl'ovyi's "Whither Go?" let us answer: *Ad fontes,* to the original sources, to the roots.[30]

.   .   .

In our literary life there is still very little real culture, little knowledge, little education, while our scholarship is at a disadvantage. Second-hand knowledge, lack of direct contact with those theories we accept, create for us all kinds of fantastic illusions and we live among them without being aware of their unreality. . . . Khvyl'ovyi is right. A young writer must get rid of his illiteracy in the field in which he wishes to work; he must learn his trade before he decides to appear

27 *Dumky proty techiï,* p. 49.
28 "Evropa-Pros'vita-Os'vita-Liknep," "Evraziis'kyi renesans i poshekhons'ki sosny," "Zmitsnena pozytsiia," all reprinted in *Do dzherel* (Kiev, 1926).
29 *Do dzherel.*   30 *Ibid.,* p. 118.

before the reader. Such self-education will be the first step to what Khvyl'ovyi called "Europe." We can conquer Europe only when we make their achievement our own. Whether we like it or not, from the times of Kulish, Drahomanov, Franko, Lesia Ukraïnka, Kotsiubyns'kyi, and Kobylians'ka—European forms and themes have penetrated our literature and stayed there.

The whole crux of the matter is how we shall pass through this process of Europeanization: as pupils, as unconscious provincials who can only copy the exterior, or as mature and grown-up people—who know the nature and the consequences of such an appropriation of culture and therefore take from its inner core what is most essential. We must be well in front, not lagging behind; we must approach the sources themselves (*juvat integros accedere fontes*), and not accept anything on trust; we must learn how to read music, not learn, like children, by ear.[31]

For Zerov, the sources of literary culture lay chiefly in Greek and Roman poetry and art, and the French Parnassians. Three conditions which, according to him, were necessary for the "development of our literature" were:

(1) To become fully acquainted with the vastly experienced world literature: that is, to gain a good literary education and work persistently and systematically on translations. (2) Clarification and re-valuation of the Ukrainian literary tradition and heritage. (3) Artistic refinement and higher standards for young writers.[32]

It is not surprising, therefore, that although differing on many questions, Zerov and Khvyl'ovyi became allies in 1925. Khvyl'ovyi, who wrote that "the Zerovs sensed the spirit of our age," declared that "if Zerov knows this Europe (and he does) we shall stretch out our hand to him." [33] It was under Zerov's influence that Khvyl'ovyi's concept of an "Asiatic renaissance" expanded to embrace the classical tradition of Western Europe. "The Asiatic renaissance," he wrote in 1926, "will be an epoch of European regeneration plus the incomparable, exhilarating and joyous Greek and Roman art." [34]

However much opposed they may have been to the Communist "proletarian" idea of art as subordinated to the state, the Neoclassicists regarded themselves, not without some right, as better Marx-

---

[31] *Ibid.*, pp. 111–12. [32] *Ibid.*, p. 122.
[33] Khvyl'ovyi, *Kamo hriadeshy*, p. 42. [34] *Ibid.*, p. 61.

ists than those who followed Lenin's precepts. In an article in *Chervonyi shliakh* [35] Zerov elaborated skillfully on Marx's famous observation on Greek art.[36]

In the same article Zerov defines once more the convictions of the Neoclassicists:

Allowing enough space for everyone, they [the Neoclassicists] never constructed any rigid framework for all. They translate the sonnets whether of German proletarian poets or ancient Romans or of Polish romanticists, and . . . they are equally familiar with hexameter, with octaves, four-foot iambics, and vers libre. That is why . . . they will never subscribe to the manifesto of the Russian Neoclassicists and will not say that they create on the basis of pure classicism. That is why they prefer to put the appellation "Neoclassicists" in quotation marks, and will never agree . . . that art exists for art's sake, and that classical art is the alpha and omega of all artistic achievement. The Neoclassicists think that Greek and Roman writers can be of value in the creation of a "great style," but they will never regard the ancient authors as the world's pinnacle.[37]

The strength and influence of the Neoclassicists lay equally in poetry and in theory. Unlike the other groups, they created more than they preached, and thus enriched modern Ukrainian literature not only with their theory of art but with some of the finest examples of poetry.

In sharpest contrast to the Neoclassicists and also to Khvyl'ovyi stands another literary debater, Andrii Khvylia. In his speech before the First Congress of VUSPP, Khvylia made the following denunciation:

If in our [literary] development, the Ukrainian bourgeois intelligentsia, so hostile to us, pretends to be on our side, it tries, in fact, to exploit this development . . . in order to carry on its work of consolidating not the working class in the cause of socialist culture, but the nationalist culture aimed against the Soviet Ukrainian republic, against the socialist Ukraine.

[35] M. Zerov, "Nashi literaturoznavtsi i polemisty," *Chervonyi shliakh,* No. 4, 1926, pp. 155-57.
[36] In his *A Contribution to the Critique of Political Economy* (1859), Marx observed that although Greek art and epic poetry reflect certain forms of the social development of their time, they continue to give esthetic pleasure, and to some extent remain the highest models for the artist. Marx explained this phenomenon as an everlasting appeal which the childhood of mankind has for those in later and higher stages of development.
[37] Zerov, "Nashi literaturoznavtsi i polemisty," *Chervonyi shliakh,* No. 4, 1926, p. 172.

The literary front is the most sensitive of all; it reflects all contemporary moods, all political tendencies of those elements which stimulate the growth of the Ukrainian bourgeoisie.

We have in mind the so-called Neoclassicists. Until very recently some members of the Party considered this question from the following viewpoint: We have the resolution of the Central Committee of the All-Union Party which expresses a certain "neutrality" and non-interference with literary affairs and is against any administrative interference in literature which can be represented by various schools and groups, none of them having the right to claim a monopoly. This is supposed to dictate our practical policy in the field of literature.

Why, then, wonder if the Neoclassicist poets write about Hellas and Rome? Let them write; it is useful for us if they work on translations of the classics. Comrades, I wish to say here that the Party organization in the Ukraine never thought of combating the Neoclassicists as a certain literary school, because we do not like their translations from Horace or Virgil, or because they sing of ancient Rome. No, we are fighting against them for different reasons. We do not fight them as a literary school, but we fight the Ukrainian bourgeoisie which has sprouted among them. We are fighting against their policy, against their Neoclassicist ideology.[38]

An even stronger accusation is leveled by Khvylia at Khvyl'ovyi, whom he could not forgive his disobedience to clear Party directives.[39] He warned him that, "if the comrades from VAPLITE, Khvyl'ovyi, Dos'vitnyi, Ialovyi, continue to follow this road, they will fall into the mire of nationalism." [40]

All the issues arising during the Literary Discussion had, for Khvylia, political significance. A faithful watchdog of the Party's supremacy, he tried on every occasion to unveil and expose its actual and potential enemies:

In the end, the Literary Discussion assumes a political aspect and we see in its separate parts the erroneous slogans of Khvyl'ovyi about our cultural construction.

The most basic error lies in the problem of cultural relations between the Ukraine and Russia. The cultural problem assumes a huge importance in the present circumstances in the Ukraine. We are solving this problem under the guidance of the dictatorship of the proletariat. Our task is to direct our cultural construction along a socialist path.

The creation of Ukrainian proletarian literature, as in all other

---

38 VUSPP Congress, p. 20.   39 Ibid., p. 25.
40 Ibid., p. 27.

cultural work, should develop in union with the cultural affairs of other peoples of the USSR and, above all, in union with socialist Russia.

Striving to find such a solution, we must unite all our forces in the fight against imperialist Russian chauvinism which, parading under the guise of a zealous law maker of Soviet power, wants at some time to reunite Greater Russia, reestablishing old relations between the mother country and the colonies, between the ruling imperialist nation and the subjugated peoples.

There are some fools who believe in the reestablishment of the old relationship between the peoples of former Russia.

We believe in something else: Old Russia is dead and will never rise from the grave. She was driven into it and destroyed by the proletariat. In her place there arose a union of peoples: Ukrainian, Russian, Belorussian, Tatar, Georgian, and others. He who tries to resurrect the corpse of the old Russia . . . is a criminal. . . .

At the same time we must draw our sword against national Ukrainian chauvinism. It must not be allowed to turn the formation of a Ukrainian culture into a cause of enmity between the peoples of the USSR.[41]

Khvylia saw that the roots of all nationalist deviations in Ukrainian culture and literature lay in the fact that "the revolutionary struggle in Russia and the Ukraine originated and developed under different circumstances." [42] All that was needed to rectify this anomaly was time. In due course, the proletarian consciousness of the Ukrainians would increase and completely displace their national feelings. Then socialism, under the leadership of Russia, would be accepted by all without reservations. Khvyl'ovyi, that is, with his idea of an Asiatic renaissance and his skepticism toward Russian literature and art, was simply out of step with the course of events. The destiny of Soviet Ukrainian literature, thought Khvylia, lay in the closest collaboration with Russian culture, although, as he was anxious to emphasize, "we go forward as equals and shall defend this principle." [43]

Mykola Skrypnyk, who early in 1927 became the Ukrainian Commissar for Education, had by virtue of his office an important voice in the Literary Discussion. His was not, however, merely the voice of an official, but rather that of an intellectual leader and a great

[41] A. Khvylia, *Pro nashi literaturni spravy*, pp. 3–5.   [42] *Ibid.*, p. 13.
[43] *Ibid.*, p. 40.

personality. Unlike Khvylia, he believed that a parallel and balanced development of Ukrainian and Russian culture could only be satisfactory if the boundaries between these cultures as well as between the states were well defined, even though the Party were the supreme arbiter in all matters of cultural policy.

At the same time Skrypnyk was much more aware than most Ukrainian Communists of the inherent conflict underlying Russian-Ukrainian relations. In fact, it is hardly possible to draw any comparison between Khvylia and Skrypnyk; they were men of different stature. There is an interesting and intimate impression of Skrypnyk in the recently published account of the meeting between him and Professor I. Borshchak in Paris in 1927.[44] In Borshchak's account Skrypnyk emerges in his true likeness. An enthusiast for Ukrainization, he was deeply convinced that Soviet Ukrainian culture could flourish in the Soviet Ukrainian Republic, the building of which he regarded as still incomplete. Intensely interested in cultural relations between the Ukraine and the West, Skrypnyk thought and acted as a Ukrainian intellectual and statesman, not a Party representative.

Skrypnyk analyzed the position of the chief adversary of the Party, Khvyl'ovyi, with the detached air of a Marxist and a Leninist:

> If Khvyl'ovyi is against this or that Ukrainian or Russian literary trend and opposes their form and style, pleading for a new form and style, then in such a case he has *carte blanche* and we do not hold anything against him.
>
> Yet we should like to put this question to comrade Khvyl'ovyi: Is he against Russian literary trends and their forms because the latter are bad or because they are Russian? Khvyl'ovyi's objections to Russian literary trends are simply because they are Russian. That this is so, is confirmed by his own words that Ukrainian literature has to direct a course "on no account toward the Russian; this is unconditional."
>
> Comrade Khvyl'ovyi thinks unconditionally that the only possible way is that of counterpoising Ukrainian literature against Russian literature, that of struggle between two cultures.[45]

---

44 I. Borshchak, "Dvi zustrichi," *Ukraïna*, No. 4, 1950.

45 M. Skrypnyk, *Do teoriï borot'by dvokh kul'tur,* first printed as a series of articles in *Kommunist* (1926); appeared in booklet form in 1926; here quoted from B. Borev, *Natsional'ne pytannia*, pp. 148, 149.

Skrypnyk considered Khvyl'ovyi's attempt to separate culture from politics naive and un-Marxian (although he, Skrypnyk, did the same), but he did not make this an excuse for abuse and castigation:

Here is the clue to Khvyl'ovyi's attitude. For him the connection and influence of Russian literature become an obstacle to the self-determination of national culture. He declares that one must not confuse political union with literature. . . . The ideological camouflage of Khvyl'ovyi's attitude does not hide its real nature which is not literary but political, based on the theory of struggle between two cultures. . . . This is a nationalist approach, which is not the one discovered by the October Revolution. . . . It all started with the literary theory of Formalism, the roots of which are in the bourgeois outlook; then came the concept of union with the Ukrainian bourgeois intelligentsia; hence orientation against Soviet Russia.[46]

The true explanation of the basic error of "nationalist" deviationists is given by Skrypnyk in his classic piece of Leninist interpretation of history:

Where is the root of the theory of struggle between two cultures? What is the reason why the relationship between two cultures in one country should be regarded as a struggle?
The reason lies, of course, not in the mere fact of the existence in one country of two languages or two cultures. It is this: These views arise because of the transference to the Soviet Ukraine of the modes of development which the national culture of a subjugated people followed in a bourgeois capitalist state.[47]

This opinion is supported by another article of faith:

Whereas in a capitalist country a young culture of a nation formerly oppressed could express itself only through opposition to and struggle against the culture of the ruling nation, after the victory of the proletariat this relationship has been altered. Not opposition and struggle, but brotherly collaboration, friendly mutual influence, and a striving toward a common goal are now the means toward cultural fulfillment.[48]

Skrypnyk's disciple, Hirchak, broadened this concept to cover Ukrainian ideological divergencies.

Khvyl'ovyi's main error which gave rise to all his other errors is his misunderstanding of a national rebirth under conditions of prole-

---

46 Borev, *Natsional'ne pytannia*, pp. 150–51.   47 *Ibid.*, p. 151.
48 *Ibid.*, p. 152.

tarian dictatorship and socialist construction. He imagines that the process of national regeneration under the conditions of proletarian dictatorship, at a time when the workers and the toiling masses have created several independent proletarian states which have voluntarily joined in a Union, will proceed along the same path as the regeneration of nations under conditions of bourgeois democratic revolution against feudalism.

That is why he is always attracted by the heroes of bourgeois national revival, why he was under its influence and used analogies with the bourgeois national regeneration. . . . Such a view is not Leninist, it is not dialectical. The path of national regeneration under the conditions of ruling capitalism is a path of struggle between the culture of one nation with the culture of another nation, it is the path of oppression, exploitation, and subjugation of one nation by another, it is the path of struggle of national states.

The whole history of the development of capitalist society is the best testimony to it. Under the conditions of capitalism (not to speak of conditions of imperialism) the national problem was not and could not be solved. There, the evolution was such that a nation subjugated and without any national rights today, then liberated by a revolution or war, tomorrow became the country which oppressed other nations (France during the revolution, Italy, Germany). There is hardly any need to point out that under conditions of proletarian revolution the path of national regeneration is a path of real liberation of that nation, is a path of brotherly collaboration between the liberated nations, who have won their independence, and created their states.[49]

Against such explicit Leninist beliefs Soviet Ukrainian writers could not openly advance any arguments since they themselves subscribed to the Marxian doctrine. We saw that Khvyl'ovyi could not accept the simple article of faith—that national oppression is impossible in a Soviet state. Many other writers who took part in the Literary Discussion did point to the practical aspects of the actual national policy in the Ukraine which demanded a clearer answer than that provided by Skrypnyk or Hirchak.

Not only writers from Khvyl'ovyi's camp, but his opponents too, expressed concern about the results and the pace of the Soviet Ukrainization policy. In 1927, Koriak, one of the founding members of VUSPP, declared that

the day before this Congress the paper *Komunist* published figures about our trade unions. They show that of 569 workers' clubs in the

49 Ie. F. Hirchak, *Shumskizm i rozlam v KPZU*, pp. 89–90.

Ukraine only 240 are clubs in which Ukrainian workers predominate. The clubs as a whole have in their libraries 2,400,703 books—among them 155,000 Ukrainian. This means that there are over a hundred and fifty thousand Ukrainian books to two million Russian. . . . Ten years after the Revolution Ukrainian books have failed to reach our proletariat.[50]

VUSPP, VAPLITE, and Pluh were eager to mobilize around their platforms Ukrainian writers and critics for the purpose (among others) of remedying these conditions. Both camps, the Vaplitians and the Vusppists, claimed for literature the role of intellectual avant-garde in the development of Ukrainian culture. It was at this point that Skrypnyk took issue with them and advanced a theory which was best expressed by him at the closing session of the Literary Discussion. He deplored the fact that "our literary organizations were, and for the most part still are, not organizations with literary or artistic aims, but literary-political organizations slightly reminiscent of the organizations of the Russian intelligentsia in 1905, such as the unions of engineers, teachers, and so on, all founded on a certain social and political platform": [51]

Two conclusions may be drawn from this fact: first, that our literature has not yet passed the stage of a primitive and provincial existence; secondly, the achievements of our literature are higher than the forms of our literary organizations.[52]

For me, the newly established organization Nova Generatsiia has more meaning in comparison with other groups because it was formed for artistic and literary purposes. Its existence will force other writers to declare themselves as artists.[53]

Writers, in other words, should be concerned, according to Skrypnyk, with literature as one of the arts and not as the expression of ideological tendencies of a culture. This view he defended against several attacks in the last days of the debates and he re-emphasized that for writers to group themselves according to artistic principles means "that they should work on their styles and form, and that they should improve their choice of images, and their depth." [54]

He condemned, therefore, both VAPLITE and VUSPP for trying to assume ideological leadership:

---

[50] VUSPP Congress, p. 33.   [51] M. Skrypnyk, *Nasha literaturna diisnist'*, p. 7.
[52] *Ibid.*   [53] *Ibid.*, p. 9.   [54] *Ibid.*, p. 36.

I said that today we are taking part in the funeral of the deceased VAPLITE. At the same time we have witnessed the burial of an attempt by another organization [VUSPP] to monopolize literature.[55]

Two years later, reflecting on the Literary Discussion, Skrypnyk still thought that it became a "political contest." "Today," he declared, "we cannot allow that literature can transform political life and can attempt to determine the relationship in our cultural and political life." [56]

Although Skrypnyk's endeavor to force the Literary Discussion on to a purely esthetic level may be regarded as un-Marxian, it was probably the result of purely practical considerations. By telling writers to attend to their writing and not to meddle in politics, Skrypnyk was on the one hand trying to protect them from the pitfalls of deviationism, while on the other he was hoping to reserve any decisions in literary policy for himself, as the representative of the Party and the Commissar for Education. However, his attempts were doomed to failure. It became increasingly difficult to follow the policy with which Skrypnyk had intended to please both the Ukrainians and the Kremlin. During the last session of the Discussion, held from February 18–21, 1928, it became clear that the literary debate was straying for beyond the field of style and form. Too many challenges and daring inquiries were being allowed, covering the entire field of Soviet Ukrainian culture, to be suddenly laid aside or rendered fruitless. Two hostile ideological camps (VAPLITE and VUSPP) were still facing each other, determined to win or die in battle. In their exchanges many lengthy and ponderous utterances by such prominent participants as Pylypenko and by others without clear slogans of their own were all but drowned.

The Outcome of the Debate

The literary battle in the Ukraine was joined in April, 1925. Then, according to one of the debaters, Mohylians'kyi, "the impression, after Khvyl'ovyi's article, was as if in a room so stuffy that breathing was difficult, the windows had been suddenly opened, and the lungs felt the air again." [57]

55 *Ibid.,* p. 37.   56 M. Skrypnyk, *Pereznaky tvorchoho terenu,* p. 37.
57 *Shliakhy rozvytku suchasnoï literatury; Dysput 24 travnia 1925,* p. 43.

Perhaps the greatest value of the Literary Discussion was the freedom with which writers expressed their views. For once the platforms and policies of various groups and organizations gave place to the fundamental issues of the time: content, form, and the orientation of Soviet Ukrainian literature. The Neoclassicists and fellow travelers (Pidmohyl'nyi, Antonenko-Davydovych, Ivchenko) felt free to support Khvyl'ovyi, who attempted to rally behind him some of the fellow travelers and the "inner emigrants." "Khvyl'ovyi's article," said Zerov, "makes it clear that for him Europe symbolizes a strong cultural tradition, strict, lifelong competition, an unwavering artistic choice." [58]

Khvyl'ovyi's demand that the illiterate scribbling of Communist graphomaniacs should not be classed as literature found wide support among the debaters. Ryl's'kyi spoke on their behalf when he said: "We are in the midst of a literary crisis not because our writers are few but because they are many. To those who spoke of the necessity of strictures I shall say that free thought will always overcome strictures. The only strictures which are necessary are for those without any talent [applause]." [59] In fact, the general impatience with the dull products of some would-be proletarian writers was so pronounced at the opening debate in the Academy of Sciences that the defenders of the scribblers were driven to desperation. "We protest against such a dispute," cried Kovalenko, the representative of the Kiev Hart, "and we declare that we shall reach an agreement with the masses of workers and peasants over your heads [applause, laughter, and also cries of 'shame,' 'disgrace']." [60]

The strongest appeal of Khvyl'ovyi's challenge was in his plea for a pro-Western orientation of Ukrainian literature, for its independence from Moscow. There was no cogent reason to assume that Ukrainian literature must have a pro-Moscow orientation. None of the staunchest defenders of the Party policy dared to declare openly that the political dependence of the Ukraine on Russia also meant cultural subservience. On the contrary, much ink was spilled on stressing the cultural independence of the Ukraine and of the other non-Russian Soviet republics. Khvyl'ovyi was the first Ukrainian (and a Communist at that) who voiced the doubt which must have been shared by thousands of others: was it really possible to follow

[58] *Ibid.*, p. 24. [59] *Ibid.*, p. 79. [60] *Ibid.*, p. 80.

an independent cultural policy in the Ukraine while being politically and economically tied to Russia? He put it to the test by issuing his call "away from Moscow."

The result unmasked in a most dramatic way the actual state of
affairs. While Khvyl'ovyi's ideas stirred wide response, the Party
trampled them into the dust, crushed their exponents, and forced
the groups upholding them to dissolve. To a Ukrainian intellectual, reared in the spirit of national emancipation, rooted in the
prerevolutionary struggle for national liberation, and nurtured on
glowing Bolshevik promises of self-determination, what could be
better evidence of Moscow's imperialism and his own country's
impotence?

However, in spite of the vituperation heaped upon Khvyl'ovyi,
and ignoring the strictures and bans on his works and ideas, a considerable section of the Soviet Ukrainian intelligentsia, particularly
the writers, supported him in the battle against Party controls while
struggle was still possible. In the Literary Discussion, this opposition became most vocal. The period of the discussion (1925–28)
may be studied from many points of view. One rewarding approach
would be to analyze it in the light of the anti-Moscow feelings of
Ukrainian writers and artists. These feelings found their expression as soon as an opportunity offered itself. To these rebellious
writers as well as to all those who looked upon the future of Ukrainian culture as separate and independent of Russia, Khvyl'ovyi's
part in the Literary Discussion resembled, in Hordyns'kyi's opinion, "the fiery words of Shevchenko." [61]

[61] Hordyns'kyi, *Literaturna krytyka,* p. 59.

[VI]

A GLANCE AT THE INTRACTABLE
LITERATURE

Orientation toward Western European Art

Had the Ukrainian opposition to the Party policy expressed itself merely in literary theorizing and pamphleteering, it would have lacked the dynamic vitality which, in fact, informed it. It was sustained by a rich efflorescence in all genres of literature: the novel, the short story, poetry, and drama. In a very brief survey of those works which were subsequently placed on the "index," it might be fitting to glance first at some of the writings of Mykola Khvyl'ovyi.

Considered "one of the most outstanding writers of the proletarian age," [1] Khvyl'ovyi (pseudonym of M. Fitilov, b. 1893) began his literary career as a poet with two collections of verse, *Molodist'* (Youth, 1921) and *Dos'vitni Symphonii* (The Morning Symphonies, 1922), and a long poem, *Elektrychnyi vik* (The Age of Electricity, 1921). It was, however, his first collection of short stories, *Syni etiudy* (The Blue Etudes, 1923), which brought him fame. All of them were concerned with the Revolution in the Ukraine, which Khvyl'ovyi had greeted with enthusiasm. For him, indeed, this revolution was much more profound and far-reaching than the revolution in Russia. In the Ukraine the Revolution aimed at both social justice and national liberation, and in its intensity it reached even the extremes of anarchism (the rebellion of Makhno). Moreover, he regarded the Revolution of 1917 in the Ukraine as a continuation of the Cossack risings in the seventeenth

[1] O. Doroshkevych, *Pidruchnyk istorii ukrains'koi literatury*, p. 304.

century and the peasant rebellions of the eighteenth and nineteenth centuries. In Khvyl'ovyi's view, what hindered and ob-
structed the fullest and most complete revolutionary process in the
Ukraine was the activity and the mentality of the new proletarian
philistines, whom he defined as the "pan-federal petite bourgeoisie." They were the opportunists who regarded the Revolution as
a mere change of government and hastened to hang Lenin's picture
instead of that of the tsar (*Zaulok*), the Party and government
officials who occupied the houses of the former bourgeoisie and
differed from them only in enjoying the good things in life with
less ostentation than their predecessors did. Khvyl'ovyi's early short
stories (a second collection, *Osin'* [Autumn], was published in 1924)
are full of sketches of these new parasites of the Revolution, drawn
with all the vehemence and contempt of a genuine though romantic revolutionary.

Another problem which began to manifest itself early in his
works arose out of Khvyl'ovyi's analysis of the Ukrainian revolu-
tionary leadership. Disillusioned in the leaders of the Communist
Party, Khvyl'ovyi, himself a member of the Party, attempted to
define the ideal qualities of a Communist leader in the Ukraine.
Here, however, he was at once faced with the most serious dilemma:
is it possible to be a good Communist and at the same time a good
Ukrainian? Theoretically, the answer was "yes," yet in practice
Khvyl'ovyi found it impossible to reconcile these two elements.
"Am I really superfluous because I love the Ukraine madly?" editor
Kark (in the story "Editor Kark"), an assistant to a half-illiterate
Russian, who is a protégé of the Party, asks himself. Kark concludes
that if he wants to keep his job and thus serve "centralist Moscow,"
he will have to thrust aside the burning problem of Ukrainian
national development and self-expression. The Ukrainian people
is symbolically represented in this short story by a blind invalid
of the Civil War who asks passers-by to show him the way. Kark
lives through a great internal crisis and approaches the verge of
suicide, since he is helpless to remedy the betrayal of the Revolution. Kark, like Shevchenko, loves his Ukraine so much that he is
prepared to "give his soul for her," yet the question which torments
him, and obviously the author himself, is "how to lose one's soul."
The conflict between the Communist dream and real life reaches

genuinely tragic proportions in Khvyl'ovyi's story "Ia" (Myself) in which a member of the Che-ka, out of a feeling of duty and devotion to the Revolution, executes his own mother, an alleged enemy. Having committed this act, the hero realizes his crime and becomes utterly disillusioned with Communism and its dogma that "ends justify means." In his first short novel, *Sanatoriina zona* (In the Sanatorium District, 1924), Khvyl'ovyi works out the problem of the betrayed Revolution in a more subtly symbolic manner. In the sanatorium which represents life in the Soviet state, various characters meet, all of whom are victims in one way or another of the regime. Two men, Khlonia, a former Communist idealist, and Anarkh, the ex-leader of a Ukrainian peasant revolt, are now both very sick. Khlonia prophesies that "years will pass, one, two, ten, twenty, and, believe me, the unknown enemy will avenge himself. I can see even now how the thoughts of my teacher [Lenin] are overlaid by a great pile of dirty rubbish and petty distortions. The world's rabble making their way to the Holy of Holies will hide there behind his name and will turn him into a foul instrument of human regress" (*In the Sanatorium District*). Anarkh, an enthusiastic but frustrated Ukrainian rebel, falls in love with Maia, a beautiful girl who is revealed to be a spy of the GPU. In the end both men take their lives while the depressing atmosphere of the sanatorium grows even more forbidding.

Yet another aspect of the same disappointment in the Revolution is treated by Khvyl'ovyi in the short story "Sentymental'na istoriia" (A Sentimental Tale, 1928.) The heroine, the innocent and vigorous peasant girl Bianca, leaves her native village for the town eager to partake of the radiant socialist reality. Very soon, however, surrounded by selfish, vulgar, and lecherous comrades, she becomes utterly disappointed. The only man who offers her any hope of fulfillment is the artist Charhar, who is constantly afraid of denunciations by those who condemn his art on political grounds. Charhar fails to gather enough moral courage to overcome his anxiety and save Bianca by accepting her love; he begins to see in Bianca merely a source of physical pleasure. Yet even in this he fails, for he is afraid of the consequences. Torn between the forces of good and the much more powerful forces of evil, Bianca, to revenge herself on Charhar, gives herself to a disgusting and corrupt official, Kuk. Her innocence lost, she also loses for ever the beautiful dream of a new Soviet society.

Another of Khvyl'ovyi's heroines is Ahlaia in *Val'dshnepy* (The Woodsnipes, 1927). Unlike her namesake in Dostoevskii's *The Idiot,* she is a kind of Ukrainian Jeanne d'Arc. She destroys the unhappy marriage of the Communist Karamazov and his wife Hanna in order to purify Ukrainian Communism. She makes Karamazov realize that his party is doomed and that he must (with her help) renew its revolutionary faith. She mercilessly unmasks her distant relative, the Russian Evgenii Valentinovich: "Zhenia, tell us more clearly how you are building socialism in one country? . . . He is the same old Russian intellectual—the internationalist who gladly talks about the self-determination of nations . . . only not those in the Soviet Union; who sees 'Petliurovism' [2] everywhere and does not notice his own 'Ustrialovism'; [3] who even now believes that Ukrainian culture exists as the result of an Austrian plot. . . . In a word, it is the same old internationalist who under his cosmopolitanism hides the most ordinary 'zoological' nationalism." The novel was never published in its complete form, because of the ban placed on it after the first part appeared. Among the later works of Khvyl'ovyi, two of his short stories deserve to be mentioned. They are "Ivan Ivanovych" and "Revizor" (The Inspector General), both excellent satires on Soviet officialdom. Only a few of Khvyl'ovyi's stories are genuine short stories; most of them are dramatic character sketches full of philosophical and historical digression, almost plotless, and soaring into intense lyrical passages. Yet they are masterpieces of specifically revolutionary romanticism, and their unconventional forms and contrapuntal style are the marks of a truly great writer whose promise was only half-fulfilled.

The revolutionary and national romanticism which permeated the earlier works of Khvyl'ovyi was also the central theme of two

[2] Symon Petliura, the head of the Direktoriia, the government of the Ukrainian People's Republic.

[3] Ustrialov, a prominent representative of the Smena vekh (Change of Landmarks), a Russian émigré group which advocated reconciliation with the Soviet regime. According to E. H. Carr, Ustrialov "expressed the spirit of Great Russian chauvinism in its purest form" (E. H. Carr, *The Bolshevik Revolution,* I, 372).

Quotations from the unpublished part of *The Woodsnipes* are taken from Khvylia's *Vid ukhylu v prirvu,* p. 29.

other prose writers: Hryhorii Kosynka (real name Strilets', 1899–1934) and Iurii Ianovs'kyi (1902–54). A talented representative of the Ukrainian peasantry, Kosynka published his first collection of short stories, *Na zolotykh bohiv* (Against the Golden Gods), in 1922. Written in a highly impressionistic style, they dealt with the Revolution in Ukrainian villages and masterfully revealed the mentality of the peasants, their deep love of freedom and intense hatred of all kinds of government, characteristics sometimes attributed to the Ukrainian people as a whole. Kosynka is first of all an acute observer of peasant psychology; his stories lack ideological content and his peasants remain on the whole unfriendly to the Soviet regime. Some of his best short stories appeared in the collection *V zhytakh* (In the Wheatfields, 1926). In 1932 Kosynka wrote the novel *Harmoniia* (Harmony) which was condemned as "chauvinist."

Iurii Ianovs'kyi is considered by many critics to be the most outspoken nationalist after Khvyl'ovyi in the early Soviet Ukrainian novel. This reputation is based on his novel *Chotyry shabli* (The Four Sabres, 1929), now omitted from all Soviet editions of his works, although later Ianovs'kyi became reconciled to the demands of the Stalinist regime. *The Four Sabres* is more like a poem in prose than a novel; at a breathless pace with swiftly shifting scenes it takes us into the midst of a fighting band of rebel peasants in the Ukraine. Their leader, Shakhai, is a modern Ukrainian Taras Bul'ba, who wishes to restore the best qualities of the old Zaporozhian Cossack Host—their indomitable courage and the honor of the fighting man. "I swear," he says, "by my honorable kin; I swear by my great-grandfather, a serf, and my grandfather, a Zaporozhian Cossack, that honor and valor have not yet perished." (*Chotyry shabli*, p. 19.) The scenes of battle are written in the best tradition of heroic poetry, although at times tinged with irony; they convey to the reader the picture of wild steppes and brave fighting men with a vividness surpassing that of Stephen Crane. In the last part of the novel, one of the heroes, Ostiuk, finds himself in Paris. He is overcome by intense homesickness for the Ukraine and his dream of his country takes the following form:

In the middle of the Dnieper there is a granite island—its size three by six kilometers. A mass of granite of enormous depth. Next to the island—the world's greatest power station, and far around the steppe with rich ores, coal, oil, and wheat. The island like steel. These are not the Finnish marshes, where St. Petersburg had to be built on the bones of your forefathers. This is not the island of Manhattan where stands New York, this is the famous rocklike Khortytsia [4] which can support structures of any size.[5]

This electrified Dnieper island of the future, Khortytsia, is the same island which in the seventeenth century was the seat of the Zaporozhian Sich. It is for Ianovs'kyi the symbolic capital of a powerful Ukrainian state to come. Ianovs'kyi's early collection of sea poems, *Prekrasna Ut* (The Beautiful Ut, 1928), and the novel *Maister korablia* (The Master of the Ship, 1928) are more original but less romantic.

A totally different, nonheroic, and nonromantic approach to the Revolution may be found in the short stories and novels of Valeriian Pidmohyl'nyi (b. 1901). His first collection of short stories, *Tvory* (Works, 1920), is greatly influenced by the Russian writers Leonid Andreev and Anton Chekhov, while his later works show the influence of the French realist writers. Protracted plots, long dialogues, realistic portrayal of characters, and love for detail characterize this writer who received the Revolution with caution and seriousness. Pidmohyl'nyi's first novel, *Ostap Shaptala* (1922), has been described as "an apotheosis of death," [6] and has been criticized even by such mild proletarian critics as Doroshkevych, who saw in it "a long and boring theme with endless 'sufferings' and the unnecessary meditations of Shaptala." [7]

Pidmohyl'nyi's short story "Tretia revoliutsiia" (The Third Revolution, 1926) was an attempt to write on a revolutionary theme. The story is set in a village dominated by the Ukrainian anarchist peasant leader Makhno. However, the Soviet critics did not like Pidmohyl'nyi's treatment of the Ukrainian Revolution. "The story suggests," wrote Khvylia, "that Makhno was the leader of the revolutionary movement . . . and that the Communist Party was a group of schemers with no ties with the masses, who by sabotage and conspiracy exploited the heroic deeds of others." [8] In 1928 Pidmohyl'nyi wrote the novel *Misto* (The City), a comparative study of city and and village life. The hero, Stepan Radchenko,

[4] Khortytsia—the island on the Dnieper above the rapids.
[5] Iu. Ianovs'kyi, *Chotyry shabli* (Prague, 1941), pp. 163–64.
[6] Iefremov, *Istoriia ukraïns'koho pys'menstva*, II, 402.
[7] Doroshkevych, *Pidruchnyk*, p. 318.   [8] A. Khvylia, *Iasnoiu dorohoiu*, p. 130.

who comes to the city (Kiev) from the country, finds there bureaucracy, prostitution, and corruption; yet he remains inviolate and symbolizes the triumph of the village over the city. Pidmohyl'nyi's novel was attacked as anti-proletarian and reactionary and was singled out by Postyshev in 1935 as an attempt to portray the city as hostile to the village. Pidmohyl'nyi's last masterpiece was a novel, *Nevelychka drama* (A Little Drama), printed in *Zhyttia i revoliutsiia* (1930).

Another gifted writer, Borys Antonenko-Davydovych (b. 1899, real name Davydov) was condemned on similar grounds. In 1925 Antonenko-Davydovych published his first collection of short stories, *Zaporosheni syliuety* (Dusty Silhouettes), and two years later he wrote his novel *Smert'* (Death). The hero of the novel, Kost' Horobenko, is a petit-bourgeois nationalist who joins the Communist Party for doubtful reasons. He fails, however, to acquire a "Bolshevik soul," although he tries to conquer his old self by engaging in punitive expeditions against Ukrainian peasants. He is portrayed as a most despicable renegade and hypocrite. The novel was attacked for being hostile to the interests of the working class. In 1930 there appeared a series of travel sketches and essays, *Zemleiu ukraïns'koiu* (Across the Ukrainian Land), which, however, was withdrawn from the bookstores.

A novel by another Soviet Ukrainian writer, Volodymyr Gzhyts'kyi, *Chorne ozero* (The Black Lake, 1929), caused an uproar among Soviet critics. Its action is set in the Altai region in Central Asia. The main characters are divided sharply into two groups according to their stand on the national problem of the Altai. Ivan Makarovych, Tania, and Temir are in favor of Altaian autonomy and have sharp words to say about Moscow and the central Soviet government, while the Russian Lomov is represented as a Soviet imperialist. The Soviet critics described this novel as a well-camouflaged expression of Ukrainian nationalism. Gzhyts'kyi's other novels, *Zakhar Vovhura* and *Dovbush,* were also banned.

A similar device for expressing a point of view on the national problem in the Ukraine was adopted by Mykhailo Ivchenko (b. 1890), whose short stories, *Shumy vesniani* (Spring Clamours), first appeared in 1919 and in 1926 were included in an expanded collection, *Imlystoiu rikoiu* (The Misty River). Basically a lyricist, Ivchenko did not greet the Revolution as a world-shaking event; for him the human problems remained as difficult to solve as they were before the Revolution. Ivchenko was concerned in particular with the character of the Ukrainian people. In his novel *Robitni syly* (The Working Forces, 1929) he dealt in Aesopian language with the problem of national regeneration. The hero of the novel, Savlutyns'kyi, a professor of biology, finds that the ordinary type of sugar beet growing in the Ukraine is too soft and tender to resist the severities of the climate. Hence he decides to impoverish the soil and so to increase the plant's resistance. The idea behind this, of course, is that the rich and fertile Ukraine makes the Ukrainians too soft. In their character, instincts and emotions prevail over the will. Savlutyns'kyi aims, therefore, at a transformation of the Ukrainian people by making them less susceptible to their mellow surroundings. The hope of such a regeneration is held out by Orysia, whom the professor marries. The Soviet critics charged that the novel preached the purity of the Ukrainian race. A defendant in the trial of the Union for the Liberation of the Ukraine (1930), Ivchenko was forced to leave the Ukraine and live in the Caucasus.

The proletarian writer H. Epik was censured for his novels *Bez gruntu* (Without Ground), *Persha vesna* (The First Spring), and *Petro Romen*. The first of these he rewrote to conform to the demands of the critics.

A worse fate overtook the first Ukrainian proletarian novelist, Dos'vitnyi, who in 1924 published the novel *Amerykantsi* (The Americans). The critics hailed this work, which contained some of the sharpest and crudest ridicule of American policies in the Far East and especially in Korea during the Revolution, but Dos'vitnyi's other works (the novels *Nas bulo troie* [There Were Three of Us, 1929] and *Kvartsyt* [Quartzite]) were condemned as nationalistic. According to Shchupak, Dos'vitnyi's novel *Quartzite* was an attempt to rehabilitate the writers of the suppressed VAPLITE group. "Dos'vitnyi," writes Shchupak, "perpetuates the malicious fable invented by the VAPLITE that Khvyl'ovyi's followers did more for the cause of the Revolution than the writers who were members of VUSPP. Dos'vitnyi glorifies the past of the Khvyl'ovists, portraying them as real Ukrainian heroes." [9]

9 S. Shchupak, *Borot'ba za metodolohiiu*, p. 221.

The greatest Ukrainian humorist of the Soviet period, Ostap Vyshnia (pseudonym of Pavlo Hubenko, b. 1889), the author of *Us'mishky* (Smiles, 1928), was deported under a long sentence for his outspoken ridicule of industrialization. After serving his term, however, he reappeared on the literary scene in the early 1940s, a few years before the great Russian humorist Zoshchenko suffered his eclipse. Another Ukrainian satirist, Iurii Vukhnal', the author of *Humoresky* (Humoresques, 1929), also disappeared.

Other Ukrainian prose writers who suffered as a result of literary discrimination and purges were Maik Iohansen, a poet (*D'hori* [Upwards, 1921]; *Doribok* [Gleanings, 1924]) and the author of several travel sketches (e.g., *Podorozh liudyny pid kepom* [Travels of a Man in a Cap, 1929]); Oleksa Slisarenko, a gifted poet (*Baida,* 1928), novelist (*Chornyi anhel* [The Black Angel, 1929]), and short story writer whose "Tvaryna" (The Animal) is a superb short story; and Arkadii Liubchenko, the author of *Buremna put'* (Stormy Passage, 1926) and *Vertep* (The Puppet Show, 1929). The last work can best be compared to a medieval mystery. It conveys through a series of fragmentary, allegorical scenes a philosophical conception of Soviet Ukrainian history against a background of the universal scheme of things. Perhaps the most memorable is the part "Naimenniam zhinka" (Thy Name Is Woman) where, as Iurii Sherekh has so well expressed it, "the traditional Ukrainian cult of woman and mother has assumed for Liubchenko a manifestation of the life forces of the renascent Ukrainian people, and their deep roots in the black earth of the Ukrainian steppes. . . . Eternal youth, eternal fertility, eternal purity, life eternal, and the Ukraine eternal—this is the meaning of this image." [10]

Several writers who were at first followers of Khvyl'ovyi and later went over to the Communist camp had to rework some of their writings. Thus the novelist A. Holovko, author of *Burian* (Weeds, 1927), had to alter his novel *Maty* (Mother, 1934) after it was censured by the Soviet critics as giving too much prominence to the role of the Ukrainian intelligentsia in the 1905 revolution.

[10] Iurii Sherekh, "Kolir nestrymnykh palakhtin'," *Mur Al'manakh,* I (1946), 168–69.

Poetry—the Mirror of Revolution

The Ukraine had always had a strong poetic tradition. In the post-revolutionary period also the Ukrainian poets became the literary avant-garde and achieved the fullest artistic maturity. Among them the most outstanding was Pavlo Tychyna, justly called "the poet of the Ukrainian Revolution."

Tychyna (b. 1891) began writing poetry in 1910 under the influence of the Symbolist school. His talent first reached the height of its expression in 1918 with the publication of his collection of poems *Soniashni kliarnety* (The Clarinets of the Sun). The poetic achievement of Tychyna lay in his successful fusion of folksong and poetry, or rather in the transformation of folksong into poem. The poet's enthusiastic welcome of what he believed to be the national freedom expresses itself here in lyrical and elegiac moods, pervaded by musical chords of cosmic harmony.

Tychyna's philosophy is pantheistic; music is at the heart of nature and the universe, and man must submit himself to it.

The national Ukrainian revolution of 1917 to him was an awakening of the inner music of the world, which till that time had slumbered in the Ukrainian nation. He glorified it in the image of the "Golden Harmony" (Zolotyi homin) that rings from the churches of St. Sophia and the Lavra in Kiev, and echoes in the soul of every Ukrainian. This inner musicality cannot be produced through the play of words. . . . Tychyna sought it in unusual groupings of words, and in images full of unusual meaning. In his poetry the Ukrainian word for the first time acquired a manifold meaning, as in the poems of the Western European Symbolists.[11]

Tychyna's second collection of poems, *Pluh* (Plough, 1920), shows greater preoccupation with the social aspects of the Revolution and with the Civil War. The poet remains optimistic, although reflection and calm have replaced his earlier feelings of joy. Tychyna's third collection, *Viter z Ukraïny* (The Wind from the Ukraine, 1924), is perhaps his highest poetic achievement. His faith in the people and his detachment from politics, together with his deep concern with human issues, blend here in an unsurpassed harmony. A long unfinished philosophical poem by Tychyna, *Skovoroda*

11 Iurii Sherekh, "Trends in Ukrainian Literature under the Soviets," *The Ukrainian Quarterly*, No. 2 (Spring, 1948), p. 152.

(1923), showed a high level of sustained poetic expression. In 1925 Tychyna joined VAPLITE and, although he never took an active part in the literary debates, there is no reason to doubt that until the literary troubles in the late twenties he was on the side of the literature of resistance.

In 1927, when he was accused by the Chairman of the Ukrainian Council of the People's Commissars, Chubar, of "peddling a nationalist opiate under the banner of proletarian literature," in one of his poems published in *Vaplite Al'manakh*, Tychyna wrote the following unrepentant letter to the newspaper *Komunist:*

Having read in your paper *Komunist*, No. 11, the speech by comrade Chubar at the Kharkov District Party Conference, I was very much surprised when I found in it a quotation from my work "Mother Peeled the Potatoes," still more because it was described as . . . "peddling a nationalist opiate under the banner of proletarian literature." Allow me to state that nowhere and never have I peddled nationalist opiates. The published poem is merely an introduction to a larger poem on which I have already been working for several years. In this introduction I opposed two forces, the old one which is receding and not catching up with life (represented by the mother) and a new, revolutionary, and victorious force, which is symbolized by her Communist son. The events described took place at the beginning of the establishment of Soviet power, and the village is portrayed as it then was (famine, scarcity of land, belief that Lenin was Anti-Christ). The interpretation of the mother's words about the Ukraine specially astonished me. It should be obvious that her words, which could in no way be regarded as those of the author, are opposed by her son's words. Lastly, it is evident from the work itself that the author's sympathy is with the son.[12]

In 1933 Tychyna renounced his past associations and joined the fold of loyal followers of the Party. Tychyna's earlier works, which were very much a part of the Ukrainian post-revolutionary renaissance, have never been reprinted in their entirety since 1934. Today he is known in the Soviet Ukraine as the author of the *Feeling of a United Family,* for which he received the Order of Stalin, though he may still be remembered as the "poet of the Ukrainian Revolution."

A symbolist poet, Dmytro Zahul (b. 1890), produced among other works four notable collections of verse: *Z zelenykh hir* (From the

[12] P. Tychyna, "Lyst do redaktsiï," *Komunist*, November 3, 1927.

Green Mountains, 1918), *Na hrani* (On the Ridge, 1919), *Nash den'* (Our Day, 1924), and *Motyvy* (Motifs, 1927)—all of them of lasting value. He also left good translations of Balmont, Goethe, and Heine. In the thirties Zahul joined the list of those Ukrainian writers who were deported and never heard of again.

In 1922 a younger poet of a different school and of working class origin, Volodymyr Sosiura (b. 1898), published his second collection of verse, *Chervona zyma* (The Red Winter). Although essentially a lyricist, Sosiura felt the great impact of the Revolution. His second volume, *Osinni zori* (Autumn Stars, 1924), may be classed together with Khvyl'ovyi's poems as the finest examples of heroic, revolutionary verse. Sosiura's longer poems, *Mazepa* (1929) and *Taras Triasylo* (1926), dealing with two Ukrainian Hetmans, were assailed by the critics for indulging in national romanticism. Sosiura is also the author of the collection of verse *Sertse* (The Heart, 1931) which was banned soon after its publication.[13] After being for a time in disgrace Sosiura again emerged in Soviet Ukrainian literature. In 1951 his poem *Liubit' Ukraïnu* (Love the Ukraine) was condemned by Party spokesmen.[14]

Mykola Bazhan (b. 1904), the most talented of the poets of the neo-romantic trend in Soviet Ukrainian poetry, is the author of *Simnadtsiatyi patrul'* (The Seventeenth Patrol, 1926), *Riz'blena tin'* (The Sculpted Shadow, 1927), *Budivli* (Buildings, 1929), and *Doroha* (The Road, 1930). Some Soviet critics saw in Bazhan's "lyrical poems several nationalist themes," [15] while others charged that "Bazhan in his work does not measure up to the demands of the working class. . . . Only by realizing the catastrophe which awaits those who have departed from the broad path of the proletarian revolution can Bazhan arrive at a turning point in his

[13] For criticism of Sosiura's *Sertse* see P. Mel'nyk's review in *Zhyttia i revoliutsiia*, No. 11–12, 1931.

[14] Cf. "Reds in Ukraine Scored by Pravda," New York *Times*, July 3, 1951; also, Albert Parry, "Russia's Latest Witch Hunt," New York *Herald Tribune*, October 17. 1951. Ironically enough this poem was written in 1944, in conformity with the current Party line which then encouraged local nationalist feelings as a means of strengthening the resistance to the German invaders. The latter fact is in itself of the greatest significance. However, after the defeat of the German armies those writers who had been the instruments of this temporary concession to Ukrainian nationalism drew the fire of the Party.

[15] O. Levada, "Notatky pro tvorchist' Mykoly Bazhana," *Radians'ka literatura*, No. 7, 1933, p. 206.

work." [16] Bazhan obviously realized the danger; at the price of the obliteration of his earlier work he turned to eulogizing the wisdom of Stalin and earned the honor of representing the Ukrainian SSR at the United Nations.

During the Ukrainian post-revolutionary literary revival there emerged a poetic school of Neoclassicists, which made a most original contribution to Ukrainian literature and which ceased to exist in the early 1930s after the obliteration of nearly all its members. The only Neoclassicist to survive the liquidation of his school was Maksym Ryl's'kyi, who, however, was compelled to renounce his Neoclassicist past. Ryl's'kyi (b. 1895) is undoubtedly the greatest of the Neoclassicist school and many would rank him as high as or even higher than Tychyna. His first collection of verse, *Na bilykh ostrovakh* (On the White Islands, 1910), shows in yet imperfect form the romantic and passive attitude to life of this literary prodigy. Ryl's'kyi's post-revolutionary collections of verse, which established his high reputation, were *Pid osinnimy zoriamy* (Under the Autumn Stars, 1918), *Synia dalechin'* (The Blue Distance, 1922), *Kriz' buriu i snih* (Through Storm and Snow, 1925), *Trynadtsiata vesna* (The Thirteenth Spring, 1926), *De skhodiatsia dorohy* (Where the Roads Meet, 1927), and *Homin i vidhomin* (Echo and Reecho, 1929). Without in the least reflecting the impact of the Revolution, Ryl's'kyi remained in these collections a poet of the static beauty of life and of acceptance. Together with his fellow Neoclassicists he found inspiration in the detachment and the verbal and structural perfection of the Roman classical poets. "Lyric poetry," he wrote in an unpublished introduction to *The Blue Distance,* "is for me the recreation of the past in the present. I cannot write anything else." [17] This assertion proved false. Ryl's'kyi, who believed that the poet's task is to "wait until the fermentation of the present shall become the clear wine of the past," [18] was compelled by circumstances of Soviet dictatorship to take an interest in socialist construction, to follow "social command." Nevertheless his poetry remains artistically on a very high level and his translations of Mickiewicz and Pushkin belong to the best in modern literature. Yet the early, Neoclassicist period in Ryl's'kyi's work will

[16] A. Chepurniuk, "Poeziia vyshukanykh katastrof idealistychnoï filosofiï," *Chervonyi shliakh,* No. 1, 1934, p. 186.

[17] Quoted in Doroshkevych, *Pidruchnyk,* p. 298.   [18] *Ibid.,* p. 300.

remain his greatest achievement in spite of the almost complete neglect meted out to it by contemporary Soviet editors of Ryl's'kyi's works.

A poet of lesser talent but of greater personal integrity than Ryl's'kyi was the chief theorist of the Neoclassicists, Mykola Zerov (b. 1890). Zerov, who was also a distinguished literary critic, began his poetic career with the publication of some translations of Roman classical poets (Virgil, Horace, Tibullus, Propertius, Ovid) entitled *Antolohiia ryms'koï poeziï* (An Anthology of Roman Poetry, 1920). The first collection of his own verse, *Kamena* (Camena), appeared in 1924. It contained some of the most classically perfect poetry ever written in Ukrainian. In 1935, shortly before his arrest and deportation, Zerov sent one hundred and thirteen of his poems, mostly sonnets, to one of his friends. In this way the whole collection has been preserved, and it was published in Europe in 1948 under the title *Sonnetarium*. Patterned on classical poetry, these sonnets are perhaps the greatest single contribution to the Ukrainian poetic language in modern times. Upon a first reading one is left with an impression of unruffled calm which pervades every stanza of Zerov's verse. Yet upon further reading, it is possible to gain a richer comprehension of these poems, of deeper meaning hidden beneath the air of classical detachment. As Iu. Sherekh pointed out in his penetrating essay on Zerov,[19] there is in his poetry a great deal of lyrical subjectivism. It is not only the feeling of loneliness which communicates itself so intensely to the reader, but in subtle allegorical pictures a kind of personal diary is revealed by the poet who is in quest of classical beauty and creative freedom, and yet is sadly aware of the growing chasm between art and life in the Soviet Ukraine.

Two other Neoclassicist poets shared Zerov's fate in the forced labor camps. They were Pavlo Fylypovych (b. 1891), the author of *Zemlia i viter* (Earth and Wind, 1922) and *Prostir* (Space, 1925), and Mykhailo Drai-Khmara (b. 1889), the author of the collection of verse *Prorosten'* (The Sprout, 1926). Drai-Khmara died of exhaustion in a forced labor camp in 1939.[20] Iurii Klen (real name Oswald Burkhardt [1891–1947]) was the only Neoclassicist who

[19] Iurii Sherekh, "Poeziia Mykoly Zerova," *Khors*, I (1946).
[20] V. Miiakovs'kyi, "Zoloti zerniatka; pamiati M. O. Drai-Khmary," *Nashi dni*, II, No. 11 (November, 1943), 5.

managed to leave the USSR in the early 1930s. He is the author of *Prokliati roky* (The Cursed Years, 1938) and a long unfinished poem, *Popil imperii* (The Ashes of Empires, 1946), as well as of a most valuable volume of reminiscences, *Spohady pro neokliasykiv* (Memories of the Neoclassicists, 1947).

Two poets of the literary group Lanka, Ievhen Pluzhnyk and Todos' Os'machka, had their literary careers cut short and thwarted by the Soviet regime. Pluzhnyk (b. 1898) published his first collection of verse, *Dni* (Days), in 1926. Doroshkevych hailed it as the best book of Ukrainian poetry of that year.[21] Pluzhnyk's talent revealed itself in this collection as almost entirely original. His was a gift for a very personal, lyrical, and metaphysical poetry. In 1927 Pluzhnyk's second volume of verse, *Rannia osin'* (Early Autumn), appeared. His last collection, *Rivnovaha* (Equilibrium), which was written in 1933–34, was not published until 1943. It reveals Pluzhnyk at his best and is some indication of the loss which Ukrainian literature suffered through Pluzhnyk's untimely death in a Soviet concentration camp.

Todos' Os'machka (b. 1895) is a highly talented poet of peasant stock. He is the author of *Krucha* (The Precipice, 1922), *Skyts'ki vohni* (Scythian Fires, 1925), *Klekit* (Birdcall, 1929), written in the Soviet Ukraine prior to his arrest in 1932, and of *Suchasnykam* (To the Contemporaries, 1943), *Poet* (The Poet, 1947), and the novels *Starshyi boiaryn* (The Elder Boiaryn, 1948), and *Plan do dvoru* (Plan for the Court, 1950), written and published after he left the USSR in 1942. Os'machka's expressionist poetry is full of allegory and evocative metaphor which, however, do not obscure his philosophic quest. He is the poet of determined protest against the sovietization of the Ukrainian village and against attempts to suppress the spirit of Ukrainian culture. "The world in which Os'machka lives," complained one critic, "is sad and terrifying. . . . His eyes do not behold the future."[22]

A young poet of unusual promise, Oleksa Vlyz'ko (b. 1908), was executed in 1934. He was the author of *Za vsikh skazhu* (I Shall Tell for All, 1927), *Zhyvu, pratsiuiu* (I Live, I Work, 1929), *Knyha*

---

21 Doroshkevych, *Pidruchnyk*, p. 313.
22 M. Stepniak, "Ohliad potochnoï virshovanoï poeziï," *Hart* (VUSPP's journal), No. 5, May, 1929, p. 155.

baliad (A Book of Ballads, 1930), *Pianyi korabel'* (The Drunken Boat, 1933), the last possibly influenced by Rimbaud. In 1930, following a trip to Berlin, Vlyz'ko wrote *Poïzdy idut' na Berlin* (Trains Go to Berlin, 1930), and in the story "Istoriia zakordonnoho pashportu" (A Story of the Foreign Passport), published in *Nova Generatsiia,* he satirized Soviet restrictions on travel. He is a typical revolutionary romantic. One of his sea-ballads, "Baliada pro ostatochno korotkozore El'dorado" (A Ballad about a Definitely Shortsighted Eldorado), in the collection *The Drunken Boat,* ends with these lines:

Is one's own country an eternal prison
And is the better land where we are not?

A poet executed at the same time as Vlyz'ko was Dmytro Fal'-kivs'kyi (1898–1934), author of *Obrii* (Horizons, 1927) and *Polissia* (1931).

The Ukrainian Futurist poets Mykhail' Semenko (b. 1892) and Geo Shkurupii (b. 1903) vanished from literary life in the early thirties. Semenko's poems were published as collected works in 1930–31. The most noteworthy collections of Shkurupii's verse were *Baraban* (The Drum, 1923), *More* (The Sea, 1927), and *Zyma 1930 roku* (The Winter of 1930, 1934). Shkurupii was also the author of two novels: *Dveri v den'* (Door to the Day, 1928) and *Zhanna Batalionerka* (Jeanne, the Soldier, 1930).

Parody was a literary genre which could hardly be expected to flourish under the Soviet regime. However, two writers of parodies claim a place in Soviet Ukrainian literary history. The first of these was Vasyl' Blakytnyi (real name Ellans'kyi, 1895–1925), a Borot'bist leader and proletarian literary theorist. Apart from his serious, and often bombastic, verse (*Udary molota i sertsia* [The Strokes of Hammer and Heart, 1920]), he wrote under the pseudonyms of Markiz Popeliastyi and Valer Pronoza. Blakytnyi's works, like those of his Borot'bist associates Chumak, Mykhailychenko, and Zalyvchyi, have not been reprinted since 1933.

The second parodist, of wider scope and greater talent than Blakytnyi, was Kost' Burevii (1888–1934). Burevii actually created an alter ego—Edvard Strikha—thus providing himself with a fictional biography and getting his verse (supposedly written by

Strikha) published in *New Generation,* the organ of the Futurists, the very group which was the main object of Burevii's satire. The Futurists, so good were the parodies, accepted both poems and "biography" in good faith, and Semenko even held Strikha up as an example to new contributors to the magazine. This state of affairs continued until some kind person gently informed Semenko that Strikha was in fact Burevii and that the latter had had the temerity to parody the Futurists. Semenko, in order to salvage some shreds of self-respect, himself assumed the mantle of Strikha (without a word to the original author), published a few poems under the now famous name, and arranged, with pious regret, for the pseudo-poet's demise. Burevii was thus forced to find other magazines to accept Strikha's poems (his *Zozendropiia* was printed in *Avant-garde*) while he indignantly denied reports of the latter's sudden death. However, death was not to be cheated. Burevii and his brilliant creation, Strikha, were arrested and executed in 1934 in the wake of the arrests which followed Kirov's assassination. A parodist of the order of Burevii was too uncomfortable to be encouraged, especially as he satirized, through the Futurists, both the Russians and the Communists.[23] Burevii was also the author (under his own name) of a play, *Pavlo Polubotok,* published in Western Europe in 1948.

The Literary Career of Mykola Kulish

In the field of drama the 1920s were the time of a great new venture—the Berezil' Theater. Its director, the producer and writer Les' Kurbas, and the group of actors, designers, composers, and, above all, playwrights who formed the Berezil' wrote a new chapter in the history of Ukrainian drama.

P. Rulin, writing in 1929 for *Slavische Rundschau,* had this to say about Kurbas's theater:

The traditional Ukrainian stagecraft, which achieved the highest point of its growth in the work of the actors and producers Kropyvnyts'kyi, Saksahans'kyi, Sadovs'kyi, Zan'kovets'ka, Zatyrkevych, and others, had

[23] For details see George Shevelov (Yury Šerech), "Edvard Strikha: The History of a Literary Mystification," *American Slavic and East European Review,* XIV, No. 1 (February, 1955), 93–107. Strikha's works, some of them unpublished, appeared in 1955 in New York under the title *Parodezy, Zozendropiia, avtoekzekutsiia.*

reached the end of its development even before the World War. The need for a new content and new forms was strongly felt both inside and outside the world of the theater. The first seed of the coming transformation germinated within the Sadovs'kyi theater in Kiev. Les' Kurbas, a young actor and producer who because of the war moved from Galicia to Kiev where he was accepted by Sadovs'kyi, was the first to recognize the hopeless condition of the Ukrainian theater and to find supporters for his new ideas. In 1917 he issued the declaration of his newly formed Young Theater, which ushered in the beginning of a new era in the history of the Ukrainian theater. Instead of the musty folkloristic plays with their singsongs and national dances the new theater wanted to stage plays from the world repertoire.[24]

The reformist work thus begun in the Young Theater was continued by Kurbas in his new enterprise Berezil'. This new theater was formed by Kurbas in March, 1922, and was called by the Ukrainian poetic term for the month of March, yet not because it was founded in that month. According to Kurbas the name Berezil' was inspired by a poem by Björnson in which he described the month of March as a turning point in nature's course toward spring.[25] In the opinion of Rulin, March and not October was regarded by the Ukrainians as the "beginning of the Ukrainian Revolution."[26] One of the earliest successes of this first modern Ukrainian theater was Kurbas's staging of Upton Sinclair's *Jimmy Higgins* (1923), adapted for the stage by Kurbas himself. Having found congenial and gifted collaborators in the designer Meller, the musical director Meitus, and the actors Krushel'nyts'kyi, Buchma, Uzhvii, Hirniak, Chystiakova, Tytarenko, and Serdiuk, Kurbas's modern theater, emancipated completely from the old naturalist staging and the folklorist themes, was well received by Ukrainian audiences. What made Berezil' truly great, however, was its cooperation with the playwright Kulish.

Mykola Kulish[27] was born in 1892 into a poor peasant family.

24 P. Rulin, "Das ukrainische Theater in den Revolutionsjahren," Kulturchronik, *Slavische Rundschau,* No. 8, 1929, pp. 709–10.

25 D. Hrudyna, "Dekliaratsiï i manifesty: pro 'Shliakhy Berezolia,' Mystets'ka trybuna," *Krytyka,* No. 2, February, 1931, p. 102.

26 Rulin, "Das ukrainische Theater in den Revolutionsjahren," *Slavische Rundschau,* No. 8, 1929, p. 710.

27 For a brief survey of Kulish's work, see V. Revuts'kyi, "Mykola Kulish," *Novi dni,* No. 14, March, 1951. The first selection of Kulish's works, containing his plays *Narodnyi Malakhii, Myna Mazailo,* and *Patetychna sonata,* as well as his letters and his wife's reminiscences, was published in 1955 in New York.

His parents and he himself for a time earned their living as servants. His education was very scrappy and incomplete. In 1915 he fought in the ranks of the Russian army on the Austrian front in Galicia. It was here that he first came into contact with the Ukrainian national movement. After the Revolution of 1917 Kulish worked as a Party agitator, and in 1919 enrolled as a member. He then worked on the Party's behalf in Odessa, where in 1924 he was drawn into literary life by the organization Hart.

Kulish's debut as a dramatist was the performance, in 1924, of his play *97* by the Franko Theater in Kharkov under the direction of Kurbas's associate, and later rival, Hnat Iura. The play was a great success and Kulish, thus encouraged, wrote another play, *Komuna v stepakh* (A Commune in the Steppes, 1925). While still a member of Hart, Kulish met Khvyl'ovyi. In 1925 he moved to Kharkov, where for a time he was the director of Vseukrkomdrama (The All-Ukrainian Drama Committee) at the Commissariat of Education. At about the same time he joined the new literary group led by Khvyl'ovyi, VAPLITE.

In 1926 Kulish wrote his next play, *Khulii Khuryna,* an outspoken satire on the Soviet officials in the NEP period. It was followed by *Tak zahynuv Huska* (Thus Perished Huska, 1927) and *Narodnyi Malakhii* (The People's Malakhii, 1928). The latter play stirred heated controversy among the critics. The hero, Malakhii Stakanchyk, a lunatic, dreams of reforming mankind, and leaves his native village on a missionary journey to the Council of the People's Commissars, a factory, and a brothel. His plans, of course, are utterly unrealistic, or at least they are quite incompatible with Soviet reality. His ardent insistence on lighting "bonfires of universal love in the streets of our cities" finds no response whatsoever. Some reviewers thought Malakhii represented the Utopian Communists, others regarded him as an escapist, but still others held that Malakhii symbolized the Ukrainian national idea and its incompatibility with the Communist system.

Kulish's next play was *Myna Mazailo* (1929), which discussed Ukrainization in frank terms. The hero is a hard-boiled Russophile Little Russian, paying only lip service to the government's efforts to "Ukrainize" the Ukraine while changing his name from Mazailo to Mazenin. His son, Mokii, however, is a sincere Ukrainian patriot.

The conflict between father and son is further complicated by the presence of Aunt Motia, a Muscovite Ukrainophobe who declares that she would rather be raped than "Ukrainized." This comedy treated in extremely lively dramatic form one of the most important factors in Ukrainian social and political life and was attacked by the critics who saw in it an expression of Ukrainian nationalism. The play was very popular in the Ukraine and ran for a long time.[28]

In 1931 Kulish wrote what was perhaps his most accomplished work—the play *Patetychna Sonata* (Sonata Pathetique). The action takes place in 1917–19 and depicts the struggle between three camps: the national Ukrainian, the Bolshevik, and the White. The Whites are represented by General Perotskii and his two sons, Andre and George. The old general loathes the very idea of a Ukrainian state and recalls with horror as one of his bitterest experiences the time when, during his stay in a Bolshevik prison, he shared a cell with a monk who prayed in Ukrainian. His son Andre conceals behind his professed fondness for the Ukraine his schemes for the restoration of the old regime. The Bolshevik camp consists of Luka, the Communist agitator, Hamar, the believer in world revolution, Ovram, who above all wishes to avenge himself for an injury sustained in the war, and Zinka, the prostitute. The Ukrainian national side is led by the old Stupai-Stupanenko and his daughter Maryna. The old man is ridiculed because of his narrow, sentimental patriotism and his naive belief that the red flag of the Bolsheviks is the same as the red banner of the Zaporozhian Cossacks. His daughter represents the new Ukrainian generation, fully conscious of its national destiny. She believes that in time of revolution those will be victorious who have the courage to take their ideas to the scaffold.

In the first half of the play the Bolsheviks, who live in the basement of the house in which Stupai and Perotskii also reside, stage a

28 A letter from the well-known Ukrainian novelist Ianovs'kyi to Liubchenko, written in Kiev on May 4, 1929, contains the following spontaneous comment on Kulish's play: "*Myna Mazailo* was produced on May 1st. There were delegates from Moscow and Leningrad. They gave it a very cool reception. During the third act they even walked out, astonished and offended. They were certainly waiting for the *hopaks* [Ukrainian dance] and *halushky* [Ukrainian dumplings], since today *Proletars'ka pravda,* commenting on the impressions of the Leningrad workers, said that they hoped to see in Berezil' the life of Ukrainian workers and peasants—and saw *Mazailo* instead. I am so glad that I jumped for joy in spite of my appendicitis." *Holubi dylizhansy,* p. 19.

coup. The old White Russian general, who lives on the second floor, escapes to the apartment of his political enemy—Stupai—yet his son Andre is seized by the Reds. However, he is liberated by Maryna with the help of a Bolshevik sympathizer, Iuha (usually appearing as Ia [Myself]), who is in love with her. She sends him on a secret mission to the Ukrainian insurgents outside the town, now in the hands of the Bolsheviks. In the second part of the play the Ukrainian insurgents, led by Andre, seize the town from the Reds. Yet Andre betrays Maryna's confidence and now helps to restore the old regime. In the last act the Bolsheviks, led by Iuha, retake the town and arrest Maryna as one implicated in the Ukrainian nationalist conspiracy. She remains true to her ideal and is prepared to go to the scaffold. Although Iuha, the Communist, is the victorious hero, Maryna remains the real heroine of the play. It is she who gives the play its title by playing during the early part of the drama Beethoven's *Sonata Pathetique,* which reechoes till the end of the play. It is Maryna who is so devoted to the idea of national liberation that, like Antigone who loves and cannot hate, she must perish.

The play, while bearing some resemblances to Greek tragedies, is reminiscent at the same time of the Ukrainian medieval puppet show (*vertep*) with the stage divided into an upper and lower level. This device adds a great deal to the play's dramatic effect. *Sonata Pathetique* was never printed in the USSR [29] and was not performed in the Soviet Ukraine. It was, however, staged in the Kamernyi Theater in Moscow in 1931 by Tairov and ran from December 20, 1931, to March 24, 1932. At first the play received favorable notices,[30] and a review of it published in *Pravda* [31] was only mildly

[29] A German translation of *Sonata Pathetique—Die Beethovensonate* by Friedrich Wolf—was published in 1932 by Vischer Verlag in Berlin. The first Ukrainian edition of Kulish's play appeared in Crakow in 1943.

[30] Cf. Iu. Iuzovskii, "Pateticheskaia sonata: p'esa Kulisha v Kamernom teatre," *Literaturnaia gazeta,* January 4, 1932.

One of the few Americans to see a performance of *Sonata Pathetique* was Professor Philip E. Mosely, of Columbia University. In sharing his reminiscences with the present author, Professor Mosely recalled that during the performance at the Kamernyi Theater, in early 1932, the audience burst into laughter in the scene in which Stupai, momentarily accepting the inevitability of Soviet rule, exclaimed, "Long live Radians'ka Ukraina." Acquaintances in the audience took some pains to explain to Professor Mosely that this meant "Soviet Ukraine," not "Rada Ukraine," and that Stupai was being misled by what was, at bottom, a pure play on words.

[31] B. Reznikov, H. Vasil'kovskii, I. Ierukhimovich, I. Bogovoi, and A. Nazarov, "Neudavshaiasia patetika (p'esa 'Pateticheskaia Sonata' N. Kulisha v Kamernom teatre)," *Pravda,* February 9, 1932.

critical of what was termed a failure on the part of the performers to "show the real masses or genuine Bolsheviks." Otherwise the *Pravda* reviewers thought that

nevertheless the author posed the problem of national liberation correctly. He showed and he proved that the problem of national liberation is a problem of proletarian revolution. . . . Taken as a whole, *Sonata Pathetique* is a very interesting play. . . . It is unfortunate that the author has not succeeded in developing with complete clarity the picture of the proletariat's struggle for power, has failed to show fully the participants in this struggle. Nonetheless *Sonata Pathetique* belongs to the better plays of the season. . . . The Kamernyi Theater has successfully staged the multiple spectacle. Some scenes are acted brilliantly. The technical production of the play shows the cross-section of a house of several stories; the rich spectrum, the lighting effects, and the music which is interwoven with the action arouse in places a powerful social sense.[32]

Less than a month later *Pravda* printed a fierce attack on Kulish's play. In a long article (one fourth of *Pravda's* page) the author, hidden behind the nom de plume I. Ukrainets (I. Ukrainian), castigated the play which still continued to fascinate the Moscow theatergoers. "In its entirety, its basis, and its main theme, this play is not ours. Not only is it not a Party play (in spite of the fact that it was written by the Communist Kulish); but, in addition, this play reflects the philosophy of the Ukrainian national movement alien to the proletariat and the Soviet state. . . . Whether deliberately or not, comrade Kulish gave in his play in a talented form a consistent apology not for the proletarian or Bolshevik but for the nationalist philosophy of history." [33] In spite of the fact that the play was also successfully performed in Leningrad (Bol'shoi dramaticheskii teatr), it was withdrawn after such censure.

Two other plays by Kulish, *Zakut* (The Blind Alley) and *Proshchai selo* (Farewell, My Village), written after 1930, also remained unpublished and were never produced. The last play to come from Kulish's pen was *Maklena Grasa* (1933). Its theme was the attempt by the bankrupt Polish stockbroker Zbrozhek to arrange for his own death in order to gain insurance money for his family. He is killed by a small girl, Maklena, the daughter of a worker, who, by murdering Zbrozhek, wishes to help her starving father. After a

32 *Ibid.*
33 I. Ukrainets, "O 'Pateticheskoi sonate' Kulisha," *Pravda,* March 4, 1932.

trial performance, attended by members of the Ukrainian Politbureau with Postyshev, Kosior, Zatons'kyi, and Liubchenko at
the head,[34] the play was banned two weeks later. The veiled symbolism of the play (the bankruptcy of the Communist "stockbrokers,"
and the desperate act of a famine-ridden young girl) was thought
to be inappropriate at the time of the widespread famine in the
Ukraine in 1933. *Maklena Grasa* was the swan song of Kulish. Soon
after that he was arrested (1934) and brought to trial.

The achievement of Kulish entirely dominated the field of Soviet
Ukrainian drama from 1924 to 1932. A smaller though quite original talent was that of the playwright Ivan Dniprovs'kyi (pseudonym of Ivan Shevchenko, 1895–1934), the author of *Liubov i dym*
(Love and Smoke, 1926) and *Iablunevyi polon* (The Spell of the
Apple Trees). The former was described in the *Literaturnaia entsiklopediia* as "a real event in Ukrainian dramaturgy." [35] The personal correspondence of Dniprovs'kyi reveals a deep conflict
between his exceptionally delicate sensibility and the world around
him. "At one time," he wrote in 1927 in a letter to Kulish, "anticipating what has since happened, I thought that if neither mother,
wife, sister, nor friends remained to me, I should still have art
which I could cherish to the end. Yet this was in my youth, when
art did not smell of the tradesman's shears." [36]

An altogether different personality was Ivan Mykytenko, whose
works (e.g., *Dyktatura* [Dictatorship, 1930]) were written expressly
in response to "social demand." His willingness to conform, however, did not save this playwright from downfall. Other dramatists
who disappeared in the thirties were the poet Pluzhnyk, the author
of the play *Shkidnyky* (Malefactors, 1934), and Myroslav Irchan
(pseudonym of Andrii Babiuk), who wrote *Platsdarm* (Place
d'Armes). Irchan's fellow Galicians who lived and wrote in the
Soviet Union during the period of prosperity for Zakhidnia Ukraïna (V. Atamaniuk, V. Bobyns'kyi, M. Kichura, A. Krushel'nyts'kyi)
suffered a similar fate. Indeed, only three dramatists who started
their career in the 1920s were continuing to write in the 1950s.

---

[34] Mentioned by J. Hirniak, who took the part of Zbrozhek, in Khmuryi, Dyvnych,
and Blakytnyi, *V maskakh epokhy*, p. 42.

[35] *Literaturnaia entsiklopediia*, III, 321.

[36] G. Luckyj (ed.), *Holubi dylizhansy*, p. 33.

They were Ivan Kocherha (1881–1952), Leonid Pervomais'kyi (b. 1907), also a gifted poet, and Oleksander Korniichuk (b. 1905).

Literary criticism, scholarship, and translations of Western European masters also made a significant contribution to the flowering of Ukrainian literature in the twenties. Among the critics whose reputation was high until their sudden eclipse were Zerov, Fylypovych, Nikovs'kyi, Iurynets', Richyts'kyi, Iakubs'kyi, and many others. The achievement of Ukrainian scholars, particularly those associated with the Ukrainian Academy of Sciences, was notable in research on Ukrainian Romanticism and the study of Shevchenko. Among the translators the following were outstanding: Pidmohyl'nyi (France, Balzac, de Maupassant), Iohansen (E. A. Poe, Shakespeare, Aristophanes), Klen (German literature), Zahul (Schiller), Tereshchenko (Verhaeren), Ivchenko (Duhamel), and Staryts'ka-Cherniakhivs'ka (Dickens, Zola).

Although the present chapter must not be regarded as an attempt at a complete survey of the entire field of Ukrainian literature in the 1920s, sufficiently wide ground is covered to allow the following conclusions. Ukrainian literature of the period 1917–33 produced many works on national themes, some of them actually dealing with the nationality problem and in particular with Russian-Ukrainian relations. On the other hand, many works, including some of those with national themes (such as Kulish's *The People's Malakhii*), touched on wider, universal problems. Both kinds of literature were suppressed either because the works themselves were thought to be dangerous to the regime in their treatment of the national problem, or because they were produced by writers who could not or would not toe the Party line. The purges destroyed, therefore, not only the fellow travelers who still clung to the prerevolutionary view on art, but above all those Ukrainian revolutionary Communist writers who had manifested in their works a clear faith in the unfettered development of Ukrainian literature.[37]

The content of this literature in the 1920s reveals further that to many writers the burning issue was not how to reconcile their art

---

[37] The most recent Soviet history of Ukrainian literature (*Ocherk istorii ukrainskoi sovetskoi literatury*) scarcely mentions the great literary flowering of the 1920s. It merely heaps abuse upon "hostile nationalist concoctions" (p. 119).

with Communist theory and practice but rather how to isolate it from politics altogether. In spite of the lip service frequently and monotonously paid to Marxism, there remained the deep concern of the artist to focus his regard upon the problems of human existence and a yearning to have his works judged by purely artistic standards. It is thus not uncommon to discover affinities and actual links between Ukrainian "proletarian" writers and the fellow travelers or even the "inner emigrants" (e.g., Zerov and Khvyl'ovyi). Still more striking evidence of this "common front" against Communist literary politics and the vagaries of the Kremlin's cultural policy in the Ukraine may be seen in the personal correspondence of leading Ukrainian writers, contained in the Liubchenko papers. Although for obvious reasons it is not possible to quote at any length from these letters, the writers make it abundantly clear that they objected to the encroachment of politics on art and repeatedly pleaded that detached standards be applied to literature.

It is startling, even paradoxical, that the control and suppression of Soviet Ukrainian literature in that period did not curb, at least for some time, the brilliant and extensive literary accomplishment. Indeed the literary renaissance unfolded in the Soviet Ukraine in spite of the constant interference by the Party. And, for all we know, it might have assumed a different, less national character had not these controls become more rigid with time.

That Ukrainian literature flourished in spite of Party interference can be understood if one bears in mind the power and influence exercised by the Ukrainian Communists, and the relatively mild methods of Party control. Most of the literary works which were condemned and suppressed were nevertheless published, and until the early 1930s, although most of the unorthodox or rebellious writers were molested, they were not ruthlessly liquidated. In the closing years of the twenties the battle between the Party and literature in the Ukraine entered upon a new phase which augured no gains for the latter.

[VII]

LITERATURE AND THE FIRST

FIVE-YEAR PLAN

"For a Socialist Reconstruction"

Although the literary discords foreshadowed a major conflict within the political and cultural structure of the Soviet Ukraine, they were only reflections of the crisis which developed in the USSR in 1928 and 1929. The chief reason for this crisis, which precipitated a further conflict in literary affairs, was the decision to abandon the NEP and to industrialize the Soviet Union with the help of economic planning embodied in the First Five-Year Plan.[1]

For two different reasons this decision had a special significance for the Ukraine. Firstly, the Ukraine was still at that time the most important part of the Union's industrial potential. The rapid development of industry envisaged in the First Five-Year Plan was largely to be carried out in the Ukraine, with the main attention focused on the construction of the Dnieprostroi. Secondly, measures not originally planned but which, in 1929, led to the mass collectivization of agriculture, weighed most severely on the Ukraine, where the peasants, who had never lived under any system comparable to the Russian village commune (*obshchina*), fiercely resisted Soviet attempts to force them into collective farms. This situation, which led to a widespread famine in the villages and to savage repressions against the peasants by special military units, made the Ukraine the most dangerous and rebellious country in the USSR.

---

[1] The decision was taken at the Fifteenth Congress of the Party (December, 1927) when "the Congress considered the guiding lines of a Five Year Plan of national economy. The chief function of this Five Year Plan was the realization of the Leninist idea of industrialization of the country." (W. Knorin (ed.), *Communist Party of the Soviet Union: A Short History*, p. 378.)

Under these circumstances it became obvious to the Communist Party and to the Soviet planners, who never envisaged the task of industrialization without the ideological preparation for it, that they could no longer wait in the pious hope that Ukrainian writers would unite of their own accord in one organization and support the government's new and drastic policies. The time had come to consolidate proletarian literary forces in one centrally controlled organization and to crack down on fellow travelers and deviationists.

The Party's earnestness about the support which literature was ordered to provide for the Five-Year Plan can best be judged from its directive to publishers, issued in December, 1928.[2] This may justly be regarded as a cornerstone of the Five-Year Plan in literature, since it laid down a clear and definite policy for publishing which had a tremendous influence on literature as a whole. Moreover, this directive clearly departs in tone and meaning from the 1925 Party resolution on literature. It does not, in fact, regard literature as one of the arts, sovereign in its own right, but as a part of the book industry, assigned, from that time on, one single purpose—that of serving the needs of the socialist reconstruction of the USSR.

Section D of point 2 of the resolution deals with belles-lettres, which are evaluated from the same utilitarian point of view as works of propaganda or scientific textbooks. In directing publishers in the selection of books for publication, the resolution emphasizes the need for a literature dealing with present-day themes, combating hostile influences of all kinds, inspiring the masses. It further orders the publishers to give definite preference to those authors who are Communists and, of these, to select the ones who are members of proletarian literary organizations. Finally, it stresses the importance of enrolling new writers from the masses and of catering to the demands of the workers and the peasants.

Perhaps no other single resolution or action of the Party placed so much power in the hands of RAPP (Russian Association of Proletarian Writers) and its Ukrainian partner, VUSPP, as did the 1928 resolution on publishing. They were the recognized suppliers

<hr>

[2] "Ob obsluzhivanii knigoi massovogo chitatelia (Postanovlenie tsentral'nogo komiteta, 28 dek. 1928)," *Resheniia partii o pechati*, p. 119.

of what was regarded as the best Communist literary talent. From the analysis given in the preceding chapters it is clear that for VUSPP this new role was a difficult and thankless one, chiefly because of the vigorous opposition of VAPLITE and of the attitude of the People's Commissar for Education, Skrypnyk. However, after the dissolution of VAPLITE and the end of the Literary Discussion which, according to the *Literaturnaia entsiklopediia*, was terminated by order of the Party,[3] the position of VUSPP became stronger.

Proletarian Hegemony on All-Union Scale

The sharpest Russian reaction to the Ukrainian literary and political battles came from VAPP. A leading article in the organ of VAPP, *Na literaturnom postu* (On Literary Guard), entitled "And Yet the Woodsnipes Must Be Shot Down,"[4] violently attacked Skrypnyk's contribution to the Literary Discussion. "As a People's Commissar for Education," it read, "comrade Skrypnyk should know that 'On Guardism'[5] is in any case one of the Marxian trends in the literature of the Soviet land."[6] To attack it, the article implied, was tantamount to taking up an anti-Party position. Nor could the author see any reason why "the Ukrainian comrades from VUSPP who, despite some errors, have defended the interests of proletarian literature in the Ukraine on the whole quite well,"[7] should not be held in greater favor by the CP(B)U.

These words were written on the eve of the First Congress of VOAPP, which was to be a landmark in the history of Soviet literature.

The problem of literary relations between the Soviet republics assumed added importance when it was decided to start the First

---

[3] L. Pidhainyi, "Ukrainskaia sovetskaia literatura," *Literaturnaia entsiklopediia*, XI, 578.

[4] "A bit' po val'dshnepam vsëtaki nuzhno," *Na literaturnom postu*, No. 5, February, 1928, pp. 3–5. The same issue of the journal contained A. Selivanovskii's "Za iedinstvo natsional'nykh otriadov proletarskoi literatury."

[5] *Napostovstvo* ("On Guardism") was the label given to the radical position taken by VAPP's members participating in *On Literary Guard*.

[6] "A bit' po val'dshnepam vsëtaki nuzhno," *Na literaturnom postu*, No. 5, February, 1928, p. 3.

[7] *Ibid.*, p. 4.

Five-Year Plan. To be sure, an effective apparatus already existed for a single literary policy—the Agitation and Propaganda Section (after 1930, the Culture and Propaganda Section) of the centrally controlled All-Union Communist Party and the People's Commissariats of Education. But now an even closer unanimity of purpose became imperative. In heralding the First Congress of Proletarian Writers, called for April, 1928, *October,* the organ of VAPP, reviewed inter-republic literary relations. It recalled that a Federation of Associations of Soviet Writers of the RSFSR (FOSP) was created on VAPP's initiative in 1927. Apart from VAPP, it included VOKP (Organization of Peasant Writers), VSP (All-Russian Union of Writers), and since 1928 the Kuznitsa (Smithy) group, LEF (Left Front of Literature), and Pereval (the Pass, a literary group headed by Voronskii).[8]

VAPP's purpose in helping to create this federation was best expressed by Averbakh. "We wanted to build a united front of all Soviet literature," he wrote, "against those writers who are serving the neo-bourgeois cause. By creating the federation we wanted to hasten the process of ideological differentiation in the writers' midst, using the Federation as a means to bring fellow-travelers closer to us." [9]

Yet, the *October* article complained, the Federation was primarily concerned with Russian literature, and had proved unequal to the new pan-Union task:

In our contacts with other republics we have not achieved what is most important. We have not succeeded in forging the necessary cultural links between different detachments of proletarian literature. . . . The Party has told us that we should earn the right to establish a hegemony. Have we earned that right? No, this task has not yet been fulfilled. But preliminary and not insignificant steps in the direction of hegemony have already been taken. . . . It is correct to say this while taking into account the absolute and the relative growth of literature: we have entered into the zone where the literature of the fellow travelers has abandoned many of its strongholds, but these have not yet been occupied by proletarian literature.[10]

8 "Pered vsesoiuznym s"ezdom proletarskikh pisatelei," *Oktiabr',* No. 4, 1928, pp. 209–16.

9 L. Averbakh, "O sovremennoi literature," *Na literaturnom postu,* No. 11–12, June, 1928, p. 19.

10 "Pered vsesoiuznym s"ezdom proletarskikh pisatelei," *Oktiabr',* No. 4, 1928, pp. 214–15.

The fact that in this passage the hegemony of proletarian literature is linked with the plans for a pan-Union literary alliance is in
itself significant. When the Congress convened, the intentions of
the On Literary Guardists were revealed in the momentous decision to change the name VAPP to RAPP (Russian Association of
Proletarian Writers) and to create under its aegis VOAPP All-
Union Alliance of Associations of Proletarian Writers). The leading article in *On Literary Guard* assessed the "political consequences" of this act in these words:

The Congress has taken the decision to reorganize VAPP into
VOAPP. What is the meaning of this organizational transformation
within the ranks of proletarian literature? Those whose thinking is
commonplace, capable only of petty and primitive inferences, attempt
to see in this fact a struggle between groups, a victory of one of them,
a defeat for another, a collapse of the organizational structure of VAPP,
and finally decentralization of separate detachments of proletarian
literature. . . . Until the Congress VAPP did not include the Ukrainian organization of proletarian writers [VUSPP]. Hence it was not a
full-scale all-Union organization. On the other hand VAPP did not
include one of the detachments of Russian proletarian writers, organized in the Kuznitsa. From its very start, the Congress, acting in complete agreement with the policy of VAPP's executive, took the path
of uniting these organizations and thus consolidating all the forces of
proletarian literature.

The Congress warmly welcomed the entry of VUSPP and Kuznitsa
into the ranks of the new organization [VOAPP]. What is the meaning
of this organization? It consists in the creation of an organizational
framework most suitable for uniting all the detachments of proletarian
literature and for allowing the maximum freedom of development
for the national detachments while at the same time guaranteeing the
greatest possible international solidarity.[11]

From the speeches of Lunacharskii, the Secretary of the Moscow
Committee of the Party, Lazian, and the representative of the Central Committee of the Party, Krinitskii, it is evident that the Party
gave its blessing both to the creation of VOAPP and to its militant
vanguard—the RAPP. Krinitskii made a special point of emphasiz-
ing that "the task of developing national literatures faces VAPP
with all its magnitude just now," and he assured the Congress that
"for its part, the Party has helped, is helping, and will help the pro-

[11] "K politicheskim itogam vsesoiuznogo s"ezda," *Na literaturnom postu,* No. 10,
May, 1928, p. 4.

letarian writers in the ranks of Soviet literature to earn the historic right to hegemony." [12]

What is of interest to us is that aspect of the ideological strategy outlined at the Congress which was concerned with national literatures. At no previous all-Union meeting had so much time and planning been devoted to the national problem. Moreover, never before had the guiding lines of the policy in regard to national literatures been marked with such precision. The chief exponent of RAPP's and (we may with some right assume) the Party's line was Sutyrin. On May 4, he delivered before the Congress a lecture on "Proletarian Literature and the National Question," which for the first time revealed the following tenet:

> The interplay of different national cultures can express itself in two forms: one, the dissolution of a small nation in the sap of a greater culture (assimilation). This method is practiced by capitalism and is always violent. But the inclination (orientation) of a small nation to be united with the culture of a great (or leading) nation is a path diametrically opposed to assimilation.
>
> *This path alone, the path of orientation, will be trodden by all the nationalities of the USSR, which will remold their national forms first into international ones and then into international forms of the socialist world society.*
>
> The orientation toward Western European culture (Khvyl'ovyi's theory) is clearly reactionary. Proletarian literature should fight with absolute determination against similar orientations.
>
> The only correct solution of the problem of the cultural development of nations formerly oppressed by tsardom *is an orientation toward the culture of proletarian Russia. This orientation must be two-sided and presupposes a determined fight against nationalism.* One of the foremost tasks of proletarian literature is the struggle against imperialist nationalism.[13]

That this declaration caused resentment among the Ukrainian delegates from VUSPP can be seen from the words of the next speaker, Kovalenko. This most pro-Russian leader of VUSPP rose on that occasion to defend the right of Ukrainian culture to free development. He was not the first and not the last of those who in

[12] "Na pervom vsesoiuznom s"ezde proletarskikh pisatelei," *Khronika, Na literaturnom postu,* No. 10, May, 1928, p. 76.
[13] "Na pervom vsesoiuznom s"ezde prolet-pisatelei," *Khronika, Na literaturnom postu,* No. 11–12, June, 1928, p. 123 (italics mine).

the Ukraine preached dependence on Russia but in Moscow felt an inner compulsion to defend their privileges.

Kovalenko pointed out the dangers involved in the proposed policy. If all ties with Europe were to be cut, he argued, this also meant isolating oneself from the Western European proletarian literatures. He recalled the "charter of freedom" given to the writers in 1925 and then went on to cite many flagrant examples of Russian cultural imperialism in the Ukraine and insisted that the opinions of national groups be given full hearing and consideration.[14]

The next speaker, Pir, from Azerbaidzhan, accused Kovalenko of nationalist bias and of dwelling too long "on the commands, attacks, pressures, and dictation by Russia."[15] The debate grew more inflamed as Mykytenko rose to defend his fellow countryman. Finally, however, Averbakh silenced all opposition:

Comrade Kovalenko's speech was much more irreconcilable than his declaration. Comrade Kovalenko's reference to the resolution of the Central Committee of the Party on the Party policy in literature is obviously erroneous. This resolution does not contain a single hint about renouncing the principle of "democratic centralism,"[16] yet comrade Kovalenko tries to find indications of this in that passage of the resolution which mentions the necessity of competition, etc.

We must do all we can to unite with the Ukrainian comrades.[17]

From these incomplete accounts of the debate two conclusions can justifiably be drawn. Sutyrin's view that national literatures must orient themselves toward the proletarian literature of Russia was not refuted; on the contrary, it was sustained by Averbakh. It is also evident that the Ukrainian delegation did not agree with all the plans laid down by RAPP. Earlier in the discussion the Ukrainian delegate Ivan Le said that attempts to regard the Ukrainian delegation as arriving in order to present ultimata were unfounded.[18]

It has proved impossible to obtain Ukrainian accounts of the VOAPP Congress and the full story therefore must be told by fu-

---

[14] *Ibid.*, p. 123.   [15] *Ibid.*

[16] "Democratic centralism" was the theory of a "loyal" opposition within the Party which fought bureaucratic centralism.

[17] "Na pervom vsesoiuznom s"ezde prolet-pisatelei," *Khronika, Na literaturnom postu*, No. 11–12, June, 1928, p. 124.

[18] *Ibid.*, p. 119.

ture historians. Iaroslav Hordyns'kyi, whose scholarly accuracy is beyond doubt, mentions, however, that it was VUSPP's version of the VOAPP charter which was finally accepted by the Congress and that VUSPP was granted ten of fifty-two seats on the VOAPP Council.[19] This would indicate that the Ukrainians were certainly "reckoned with," though their gains were registered in the structural and organizational functioning of VOAPP, not in its political strategy.

The best evidence that VOAPP did not depart from its "national policy" as postulated by Sutyrin is the forecast of its policy made by the same writer before the First Plenum of the VOAPP Council in January, 1929. "The building up of proletarian culture in national forms," he wrote, "cannot be carried forward by means of 'independence' through independent cultural construction by each nationality of the USSR."[20] In industry and in literature alike the First Five-Year Plan led to a centralization of all power in Moscow.

In February, 1929, a delegation of fifty-two Ukrainian writers, chiefly members of VUSPP, led by Koriak and Khvylia, but also including Khvyl'ovyi, went to Moscow to discuss the "establishment of cultural relations between the brotherly republics of the Uk.SSR and RSFSR."[21] In the words of RAPP's mouthpiece, *On Literary Guard,* "the arrival of Soviet Ukrainian writers in Moscow is an event of greatest importance . . . beyond the limits of literary life."[22]

After long conferences with Russian writers and Party leaders, the Ukrainian writers were received by Stalin and Kaganovich who discussed with them for three hours the new tasks facing Soviet Ukrainian literature. According to a press report, "during the discussion, comade Stalin clarified in detail the national question and the national policy of the Soviet government under conditions of a transitory period in the dictatorship of the proletariat."[23]

About the same time a conference held at the Press and Propaganda Section of the Central Committee of the All-Union Commu-

[19] Iaroslav Hordyns'kyi, *Literaturna krytyka pidsoviets'koï Ukraïny,* p. 50.

[20] Sutyrin, "Napostovskii dnevnik; o zadachakh VOAPP'a," *Na literaturnom postu,* No. 1, January, 1929, p. 8.

[21] *Khronika, Chervonyi shliakh,* No. 3, 1929, pp. 144–45.

[22] "Za internatsional'nuiu solidarnost'," *Na literaturnom postu,* No. 3, February, 1929, p. 1.

[23] "Iednannia radians'kykh kul'tur," *Khronika, Chervonyi shliakh,* No. 3, 1929, p. 145.

nist Party was devoted to the problem of relations between Russian and Ukrainian literatures. One of the resolutions which was adopted reaffirmed in more cautious language RAPP's line:

Under present circumstances the basis of literary policy in the Ukraine is systematic work to strengthen and to consolidate further the forces of proletarian literature, to spread its influence, to combat any appearance in it of petit-bourgeois tendencies, and to continue and intensify the relentless struggle against bourgeois and nationalist elements.[24]

At the conference it was also decided that in order "to strengthen mutual understanding" the following practical program should be adopted to encourage good neighborly relations: (1) two or three books on Ukrainian literature were to be published annually in Russia; (2) Russian literary magazines were recommended to review Ukrainian books; (3) there was to be an exchange of books, reviews, etc., between Russia and the Ukraine; (4) the "International Book" in Moscow was asked to export more Ukrainian books abroad.

The creation of VOAPP, and the Moscow conference between Ukrainian writers and the Russian Party leaders, were only the first steps toward closer coordination of Soviet literature according to a definite plan, the full meaning of which became clear only much later.

How did these high-level literary politics and changes in the Soviet Ukraine appear to the ordinary reading public? What impact, if any, was made by these literary events on the mass of the people? Obviously, the sources which might provide an answer to these vital questions are very scarce. All the more valuable therefore is the material contained in a small envelope among the unpublished papers of Arkadii Liubchenko. The envelope bears the inscription: "Zapysky-zapytannia pidchas podorozhi to Artemivshchyny ta Dnipropetrovs'ka hrupy: Khvyl'ovyi, Kulish, Vyshnia, Ianovs'kyi, Liubchenko; Berezen', 1929" (Notes-questions during the visit to Artemivs'k and Dniepropetrovsk of the group Khvyl'ovyi, Kulish, Vyshnia, Ianovs'kyi, Liubchenko; March, 1929). It contains sixty-six questions, jotted down on scraps of paper by the

[24] "Rivnopravnym braters'kym spivrobitnytstvom bude zbudovano mizhnarodnu sotsialistychnu kul'turu" (Rezoliutsiia narady pry APPV TsK VKP(b) v pytanni pro zviazok ukraïns'koï i rus'koï literatury), *Visti,* May 23, 1929.

working-class listeners, and passed to the chairman of the literary meetings (Liubchenko), who with his fellow writers was visiting the districts of Artemivs'k and Dniepropetrovsk.

Apart from the usual questions as to how to get a story accepted by a newspaper, requests for the recitation of works, for a personal appearance of this or that writer, or simply to stop talking at the back of the hall, the following queries, both in Ukrainian and in Russian, were put to the chair:

Who pays the writers and how much? (U)

Comrade Liubchenko, why is comrade Sosiura not here? Where is he at present? What organizations does he now belong to? To Pluh or to Hart? Does VAPLITE still exist; if so, who among those present are members of it? (U)

Comrade lecturer, the journal *Ukrainian Bolshevik* is spreading Volobuiev's theory about construction. If you are going to build and theorize in this way, you will not get very far. (R)

Comrade Liubchenko, please tell us frankly whether it is possible to hope that Ukrainian culture will persist (such efforts are made at present), or whether all this is done just for the time being. As they say, "spent heat is soon cold." Is this only on paper, or in reality? (U)

Request that the comrades Lunacharskii, Skrypnyk, Krupskaia, Stalin, and Petrovs'kyi be appointed to the Honorary Presidium. (U)

Please tell us whether there is a demand for Ukrainian literature abroad. (U)

Comrades writers, what else do you do apart from writing? Where do you work? (U)

Why is the Ukrainian language of the newspaper *Komunist* so bad? (U)

Why are all the books in Ukrainian so expensive, so that the working man cannot buy them? (U)

In what year did the Ukrainian language originate? (R)

Why don't you writers dress in national costume? (U)

Why is comrade Holovko's description of peasant life (*Burian*) so vulgar? (U)

Which writers founded Ukrainian proletarian literature? Please answer. (U)

Please explain the main phases of the Literary Discussion and the part played in it by comrade Khvyl'ovyi. (U)

Do you have contacts with writers from the Western Ukraine? Do you go abroad? (U)

Dear comrade Khvyl'ovyi, please tell us about "Khvyl'ovism." Is it true or not? (U)

Comrade Khvyl'ovyi, please explain what Futurism is. (U)

Why should Ukrainian culture be spread among the masses? We have sold Russian-Ukrainian dictionaries from 1915 through the Ukrainian State Publishing House. (R)

Is there not among our literary circles a Russian as well as Ukrainian chauvinist deviation? What was the reason for the trip of Ukrainian writers to Moscow and their bonds with the Russian writers? Is it possible that such relations did not exist before? (U)

Without drawing a more general conclusion than this unique piece of information warrants, it is possible to point to some very interesting reactions from the floor following the appearance of this particular group of writers. Obviously the audience, although ill-informed, showed intense interest in contemporary Ukrainian literature, its ideas and forms. They were interested not only in the status of Ukrainian literature within the Soviet Union and abroad, but also in Russian-Ukrainian literary relations, and, above all, in "Khvyl'ovism" and its consequences. On the whole, while revealing antagonism between the Russian and the Ukrainian points of view, the questioners were not unsympathetic to the views of the Vaplitians.

Moscow's Lieutenants in the Ukraine and Their Problems

The Second Congress of VUSPP, held May 26–31, 1929, had an air of growing confidence about it. All the speakers, including the Russian delegates Fedin and Libedinskii, praised the growth of the organization. Skrypnyk alone, who a year earlier had opposed this hegemony, still spoke in a sobering tone: "VUSPP," he declared, "is a strong organization of writers who are on the side of the proletariat in its struggle for a new life; it is one of the factors aiding in the creation of this new life. But a factor is not identical with the controlling organization." [25] He then pleaded for a slow absorption of fellow travelers who should not be antagonized by aggressive methods.

This speech obviously meant that Skrypnyk was not yet willing to allow VUSPP to assume full charge of Ukrainian literature. In the eyes of the CP(B)U the anti-proletarian elements had been de-

[25] M. Skrypnyk, "Proty zaboboniv," Statti i promovy, V, 54.

feated but not destroyed, and to ignore them or to attempt to force them into the framework of VUSPP too quickly might mean to evoke once more their resistance and thus impede the Five-Year Plan effort. A much more suitable arrangement was the creation of a federation of Ukrainian literary organizations, envisaged long ago. Apart from VUSPP, other organizations and groups could belong to this and would later be absorbed in due course by the ruling VUSPP.

In November, 1929, a block was formed consisting of VUSPP, VUSKK (Vseukraïns'ka Spilka Robitnykiv Komunistychnoï Kul'tury—The All-Ukrainian Union of the Workers of Communist Culture, a new name for the old Nova Generatsiia), and VUARK (Vseukraïns'ka Asotsiiatsiia Revoliutsiinykh Kinematografistiv— The All-Ukrainian Association of Revolutionary Cinematographers),[26] in order to combine their efforts in support of the Five-Year Plan. Six weeks later, on December 31, 1929, the FORPU (Federatsiia Obiednan' Revoliutsiinykh Pys'mennykiv Ukraïny— Federation of Associations of Revolutionary Writers of the Ukraine) was created.[27] The declaration of its creation read: "Every revolutionary Soviet writer must be an active builder of socialism, and a disciplined fighter in the class struggle. This is our watchword and our command to the army of Ukrainian revolutionary Soviet literature." [28] It was signed by the representatives of VUSPP, Molodniak, Prolitfront, Pluh, VUSKK, Group A, and Zakhidnia Ukraïna.

The only novice among the signatories, "Grupa A" (Group A), was formed in 1929 from the scattered remnants of VAPLITE and some independent writers (Slisarenko, Smolych, Iohansen). The group was devoted to apolitical genres and tales of adventure for which it often used the *Universal'nyi zhurnal* (The Universal Journal). Its course was ephemeral and it ceased to exist in 1931.[29]

The wisdom of the CP(B)U's policy was proved in what may best be called an epilogue to the Literary Discussion which took place

26 "Dekliaratsiia v spravi bloku mizh VUSPPom, VUSKKom i VUARKom," *Visti,* November 5, 1929.

27 "Dekliaratsiia vseukraïns'koï federatsiï revoliutsiinykh radians'kykh pys'mennykiv," *Visti,* January 13, 1930; reprinted in *Prolitfront,* I (1930).

28 *Prolitfront,* I (1930), 263.

29 Vedmits'kyi, "Literaturnyi front: 1919–1931," *Literaturnyi arkhiv,* IV–V (1931), 126.

in 1929–30. The opposition to the Party line was still too powerful to be crushed at one blow. One of the strongest and most influential allies of VAPLITE throughout the Literary Discussion was the director of the Berezil' Theater, Les' Kurbas. The part he played in VAPLITE's opposition to regimentation was important not only because of the high standing of Berezil' as a theater but also because of Kurbas's influence among Soviet Ukrainian dramatists. In 1927 Kurbas had published an article in *Vaplite* expressing his passionate faith in the creative powers of Ukrainian literature:

> Only when you feel that Kharkov is your capital, that the Revolution is your own affair, will you become the real active force of the youthful Ukrainian dramatic culture.
> The Ukrainian theater contains in itself great forces and opportunities which are given to it by the new class and by a nation with a new perspective. Only the roadblocks of the citizens' inertia must be removed to give it a free passage.[30]

At that time, in spite of occasional official criticism of the plays staged by Berezil', there was a general opinion,[31] in which the CP(B)U also shared, that Berezil' was the most promising Ukrainian theater. In 1927 the Ukrainian Commissariat of Education established a special Council to Aid Berezil' (Rada spryiannia teatrovi Berezil'),[32] and a debate was arranged in the Blakytnyi Home of Literature on the "Paths of the Contemporary Theater" (Dysput: shliakhy suchasnoho ukraïns'koho teatru) which was mainly devoted to Berezil'.

This debate, although less extensive in scope than the Literary Discussion, lasted until 1929. It provides some of the most valuable evidence of the quality and extent of the anti-Party opposition in the Ukraine.

From a report on one of these sessions[33] we take speeches by Kulish, Kurbas, and Skrypnyk as the most interesting examples of the familiar ideological warfare.

Mykola Kulish, the author of such successful plays as *97*, *Narodnyi Malakhii*, and *Myna Mazailo*, spoke in support of Kurbas:

30 Les' Kurbas, "Shliakhy Berezolia," *Vaplite*, No. 3, 1927, pp. 156–57, 165.
31 See, for example, H. Kotsiuba's "Teatr 'Berezil',' " in *Kul'tura i pobut*, April 2, 1927.
32 "V radi spryiannia teatrovi 'Berezil',' " *Visti*, March 23, 1927.
33 "Shliakhy rozvytku ukraïns'koho teatru," *Literatura i mystetstvo*, June 22, 1929.

I should like to endorse in particular that part [of Kurbas's speech] which defined drama as something which must disturb and awaken [the spectator], and outline [for him] sometimes very sharply certain problems perhaps not always to his taste. . . .

Between drama, prose, and poetry there is always some sort of interrelation. I am now attempting to characterize our literature of the last two years. In this literature, lacking titanic design, lacking even in theme, but full of talent, though narrow in subject matter and written only for the present day, weakness is evident to some extent in the quality and the quantity of dramatic works. Moreover, our writers avoid such important and burning topics as, for instance, the national problem.

I am asking here, as I asked during the literary conference in Moscow: Please show me the works which reflect and elucidate the national problem in the Ukraine. Where are those works? I venture to state here that in our literature there is a tendency to avoid these problems, since they are, so to speak, from the point of view of the writer's success and career, dangerous.[34]

In his closing address, Kurbas, who earlier had defined the task of the drama and the theater as "aiming at a revolution, a kind of overthrow, a progression, in advance of the spectator," said that

the reeducation of the contemporary mentality, which is still very crude, is the only concrete task before the theater. . . . What unites [our opponents] is the obstinate tendency to look upon the watchword "art for the masses" from a single point of view, not dialectically: a tendency toward stabilization, toward acquiescence. And when Mykola Oleksievych [Skrypnyk] will not listen to Kulyk's advice to increase the interest in our theater in the form in which it showed itself up to now (that is, through the management), if Mykola Oleksievych, and I am sure he will understand that a rejection of this advice may lead to a great catastrophe, if he should disregard this counsel, then let me tell him and all my opponents: comrades, let me be a revolutionary; it is my right to suffer, to be unintelligible, to fight doggedly on my own front in my own fashion. . . .

Let me do all this, do not let me take the line of least resistance, since I cannot do what you want me to. This would mean to sit back with one's feet up and merely put on shows.[35]

To this dramatic testimony Skrypnyk had a ready answer. He noticed that "Kurbas betrays a tendency to oppose the ideological content of a work of art to its power to evoke an intuitive response;

[34] *Ibid.*, p. 3.   [35] *Ibid.*, p. 4.

this opposition may be the cause of the split between Berezil' and Kurbas on the one hand and the ideological need of our proletarian society on the other. This opposition in the theatrical art of Kurbas of ideology against intuition is most ominous." [36] For Skrypnyk the "main defect and error of Kurbas, which sets him apart from us, is this, that while creating a revolutionary theater and attempting to be an active member of our proletarian culture, he still tries to continue his work on individualist, not collective, lines." [37]

However, faithful to his policy of allowing the nonconformists to come back into the fold, Skrypnyk, as long as he was the Commissar of Education, continued to support Kurbas as the manager of the Berezil'. For his part, Kurbas, like Khvyl'ovyi, made a temporary compromise with the Party, hoping that it would not grow more rigid in its demands on individual artists.

Among the signatories to the declaration of FORPU were Khvyl'ovyi and Kulish, two former leaders of the dissolved VAPLITE. They now represented a new literary organization, "Prolitfront." Even before its formation (January, 1929), the former Vaplitians founded a literary magazine, *Literaturnyi iarmarok* (The Literary Fair), which, although officially belonging to no particular group and supported by "almost one half of the literary forces in the Ukraine," [38] served for over a year as a platform for many associates of Khvyl'ovyi. This magazine deserves more than a passing mention in the history of opposition to the Party in Soviet Ukrainian literature.

Literaturnyi iarmarok differed in appearance from most literary journals of the time. It was the last unrestrained and spontaneous reflection of the literary undercurrents in the Ukraine, symbolized by Petryts'kyi's gay and colorful dust jacket. With no official editorial board, this journal was indeed a "fair" where literary goods were sold and exchanged freely, unwrapped and often anonymous. Instead of a permanent editor, the journal had an individual writer to arrange each separate issue. The latter also wrote the introduction, a running commentary on the published material, and letters to the editor. The commentary, or as it was called after the eighteenth-century Ukrainian dramas, the "intermedium," was perhaps

---

[36] M. Skrypnyk, "Teatral'nyi trykutnyk," *Statti i promovy*, V, 160–61.
[37] *Ibid.*, p. 172.   [38] Mykola Novyts'kyi, *Na iarmarku*, p. 6.

the most intriguing part of the magazine, since it was written in Aesopian language. This literary device, used in nineteenth-century Russia and the Ukraine to circumvent tsarist censorship, was now used to evade an even more totalitarian form of control. Apart from novels, short stories, poems, and plays, *Literaturnyi iarmarok* also printed literary criticism, again chiefly in the style of the innuendo, the puff, and the "flyting." The heavy veil of artful metaphor and verbal jingle was at first so puzzling to the Marxian literary logicians that it caught them unawares and scored an initial success by its unexpected appearance.

Thus an allegorical sonnet, "Lebedi" (The Swans) by Mykhailo Drai-Khmara, published in the first issue of *Literaturnyi iarmarok*, went unnoticed for a while,[39] but soon drew sharp condemnation from official quarters. In vain Drai-Khmara tried to explain in a letter, published in the fourth issue of the magazine,[40] that the sonnet did not glorify the Neoclassicist writers but was based on a poem by Mallarmé. From that time on the Neoclassicists fell into even greater disfavor and, apart from Ryl's'kyi, who later dissociated himself from them, found it increasingly difficult to publish their poems.[41]

In spite of criticism by the Vusppists and other proletarian writers, *Literaturnyi iarmarok* continued to be published until 1930 (altogether twelve issues) and in that time sponsored many outstanding works by oppositionist Soviet Ukrainian writers. Among them were Kulish's two plays *Myna Mazailo* and *The People's Malakhii*, Gzhyts'kyi's novel *The Black Lake*, Iohansen's *The Adventures of Don José Pereira*, and Khvyl'ovyi's satires *Ivan Ivanovych* and *The Inspector General*.

What finally caused the suppression of *Literaturnyi iarmarok* [42] was the candor of its "intermedia" and the stale charge of nationalist deviation. In a satirical letter from O. Kopylenko to H. Epik, we find the following daring comment on the Five-Year Plan literature of the "social demand":

[39] B. Kovalenko even published a favorable review of the *Literaturnyi iarmarok* in *Na literaturnom postu*, No. 4–5, February–March, 1929.
[40] "Lyst do redaktsii," *Literaturnyi iarmarok*, No. 4, 1929, p. 172.
[41] V. Pors'kyi, "Lebedynyi s'piv," *Kyïv*, I (1951), 38.
[42] For an orthodox Soviet appraisal of *Literaturnyi iarmarok*, see I. Mykytenko, *Za hegemoniiu proletars'koï literatury*.

I know that you are now in a distant corner of our "Ukrainized" Ukraine, sitting on the bank of a river, catching perch and gathering material for a beautiful new short story. True, this is a deviation on your part. Other proletarian writers are now sitting high up on the chimneys of big factories, observing the workers' life, in order to write a saccharine epic entitled *The Father,* or *The Uncle,* or *Welcome, We Are Your Relatives.* And for this they will receive from the same sort of scribblers the title of honorary, proletarian, revolutionary, Soviet, people's, international, univeral scribbler.[43]

Even more outspoken criticism of the Five-Year Plan literature may be found in the "intermedia" of the second issue of *Literaturnyi iarmarok,* written by Khvyl'ovyi:

Our weekdays are not the grey days of a grey epoch. They are, in spite of all, yes in spite of all, days of Great Construction. . . . Our Fair is therefore incapable of burning with enthusiasm for these fragrant days because we (and you, esteemed reader) lack the will, or if we don't lack the will, we just want to wait a little. Today our literature has scattered itself in the crannies of the really grey life of grey people. But tomorrow, we assume, it will follow wide paths and will sparkle with all the colors of the richly colored world. . . .

Has the Zola of the black-golden Donbas perhaps already arrived? The Zola who will tell how the old grey Donbas is disappearing into the distance with its horse-drawn wagons, and in its place there comes a young, strong Donbas complete with electric power. Has he arrived who perhaps can tell us about the mentality of the Donbas man? Has he arrived? And where is he for whom the Dniprelstan is not terra incognita? He who on the basis of facts and figures will unfold to us the future of our cherry-blossomed land, our second America? Where is he who . . .

He will come and other writers too. They must come. We believe in it. We cannot disbelieve it. Our Fair will yet sparkle with all the colors of the richly colored world. But so far we can only see the bread queues.[44]

The so-called Khvyl'ovists were not alone in causing a great deal of trouble for the Party in its efforts to form a united front of writers in the cause of industrialization and collectivization. The Avant-garde group, guided by Valeriian Polishchuk, proved equally intransigent, though its objections to the Party line were dictated not by nationalism but by a kind of literary anarchism.

[43] "Lyst III: O. Kopylenko do Hr. Epika," *Literaturnyi iarmarok,* No. 7, 1930, p. 101.
[44] "Do knyhy sto trydtsiat' druhoï," *Literaturnyi iarmarok,* No. 2, 1929, pp. 3–4.

After the publication of *Avant-garde No. 3,* VUSPP, Pluh, Molodniak, and Nova Generatsiia published a joint letter in *Visti* condemning it as an expression of an ideology hostile to the proletarian class and as pornographic.[45] Two days later, the Russian *Literaturnaia gazeta,* the organ of the Federation of the Associations of Soviet Writers, published a rebuke to the Avant-garde in the form of an open letter by Kornelii Zelinskii.[46]

Further flagrant violations of the accepted Party line were very quickly dealt with. By a resolution of the Central Committee of the CP(B)U it was declared that

the last [sixteenth] issue of the newspaper *Red Pepper* for 1929 consists almost entirely of a lampoon directed against the constructive work undertaken by the Party and the working class in the cause of building a socialist Ukraine.

The members of the editorial board of *Red Pepper,* instead of searching out in our country the class enemy against whom battle must ruthlessly be waged, looked at the whole process of work in our republic from the philistine point of view and gave us caricatures and captions which objectively reflect hostile moods. . . .

It is therefore deemed necessary to reexamine the composition of the entire editorial board of *Red Pepper.*[47]

Criticism seems *de facto* to have become the monopoly of the Party [48] and the so-called *samokritika* (self-criticism) was reduced to a public admission of sin. Accusations of nationalist deviations were repeated *ad nauseam,* and the literary atmosphere was stifled with accusations, denunciations, and self-condemnations.

A great sensation was caused at the end of 1929 by the uncovering of what was claimed to be the SVU (Soiuz vyzvolennia Ukraïny— The Union for the Liberation of the Ukraine). At the head of this underground organization, it was charged, stood Professor Serhii Iefremov, a well-known literary historian and a member of the Ukrainian Academy of Sciences in Kiev. Among the accused were several writers and critics (L. Staryts'ka-Cherniakhivs'ka, M. Iv-

---

[45] "Lysty do redaktsiï," *Visti,* November 16, 1929.

[46] K. Zelinskii, "Otkrytoe pis'mo ukrainskim konstruktivistam-spiralistam po povodu sbornika *Avangard 3,*" *Literaturnaia gazeta,* November 18, 1929.

[47] "Postanova TsK KP(b)U pro zhurnal 'Chervonyi perets,' " *Literatura i mystetstvo,* October 20, 1929, p. 1.

[48] The new magazine devoted to literary criticism, *Krytyka,* founded in 1928, very soon became the mouthpiece of the Party, changing its title to *Za markso-lenins'ku krytyku.*

chenko, A. Nikovs'kyi). In a public trial held at the beginning of 1930 great publicity was given to the wickedness of these Ukrainian scholars and intellectuals who were allegedly plotting to overthrow the Soviet regime.[49]

It is clear that the Party was very anxious to exploit the SVU trial for its own purposes. Although literature was not directly involved in this issue, and the blow at Iefremov and others was aimed against Ukrainian scholarship and science, Soviet Ukrainian writers were prompted to declare their loyalty to the Soviet state by public denunciation in the press. During the actual trial of the SVU in Kharkov, which lasted several months, writers appeared both as witnesses and "people's prosecutors." Thus Zerov was asked to testify during the cross-examination of Ivchenko. Zerov condemned the "literary group of the SVU" as "anti-Soviet, counterrevolutionary, and very harmful." At the same time he declared that the "conditions for the development of literature in the Soviet Ukraine are very favorable," and that "Ukrainian culture has achieved gigantic successes." [50] Another writer, Oleksa Slisarenko, made an impassioned speech as a member of the people's jury.[51] The trial ended with relatively mild sentences, the chief defendants being deported for ten years. One of the results of the trial, however, was the discontinuation of the literary symposia *Literatura* which were guided to a large extent by the Neoclassicists (Fylypovych, Zerov) and the first issue of which appeared in 1928. It was only after the purges of 1932 and 1933 that Soviet Ukrainian writers, in particular the Neoclassicists, were accused of very close collaboration with the SVU.

As a result of denunciations, the unceasing vigilance of the Party,

[49] For the Soviet interpretation of the SVU trial, see L. Akhmatov, "Literatura i SVU," *Literaturnyi arkhiv*, I–II (1930). An account by the only survivor of the trial was written by K. Turkalo ("Sorok pyat'," *Novi dni*, Nos. 34, 35, 36, 37, 38, 39, 40, 1952–53.

Among several theories advanced in order to get behind the Soviet version of the trial, there is one which claims that no SVU ever existed and that it was created by Soviet provocation. This finds some support in the fact that in 1930 similar "underground organizations" were uncovered in other Soviet republics (e.g., "The Union for the Liberation of Belorussia"). There is little doubt that the SVU existed as a community of spirit and ideas.

[50] "Dopyt s'vidka Zerova; Sprava 'Spilky vyzvolennia Ukraïny,' " *Visti*, March 23, 1930. See also the declaration of VUSPP and Molodniak against Iefremov in *Visti*, November 23, 1929.

[51] "Sprava 'Spilky vyzvolennia Ukraïny,' " *Visti*, March 23, 1930.

156   LITERATURE AND THE FIRST FIVE-YEAR PLAN

and the constant appeals for a united front, the general atmosphere of Ukrainian literary life in 1930 became increasingly tense and demands upon literature grew more stark and inflexible. One of the grimmest cases of unadulterated persecution of writers at that time is provided by the ruthless treatment of Zerov. Attacked from all sides and accused of many sins he had never committed, Zerov published a penitent letter in *Proletars'ka pravda* (Proletarian Truth), February 25, 1930, declaring his willingness to become "just an ordinary worker in the socialist construction of our country." Even this letter, however, was severely attacked [52] for its alleged insincerity and was regarded as an attempt to camouflage counterrevolutionary ideas. Zerov was driven to leave the Ukraine, but after unsuccessful attempts to obtain work in Moscow, he was arrested and deported. [53]

The Party's attempt to measure the nature and degree of the ideology and organization of one literary group or another, by the outcome of the Literary Discussion, [54] partially failed because of the able maneuvering and tactics of the opposition still led by Khvyl'ovyi and the former Vaplitians. Their strategy was to refuse to be classed as deviationists or to be condemned as antiproletarian. They constantly regrouped their forces and changed organizations, forming new ones in place of those dissolved; they were willing to recant and plead guilty (open admission of political sins was regarded as a virtue in Communist ethics); and yet they never surrendered their basic premises, their fondest hopes—that they would share in and influence Ukrainian Communist culture.

While taking leave of the readers on behalf of the editorial group of *Literaturnyi iarmarok*, Khvyl'ovyi wrote "au revoir in the new journal *Prolitfront*." [55] This new organ, published by the ex-Vaplitians in their final manifestation, had to make obeisance to the latest official demands in order to exist.

With the first manifesto Prolitfront declared itself to be in the vanguard of the "fight against bourgeois art, against a hostile ideology . . . against nationalist manifestations." It opposed VUSPP and Pluh merely on esthetic grounds ("false ideas about style and

[52] Kost' Dovhan', "Z pryvodu odniieï dekliaratsiï," *Krytyka*, No. 3, 1930.
[53] Iurii Klen, *Spohady pro neokliasykiv*, p. 31.
[54] A. Leites and M. Iashek, *Desiat' rokiv ukraïns'koï literatury (1917–1927)*, II, 424.
[55] "Proloh do knyhy sto sorok druhoï," *Literaturnyi iarmarok*, No. 12, 1930, p. 4.

theme, vulgarization of the tasks of Marxian criticism, identification with the Party"),[56] and called for a united front in literature. Prolitfront also had a section of Jewish writers. One of the first acts of Prolitfront, obviously designed to win the confidence of the Party, was the attack on the "fascist nationalism" of the Nova Generatsiia."[57]

Moreover, Khvyl'ovyi wrote an article in the Party organ, *Komunist*, bitterly denouncing his past and what had come to be known as "Khvyl'ovism."[58] In February of the same year Khvyl'ovyi joined one of the writers' brigades visiting collective farms.[59]

In March, 1930, the obdurate Semenko capitulated and on behalf of Nova Generatsiia joined VUSPP together with other well-known Ukrainian Marxian critics and writers—Sukhino-Khomenko, Hirchak, Demchuk, Ovcharov, and Novyts'kyi.[60] However, it was a doubtful advantage for VUSPP to have in its ranks such an old rebel as Semenko, and in May, 1930, serious objections were raised against Nova Generatsiia at the first plenum of VUSPP.[61] The union between the Futurists and the Vusppists was shattered when, according to Vedmits'kyi, the Nova Generatsiia, "having opposed itself to VUSPP, had become the mouthpiece for the anti-proletarian elements."[62] As a result of an internal crisis, the Nova Generatsiia dissolved itself on January 11, 1931. Some of its members were then accepted into VUSPP, but Semenko and Shkurupii preferred to stay out.[63]

Literary Shock Workers

The pace of unification quickened as the Five-Year Plan approached its period of test. In the Ukraine as in Russia, writers were press-ganged to participate in the general effort. VUSPP, Molod-

[56] "Do chytacha," *Prolitfront*, I (April, 1930), 5–6.
[57] See, e.g., I. Senchenko, "U parkakh zblidlykh fantazii," *Prolitfront*, II (1930); Varvara Zhukova, "Fashyzm i futuryzm," *Prolitfront*, III (1930).
[58] M. Khvyl'ovyi, "Kruchushche bozhyshche," *Komunist*, January 27, 1930.
[59] *Literatura i mystetstvo*, No. 7, February 16, 1930.
[60] *Ibid.*, No. 9, March 2, 1930.
[61] "Za hegemoniiu proletars'koï literatury. Pidsumky pershoho poshyrenoho plenumu VUSPPu," *Visti*, May 27, 1930.
[62] Vedmits'kyi, "Literaturnyi front: 1919–1931," *Literaturnyi arkhiv*, IV–V (1931), 125.
[63] *Ibid.*

niak, and Nova Generatsiia accepted the "challenge of the Kharkov Komsomol" and proclaimed "socialist competition for the best literary works on the Tractor Factory." [64] Throughout the country VUSPP organized hundreds of literary *udarniki* (shock workers).[65] The FORPU declared itself mobilized and decided "to take an active part in the realization of the resolution of the Central Committee on the liquidation of 'breakages' and on the preparation of the third year of the Five-Year Plan." It was also decided to send shock brigades to Donbas. On behalf of the presidium of the FORPU this declaration was signed by Mykytenko, Khvyl'ovyi, and Pylypenko.[66]

The drive for enrolling shock workers in literature, practiced as it was on a large scale throughout the Union, had a special character in the Ukraine. It was given great prominence in all the Ukrainian literary magazines [67] and was supported by VUSPP in collaboration with the Ukrainian Trade Unions (VURPS), and no doubt reflected the resolution of the Central Committee of the All-Union Party of November, 1929, on the cultural work in Ukrainian villages. This resolution, passed at the time when collectivization was just beginning, declared that

the Party organization of the Ukraine must intensify its work to organize and raise the cultural level of the proletarian masses of the village to increase and unify the activities of the poor masses, and to assure its union with the "middle peasant" (*seredniak*) for the decisive advance against the kulak.[68]

This campaign was by 1930 already producing tangible results in the form of collections of prose and poetry (such as *Kuz'nia heroïv* [The Smithy of Heroes] by the shock workers of the Kharkov Tractor Factory; *Udarnyi Kharkov,* in Russian, by the shock workers of the Kharkov engine building plant). In 1931 VUSPP began to publish a special journal, *Literaturnyi prizov* (Call to Literature).

<hr/>

[64] "VUSPP, 'Molodniak' i 'Nova Generatsiia' pryimaiut' zaklyk kharkivs'koho komsomola," *Visti,* March 4, 1930.

[65] According to Vedmits'kyi, by 1930 VUSPP mobilized 1,500 and Pluh 700 *udarniki.* "Literaturnyi front: 1919–1931," *Literaturnyi arkhiv,* IV–V (1931), 122.

[66] "Vseukraïns'ka federatsiia revoliutsiinykh radians'kykh pys'mennykiv oholoshuie sebe mobilizovanoiu," *Literatura i mystetstvo,* September 14, 1930, p. 6.

[67] See, e.g., "Do robitnykiv udarnykiv Ukraïny," *Krytyka,* No. 11, 1930.

[68] "Noiabrskyi plenum TsK VKP(b) 1929," *Ot XVI konferentsii do XVI s"ezda VKP(b),* p. 112.

Some of the more talented shock workers of the pen were later accepted as members of VUSPP.

The Party leaders in the Ukraine did all in their power to whip up enthusiasm for literature by "social demand." Skrypnyk, addressing the First Congress of "Zakhidnia Ukraïna" (Western Ukraine) January 6, 1930, said that "Ukrainian culture has now become not only the culture of song, music, dance, theater, literature, cooperation, and education; Ukrainian culture is now the culture of factories and plants, the culture of the Dniprelstan and Donbas. It is the culture of the new millions of proletarian masses, the culture of collectivization, agriculture, and socialist reconstruction of the whole land." [69]

The Secretary General of the CP(B)U, Kosior, pleaded in his speech before the Eleventh Congress of the CP(B)U that "the time has come to stop throwing his old sins at Khvyl'ovyi as some of our fiery and principled comrades often do." [70] Kosior also upheld the validity of the 1925 Party resolution on literature. "Some of our comrades demand that all writers should join VUSPP. It is clear that VUSPP is the organization closest to us; it unites our most trusted literary cadres. This is self-evident, but it is not everything." He went on to remind his audience that the 1925 resolution expressed itself against any monopoly. "Recently," Kosior continued, "demands have been made by some literary quarters that a literary discussion should be opened since many problems, it is claimed, have arisen and a consolidation is taking place. We have, however, absolutely refused such demands. It must be admitted that writers sometimes like to create a storm in a teacup." [71]

The Sixteenth Congress of the Party and the Fate of Proletarian Literature

The Eleventh Congress of the CP(B)U was held only one week before the Sixteenth Congress of the All-Union Party convened in Moscow on June 26, 1930. The Sixteenth Congress, which went

[69] Mykola Skrypnyk, "Novyi etap, novi zavdannia," *Statti i promovy*, V, 75.

[70] "Politychnyi zvit TsK KP(b)U; Dopovid' tov. S. V. Kosiora," *Visti*, June 17, 1930. A part of Kosior's speech, under the title "Literaturni spravy," was reprinted in *Prolitfront*, No. 4, 1930.

[71] *Prolitfront*, No. 4, 1930, pp. 5, 7.

down in the annals of Soviet history as "the congress of the general offensive of socialism along the entire front," while the Party was "ushering in the period of socialism in the USSR," [72] also revealed the latest precepts of Party policy in the literature and culture of the national groups. Stalin's well-known discourse on the concept of culture as "socialist in content and national in form" will be considered in detail in the next chapter of this study. For the Ukraine, however, this congress was most important, not only because "great-state Russian chauvinism" was declared to be the greatest danger. The place of national culture in a Communist state was also upheld. The Congress had its undertones and warning signals too. These were directed against RAPP, which was criticized for its failure to provide literary works worthy of the industrial and economic achievement of the Five-Year Plan. It is true that the Rappists gained some applause. *Na literaturnom postu* noted with pride that "at no previous congress of the Party has so much attention been paid to the problems of literature (public appearances of Serafimovich, Kirshon, Bezymenskii). Such respect [for literature] is due to the success of proletarian literature." [73]

But from the general tone of speeches dealing with literature, unmistakable dissatisfaction with RAPP could be detected. So far the differences between the Party and RAPP were not serious; each needed the other and they were prepared to work together. The history of their alliance has been subjected to a penetrating analysis by Edward J. Brown,[74] who came to conclusions (well supported by evidence) which may at first appear surprising. His analysis revealed a strange anomaly of this alliance which was due in part to a basic disharmony between the theory and the practice of RAPP. In theory, it appears, RAPP was opposed to the Party literary policy of "social demand" and to its utilitarian approach to the problems of proletarian literature. In practice, however, RAPP functioned as the literary handmaid of the Party. This disparity finally led the Party to discredit RAPP's literary method and theory.[75] It is doubt-

[72] W. Knorin (ed.), *Communist Party of the Soviet Union: A Short History*, p. 435.

[73] "Ko vsem chlenam RAPP," *Na literaturnom postu*, No. 13–14, July, 1930, p. 4.

[74] Edward J. Brown, "The Russian Association of Proletarian Writers; 1928–1932" (Dissertation, Columbia University, 1950); published in condensed form as *The Proletarian Episode in Russian Literature, 1928–1932*.

[75] Brown, *The Proletarian Episode in Russian Literature, 1928–1932*, pp. 220–21.

ful, however, if RAPP's downfall can be adequately explained without a study of the changes in the Kremlin's policy toward non-Russian literatures.

In the Ukraine the ensuing struggle between the Party and RAPP during the years 1931 and 1932 left a deep impression. As early as the end of the Sixteenth Party Congress significant repercussions were noticeable in the Soviet Ukraine.

Skrypnyk, who had never shown any great esteem for On Guardism, regarded the Sixteenth Congress as a victory for the cause of national literature and culture. He praised Stalin's insistence that the national problem had not diminished in importance and his condemnation of Vaganian, Dimanshtein, and others who thought that the time had come for the creation of a supranational, universal culture.[76] The issue of *Chervonyi shliakh* which printed Skrypnyk's speech also carried another article on "Some Problems of Literary Politics." Its author, P. Kerzhentsev, was opposed to the forced "proletarianization of literature." "Proletarian literature," he wrote, "cannot be created by sending all those who write un-proletarian literature to the Solovki Islands." [77] He recalled that "the 1925 Party resolution did not say anything about the literature of the numerous peoples of the USSR. Now this question assumes special importance since we are witnessing a rapid growth of literature and the arts in many of our republics." [78]

The Vusppists, however, like the Rappists, regarded the resolutions of the Sixteenth Congress as an endorsement of their policies.[79] Kosior's confident belief, expressed at the Eleventh Congress of the CP(B)U, that anti-proletarian forces in the Ukraine had suffered defeat, coupled with the Sixteenth Congress's call for further closing of the ranks, was interpreted by VUSPP as a demand for greater vigilance and an even bolder offensive. As a result, literary controls in the Ukraine grew more rigid; they were intensified and, as it were, fed on themselves. Literature came to be regarded exclusively as a weapon of political propaganda. Literary organizations

[76] M. Skrypnyk, "Z kraïny nepivs'koï v kraïnu sotsialistychnu," *Chervonyi shliakh*, No. 9, 1930, p. 78.

[77] P. Kerzhentsev, "Deiaki pytannia literaturnoï polityky," *Chervonyi shliakh*, No. 9, 1930, p. 86.

[78] *Ibid.*, p. 91.

[79] See Averbakh's article in *Pravda* (August 28, 1930), "Zadachi literaturnoi politiki."

were not only spoken and written of as "armies," "fronts," and "military detachments," but were treated as such for all practical purposes.

Thus the Party decided to choose the Soviet Ukraine and its literary vanguard, VUSPP, as a suitable proving ground for the activities of that literary Comintern, the International Bureau of Proletarian Literature. At a time when those Ukrainians living under Polish rule were suffering bitter persecutions, it was thought convenient to call the Second International Conference of Proletarian Literature in the capital of the Soviet Ukraine, Kharkov (November 6–16, 1930).

This gathering of many Western European leftist writers was attended by Averbakh and welcomed by Skrypnyk and Chubar, both of whom extolled the unfettered growth of Soviet Ukrainian culture. Great prominence was given to the organization Zakhidnia Ukraïna, which was officially formed to give sanctuary to Western Ukrainian writers. Its delegate, Irchan, revealed that this organization

has specific aims. It is not only a literary but also a political and social organization. It united thirty-three writers living here in the Soviet Ukraine. We regard the situation thus: there are not two Ukraines, nor two Ukrainian cultures. There is but one Ukrainian culture, one Ukrainian land. Temporarily eight million Ukrainian workers and peasants are under the heel of Polish, Rumanian, and Czechoslovakian fascism, separated from their mother country, the Soviet Ukraine. . . . It must be stressed that our organization has received the greatest support in its specific tasks from the basic proletarian organization in the Soviet Ukraine—VUSPP.[80]

There is no doubt that the applause Irchan received was genuine, for all Ukrainians wanted to be united (though not perhaps in the Soviet Ukraine) and they responded favorably to this patriotic appeal.

While organizing a literary Comintern in the borderlands of the USSR, VOAPP was fighting national deviationism in the literatures of the non-Russian Soviet republics. The Ukraine was by no means the only plague spot in the Union. Belorussia, Georgia, Armenia, and Turkmenistan also exhibited a strong inclination to

[80] "Pid haslom literaturnoho internatsionalu," *Literaturnyi arkhiv*, IV–V (1931), 145.

follow their own desires in cultural and literary development and they, too, became objects of Soviet retribution. It is important to note that at that time VOAPP was given the widest powers in these republics and any opposition to it was regarded by the authorities as anti-Soviet and counterrevolutionary. When, for instance, on November 30, 1930, the Communist Party of Georgia issued a special resolution condemning the deviation of Syrtsov and Lominadze, it emphasized that the offenders pursued policies "opposed to the literary and political line of VOAPP which was basically correct and closest to the line of the Party." [81]

It is outside the scope of the present study to investigate the contacts between various non-Russian literatures in the late twenties. Purges of writers in Belorussia, Georgia, and other Soviet republics resembled the purges in the Ukraine, although it is difficult to ascertain whether a common front of these oppositionist groups in various republics was ever contemplated. An article by VOAPP's spokesman, Selivanovskii, suggests that the Kremlin suspected and feared such an alliance of non-Russian literary "deviationists." [82]

Of particular interest to us is the relation of some Sovietophile groups of Ukrainian writers in Galicia to Soviet Ukrainian literary life, the fate of the Soviet Ukrainian literary organization Zakhidnia Ukraïna, which consisted of political émigrés from Galicia, and Galician-Soviet relations in general.

The vigorous development of Soviet Ukrainian literature and the Ukrainization movement had won the sympathy of many Ukrainians in Galicia. The writers gathered around the publications *Novi shliakhy* (New Paths), *Vikna* (Windows), and *Kul'tura* (Culture) were open admirers of the Soviet regime. The most talented among them were A. Krushel'nyts'kyi and V. Bobyns'kyi, who, together with several other enthusiasts for Soviet cultural policy, went to the Soviet Ukraine only to be destroyed a few years later. In the mid-thirties the same fate overtook all the members of Zakhidnia Ukraïna, which was created in 1927 solely to keep alive the pro-Soviet feelings of the Galicians. However, the existence of such a literary "puppet" also presented some dangers to the Soviet

81 "Za bol'shevistskuiu konsolidatsiiu sil proletarskoi literatury," *Na literaturnom postu*, No. 23–24, December, 1930, p. 71. Syrtsov and Lominadze were also linked with the Litfront opposition to RAPP (see *Literaturnaia entsiklopediia*, VI, 507–8).
82 A. Selivanovskii, "Na pochatkovi novoho etapu," *Krytyka*, No. 10, 1930.

regime. The expatriate Galicians in the Soviet Ukraine and Communist sympathizers in Galicia, although under strict supervision by the Party, were not only providing channels for Soviet propaganda in Galicia but were informing the Soviet Ukrainian public of Western Ukrainian life. Even though the picture they painted was very dark, it nevertheless offered a means of contact with a non-Soviet Ukraine. Such contacts in terms of polemics and recriminations between the Soviet Ukrainian writers on the one hand and the Galicians and the émigrés on the other had a definite bearing on Ukrainian literary life. That the effect was not what the Kremlin desired may be seen from the fact that after 1932 all Soviet attempts to court the attention of Galician writers were abandoned.

In many respects Soviet policy toward Ukrainian writers in Galicia and Western Europe was seemingly inconsistent. Thus, for instance, the Soviet government sent financial assistance to non-Communist writers (e.g., Vasyl' Stefanyk in Galicia and Ol'ha Kobylians'ka in Bukovina) and allowed the publication in the Soviet Ukraine of the works of Vynnychenko who, while living abroad, was a supporter of the Soviet regime. The latter's novels and dramas enjoyed wide popularity in the Soviet Ukraine. The over-all objective of Soviet propaganda was to attract as many well-known literary figures to the Soviet system as possible and to divide even further the already divided émigrés. Yet at the same time, by appearing to make concessions to the national aspirations of the Ukrainians both abroad and at home, it recognized the validity of the demands for an all-Ukrainian cultural and political unity.

In the late twenties there was still lively contact (usually skirmishing) between the Galicians and the Soviet Ukrainians. Khvyl'ovyi had followers among both groups. Although he won plaudits from some Galicians for attacking the Russians, this certainly did not strengthen his position in Kharkov but did raise him and the movement he headed to an all-Ukrainian significance. Ukrainian writers in L'vov, Prague, Warsaw, Vienna, and Paris were eagerly watching events in their homeland, taking sides in the vital dispute. In the Ukraine, in the meantime, the drive to consolidate proletarian literature demanded another sacrifice upon the altar of the eternal purge.

At the end of 1930 Prolitfront came under heavy fire from Vusppist and pro-Party critics. It was charged with inadequate criticism of its own members, reluctance to collaborate with VUSPP, and too much toleration of the fellow travelers. Acting in self-defense, on January 9, 1931, Prolitfront published a "Resolution of the General Meeting of the Prolitfront concerning the Consolidation of the Forces of Proletarian Literature." "Prolitfront," the statement reads, "could not rise to the level of a thorough criticism of the petit-bourgeois and nationalist works of some of its members." Moreover, "Prolitfront has committed a bad political error in its reply to the questionnaire of VOAPP and the International Bureau of Proletarian Literature. From this reply it might appear that Prolitfront accused the Headquarters of the All-Union proletarian literary movement—VOAPP—of imperialist chauvinism. This we categorically deny and condemn." [83]

The resolution also included a list of thirty-five names of members of Prolitfront who were willing to join VUSPP. Among them was Mykola Khvyl'ovyi. Such then was the sorry end of his last creation—Prolitfront. On February 11, 1931, when eighteen out of thirty-five applicants, among them Khvyl'ovyi, Tychyna, Kulish, Ianovs'kyi, and Vyshnia, who thus far had never belonged to Party-sponsored organizations, were accepted as members of VUSPP,[84] the curtain fell on a long period of organized resistance by Soviet Ukrainian writers to the Party, which thus emerged from the hard contest as a final victor. Yet, to borrow the frequently used Marxian jingle, the struggle went on, assuming new forms.

It is impossible to evaluate correctly the complex motives involved in the final capitulation of Khvyl'ovyi and his group. To say that "force can never conquer; it can only subdue," may be true only in the absolute. The history of totalitarian states proves the opposite. It is even easier for those who possess force to conquer enemies if the latter share their basic creed. Yet even then no generalization can express all the nuances of a particular human or social situation and we must allow a margin of doubt as to whether Khvyl'ovyi's opposition to force had been conquered or only temporarily subdued.

[83] "Rezoliutsiia zahal'nykh zboriv 'Prolitfrontu' v spravi konsolidatsiï syl proletars'koï literatury vid 19 sichnia 1931 roku," *Prolitfront*, No. 7–8, 1930, pp. 322–23.
[84] "Khronika," *Chervonyi shliakh*, No. 3, 1931, p. 202.

In a speech before the Kharkov branch of VUSPP Khvyl'ovyi explained that Prolitfront was dissolved without any external pressure.[85] While VUSPP from the beginning possessed a "healthy proletarian kernel," Prolitfront had merely carried on the tradition of VAPLITE and could not rid itself "of old deviationist traditions and tendencies." [86]

Whether there was a suspicion that Khvyl'ovyi was talking tongue in cheek, or whether VUSPP feared contamination by ex-Vaplitians, it was quick to take Khvyl'ovyi to task for alleged errors and heresies in this speech. A special declaration issued by the Communist faction of VUSPP condemned Khvyl'ovyi for misrepresenting VUSPP's drive for hegemony, for not making a clear distinction between VUSPP and Prolitfront, and for being in favor of a "mechanical consolidation." [87]

In 1931, therefore, FORPU was bereft of three units (Prolitfront, Nova Generatsiia, Group A), but this only strengthened VUSPP. The journals *Chervonyi shliakh, Zhyttia i revoliutsiia,* and *Literaturna hazeta* became the organs of the Federation.[88]

Writing in the middle of 1931, the Ukrainian Marxist critic, Samiilo Shchupak, still divided the "anti-proletarian remnants" in Soviet Ukrainian literature into four groups. According to his classification, they were (1) the Futurists of the Nova Generatsiia, some members of which he believed might yet become genuine proletarian writers; (2) fellow travelers, like Smolych and Slisarenko; (3) apolitical writers, like Iurii Ianovs'kyi; and (4) the "Right front," in which he placed such prominent poets as Ryl's'kyi, Pluzhnyk, Os'machka, and the novelists Pidmohyl'nyi and Antonenko-Davydovych, who "display in their works motifs of national voluntarism" and "idealize the kulaks and the bourgeoisie." [89]

After Prolitfront merged with VUSPP such small unsubmissive groups lost the significance and the influence they had previously

85 M. Khvyl'ovyi, "Za konsolidatsiiu," *Chervonyi shliakh,* No. 4, 1931, p. 89.
86 *Ibid.,* pp. 90, 91.
87 "Postanova biura kom. fraktsiï VUSPPu v spravi konsolidatsiinykh zboriv kharkivs'koï orhanizatsiï VUSPPu," *Chervonyi shliakh,* No. 5, 1931, pp. 112–13.
88 Vedmits'kyi, "Literaturnyi front: 1919–1931," *Literaturnyi arkhiv,* IV–V (1931), 128.
89 Samiilo Shchupak, "Literaturnyi front na Ukraïni," *Zhyttia i revoliutsiia,* May-June, 1931, p. 115.

possessed. The stage was left free for VUSPP and its satellites, who were becoming ever more dependent on VOAPP and its controlling brain—RAPP.

The Decline and Dissolution of RAPP, VOAPP, and VUSPP

Ironically enough, at the moment when all obstacles had been removed to the attainment of the hegemony of proletarian literature, and when it seemed that no power could stop the fulfillment of this "historic right," there began, at first almost imperceptibly, a gradual decline in the power of VOAPP and RAPP. Outwardly VOAPP exhibited great confidence in its victory. In the English-language magazine *Literature of the World Revolution,* published in Moscow as the central organ of the International Union of Revolutionary Writers, Averbakh described VOAPP in these terms:

We, the All-Union Federation of Associations of Proletarian Writers (VOAPP), have every reason to feel proud of the struggle that was waged by our organization as a whole and by its component parts against all and every manifestation of bourgeois ideology. Of course, there were also mistakes and drawbacks in our activity. Yet notwithstanding the numerous mistakes and shortcomings, during the last two or three years the proletarian writers of the Soviet Union have gone through a vast school of political training, and this is one of the highly important reasons why we can now speak of the leading role of VOAPP organizations in literary life. Soviet literature is now already led and headed by the proletarian writers. This is a reflection of the successes of the proletarian cultural revolution as a whole. It demonstrates the manner in which the question "who will win?" is being solved in this country. And the unity of VOAPP in all our recent battles denotes the growth of international solidarity in the proletarian ranks of the national literatures. . . .

We must be in the front ranks of the struggle for international proletarian culture against national exclusiveness, against the conservation of any lingering animosity among the toilers, against nationalistic provincialism, and for the broad horizons of the soldiers in the army of World Revolution. We must bring even closer together all the national sections of VOAPP, ruthlessly resisting the least manifestations of imperialist sentiment—the chief enemy—and clearing a path for ever greater unity of the toilers of all nations.

Comrades, not so long ago we had to admit that we were more on the defensive than on the offensive. It was one of the most critical moments of transition to the new stage, to the new tempo of reconstruction, to the strengthening of the struggle for bolshevization of proletarian literature under the new circumstances. That phase has rapidly passed away. Our organization has managed to repulse the opponents of the general policy of VOAPP, to demonstrate its loyalty to the policy of the Party, and, despite numerous mistakes and shortcomings, to find the basic keys for further progress. In our domain, in conformity with the policy of the Party, we are today unfolding the socialist offensive. We are the Bolshevist vanguard of Soviet literature.[90]

The firm voice of the RAPP leader was used to conceal his own insecurity. The Party now showed openly its displeasure with RAPP. Thus *Pravda* criticized it for being concerned with administrative rather than educational and ideological issues.[91] It rebuked RAPP on several occasions in its literary page, which became a regular feature of this Party daily on February 17, 1930.

Furthermore, on August 15, 1931, the Party adopted an important resolution on publishing, thus once more taking the initiative by interfering in the literary affairs of the USSR. This resolution had also received wide publicity in the Ukraine; it was published not only in the daily press but also in literary periodicals.[92] Perhaps the most significant article of the preamble to this directive declared that

the character and content of a book must completely correspond to the tasks of socialist reconstruction. A book must have a fighting spirit and political relevance; it must arm the widest masses of the builders of socialism with Marxian-Leninist theory and with technical and productive skills. A book should become the most powerful weapon for educating, mobilizing, and organizing the masses around the tasks of economic and cultural construction. The quality of a book must satisfy the cultural demands of the masses, demands which are ever growing.

The form of a book, its content and language, must harmonize with its purpose and with the level and the demands of the group of readers for whom it is intended.[93]

90 L. Averbakh, "Proletarian Literature and the Peoples of the Soviet Union; For Hegemony of Proletarian Literature," *Literature of the World Revolution*, V (1931), 114, 115 (verbatim).
91 "Za proletarskuiu literaturu," *Pravda*, April 19, 1931.
92 See, e.g., "Pro vydavnychu robotu," *Krytyka*, No. 9, 1931.
93 *Ibid.*, p. 4.

Kost' Dovhan' in the article "How Are We Fulfilling the Fighting Directive of the Party?" [94] stressed that the decree "has historic importance . . . for the whole front of the cultural revolution in the USSR."

Finally Stalin himself indicated that the militant and uncompromising attitude of RAPP needed revision. In a speech delivered before the industrial managers on June 23, 1931, he said that "whereas in the period of greatest wrecking activities our attitude to the old technical intelligentsia was mainly expressed by a policy of destroying them, now, in the period of the return of this intelligentsia to the side of the Soviet government, our attitude to them must be expressed most of all in a policy of enlisting them and of solicitude for them. It would be wrong and undialectical to continue our former policy under the new and changed conditions." [95]

It is interesting to note that both RAPP and VUSPP missed the hint given here by Stalin that the time had come to enlist the help and experience of the non-Communists in the gigantic tasks of reconstruction. In the resolution of the Plenum of RAPP [96] the old Rappist slogan of "enemy or ally" was repeated. In an article in *Krytyka* Averbakh was engaging in a familiar old witch hunt against Ukrainian fellow travelers, branding the Neoclassicists as the "literary center of the Union for the Liberation of the Ukraine." [97]

The Ukrainian proletarian writers must have been aware of the conflict between the Party and RAPP. While preserving some semblance of loyalty to VOAPP and RAPP, they began to differ over the extent of collaboration with them. A more radical group of Ukrainian On Guardists came into being within VUSPP itself. It was led by Kovalenko, who claimed that "in its work On Guardism had met with the Party's approval as evidenced by the fact that RAPP was recognized as a basic organization of proletarian literature, carrying out the Party line. However, On Guardism has outgrown the boundaries of the RSFSR." [98] Summing up the debates

---

[94] Kost' Dovhan', "Iak my vykonuiemo boiovu dyrektyvu partiï," *Krytyka*, No. 11–12, 1931, p. 3.

[95] J. Stalin, *Sochineniia*, XIII, 72.

[96] "O poputnichestve i soiuznichestve," *Na literaturnom postu*, No. 26, 1931.

[97] L. Averbakh, "Boiovi zavdannia proletars'koï literatury URSR," Part II, *Krytyka*, No. 9, 1931, p. 17.

[98] Kovalenko, "Za vsesoiuznoe napostovstvo," *Na literaturnom postu*, No. 18, June, 1931, p. 4.

of the Plenum of VOAPP, Kovalenko also suggested that the Communist Academy should be given the task of working out a theory of national culture and literature in the Soviet state.[99]

Yet Kovalenko's eagerness to become Averbakh's lieutenant met with a cool response from the latter. "We cannot lend our organization to those who feel themselves On Guardist," [100] replied the leader of RAPP. In the same article he had more to say about the literary relations between the Soviet republics:

We talk a great deal about international unity, but in reality there is still a very strict national insularity and cleavage. If, for instance, writers' brigades are going into the country, then the Ukrainian brigades travel across the Ukraine, the Russian ones across Russia, and so on. Instead, there is no reason why the Ukrainians should not only learn of achievements in the Ukraine but also be sent to the Urals, and the Uralians to the Ukraine, and so on.[101]

Moreover, Averbakh had a very clear conception of the future image of Soviet socialist literature as developed by VOAPP. "It is necessary," he wrote, "to find scores of new ways to break down the old national isolation, which would demonstrate that we are not a mechanical association of national detachments, but that we are really a strong, mighty, and single union of proletarian literature." [102]

As we shall see later, Averbakh's concept of the unity of all national literatures was not fundamentally different from that which the Party adopted a year later. Why then were RAPP and VUSPP subjected to attacks for doing what the Party wanted? The answer may well be that for purely political reasons the Party objected to Averbakh's personality, to the "Trotskyite" views of some of the prominent Rappists (Selivanovskii, Libedinskii), and that it had decided to follow Gorky's advice by forgiving the Russian intelligentsia all their sins. None of these reasons applied to the Ukraine, yet blame was automatically attached to VUSPP—the sister organization of RAPP.

In the meantime, Kovalenko was getting nowhere in his cam-

---

[99] Kovalenko, "Vsesoiuzny smotr proletarskoi literatury; itogi plenuma VOAPP," *Na literaturnom postu*, No. 17, June, 1931, p. 3.

[100] Averbakh, "Trevoga a ne samodovol'stvo," *Na literaturnom postu*, No. 18, June, 1931, p. 4.

[101] *Ibid.*, p. 10. [102] *Ibid.*

paign for Ukrainian On Guardism. Perhaps his only success, of a highly fictitious nature, was his election to the editorial board of *Na literaturnom postu* in August, 1931. His persistent demand [103] that Molodniak be merged with VUSPP remained unanswered by VOAPP.

When the Fifth (and last) Plenum of RAPP convened in December, 1931, the Party representatives again accused RAPP of lagging behind. The slogan under which the plenum was held ("For Magnitostrois of Literature") was suggested to RAPP by the Party.[104] There is ample evidence that RAPP resented this directive [105] and thus hastened the climax of the growing crisis. The new role which the Party imposed upon RAPP and VOAPP was not that of a master organizer of all Soviet literature but that of a performer of two special functions: the creation of works dealing with the construction of the gigantic plants, and the destruction of class enemies in literature.[106]

In vain RAPP and VUSPP tried to reorganize themselves.[107] Kovalenko's assurances that "the Ukrainian On Guardists in VUSPP and Molodniak have, on the whole, fought correctly in defense of the Party line," [108] sounded more like the plea of a defendant than of one charged with the task of reconstruction. After a long period of hesitancy the Party finally decided to take a drastic step. By a resolution of April 23, 1932, it dissolved in effect all literary organizations in the USSR, including RAPP and VOAPP. In their place a single Union of Soviet Writers was to be formed.[109]

The effect of this act was stunning, and the immediate reaction to it in Russia and in the Ukraine was similar. The Russian *On Literary Guard* failed to print the Party resolution and *Literary Gazette* tried to minimize its importance.

[103] Kovalenko, "Ukrainskaia literatura pered novimy zadachami," *Na literaturnom postu*, No. 30, October, 1931, p. 6.

[104] See, e.g., Stavskii, "Litsom k tvorchestvu," *Pravda*, December 23, 1931.

[105] Brown, "The Russian Association of Proletarian Writers; 1928–1932," p. 347.

[106] "Pis'mo tov. Stalina i zadachi VOAPP," *Na literaturnom postu*, No. 35–36, December, 1931.

[107] "Pro zavdannia perebudovy VUSPPu," *Zhyttia i revoliutsiia*, January, 1932, pp. 130–33.

[108] Kovalenko, "Cherhovi zavdannia perebudovy roboty VOAPPu," *Zhyttia i revoliutsiia*, January, 1932, p. 108.

[109] "O perestroike literaturno-khudozhestvennykh organizatsii," *Pravda*, April 24, 1932. For a complete text see Appendix G.

In the Ukraine, too, VUSPP showed no enthusiasm about the news. The Party organs had to exert all their pressure to evoke the desired response from those proletarian writers who had believed themselves to be so firmly in the saddle. "For ten days after the publication of the resolution they were silent," said Skrypnyk, "until called by the Central Committee." [110] In the same address Skrypnyk sharply criticized the Vusppists, and especially Mykytenko, for their reservations against the resolution. He insisted that they should dissolve without delay, and he minced no words about VUSPP. It was, he said, "a literary-political organization, created by the Party in order to fulfill certain political tasks." [111] As a result of this tongue-lashing VUSPP called a special meeting which was to be its last. On May 7, 1932, before a large gathering of Party officials and writers, the Party resolution was read by Mykytenko and it was greeted with great applause.[112] It was significant, however, that the audience elected to the Honorary Chairmanship of this meeting Postyshev, the newly appointed special Party representative in the Ukraine. The dissolution of RAPP and all other literary organizations was one of the symptoms of the radical change in the cultural policy of Stalin toward the non-Russian republics.

The April resolution was indeed a landmark in the history of Soviet Ukrainian literature. But before examining its special significance for the Soviet Ukraine, it is once more necessary in an unavoidable digression to turn our attention to the ideological strife and deep internal changes taking place within that country during the critical period of the early 1930s.

110 M. Skrypnyk, "Perebuduvatysia po spravzhn'omu; Vystup na lit. naradi v TsK KP(b)U 2.V.1932 v spravi realizatsii postanovy TsK VKP(b) vid 23.IV.1932," *Chervonyi shliakh*, No. 5–6, 1932, p. 103.

111 *Ibid.*, p. 108.

112 "Pys'mennyky Ukraïny vitaiut' istorychnu postanovu TsK VKP(b)," *Visti*, May 11, 1932.

[VIII]

THE GREAT CHANGE

Like many modern students of the Soviet Union Max Beloff arrived at the following conclusion:

The years after 1929 witnessed psychological and moral changes in the USSR . . . which led to the development of the earlier internationalism of the Revolution and its leaders into something which can best be described as Soviet patriotism or even as Soviet nationalism.[1]

But while a great deal has been written about the changes in Soviet foreign policy, and about the social and economic structure of the USSR at that time, the national problem has been almost untouched. Yet it is here, in the Soviet nationality policy during the early 1930s, that the most drastic changes in the Soviet system took place, illustrating most strikingly the transition from the "earlier internationalism" to "Soviet nationalism," and revealing at once the motives and the intentions of the Soviet rulers. It is also important to bear in mind that they themselves regarded the years 1929–30 as the crucial turning point in the history of the USSR. Stalin made it clear in his speech before the Sixteenth Congress (June 26–July 13, 1930) by declaring that "our country has already entered the period of socialism." [2] The next Party Congress (Seventeenth, 1934) is known in the official history of the Party as the "Congress of the victors." [3]

A victory presupposes, of course, an enemy who has been defeated and a strategy which made this triumph possible. Here, however, the Soviet interpretation of their own history must and can be refuted if we are to gain any insight into the real history of that

---

[1] Max Beloff, *The Foreign Policy of Soviet Russia*, I, 178.
[2] W. Knorin (ed.), *Communist Party of the Soviet Union: A Short History*, p. 435.
[3] *Ibid.*, p. 496.

period. The Soviet view that the victory was that of the proletarian class under the leadership of the Party, guided by Marxism and Leninism, over the hostile classes (bourgeoisie, the kulaks), over the bourgeois nationalist and other deviations, and finally over the remains of the capitalist system of ownership and production is completely inadequate to explain what really happened.

The task which the Party (predominantly Russian in its composition) faced at the beginning of the First Five-Year Plan was not only the preservation of the Soviet multinational state but its complete economic reconstruction. This could be done either by sharing their labors with the non-Russian peoples or their respective governments (something to which they were entitled by virtue of their constitutional powers and their historical development within the USSR) or by centralizing and concentrating all power in the Party's own hands. The Party chose the latter; the ultimate reasons for this choice, however, will not be our concern here, but rather the Party's policies—and the supporting theories—in one particular sector of its vast endeavor: that of national culture and literature.

Theory of National Culture in a Socialist State

It was not until 1930 that Stalin made a determined attempt to redefine and establish the place of the national cultures and literatures within the framework of a socialist state, and this fact is significant. The theory of national culture received special attention in the USSR after the beginning of 1930. Thus the review *Revoliutsiia i Natsional'nosti* (The Revolution and the Nationalities) was founded in that year, a symposium on the national problem was published by Velikovskii, and in the Ukraine the Ukrainian Institute of Marxism and Leninism was given a new lease on life.

This did not mean that no clear conception of a national culture existed earlier, but it did show that now it suddenly became imperative to have a theory adapted to new conditions. In fact, it may justly be said that during the twenties the Ukraine was the chief testing ground for the nurture of a national culture in the Soviet Union. Based on the principle of self-determination, espoused by

Lenin, the theory and practice of national culture in that country followed a definite process of fruition and fulfillment. The most outstanding theorist and administrator of it was Skrypnyk, for whom Communist Revolution was often synonymous with national liberation. Under his protection Soviet Ukrainian culture made significant advances, providing an example to the oppressed peoples of the world of the beneficence of the Soviet regime toward the cultural self-expression of all nations.

However, Skrypnyk's interpretation in the twenties of the role of a national culture in the Soviet state deviated as much from Marxian theory as did Stalin's practice in that field in the thirties. To see this one must glance at the fountainhead.

The Bolshevik theory of national culture within the Soviet state is rooted in the Marxian conception of the nation as something which is not permanent and immutable but simply a phase of historical development occurring during the rise of capitalism. Marx did not believe in the self-determination of nations, and in underrating national sentiment he "proved a poor guide for his followers, who were later harassed by the intricate problems arising from the growing strength of nationalist movements." [4]

The opinions of Lenin and Stalin on the place of national culture in a socialist state are, therefore, of far greater importance. Although for Lenin, as for Marx, the question of nationality did not exist per se, but was one of the problems of the social revolution, it was very extensively treated by him and was also analyzed in its cultural content. Lenin wrote:

Developing capitalism knows two historical tendencies as far as the national problem is concerned. First, the awakening of national life and national movements accompanied by struggles against all kinds of oppression of a nation, and the formation of national states. Secondly, the development and intensification of all types of relations between nations, the breaking of national barriers, the creation of an international unity of capital, economic life in general, politics, sciences, etc. Both these tendencies are fundamental to capitalism. The first dominates the beginning of its development, the second is characteristic of the ripe capitalism which is moving toward socialism. [5]

[4] Solomon F. Bloom, *The World of Nations: A Study of the National Implications in the Work of Karl Marx*, p. 201.
[5] Lenin, *Sochineniia*, XVII, 140.

Hence Lenin believed that in the second period, within a people still living in a capitalist state, there would be formed the embryo of an international, even a socialist, culture. He clarified this point in two additional statements:

There are two nations in every contemporary nation. There are two national cultures in every national culture. There is the Great Russian culture of a Purishkevich, a Guchkov, or a Struve, but there is also another Russian culture, that of Chernyshevskii and Plekhanov. Two such cultures exist also among the Ukrainians, as well as in Germany, France, England, etc.[6]

In each national culture there are elements of democratic and socialist culture. . . . Following the slogan "for an international culture of democracy and for a universal workers' movement," we take from every national culture only its democratic and socialist elements; we take them in opposition to the bourgeois culture, to the bourgeois nationalism of every nation.[7]

This strictly pragmatic view of national culture became the cornerstone of the Leninist doctrine and should always be borne in mind. National culture, for Lenin, was something to be used in the achievement of the socialist revolution, it was a means to an end.

Lenin's theorizing on national culture applied *ipso facto* to national literatures. Thus Nusinov, writing before 1934, argued that "at first, a national literature tended to reflect the national struggle and the awakening of a national consciousness as well as stressing the separate national characteristics." [8] This, in accordance with Lenin's view, occurs during the first period of a people's existence as a nation. In the second period ("the breaking down of national barriers") there is a tendency to establish contacts between national literatures.

However, Nusinov is anxious to point out that "this does not mean that even during capitalism the boundaries between the various national literatures will disappear, and that by a process of assimilation all literatures will merge into one. Lenin, and later Stalin, maintained that this task would only be solved in a socialist country." [9]

It is precisely on this point that Leninist theory proved later on to be a bone of contention among Soviet ideologists. This process

[6] *Ibid.*, p. 143.   [7] *Ibid.*, p. 137.
[8] I. Nusinov, "Natsional'naia literatura," *Literaturnaia entsiklopediia*, VII, 631.
[9] *Ibid.*, p. 632.

of fusion (or should it be called a transformation?) of national cultures and literatures in a socialist state would, according to Lenin, be a very long one. He said, "National differences will remain for a very long time after the realization of the dictatorship of the proletariat on a world scale." [10]

Stalin's Contribution

Lenin's statement served as a basis for Stalin's formulation of the well-known theory of culture "socialist in content and national in form." The first complete argument for it was given by Stalin in 1925 in his lecture "The Political Tasks of the University of the Peoples of the East":

I then spoke about raising the national cultures in the Soviet republics of the East. What then is a national culture? How can it be combined with a proletarian culture? Did not Lenin tell us even before the war that there are two cultures, bourgeois and socialist, that the slogan of a national culture is a reactionary slogan of the bourgeoisie which is trying to poison the consciousness of the workers with the poison of nationalism? How to combine the construction of national culture, the development of schools and courses in the native languages, and the production of cadres from local people with the building of socialism, the building of a socialist culture? Is there an impassable contradiction here? Of course not!

We are building a proletarian culture. This is quite true. But it is equally true that a proletarian culture socialist in content accepts different forms and modes of expression in different peoples absorbed in socialist construction, depending on differences in language, customs, etc. Proletarian in its content, national in its form, such is the universal culture toward which socialism is advancing.

Proletarian culture does not abolish national culture; it fills it with content. And vice versa, national culture does not abolish proletarian culture. It gives it form. The slogan of national culture was bourgeois as long as power was in the hands of the bourgeoisie and the consolidation of nations was carried on under the protection of a bourgeois order. The slogan of national culture became proletarian when power came into the hands of the proletariat and when the consolidation of nations began to take its course under the aegis of Soviet government. Whoever has not understood the basic difference between these two situations will never understand Leninism or the nature of the national problem.[11]

10 Lenin, *Sochineniia*, XXV, 229.   11 Stalin, *Sochineniia*, VII, 137–38.

As in the Soviet theory of government the Marxian tenet of the withering away of the state has been indefinitely postponed, so in the field of Soviet culture Stalin's formula has replaced the belief in a gradual fusion of national cultures into an international culture with an international language, held by some early Marxists.

Stalin made his pronouncement in 1925 at a time when NEP was still in full swing and he was himself fighting for the right to don Lenin's mantle. It was therefore of little practical importance to Soviet literature at that time. Five years later, however, the situation had radically changed. Stalin was at the helm of the Soviet state and proletarian literary organizations supported by the Party were playing the leading role in Soviet literature. It was necessary, therefore, to restate the dogmas of national culture in a country that, according to the official proclamation, was entering the era of socialism.

Yet these were not the only reasons for Stalin's statement on national culture during the Sixteenth Congress of the Party in 1930. The development of the national cultures within the USSR in the decade following the Civil War was characteristically national. Each of the peoples was aroused to promote its culture independently. As Lenin foresaw, national characteristics showed no tendency to disappear; on the contrary, they were intensified to an extent which would certainly have surprised him.

We have already seen how the renaissance of Ukrainian literature and literary theory was greeted by the Party with mounting alarm. Similar cultural developments were taking place in other Soviet republics. If these national and cultural movements were allowed to grow (and their impetus was far from being exhausted), the unity of the Soviet state and the solidarity of the proletariat might be seriously undermined. A bold move was needed to save the monolithic state and to parry the resultant divisive forces without offending the various non-Russian nationalities. This move was made by Stalin in his report to the Sixteenth Congress of the Party in 1930:

Those who are deviating towards Great Russian chauvinism are profoundly mistaken in believing that the period of building Socialism in the USSR is the period of the collapse and liquidation of national cultures. The very opposite is the case. Actually, the period of the proletarian dictatorship and of the building of Socialism in the USSR is the period of the *efflorescence* of national cultures that are *socialist* in content and national in form; for under the Soviet system, the nations themselves are not the ordinary modern nations, but *socialist* nations, just as in content, their national cultures are not the ordinary bourgeois cultures, but *socialist* cultures.

Obviously, they fail to understand that national cultures must develop *with renewed force* with the introduction and firm establishment of compulsory universal elementary education in the native languages. They fail to understand that only if the national cultures are developed will it be possible really to draw the backward nationalities into the work of socialist reconstruction.

They fail to understand that this, precisely, is the basis of the Leninist policy of *helping* and *promoting* the development of the national cultures of the peoples of the USSR.

It may seem strange that we who stand for the future merging of national cultures into one common (in form and in content) culture, with one common language, should at the same time stand for the *efflorescence* of national cultures at the present time, in the period of the proletarian dictatorship. But there is nothing strange about it. The national cultures must be allowed to develop and unfold, to reveal all their potentialities, in order to create the conditions for merging them into one common culture with one common language in the period of the victory of Socialism all over the world. The efflorescence of cultures that are national in form and socialist in content under the proletarian dictatorship in one country *for the purpose* of merging them into one common socialist (in form and in content) culture with one common language, when the proletariat is victorious all over the world, when Socialism has become the way of life—herein, precisely, lies the dialectics of the Leninist presentation of the question of national culture.

It may be said that such a presentation of the question is "contradictory." But is there not the same "contradiction" in our presentation of the question of the state? We stand for the withering away of the state. At the same time we stand for the strengthening of the proletarian dictatorship, which is the mightiest and strongest state power that has ever existed. The highest development of the state power with the object of preparing the conditions for the withering away of the state—such is the Marxist formula. Yes, it is "contradictory." But this is the contradiction in life, and it fully reflects Marx's dialectics.

Or, for example, Lenin's presentation of the question of the right of nations to self-determination, including the right to secession. Lenin sometimes depicted the thesis on national self-determination in the shape of the simple formula: "disunion for union." Think of it— disunion for union. It even sounds like a paradox. And yet, this "contradictory" formula reflects the living truth of Marx's dialectics which enables the Bolsheviks to capture the most impregnable fortresses in the sphere of the national question.

The same may be said about the formula on national culture: the efflorescence of national cultures (and languages) in the period of the proletarian dictatorship in one country with the object of preparing the conditions for their withering away and merging into one common socialist culture (and into one common language) in the period of the victory of Socialism all over the world.

Whoever has failed to understand this peculiar feature and "contradiction" of our transitional period, whoever has failed to understand these dialectics of the historical processes, is doomed for Marxism.

The misfortune of our deviators is that they do not understand and do not wish to understand Marx's dialectics.

That is how the matter stands with the deviation towards Great Russian chauvinism.

It is not difficult to understand that this deviation reflects the striving of the moribund classes of the formerly dominant Great Russian nation to recover their lost privileges.

Hence the danger of Great Russian chauvinism as the chief danger in the Party in the sphere of the national question.

What is the essence of the deviation towards local nationalism?

The essence of the deviation towards local nationalism is the striving to separate and shut oneself up within the shell of one's own nation, is the striving to tone down class antagonisms within one's own nation, is the striving to protect oneself from Great Russian chauvinism by deserting the general stream of socialist construction, is the striving not to see what draws together and unites the laboring masses of the nations of the USSR and to see only what can draw them apart from one another.

The deviation towards local nationalism reflects the discontent of the moribund classes of the formerly oppressed nations with the regime of the proletarian dictatorship, their striving to isolate themselves in their national bourgeois state and to establish their class rule here.

The danger of this deviation lies in that it cultivates bourgeois nationalism, weakens the unity of the working people of the different nations and plays into the hands of the interventionists.

Such is the essence of the deviation towards local nationalism. The Party's task is to wage a determined struggle against this deviation and to ensure the conditions necessary for the international education of the laboring masses of the peoples of the USSR.[12]

This speech was welcomed by the non-Russian delegates (among them by Skrypnyk) and was regarded as a deathblow to the theory

[12] J. Stalin, *Political Report of the Central Committee to the Sixteenth Congress of the CPSU(B)*, pp. 173–78.

of those Russian representatives (for instance, Larin) who had expressed themselves in favor of an international proletarian culture and who were often before accused of pro-Russian bias. They were obviously pleased to hear that Stalin branded Great Russian chauvinism a greater danger than local nationalism.

The question is, of course, how this speech should be interpreted. It is obvious that it had a tactical purpose and was meant to reassure the nationalities of the USSR that they could retain their national forms in culture and literature in spite of the growing centralization and regimentation induced by the Five-Year Plan.[13] But this is not a complete explanation. We gain a better insight into the meaning of Stalin's speech when we turn to Stalin's "The National Question and Leninism; Reply to Comrades Meshkov, Kobal'chuk, and Others," which was written in 1929 but appeared in print for the first time in 1949.[14]

After repeating his belief that only under socialism could a national culture reach its highest development, Stalin emphasized the importance of the October Revolution for all the nations within the Soviet Union. In fact, he introduced a new term: "bourgeois nation." Among these "bourgeois nations" were, in his opinion, the French, the English, the Americans, etc. The Russians, the Ukrainians, the Armenians used to belong to bourgeois nations until the time of the October Revolution. "With the fall of capitalism," wrote Stalin, "such nations must leave the stage of history. Today there are in the world other nations: Soviet nations. The working class and its international Party strengthen and guide these new nations. Such nations are socialist nations." [15]

The idea that the Revolution would tip the balance in the development of a national culture in favor of the socialist element within that nation was already present in Lenin's works.[16] But never before had the line between "bourgeois" and "Soviet" nations been so clearly and decisively drawn as it was now by Stalin.

---

[13] Some Russian comments on Stalin's speech emphasized the socialist rather than the national aspect of Soviet culture. Thus M. Velikovskii wrote: "International accord will be all the greater when the cultures of different nationalities will merge into one common culture, socialist in content as well as in form." (M. Velikovskii, "Zadachi natsional'noi politiki v svete reshenii XVI s"ezda," *Revoliutsiia i natsional'nosti*, Nos. 4–5, 1930, p. 20.)

[14] Stalin, "Natsional'nyi vopros i Leninizm; Otvet tovarishcham Meshkovu, Kobal'chuku i drugim," *Sochineniia*, XI, 333–55.

[15] Stalin, *Sochineniia*, XI, 338.   [16] Lenin, *Sochineniia*, XVII, 139.

That "Soviet" nations are "socialist" is for Stalin an accomplished fact. The October Revolution brought about a qualitative change within a "nation." In 1913 Stalin believed that the nation was "a historical category of a definite epoch, the epoch of rising capitalism," [17] being apparently convinced that nations would tend to disappear with the abolition of capitalism. In 1929 he modified this concept of the nation by declaring that there are now two kinds of nations—"bourgeois" and "Soviet." From this new premise Stalin then drew the startling conclusion which in his speech to the Congress he describes as based on "Marxian dialectics." The nationalism of a "Soviet" nation is no longer a reactionary and bourgeois sentiment, but something new which must be encouraged.

I reject the thesis which would have us believe that with the victory of socialism in one country, in our own, for instance, national languages will apparently wither away, and nations will merge, and instead of several languages there will appear one language. This is impossible. On the contrary, this period [of socialism in one country] creates favorable conditions for the rebirth and flowering of nations. . . . In this connection the Party thought it necessary to help the reborn nations of our country to reach their full stature, to encourage schools, theaters in their own languages, etc. This means that the Party is supporting and will support the development and flowering of national cultures of the peoples of our country. However, the national cultures of the Soviet nations are socialist in their content.[18]

So much for the theory. Stripped of verbiage, this and earlier pronouncements of Stalin on "socialist culture, national in form" need further scrutiny on the following points: (1) What precisely does the content of a culture as distinct from its form mean? (2) Does Stalin's theory refer to 1930 or to the future? In 1930 there was no fully developed socialist culture in the USSR. It was only beginning and was created under strong pressure from the Party against the anti-proletarian forces. (3) What are the criteria for the establishment of socialist content in a culture? (4) If the national cultures were to be encouraged (as long as they were socialist in content), did this apply also to the Russian culture, or did this particular culture enjoy special privileges (of leadership)? (5) Since the concept of a nation and national self-determination was modified and applied as a means to further the advent of socialism

---

[17] Stalin, *Sochineniia*, II, 303.   [18] *Ibid.*, XI, 353.

abroad and the consolidation of the Party rule at home, can the encouragement of national culture, socialist in content, be regarded as a principle, or only as another expedient move in Party policy? Finally, (6) is the "dialectic" approach to the problem of national culture, in which the Party reserves the right to pronounce changes in "historical condition," anything but "double talk," used here to cover up the policy of assimilation and unification?

Partial answers to these and other questions raised by Stalin's theory can be gathered from a study of the relation between this theory and its practice. Before analyzing events in the Ukraine between 1930 and 1933, it is well to remember that although it left many questions unanswered, Stalin's speech at the Sixteenth Congress (1930) generally confirmed the earlier interpretation of Lenin's theory of national culture. It reiterated that Great Russian chauvinism was the major threat to the Soviet system, and that local nationalism, both in politics and culture, was the inevitable reaction; and that further development of national culture was not only desirable but imperative, since this did not imperil in any way the creation of a socialist society, now that all Soviet nations had entered the era of socialism.

The Debacle in the Soviet Ukraine

The CP(B)U was still committed to a policy of Ukrainization. It was becoming exceedingly difficult to implement this to its full extent for two reasons. First, there was still considerable passive opposition to Ukrainization from Russian officialdom and the proletariat in the Ukraine. The daily Soviet Ukrainian press contains in the years 1926 to 1930 scores of complaints to that effect. However, the second difficulty was even greater. It was defined most clearly as far back as 1922 by the Central Committee of the CP(B)U:

The Ukrainian proletarian state is faced with a difficult task. While creating the Ukrainian socialist state, Ukrainian schools, giving equal rights to the Ukrainian and the Russian languages, to the language of the Ukrainian peasantry as well as to the language of the Ukrainian proletariat, the Ukrainian counterrevolution must not be allowed to exploit Ukrainian national socialist statehood for class purposes. The efforts of the Ukrainian counterrevolution to take possession of the cultural life of the country have manifested themselves all the more obviously after the failure of Ukrainian nationalists to establish their rule by force in the Ukraine.[19]

Since 1922 the CP(B)U had experienced some of its worst inner crises (Shumskism, Khvyl'ovism), all of which had their roots in what was branded as "Ukrainian nationalism." To allow, therefore, further Ukrainization might lead to further deviations. On the other hand it was impossible for the Party to change course in such a basic policy. Ukrainization could not be officially repealed, if only to fulfill the promises and to satisfy the demands of the Ukrainian public.

It is significant that the 1922 resolution speaks of the "Ukrainian socialist state" as something sovereign and real. The same language was often used by People's Commissar Skrypnyk, the individual most responsible for the determination with which the policy of Ukrainization was carried out up to 1932.[20]

In 1930, a resolution of the Third Plenum of the Central Bureau of the PS of the Ukraine expressed concern over the "fierce resistance to the Ukrainization on the part of imperialist Russian elements." It was also perturbed over the "catastrophic state of provision of Ukrainian textbooks in the higher institutions of learning," and advised the student organizations to "watch over the advancement of Ukrainian students in scholarly work." [21]

Some indication of the growth of Ukrainization is provided in the statistics supplied by Zatons'kyi [22] dealing with book production: [23]

[19] "Dyrektyvy plenumu TsK KP(b)U v natsional'nomu pytanni," *Istoriia KP(b)U v materialakh i dokumentakh,* pp. 631–32.

[20] See M. Skrypnyk, *Stan ta perspektyvy kul'turnoho budivnytstva na Ukraïni,* pp. 52–53.

[21] See M. Skrypnyk, *Novi linii v natsional'no-kul'turnomu budivnytstvi.*

[22] V. P. Zatons'kyi, *Natsional'no-kul'turne budivnytstvo i borot'ba proty natsional-izmu: dopovid' ta zakliuchne slovo na sichnevii sesiï VUAN.*

[23] *Ibid.,* p. 12. Zatons'kyi omitted the figures for Russian books published in the Ukraine. In order to complete the table the following figures must be added for 1928: Russian titles, 2,216 (38.9 percent); copies, 10,360 (27.2 percent); and for 1932: Russian titles, 982 (13.7 percent); copies, 6,824 (9.9 percent). The final table does not prove any great advances in Ukrainization if we bear in mind that in the year in which Zatons'kyi made this statement (1934) the respective figures were: total copies, 4,711; Ukrainian, 2,750 (58.5 percent); Russian, 1,459 (30.8 percent); national minorities, 502 (10.7 percent) (V. Doroshenko and P. Zlenko, "Vydavnytstva i presa," *Entsyklopediia ukraïnoznavstva,* III, 977). It should also be remembered that Russian books published in Russia are sold in the Ukraine in addition to those published in the Uk.SSR.

	TOTAL		IN UKRAINIAN			IN LANGUAGE OF NATIONAL MINORITIES		
YEAR	Titles	Number of Copies	Titles	Per-centage	Number of Copies	Per-centage	Titles	Per-centage	Number of Copies	Per-centage
1928	5,695	38,336	3,201	56.2	27,018	70.5	278	4.9	958	2.3
1932	7,157	80,895	5,134	71.7	69,870	84.7	1,041	14.6	4,201	5.4

These figures were given by Zatons'kyi who, in 1932, replaced Skrypnyk as the People's Commissar for Education. He noted, too, the national composition of the proletariat in the Ukraine, which was: [24]

YEAR	UKRAINIANS
1926	41 percent
1933	53 percent

These last figures, though possibly unreliable, are more vital for an understanding of the national problem in the Ukraine than those for schools and book production. As late as 1933 the proletariat, this vanguard of the Soviet power, was only 53 percent Ukrainian. Stalin, speaking at the Twelfth Congress of the Party, said that "the class nature of the national question is dependent on the correct relation between the proletariat of the formerly sovereign nation and the peasantry of formerly subjugated nations." [25] In the Ukraine this relationship could not be at its best when half the proletariat was Russian and the Party was conducting a campaign for the destruction of the (Ukrainian) kulaks as a class.

In 1932, the goal of Ukrainization was far from being achieved. If Stalin's dicta on the flowering of national cultures in a socialist state were to be taken literally, then there was no reason why Ukrainization should not have been continued. Writing in 1929, Skrypnyk, in line with the Party's official policy, declared that "we are building a Ukrainian national culture just because we are internationalists." [26]

Skrypnyk's conception of national culture in a socialist state was rooted in his interpretation of Ukrainian history. The revolution in the Ukraine was for him a three-cornered fight between the proletariat (Russian and Ukrainian), the Whites, and the bourgeois nationalists. The defeat of each of the two latter contestants, however, affected the victorious Ukrainian Communists differently.

[24] Zatons'kyi, *Natsional'no-kul'turne*, p. 14.   [25] Stalin, *Sochineniia*, V, 239–40.
[26] M. Skrypnyk, "Bez zaboboniv," *Statti i promovy*, V, 57.

Both the Ukrainian nationalists and the Ukrainian Communists had fought for the national liberation of their country, although they differed sharply on the political, social, and economic order to be established. There were, however, many nationalists and Ukrainian Communists (Borot'bists, Ukapists) who eventually went over to the Bolshevik camp and became loyal citizens of the Soviet Ukraine. They were regarded by Skrypnyk as allies, especially useful in the further development of Ukrainian culture and literature. The national culture represented to him not something charitable donated to the formerly oppressed Ukraine by the beneficent proletarian Revolution, but a hard-won prerogative of the Ukrainian national revival. "There is a tendency," he declared at the Eleventh Congress of the Russian Communist Party in 1922, "to liquidate the statehood of the workers and peasants, which was won by the workers and peasants of this country. The question of the liquidation of the statehood of the workers and peasants of the Ukraine has been raised here by some followers of the 'Change of Landmarks' group." [27]

Skrypnyk's intention was to let the bulk of the Ukrainian intelligentsia be slowly absorbed into the Soviet system. He was convinced that they could contribute a great deal to the development of Ukrainian culture, if properly guided by the Party. On one occasion, therefore, he openly accused the Party of fearing the Ukrainian Borot'bists. In one of his speeches he said:

We have succeeded in winning over to our cause the Ukrainian Communist Party of the Borot'bists, which has merged with us, and its 4,000 members have entered our ranks to become transformed members of our Party in the full sense of the word. Have we accomplished this [transformation]? No! How many of the former Borot'bists are there left? Right now there are only 119 Borot'bists in the [Communist Party of the Bolsheviks of the] Ukraine. [28]

From a report of a speech by P. Liubchenko we also learn that Skrypnyk wanted to attract 1,500 teachers from Western Ukraine to remedy the shortage of teachers in the Soviet Ukraine. [29] While

[27] M. Skrypnyk, "Vid postanov do dila u natsional'nii politytsi," *Statti i promovy,* II, Part 2, pp. 6–7.
[28] M. Skrypnyk, "Za zdiisnennia teoriï na praktytsi," *Statti i promovy,* II, Part 2, p. 12.
[29] *Proletars'ka pravda,* December 14, 1933.

any such move to win over Western Ukrainians to the Communist cause would have been welcomed before 1928, it was afterwards regarded as inviting so many hundreds of foreign spies into the USSR.

In his national policy Skrypnyk therefore followed the theory of Lenin and Stalin with scrupulous consistency, but for that very reason he departed from their practice. If the accepted view of the Party is that imperialist Great Russian chauvinism is a greater danger than local nationalism, argued Skrypnyk, why then is nothing done about it? He himself always had the courage to point out instances of Great Russian chauvinism, not only in single cases or personal remarks by well-known Communists, but in the actual application of the self-determination principles by the CPSU [30] to the non-Russian peoples of the USSR. The records of the Central Committee of the Soviet of the Nationalities contain many a fearless defense by Skrypnyk of the rights of non-Russian republics.[31]

The two most famous instances of Skrypnyk's opposition to the centralist policies of the CPSU occurred in defense of his own country. In the debate on the all-Union law on the use of the land, Skrypnyk spoke against the proposed measure:

The first clause of the Union law on the use of land declares that all land is the property of the USSR. I regard this statement as false in principle, since it contradicts the resolutions of the Party on the relations between the Union and the Union Republics.

The new law concerning the use of land declares that the land is not the property of the Republic, but of the whole Union. If we should pass such a law it would mean that the sovereignty of the individual Republics is limited to the fact that they merely have their own governments, but no territory. I think that all such tendencies must be rejected.[32]

It was also well known that Skrypnyk showed great concern for the Ukrainians living outside the Soviet Ukraine, not only in the West, but also in the East, i.e., not only in Poland, Rumania, and Czechoslovakia, but also in those parts of the RSFSR adjacent to the Ukraine (especially in the provinces of Kursk, Voronizh, and in

[30] CPSU (Communist Party of the Soviet Union), in Russian VKP(b)—Vsesoiuznaia kommunisticheskaia partiia bol'shevikov.
[31] See, e.g., "Do natsional'noï problemy na Zakavkazzi," *Statti i promovy*, II, Part 2.
[32] Quoted in Postyshev's "Radians'ka Ukraïna—nepokhytnyi forpost velykoho SRSR," *Chervonyi shliakh*, No. 8–9, 1933, p. 254.

the Kuban'). On several occasions he demanded that they be included in the Soviet Ukraine.[33]

But above all Skrypnyk was concerned with the practical application of Leninist principles to the national problem. Hence he was skeptical about Stalin's constant theorizing and of his dialectical approach. At the Twelfth Congress of the Russian Communist Party Skrypnyk censured him in the following words:

As far as practice is concerned, why do we tramp about the same piece of ground; in spite of the solution of the national problem in principle, we are in reality powerless. The reason is that all the time we are dithering in the field of one national problem. Some are continually attempting to find a middle course. Each directive concerned with imperialist chauvinism they feel it necessary to counterpose with an opposite directive—about the chauvinism of the formerly stateless nationalities—and so there is always a double bookkeeping. Each mention of Great Russian chauvinism is always to be discounted. . . .

It is true that theoretically comrade Stalin sets side by side both nationalisms: that of the formerly imperialist nation and of the formerly oppressed nationalities. However, does not comrade Stalin stretch this too far? Will not this counterposing of two nationalisms provide a pretext for many of those who are in opposition, trying to excuse their passivity toward the whole national problem? I am very much afraid of this.[34]

It may be that the very fact of his opposition to Stalin, which Skrypnyk must have shown on other occasions as well, made him an enemy of the General Secretary of the Party at a time when the latter's infallibility was beginning to be officially established.

At the end of 1932 a drastic change occurred in the Soviet Ukraine. Peasant opposition to collectivization and discontent among the Ukrainian intelligentsia were seriously threatening the success of the Five-Year Plan. Faced with Stalin's grandiose plans, the Bolshevik theories of "self-determination of nations" and of "efflorescence of national cultures" lost whatever remaining validity they had. These plans called for nothing less than the harnessing of all the Soviet republics in a single effort to industrialize the Soviet Union. Because of her mineral and agricultural resources,

[33] See P. Liubchenko's speech in *Visti*, June 6, 1933.
[34] Quoted in Kosior's "Pidsumky i naiblyzhchi zavdannia natsional'noï polityky na Ukraïni," *Chervonyi shliakh*, No. 8–9, 1933, pp. 235–36.

the Ukraine came to play a crucial part in the building of Stalin's new empire.

The Third All-Ukrainian Party Conference of the CP(B)U convened in July, 1932, primarily in order to investigate the "lagging" and "dislocations" in the harvesting of crops in the Ukraine. The records of this conference [35] show clearly that the Soviet Ukrainian government headed by Chubar, Zatons'kyi, Skrypnyk, and Shlikhter clearly rejected the accusations made by the delegates of the CPSU—Molotov and Kaganovich—that the Party organization in the Ukraine was to blame for the setbacks in agricultural production. They courageously explained to their masters from Moscow that the demands made by the Five-Year Plan on the Ukrainian peasants were too high and that the economic plans designed for the Ukraine were faulty.

Having listened to all that the Ukrainian Communist leaders had to say, Molotov and Kaganovich reiterated that there were to be "no retreats or vacillations" in the fulfillment of the economic plans accepted by the Party.[36] The will of the Party to subdue the starving yet still rebellious peasants of the Ukraine was inflexible. Even more ruthless measures than those used hitherto were ordered by the Party on the eve of the Second Five-Year Plan. The Central Committee of the Party decreed that "political detachments" (politotdely) were to be created in each MTS (Machine and Tractor Station) [37] in order to guarantee "that the collective farms and all their members fulfill their duties to the state unconditionally and on time." [38] As motive for such an action the following reasons were cited:

The anti-Soviet elements in the villages show ferocious resistance to the successful fulfillment of these tasks [of collectivization]. The kulak, economically destroyed but not yet utterly deprived of his influence, former White officers, former priests, their sons, former land agents and sugar producers, former officials, and other anti-Soviet elements from the bourgeois nationalists, including SR and Petliurist in-

[35] See *Pravda*, July 9, 1932; *Visti*, July 11, 1932.
[36] For the resolution on the Third All-Ukrainian Party Conference see *Pravda*, July 15, 1932.
[37] "Ob"edinënnyi plenum TsK i TsKK VKP(b) 7–12 ian. 1933," *VKP(b) v rezoliutsiiakh i resheniiakh s"ezdov, konferentsii i plenumov TsK*, Part II, p. 525.
[38] *Ibid.*, p. 526.

telligentsia, having settled in the villages, are attempting by all means in their power to disorganize the collective farms, to break down the measures which the Party and the government have issued for agriculture, exploiting for these purposes the ignorance of some collective farm members against the interests of collective farming and collective farm peasantry.[39]

This accusation made against the Ukrainian intelligentsia and peasantry was followed by another stern resolution. On January 24, 1933, the Central Committee of the CPSU expressed its dissatisfaction with the CP(B)U since it had failed to fulfill the plan for harvesting the grain. In view of this, it was decided to send to the Ukraine a special plenipotentiary of the Party, Postyshev, whose task it would be to correct the errors of the CP(B)U in the field of grain collection.[40]

This unprecedented step ushered in what is known in Soviet Ukrainian history as the "Postyshev reign of terror." Postyshev did not come to the Ukraine alone. His entourage consisted, as he later admitted,[41] of 1,340 picked Communist organizers from Moscow. Simultaneously with Postyshev, V. Balitskii was sent to the Ukraine and put in charge of all the forces of the NKVD.

It is no wonder, therefore, that the Ukrainians gave Postyshev a chilly reception. This was demonstrated particularly during the meeting of the Kharkov district committee on January 29, 1933. In a speech delivered a few days later Postyshev complained that

it would seem that the resolution of the Central Committee of the CPSU, dated January 24, 1933, ought to have been used by the leadership of the Kharkov Party organization in order to mobilize the Kharkov Bolsheviks for the purpose of correcting the errors which were committed. In reality, comrades, something quite different has occurred. . . . It is a fact that the Plenum of the District Committee which was held on January 29, 1933, lasted only twenty minutes and did not express [an opinion] in any manner upon this most important resolution of the CPSU.[42]

[39] *Ibid.*

[40] This resolution has not been made public. Excerpts from it were quoted by S. Kosior in his speech "Itogi i zadachi KP(b)U v bor'be za podniatie sel'skogo khoziaistva Ukrainy," printed in *Pravda*, February 15, 1933.

[41] Postyshev's speech at the November Plenum of the CP(B)U, "Itogi 1933 sel'skokhoziaistvennogo goda i ocherednye zadachi KP(b)U; Rech tov. P. P. Postysheva na plenume TsK KP(b)U 19 noiabria 1933 goda," *Pravda*, November 24, 1933.

[42] *Proletars'ka pravda*, February 8, 1933.

But, most significantly, instead of busying himself with the Ukrainian economy, Postyshev launched a vigorous campaign of terror against Ukrainian cultural, literary, and learned institutions. As if in accordance with some well-conceived plan of the Kremlin aimed at the destruction of the spiritual and ideological backbone of the Soviet Ukrainian state, Postyshev applied himself with the utmost thoroughness to the annihilation of the cultural achievement of the fifteen years of Soviet regime in the Ukraine.

Two months after Postyshev's arrival the famous Ukrainian Marxist historian Matvii Iavors'kyi, whose role in the Ukraine was often compared with that of M. Pokrovskii in Russia, was arrested and charged with belonging to the counterrevolutionary Ukrainian Military Organization. In January, 1934, Postyshev listed as counterrevolutionists the following Ukrainian historians, members of the VUAMLIN (Vse-Ukraïns'ka Asotsiiatsiia Markso-Lenins'kykh Instytutiv—The All-Ukrainian Association of the Marx and Lenin Institutes): M. Iavors'kyi, A. Richyts'kyi, M. Chechel', V. Mazurenko, V. Holubovych, P. Khrystiuk, V. Lyzanivs'kyi, and eighteen others.[43] M. Ravich Cherkasskii, the historian of the Ukrainian Communist Party, met a similar fate.

At the same time the final blow was delivered to Academician Mykhailo Hrushevs'kyi and his collaborators in the Ukrainian Academy of Sciences. The doyen of Ukrainian historians was deported and died in 1934.

By a special resolution of the CP (B)U, Professor V. Iurynets', the President of the Institute of Philosophy of the VUAMLIN and member of the Ukrainian Academy of Sciences, was branded as a "bourgeois philosopher" [44] and expelled from the Party and the Academy of Sciences.

According to Postyshev himself, "the Academy of Sciences and the University of Kiev have had three hundred members purged." [45]

In his drive to extirpate the original national content from

[43] "Radians'ka Ukraïna na novomu pidnesenni; Politychnyi zvit TsK KP(b)U zïzdovi KP(b)U. Dopovid' tov. P. P. Postysheva 20 sichnia 1934 roku," *Visti*, January 24, 1934.

[44] M. Popov, "Pro natsional'ni ukhyly v lavakh ukraïns'koï partorhanizatsiï i pro zavdannia borot'by z nymy," *Visti*, June 12, 1933.

[45] "Itogi 1933 sel'sko-khoziaistvennogo goda i ocherednye zadachi KP(b)U; Rech tov. P. P. Postysheva na plenume TsK KP(b)U, 19 noiabria 1933 goda," *Pravda*, November 24, 1933.

Ukrainian culture Postyshev sometimes used methods which were unbecoming even to a dictator. Only a few months after his arrival in Kharkov, the monument to the Borot'bist-Communist poet Ellan Blakytnyi was removed during the night after an alleged accident in which it was damaged by a truck. The monument, in spite of assurances given in the press, was never reerected.[46] In order to remove any remaining inhibitions in his moves against Ukrainian culture Postyshev turned against the bulwark of Ukrainization—the People's Commissariat of Education—and its head— Skrypnyk.

This most dramatic struggle between Postyshev and Skrypnyk was really the climax of the long-drawn-out antagonism between Russian and Ukrainian Communism. In spite of the theories of Marxian dialectics, this antagonism could only be resolved in practice by the victory of one over the other. The victor in this case was not so much Postyshev personally as it was the Russian centralist CPSU.

The open campaign against Skrypnyk started in May, 1933. It must have been a shock to the average Ukrainian when he read in the press that this member of the Bolshevik old guard, who only a few months before had been praised as a stalwart of the Party and who was generally regarded as the foremost Ukrainian Communist leader, was suddenly denounced as a most dangerous enemy of the state—that is, as a nationalist. It must also be borne in mind that Skrypnyk was one of the key men in the All-Union Party hierarchy and in 1931, together with three other Ukrainians (Manuil's'kyi, Petrovs'kyi, and Chubar), was a member of the Central Committee of the CPSU which at that time consisted of seventy-one members.

In June, 1933, for the first time, Postyshev openly attacked Skrypnyk during the Plenum of the CP(B)U for abetting and shielding Ukrainian nationalists and "agents of foreign intelligence services" in the cultural and educational institutions. There is no doubt that Skrypnyk defended himself vigorously. Yet how strange, even ominous, must have been the fact that his reply to Postyshev was not printed by a single newspaper.

[46] I am indebted for this detail to H. Kostiuk: "Stalinskaia chistka Ukrainy," manuscript at the Research Program on the USSR, New York.

We learn from a later admission by Postyshev [47] that Skrypnyk charged his accusers with perverting the old principles of the Soviet nationality policy and with suddenly reversing its course by turning against all those who had previously been regarded as the main executors of this policy.

The star of one of the founders of the Ukrainian SSR was rapidly fading. How would this "old guardist," possibly the most popular man among the rank and file in the CP(B)U and among the people, receive this challenge? This was a question to which even the omnipotent Postyshev had no answer.

To beat up the frenzy of public accusations, several other members of the Ukrainian Politbureau sullied Skrypnyk's name in widely publicized speeches.

Panas Liubchenko, speaking before the Congress of the *Komsomol* in June, 1933, charged that Skrypnyk (1) supported Vynnychenko's theory of the Ukrainian nation as being without a bourgeois class; (2) paid too much attention to the national problem and to the national character of the Revolution in the Ukraine; (3) demanded that the Kuban' and Taganrog, which had a predominantly Ukrainian population, be included in the Ukrainian SSR.[48]

The first two charges are without foundation, but the third one, although true, was yet very startling. Skrypnyk's request that those Ukrainian territories to the east of the Soviet Ukrainian boundaries, which according to the statistics were Ukrainian, be incorporated into the Soviet Ukraine was strictly consistent with the theory though not with the practice of the Soviet nationality policy. Skrypnyk's demands were made, as Liubchenko pointed out, so that by such an act an example of the self-determination of the peoples in the USSR might be set for the Ukrainians living in Poland, Rumania, and Czechoslovakia. It seems, however, that while the Soviet leaders were only too eager to conduct propaganda for the reunion of all Ukrainians in the west, they were reluctant to encourage it in the east. In the meantime Ukrainians living in the non-Ukrainian territories of the USSR were condemned to a slow Russification.

[47] "Mobilizuem massy na svoevremennuiu postavku zerna gosudarstvu: Rech tov. P. P. Postysheva na plenume TsK KP(b)U 10 iiunia 1933," *Pravda*, June 22, 1933.
[48] "Pro deiaki pomylky na teoretychnomu fronti: Z promovy tov. P. P. Liubchenka na plenumi TsK LKSMU," *Visti*, July 6, 1933.

On June 30, *Visti* printed two other attacks on Skrypnyk. An article by Khvylia [49] accused Skrypnyk of complicity in the anti-Soviet plot which the Ukrainian linguists were hatching by introducing too many archaic Ukrainian words and artificial scientific terms into the Ukrainian language and thus separating it from Russian. Another, more serious charge was contained in a resolution condemning Skrypnyk. Finally, on July 31, 1933, *Pravda* carried a report of the speech before the Plenum of the Kharkov District on June 14, 1933, by Postyshev, the man who was responsible for the unveiling of all of Skrypnyk's "crimes."

The enemy is trying to hide behind comrade Skrypnyk's back. This shows us once more the serious mistakes [made by] comrade Skrypnyk in his literary work in the field of the national problem and of cultural construction, as well as in his practical work in supervising the educational system in the Ukraine. However, it is in vain that the enemy tries to hide behind comrade Skrypnyk's back. Now comrade Skrypnyk himself is lashing his own back with a birch rod, but not hard enough; we shall have to help him.[50]

On July 8, 1933, *Visti* printed the following obituary:

The Central Committee of the CPSU announces the death of a member of the Central Committe of the CPSU, comrade M. O. Skrypnyk, which came as a result of suicide.
Regarding the act of suicide as an act of faintheartedness particularly unworthy of a member of the Central Committee of the CPSU, the Central Committee deems it necessary to inform members of the Party that comrade Skrypnyk fell victim to the bourgeois-nationalist elements who, disguised as formal members of the Party, gained his confidence and exploited his name for their anti-Soviet, nationalist purposes. Having become entangled with them, comrade Skrypnyk committed a series of political errors and upon realizing this he could not find the courage to overcome them in a Bolshevik manner and thus resorted to the act of suicide.[51]

Another, almost identical obituary notice was from the Central Committee of the CP(B)U. A longer account of Skrypnyk's life and work was published on the last page of the same issue of *Visti*, while *Pravda* wrote that Skrypnpk's death should be a stimulus to the

---

[49] "Stan na movnomu fronti; dopovid' A. Khvyli," *Visti*, June 30, 1933.

[50] Postyshev, "Osobennosti klassovoi bor'by na nyneshnem etape sotsialisticheskogo nastupleniia," *Pravda*, July 3, 1933.

[51] The same obituary notice appeared in *Pravda*, July 8, 1933.

Party "to sear with red-hot iron all chauvinist Petliurian elements under no matter what falsely-national flag they would parade." [52]

The venom which characterized all official reaction to Skrypnyk's death betrayed the vexation which Postyshev and his lieutenants must have felt when their victim instead of surrendering succeeded in escaping them. Strict orders were issued not to allow the public to witness the funeral procession which consisted only of the representatives of the Party and some citizens. Yet although streets were cleared by the NKVD,[53] at the hour of the funeral huge crowds gathered at the windows and on the roofs of houses along Sums'ka street. Silently they bade farewell to the man who had epitomized the Soviet Ukrainian state for over fifteen years.

Skrypnyk's death, which was followed by a severe purge of the Ukrainian Commissariat of Education, did not put an end to the Party's crusade against him. The Central Committee of the CP(B)U passed a resolution, declaring that in some republics of the USSR, especially in the Ukraine, the main danger was the local (Ukrainian) nationalism which comes close to the imperialist interventionists.[54]

The speeches and resolutions of this November Plenum of the CP(B)U provide us with the best evidence of the severity with which Postyshev applied himself to the "reconstruction" of Ukrainian cultural life after Skrypnyk's death. He always linked the nationalist deviations to the general Five-Year Plan efforts in the Ukraine:

It is just these errors and deviations committed by the CP(B)U in the realization of the national policy of the Party which have been one of the main causes for breakdowns in the agricultural production of the Ukraine in 1931–32.[55]

The resolutions consisted of a series of directives brutally formulated. Even the usual honeyed words about the growth of Ukrai-

52 "N. A. Skrypnik," *Pravda*, July 8, 1933.

53 I am indebted for this information to H. Kostiuk.

54 "Rezoliutsiï obiednanoho plenumu TsK i TsKK KP(b)U," *Chervonyi shliakh*, No. 8–9, 1933, pp. 267–68.

55 P. Postyshev, "Radians'ka Ukraïna—nepokhytnyi vorpost velykoho SRSR," *Chervonyi shliakh*, No. 8–9, 1933, p. 245. For the translation of a part of the resolutions passed by the November Plenum see Appendix H.

nian proletarian literature were missing on this occasion. This was no longer a guiding directive, but a military command demanding complete subordination.

An article in the Party organ, *Komunist,* defined Skrypnyk's basic errors thus:

(1) He exaggerated the importance of the national problem, assigning to it an independent role and denying its dependence on the dictatorship of the proletariat.

(2) He substituted the struggle against imperialist chauvinism for the struggle against two fronts in the realization of the nationality policy.

(3) He regarded cultural construction as limited only by the national development.

(4) He was also responsible for the introduction of forced Ukrainization in schools.

(5) His attitude was harmfully nationalist on the questions of terminology and orthography which were leading to a break between the Ukrainian toiling masses and the language and culture of the toiling masses of Russia.[56]

Similar charges were repeated by nearly all the prominent Ukrainian Communists, and Kosior made a special point of reminding his listeners that "the nationalist errors of Skrypnyk follow the line which wishes to tear Ukrainian culture away from the Russian proletarian culture"; [57] therefore, according to Kosior, "the foremost and fundamental task" for Ukrainian culture and literature is "bringing up the masses in an international spirit and consolidating the fighting revolutionary unity of the peoples of the USSR, the shield of the proletarian world revolution." [58]

This is a marked departure from previous Communist proclamations on the role of national culture, which incidentally is hardly mentioned here. It has become a tool in the hands of the Party in the Ukraine just as it has in Russia. But there was a very great difference between the cultural and literary policies of the Party in

[56] *Komunist,* No. 172, 1933.

[57] "Za rishuche perevedennia lenins'koï natsional'noï polityky: Za bilshovyts'ku borot'bu proty natsionalistychnykh ukhyliv. Vystup tov. S. V. Kosiora na zborakh aktyvu Kharkivs'koï partorhanizatsiï 9 lypnia 1933 roku," *Visti,* July 23, 1933.

[58] S. Kosior, "Pidsumky i naiblyzhchi zavdannia natsional'noï polityky na Ukraïni," *Chervonyi shliakh,* No. 8–9, 1933, p. 224.

Russia and in the Ukraine at that time. While Russian literature and culture never experienced a purge like Postyshev's and were never branded outright as counterrevolutionary, in the Ukraine the whole stratum of the Ukrainian Communist intelligentsia together with many writers who had put their faith in Skrypnyk were suddenly declared to be enemies and traitors. Those who were left were told to work for the cause of Russian-Ukrainian solidarity. It is interesting to note that while at first Skrypnyk was represented by his henchmen as merely a screen for the nationalists, he was later described as the real culprit. Postyshev took great pains to blacken his memory. He wrote:

> The nationalist deviation headed by Skrypnyk was a direct continuation of Shums'kyi's deviation in 1927. Both Shumskism and Skrypnyk's deviation were nurtured by the same roots and sap. Both worked for the separation of the Ukraine from the Soviet Union, for the imperialist enslavement of Ukrainian workers and peasants. Both strove to break away from Moscow—the center of the world proletarian revolution.
>
> But the point is that Shums'kyi was uncovered by the Central Committee of the CP(B)U in 1926–27 and Shumskism was annihilated by the CP(B)U. Skrypnyk's deviation, on the other hand, was unnoticed by the CP(B)U—and this also happened at the moment of the sharpest class struggle.
>
> Whereas at the June plenum I spoke of Skrypnyk as merely a screen for the nationalist elements, I can say now, after digging a little through his archives, that Skrypnyk was not a screen but a direct tool, even if an unconscious one, of these nationalist elements.
>
> The last year was the year of the rout of the nationalist counterrevolution, the discovery and rout of the nationalist deviation with Skrypnyk at its head, and of the great unfolding of the efforts to build up Soviet Ukrainian culture.[59]

What did Stalin have to say about events in the Ukraine? How was he to explain that, in spite of his pronouncement in 1930 (that it was the imperialist chauvinism which presented the greatest danger to the Soviet state), the Party had spent the last three years annihilating what was branded as "Ukrainian nationalism"? Which of the deviations was more serious in 1934?

In his speech during the Seventeenth Congress of the Party

---

[59] "Sovetskaia Ukraina na novom pad"ëme; Politicheskii otchët TsK KP(b)U na XII s"ezde KP(b)U. Doklad tov. P. P. Postysheva," *Pravda,* January 24, 1934.

(January, 1934) Stalin gave this analysis of the recent situation in the national problem:

Here, too, in the sphere of the national problem as in other questions, in some sections of the Party there is a confusion of views which represents a certain danger. I have spoken of the tenacity of the survivals of capitalism. It is necessary to note that the survivals of capitalism in the consciousness of men remain more alive in the field of the national problem than in any other field. They are more tenacious since they can well masquerade in national costume. Many think that the fall of Skrypnyk is a solitary instance, an exception to the rule. This is not true. The fall of Skrypnyk and his group in the Ukraine is not an exception. Such "dislocations" can be observed among individual comrades in other national republics.

What is deviation toward nationalism—it matters not whether we speak about a deviation in the direction of Great Russian nationalism or of local nationalism? The deviation toward nationalism is an adaptation of the internationalist policy of the working class to the nationalist policy of the bourgeoisie. The deviation toward nationalism reflects the attempts of a particular national bourgeoisie to undermine the Soviet system and to reestablish capitalism. The origin of both deviations as you see is the same. It is a departure from Leninist internationalism. If you want to keep both deviations under fire it is necessary, first of all, to mark this source, those who depart from internationalism, regardless of whether the deviations are toward local nationalism or toward Great Russian nationalism.

There is some argument as to which deviation represents the major danger—the deviation to Great Russian nationalism or the one toward local nationalism. Under present conditions this is a formal and therefore pointless controversy.

Until quite recently the deviation toward Ukrainian nationalism in the Ukraine did not represent the major danger; however, when we ceased to fight it and allowed it to grow to such an extent that it merged with the interventionists, this deviation became the major danger.[60]

The facts fail to support this analysis by Stalin. The fight against Ukrainian nationalism never did cease and after the defeat of Shums'kyi it continued to claim hundreds of victims every year. The accusation of a merger with the interventionists, based on the uncovering of the alleged UVO (Ukraïns'ka Viis'kova Orhaniza-

    [60] "Semnadsiatyi s"ezd VKP(b)," *VKP(b) v rezoliutsiiakh i resheniiakh s"ezdov, konferentsii i plenumov TsK,* Part II, pp. 567–68.

tsiia—Ukrainian Military Organization) and such traitors and spies as Professor Iavors'kyi or Andrii Richyts'kyi, was in all probability sheer fabrication. Later similar accusations of treason and espionage against Russian Communist leaders (in 1934, 1937, and 1938) and the absence of any evidence to link the purged Ukrainian Communists with Western powers seem to confirm the impression that these charges were brought against Skrypnyk and others only in order to discredit them in the eyes of the people and to justify the use of terror. On the other hand, there are clear indications that Hitler's rise to power in 1933 caused great concern to the Soviet leaders. The repressions in the Ukraine were also designed to strengthen the defenses of the Soviet Union against possible German expansion.

Finally, one more oblique explanation of Stalin's nationality policy may be submitted here. It is based on a deduction from his earlier tactics. In 1926–27, when Stalin fought the "Left Opposition" of Trotsky, Zinov'ev, and Kamenev, he opposed them because of their insistence on a speedier development of industry and a swifter pace for the proposed collectivization of agriculture. Yet after defeating the "Left Opposition," Stalin assumed their position both in theory and practice throughout the whole of the First Five-Year Plan. Later, after destroying the "Right Opposition" of Rykov, Tomskii, and Bukharin, Stalin also accepted many of their tenets. Similarly in the national problem Stalin seems to have followed a line of saying one thing and doing another, of denouncing those who regarded local nationalism as the major danger but in fact concentrating on destroying whatever went by that name while talking about the danger of Great Russian chauvinism. The counterposing of two nationalisms was, as Skrypnyk rightly suspected, merely a subterfuge for the actual policy. Theory and ideology, that is, were used as means to a political end—that of the centralization in Moscow of absolute power over the whole USSR. This was admitted to some extent by Stalin in his speech before the Seventeenth Congress when he referred to the "pointless controversy" as to which of the two nationalisms constituted the major danger. He asked the Party to destroy the kind of nationalism which was just then raising its head. Here the record of the Party's actions speaks for itself. At no time had it ordered mass purges, deportations, or trials for deviation toward Great Russian chauvinism.

Socialist in Content, National in Form—Final Version

Under the conditions which developed in the Ukraine in 1932 and 1933, what were the prospects for the creation of a specifically Ukrainian theory of proletarian culture and literature? Could the Ukrainian writers and critics participate in the construction of the new theory, so vital to all Soviet writers and in particular to the Ukrainian whose works were to be "socialist in content and national in form"?

As far back as 1930 Skrypnyk had been aware of the importance of this problem, long before it was publicly heralded on April 23, 1932:

Now it is not enough to say that we want to work in an immediate relation to the construction of Ukrainian culture, national in form and material and socialist in content, that we wish to serve socialism. . . . This is not enough. That is the past phase of historical development. Now we must imagine in which way these tasks which the new period of our cultural and economic life puts before us may be fulfilled.[61]

Scores of authors writing in 1930–33 showed great eagerness to clarify and develop a theory of culture national in form and socialist in content. Some Ukrainian critics were attracted to the literary theory worked out by RAPP. One of them, Koriak, wrote that "the application of dialectical materialism is based on a consistent materialist recreation of life not as it is (in the spirit of naive naturalism) and not as it should be (romanticism), but as it is becoming before our eyes—during the period of reconstruction. Collectivism and anti-individualism, Party spirit and class truth, activism and an endeavor directed to the fulfillment of the tasks of the workers' party and class—these are the basic conditions of the application of dialectical materialism to artistic creation."[62] This conception comes close to the Rappist ideal of the "living man." However, the

[61] M. Skrypnyk, *Pereznaky tvorchoho terenu*, p. 92.
[62] V. Koriak, "Khudozhnia literatura na suchasnomu etapi sotsiialistychnoho budivnytstva," *Chervonyi shliakh*, No. 6, 1931, pp. 86–87.

1932 resolution on literature put an end to RAPP and its theory.
The quest for the Marxian theory of literature in the Ukraine in
these years was thus described by I. Lakyza:

> What do we have in Ukrainian Marxian literary scholarship? We
> have a great deal of literary practice, but very little theory. This is most
> striking. Whereas in the RSFSR all literary scholarship was conducted
> on the basis of theory . . . we can say that in the Ukraine there reigned
> and still reigns an indifference to theoretical and methodological prob-
> lems.
> We do not take the trouble for instance to pull apart a literary
> faction which is hostile to us. Thus, jesting aside, it was the GPU,
> through the arrest and trial of the Union for the Liberation of the
> Ukraine, which has awakened a deeper interest in the study of Iefre-
> mov's teachings.[63]

Purged as it was of the literary theories of the Neoclassicists,
Khvyl'ovyi, the Futurists, and the Symbolists, Soviet Ukrainian
literature was a vacuum which could not be filled by clichés about
socialist literature. As in all other provinces of Soviet life, the Party
leaders also became supreme arbiters of literary theory and Moscow
became its sole source. Theirs was not only the task of channeling
all literary life into a single stream and of herding all writers into
one organization directly under the control of the Party, but also of
playing the role of literary pundits. Pronouncements on literature
and on socialist culture by Stalin and Kaganovich were now regarded in the same way as those of Plekhanov and Lenin were before 1930, that is, as revelations of supreme wisdom.

A true inkling of what Stalin's attitude was to the national literatures of the USSR and of his conception of literature as a service to
the state may be gleaned from his letter to the Russian writer
Demian Bednyi, written on December 12, 1930, but published for
the first time in 1951:

> The whole world now acknowledges that the center of the revo-
> lutionary movement has transferred itself from Western Europe to
> Russia. The revolutionaries of all lands look with hope to the USSR
> as to the hearth of the struggle for liberation of the workers of the
> whole world, acknowledging it as their only home. The revolutionary
> workers of all countries unanimously applaud the Soviet working class
> and above all the *Russian* working class, the vanguard of the Soviet

---

[63] I. Lakyza, "Na literaturnomu fronti," *Literaturnyi arkhiv*, III (1931), 7.

workers, as its recognized leader carrying out the most revolutionary and active policy ever dreamt of by the proletarians of other countries. The leaders of the revolutionary workers of all lands eagerly study the instructive history of the working class in Russia, its past, Russian history, knowing that apart from the reactionary Russia there existed also a revolutionary Russia, the Russia of the Radishchevs and the Chernyshevskiis, the Zheliabovs, the Ulianovs, the Khalturins, and Alekseevs. All this fills (it cannot do otherwise) the hearts of the Russian workers with a feeling of revolutionary national pride, which can move mountains and perform miracles.

And you? Instead of realizing this grand development in the history of the revolution and raising the bard of the leading proletariat to the height of his powers, you have gone off somewhere into a hollow and have lost yourself in dull quotations from the works of Karamzin and no less boring aphorisms from "Domostroi," and have begun to proclaim to the whole world that Russia in the past represented a vessel of meanness and abomination, that contemporary Russia represents a continuous recess, that laziness and a desire to "sit behind the stove" is an almost characteristic feature of all Russians, and that also includes the Russian workers who, having accomplished the October Revolution, have, of course, not ceased to be Russians.

And this is what you call Bolshevik criticism. No, esteemed comrade Bedny, this is not Bolshevik criticism; it is a slander against our nation, the dethronement of the USSR, the dethronement of the proletariat of the USSR, the dethronement of the Russian proletariat.

And after all this you want the Central Committee to remain silent! What are you taking the Central Committee for? [64]

One could hardly find a better example of deviation toward Great Russian chauvinism. The national pride in the Russian proletariat, the vanguard of all other Soviet workers, and in the Russian culture and literature here reaches truly messianic proportions. On the other hand, scorn for the writers who even temporarily cannot share his vision is equally profound. This, then, was the outlook on literature and the service he believed it ought to render to the Russian proletariat of the man who, after 1930, became the dictator of the Soviet Union. It could hardly be regarded as a good augury for the non-Russian nationalities and their literatures.

[64] J. Stalin, "Tov. Demianu Bednomu," *Sochineniia*, XIII, 24–26.

[IX]

THE FORMATION OF THE

WRITERS' UNION

APRIL, 1932-AUGUST, 1934

The resolution of the Party issued on April 23, 1932, which in effect dissolved all literary organizations in the USSR, came as a surprise to most Soviet writers. Some of them tried to see in it merely the termination of the dictatorship of RAPP and were therefore inclined to regard it as a "magna charta" of literary liberties. To others it must have been plain that this resolution obliterated for ever the possibility of the free expression of views which up till this time had, to a certain extent, been voiced through literary organizations. It is important to bear in mind that *Pravda,* in Iudin's article which appeared the day before the resolution, pointed out, as one of RAPP's errors, the fact that it was not abreast with the developments. RAPP, it charged, was still concerned with proletarian literature, while the time had come to talk about socialist literature. Soviet literature was entering a new era in which some of the former confirmed fellow travelers were emerging as socialist writers.[1]

For Ukrainian literature the April resolution was significant chiefly because it abolished the autonomy of Ukrainian literary organizations. The Ukrainian writers lost more than their Russian colleagues, since they were henceforth entirely dependent on the Writers' Union, an organization in which they could never hope to exercise a decisive influence. The decision to create a central Union of Soviet Writers therefore reduced non-Russian writers to

---

[1] P. Iudin, "Protiv izvrashchenii Leninskogo ucheniia o kul'turnoi revoliutsii," *Pravda,* April 23, 1932.

the role of a minority in this new republic of letters, which soon proved to be yet another facet of the Muscovite regime.

The nature of this new move by the Party became clear only a few years later. In 1932, in spite of the shock which it produced, the resolution was received with mixed feelings. The work of the Organizational Committee [2] which was set up in order to prepare the way for the formation of the Union of Soviet Writers was partly responsible for the false hopes that RAPP's liquidation might bring a brighter future.

The Orgkomitet Begins Its Work

The selection of members for the Russian Orgkomitet must have been regarded at the time as a conciliatory gesture toward fellow travelers and nonproletarian writers. In the Russian Orgkomitet such well-known fellow travelers as Vsevolod Ivanov, Leonov, Tikhonov, Fedin, and Slonimskii sat side by side with the former Rappists Kirpotin, Bezymenskii, Fadeev, and Chumandrin, all happy under the President, Gronskii, editor of *Izvestiia*.

In the Ukraine, however, the adjustment between proletarian and nonproletarian writers was far less of a compromise. The following were elected to the Ukrainian Orgkomitet: Kulyk (Chairman), Bazhan, Fefer, Gorodskoi, Holovko, Hrudyna, Irchan, Khvyl'ovyi, Korniichuk, Kushnarëv, Kyrylenko, Le, Liubchenko, Mykytenko, Panch, Shchupak, Shishov, Semenko, Tereshchenko, Tychyna, Vyshnia.[3] Of these, seven (Bazhan, Khvyl'ovyi, Liubchenko, Panch, Semenko, Tychyna, Vyshnia) might be classed as "resisters," while all the others belonged to the category of "cooperators." Two of them were relatively minor Russian writers living in the Ukraine (Gorodskoi, Shishov), and two (Fefer, Kushnarëv) were Jewish representatives. The relative strength of those writers loyal to the Party was, therefore, much greater than that of its opponents. Key positions in the Orgkomitet were given to VUSPP.

[2] This body will be designated from now on by the Russian abbreviation Orgkomitet.

[3] "Perestroika literaturnykh organizatsii," *Literaturnaia gazeta*, June 5, 1932. Through a misprint Khvyl'ovyi's name appears in this article as Shtilevoi. For the Ukrainian record of the composition of the Orgkomitet see "Khronika; literaturne zhyttia," *Chervonyi shliakh*, No. 5–6, pp. 144–46.

The task which the Ukrainian Orgkomitet faced was a difficult one. It had to prepare for the All-Ukrainian Congress of Writers and also make a list of candidates to be admitted into the Writers' Union. The fact that these duties had to be performed in the name of the Central Orgkomitet in Moscow, of which the Ukrainian committee was a branch, at a time of dreadful purges of Ukrainian culture and of the Ukrainian Commissariat of Education, added considerably to the difficulties. There was uncertainty as to the final form which the Party's practice in the field of national culture and literature would assume. At the end of 1932, despite widespread discussion of the theoretical aspects of national culture, this uncertainty greatly increased when accusations were leveled against Skrypnyk, who until then was regarded as the loyal executor of the Party line.

We gain a revealing intimation of what was to come from the Stenographic Report of the First Plenum of the Orgkomitet, held in Moscow from October 29 to November 3, 1932. In his opening address Gronskii once more stated the main reason for the dissolution of RAPP:

If we want to be Bolsheviks, the pupils of Marx, Lenin, and Stalin, we should turn toward the old intelligentsia, toward the old writers, remembering that the old intelligentsia, the old writers, have very great culture, wide, indeed, very wide, experience, of which we, the young class, have little and which we, as a young victorious class, should value.

And here is RAPP, a special organization of proletarian writers, which was created at a certain stage of the development of the Revolution in order to lead the proletarian writers, to fortify the position of the working class, and to strengthen the position of proletarian literature in our country's literature as a whole—this organization, representing the Party and directing literature in the name of the Party, did not grasp the changed situation, has failed to face the writers who are returning to the side of the Soviet government, has failed to recognize a turning point in literature. Therein lies the basic and chief error of RAPP, and of RAPP's leadership.[4]

In view of this it might be assumed that the Party's demand to attract and utilize the old intelligentsia and old writers would now be fulfilled all over the Union, not only in Russia. Yet here the results of the 1932 resolution proved to be different in Russia and

4 *Sovetskaia literatura na novom etape; Stenogramma pervogo plenuma orgkomiteta soiuza sovetskikh pisatelei*, p. 7.

in the Ukraine. While the old Russian intelligentsia and writers were being reinstated (at the First Plenum were present Andrei Belyi, Prishvin, Panteleimon Romanov, and Slonimskii), Ukrainian literature was deprived of its old cadres, who were declared to be bourgeois nationalists and counterrevolutionaries. Only one of the Neoclassicists (Maksym Ryl's'kyi) and very few of the fellow travelers were admitted at that time to the Writers' Union, and Pavlo Tychyna gave his wholehearted support to the Party only in 1933 with the publication of his poem *Partiia Vede* (The Party Leads). An open accusation was leveled at Skrypnyk for "interpreting the resolution of the Central Committee [of 1932] as an open-door policy to the nationalist writers." [5]

The dilemma which this policy of discrimination caused in the Ukraine has been described by Kulyk, who headed the Ukrainian delegation to the First Plenum:

> In the Ukraine, the problem of mastering the literary and cultural heritage of the past is acute and difficult. One must bear in mind that for a long time Ukrainian bourgeois nationalist groups and proletarian cultural and literary workers, led by the Communist Party, fought very hard battles to decide the mastery of cultural acquisitions of other classes. This problem, comrades, consists of three fundamental questions: firstly, the mastering of the historical heritage of the Ukraine. If we take the bourgeois group of Neoclassicists, whom I have already mentioned: they were, in fact, united in contrasting the "glorious past," as it were, the heroic past of the Ukraine, with our present epoch, by ignoring the present, rejecting the dictatorship of the proletariat, and contrasting it with that very same "independent" Hetman Ukraine, etc. . . .
>
> On the other hand, the problem of mastering the cultural and literary heritage of bourgeois Europe also became in the Ukraine a center of fierce and heated controversies, now long since resolved, with the organization VAPLITE at one time contrasting this bourgeois Europe with the USSR and Red Moscow. . . .
>
> The problem of liberating Ukrainian culture and literature from provincial narrowness has been our task. We approached it from a different angle [than VAPLITE]; we attempted to approach it critically and to transform in the Marxian way what is best in bourgeois culture; finally we approached it from the viewpoint of acquiring all of most value and significance produced by other national units of the Soviet Union. This is the third task contained in the problem of mastering

[5] D. Halushko, "Lytsari zrady," *Chervonyi shliakh,* No. 2–3, 1934, p. 194.

the heritage and enriching and widening the horizon of Ukrainian literature and culture.

We can now say that Ukrainian literature is no longer provincial and limited as it was in the past by the tsarist yoke and as Ukrainian bourgeois chauvinists attempted to preserve it. We can proudly say that Ukrainian literature takes one of the most honorable places on the general background of Soviet literatures, although this, comrades, must not allow us to rest on our laurels and be content. It is imperative to resolve the problem of permanent contact between the republican literatures, of the interchange of experience, of brigades of writers, of translation of Ukrainian works into other languages of the Soviet Union, of the translation of Russian, Tatar, Armenian, Georgian, Belorussian, and other literatures of the Soviet Union into Ukrainian.[6]

Thus while the national and European heritage of Russian literature was readmitted into Soviet socialist literature, national and European traditions of Ukrainian literature were barred as chauvinist. Instead of cultivating and utilizing the "bourgeois Ukrainian past," Ukrainian writers were thus directed either to the Russian heritage, which was tolerated and in fact admired, or to the little developed literatures of the other nationalities of the USSR.

This meant a most radical change in literary development, a change brought about not by the Communist government in Kharkov but by the All-Union Communist Party. It amounted to making Soviet Ukrainian literature and the literatures of other non-Russian nationalities subservient not only to the Russian literature of the past but also to that of the present, since Soviet Russian writers and critics had now become the acknowledged models for other nationalities.

This was the real meaning of Kulyk's demand for closer ties between the Ukrainian and Russian literatures. The Orgkomitet wasted no time in creating suitable channels for the flow of "interchange of experience and literary brigades" of which Kulyk spoke. In 1932 a special "commission for national literatures" was created, and another committee devoted its efforts to the preparation of translations.[7] We shall return to their activities later in this chapter.

As for the First Plenum of the Orgkomitet, it left no doubt in the minds of the participants as to the role which the literatures of the non-Russian republics were to assume from then on. Perhaps

[6] *Sovetskaia literatura na novom etape*, pp. 62–63.
[7] "U pisatelei," *Literaturnaia gazeta*, December 23, 1932.

this idea was expressed most clearly in the closing address by Gronskii. "At the Plenum," he said, "we have strengthened in the best possible way the brotherly union of the literature of the peoples of the USSR. The literatures of the different peoples of the USSR were at the Plenum placed in the same situation—with equal rights. The comrades who spoke here have quite rightly rejected the term 'national literature.' In place of this term the Plenum has put forward a more correct concept: 'the literature of the peoples of the Soviet Union.' " [8]

Thus even terminology was changed, but in this case it was not a mere formality. The idea behind the change from "the national literatures" to "the literature of the peoples of the Soviet Union" was in line with the general policy of the Party to eradicate the cultural traditions of the non-Russian nationalities and to force them to accept what was claimed to be a socialist and Soviet culture. The only roots which this new, superimposed culture could claim, since the roots of other national cultures were pronounced rotten, were the roots of the Russian culture and literature which were never subjected to nationalist purges and in fact were never regarded as being on the same level as other national cultures and literatures.

In the interminable discussions of the First Plenum the future development of national literatures was treated entirely in terms of the relations of these literatures to Russian literature. Time after time national delegates rose to stress the need for closer ties and for exchange of experience. Little differentiation was made between various national literatures; Ukrainian, Belorussian, Georgian, and Kirghiz literatures were all, whatever their level, regarded as achieving an unprecedented flowering during the Soviet era, and having got rid of their nationalist past, they were ready to orient themselves to Moscow. They could only complain that Moscow had not yet become acquainted with their literatures, but they hoped that all national cleavages and dispersions belonged to the past and that from now on unity and harmony would prevail.

In 1932 this unity was not yet an accomplished fact and during the next two years laborious efforts were made to achieve it. The

[8] *Sovetskaia literatura na novom etape*, p. 257.

All-Union Orgkomitet to whom this task was entrusted encountered serious difficulties in its organizational work in the non-Russian republics. The absence of complete records of its work, which was not carried on as in the old days through large congresses or the press, but through well-established permanent agencies and committees, makes it impossible to trace this interesting final phase of the struggle against the Party controls. We can only hope to establish on the basis of periodic press reports of the plena and conferences of the Orgkomitet the main course of the Party policy and some of the obstacles it encountered.

During the First Plenum of the Ukrainian Orgkomitet (January 23–26, 1933) its chairman, Kulyk, emphasized the great forward strides which Ukrainian literature had made under the guidance of the Party,[9] but deplored the "clannishness" (*hrupivshchyna*) of Ukrainian writers.[10] A month later, at the Second Plenum of the All-Union Orgkomitet (February 12–19, 1933), the Ukraine was declared to be at the same stage, in the liquidation of this "clannishness," as Russia.[11] In other non-Russian republics (Belorussia, Georgia, Azerbaidzhan) this danger still existed.[12] The determination with which "clannishness" was being eradicated, even after literary organizations had ceased to exist, shows that the Party's aim was complete subordination to it as the goal for the projected Union of Soviet Writers. "Clannishness," regarded as an inheritance from RAPP, was therefore to the Party a remnant of past evil practices; its liquidation, like the liquidation of RAPP, was imperative. There is no doubt that whatever independent thinking upon the future Writers' Union or upon relations between the republican literatures might have been done, it was very likely classed as "clannishness," and therefore condemned.

The Fourth Plenum of the Ukrainian Orgkomitet, held in January, 1933, was mainly devoted to an analysis of "clannishness." The word itself was used by the Committee chairman, Kulyk, as a

9 "Razvernutym frontom," *Literaturnaia gazeta*, February 11, 1933.
10 "Pidsumky pershoho plenumu orgkomitetu spilky radians'kykh pys'mennykiv SRSR ta zavdannia radyans'koï literatury USSR; z dopovidi tov. Kulyka," *Visti*, January 26, 1933.
11 "Literatura i iskusstvo; vtoroi plenum orgkomiteta SSP SSSR," *Novyi mir*, No. 2, 1933, pp. 248–67.
12 *Ibid.*, p. 257.

club with which to smite those writers who had not yet reached the required level of loyalty to the Party. Kulyk also made a concerted effort to explain to them what was wanted:

Our Party continually gives us forecasts on the basis of Marxism-Leninism; otherwise it would not be able to lead us politically, and we would not be able to take our full part in socialist construction. Let us take the following example: Let us consider the collective farms, the harvest, the fight against the kulak, and the combination of all these elements. . . . A writer shows that collections of grain are taking place under conditions of tense class struggle, struggle against the kulaks. But this struggle has as its aim not simply the destruction of the kulaks, but the substitution for the small property economy which had prevailed before, of a new basis—large socialist collective agricultural undertakings. Our writers often fail to combine these two ideas.[13]

An even greater obstacle to the achievement of unanimity among the Soviet writers, however, was the unwillingness of some of them to accept the Orgkomitet's demands for complete subordination to the Party. Some were obviously reluctant to accept the generous invitation of the Party, so finely declaimed at the First Plenum in Moscow, to serve under a unified command. The question of selection and preparation of candidates to the Union was considerably protracted.

This prompted Gronskii to deliver a clear ultimatum to those who were still vacillating:

As you know we must call the Congress of Soviet Writers in the middle of May. Before then the Union must be formed. We have in general accepted the Constitution, and it will be approved by the Presidium. In the immediate future we shall send our instructions to all as to who can be accepted as a member of the Union of Soviet Writers. This work must be carried out soon, so that the greater part is completed by March or the beginning of April, and the Congress of Soviet Writers may thus convene in May.

Writers who uphold the platform of the Soviet government and who wish to participate in social construction must be accepted into the Union. If anyone does not yet want to come over to the platform of the Soviet authority, let him stay outside the Union of Soviet Writers. We have waited patiently for these men for several months. But these people seem to be hopeless—let them decide their own destiny. We must not accept such people into the Union of Soviet Writers. We are

13 I. Kulyk, "Pidsumky i perspektyvy," *Chervonyi shliakh,* No. 4, 1933, p. 99.

patiently guiding the Army of Literature, but do not imagine that we shall pat the anti-Soviet or counterrevolutionary elements on the head. No, we shall fight them, shall combat them in the Bolshevik manner.[14]

This threat reechoed in the Ukraine. In an article "For a Bolshevik Vigilance," [15] Kulyk admitted that "the errors committed by the Ukrainian Party organization in the work in the villages could not but be reflected in the situation on the cultural front, in particular in literature." He also severely scolded Os'machka, a former member of Lanka, for writing a letter to the Orgkomitet in which he declared that he could not write freely and claimed in the name of Ukrainian peasantry the right to make a protest against Party controls. Another sharp rebuke was given to Valeriian Polishchuk who in one of his short stories had committed the unforgivable sin of describing the Kuban' and the Northern Caucasus as being part of the Ukraine.[16]

The Suicide of Mykola Khvyl'ovyi

From the very beginning of the Orgkomitet's existence, Khvyl'ovyi took an active part in its work. Himself a member of the Ukrainian Orgkomitet, he was elected (together with Kulyk) to the wider presidium of the First Plenum of the All-Union Orgkomitet which was held in Moscow in 1932. This fact alone shows that his loyalty to the cause of proletarian literature must have been above suspicion at that time. At the beginning of 1933 some of Khvyl'ovyi's short stories dealing with the work of reconstruction were published in *Visti*.[17]

In April, 1933, Khvyl'ovyi, accompanied by Arkadii Liubchenko, made a trip to the village of Hamaliïvka to learn, as he himself put it, about "the new, cardinal phase of socialist construction—famine." [18] The details of this visit have been preserved in Liubchenko's moving account written in 1943. "On the way," writes Liubchenko, "we talked a good deal about the shameful system of

[14] "Literatura i iskusstvo; vtoroi plenum orgkomiteta SSP SSSR," *Novyi mir*, No. 2, 1933, p. 260.

[15] I. Kulik, "Za bolshevistskuiu bditel'nost'." *Literaturnaia gazeta*, April 23, 1933.

[16] *Ibid.*

[17] "Bryhadyr shostoï," *Visti*, January 9, 1933; "Pro liubov," *Visti*, January 17, 1933; "Iz zhyttiepysu popeliastoï korovy," *Visti*, April 15, 1933.

[18] A. Liubchenko, "Ioho taiemnytsia," *Nashi dni*, No. 5, May, 1943.

state security, which makes one half of the population watch over the other half. We talked about the 'Russian dungeon of peoples,' about the stuffy Muscovite interior which was now being covered up with a red *sarafan* though of the same Riazan'-Tambov make. We talked about the blind alley into which the Revolution has entered, about the bourgeois mentality and the complete, pathological degeneration of the leading Communist stratum. How completely incapable it was of realizing the basic needs of social justice and universal progress! We talked about the absolute inevitability of the new 'Thermidor'; also about the intimidated and derided Ukrainian people with a talented but half-decimated, half-bewildered, and wholly disunited intelligentsia."

There is every reason to believe that while Khvyl'ovyi was outwardly loyal to the Party, he was yet engaged in what might be called his last and hopeless venture, the defense of the rights of Ukrainian writers. The final story of this last flicker of independence in the ideology of Communist Ukrainian literature can only be told when the records of the Orgkomitet and the testimony of the participants and eyewitnesses will be made available to the scholar and the historian. We know, however, that at the Second Plenum of the Orgkomitet (February, 1933) one of the most crucial issues was which writers should be accepted into the Union of Soviet Writers. Gronskii's speech [19] made it plain that in view of the procrastination of the fellow travelers in joining the proletarian ranks and because the Congress of Soviet Writers was to be held in May, 1933, those writers who did not uphold the platform of the Soviet government were not to be accepted (perhaps only temporarily) into the Union of Soviet Writers. In practice this would mean that to all intents and purposes they would cease to be regarded as writers. It was feared at this time that the Writers' Union would function as a writers' trade union, a fear that was later substantially borne out—those who did not belong to it were very rarely able to have their works published.

In the Ukraine, the Party through its organ, the Orgkomitet, displayed little willingness to offer an amnesty to the fellow travelers and the Neoclassicists, while in Russia fellow travelers like Alexei Tolstoi, Ehrenburg, Fedin, and others were given official dispensa-

[19] See above, p. 210.

tion. There was also a great deal of discrimination against some former proletarian writers of VAPLITE and those circles associated with it. If all these writers were to find themselves outside the official bounds of the Union of Soviet Writers, Ukrainian literature would be deprived of some of its best writers. To prevent this Khvyl'ovyi used all his influence and authority, both still very considerable.

What must have seemed very ominous to him was the speed with which the Party now hastened to complete the work of the Orgkomitet and to form the Union. The Congress to inaugurate the Writers' Union was, according to Gronskii, to meet in May. In March, 1933, the Ukrainian press printed the announcement that the Congress was to be held on June 20, in Moscow.[20] In April, the Russian organ of the Orgkomitet confirmed this date.[21] On May 10, the Ukrainian Orgkomitet met and decided to call the Congress of the Soviet Writers of the Ukraine for June 19, 1933. It also elected a committee to supervise the election of writers to the Union of Soviet Writers.[22] We do not know the composition of this committee which, of course, was decisive. Yet we know that while the Ukrainian Orgkomitet was taking these important decisions, former Vaplitians were being arrested. At the beginning of May Khvyl'ovyi's personal friend, the former president of VAPLITE, Ialovyi, was arrested.[23] An iron ring was drawn around those who had ever opposed or could oppose the Party, and for these the future held no prospect of escape. On May 13, 1933, Mykola Khvyl'ovyi shot himself.

Khvyl'ovyi's suicide came as a shock not only to his friends and disciples but also, for different reasons, to his opponents. "We, the Soviet revolutionary writers," said Panch at Khvyl'ovyi's funeral, which became a public demonstration, "have nearly all of us entered onto the path of literature inspired by the restless, fiery, and romantic Khvyl'ovyi." [24] A whole generation of Ukrainian writers who regarded Khvyl'ovyi as their leader was suddenly left defense-

[20] "Pershyi vsesoiuznyi zïzd radians'kykh pys'mennykiv," *Visti*, March 30, 1933.
[21] *Literaturnaia gazeta*, April 5, 1933.
[22] "Hotuvannia do pershoho vseukraïns'koho zïzdu radians'kykh pys'mennykiv," *Visti*, May 17, 1933.
[23] O. Han., *Tragediia Mykoly Khvyl'ovoho*, p. 75.
[24] *Literaturna hazeta*, No. 10, 1933.

less before the Party officials, irritated by Khvyl'ovyi's act of protest. They branded Khvyl'ovyi's action as cowardly, just as three years earlier they had spoken of Maiakovskii. But unlike the suicide of Maiakovskii, Khvyl'ovyi's death could not be explained away as the result of personal unhappiness. It was committed, in the words of the Secretary of the CP(B)U, as an act of "demonstration," [25] and this is why the Party did its best to sully the name of one who was becoming a legendary hero of Ukrainian resistance.

This feeling of desperate, intensified, but passive resistance became stronger after the suicide of Mykola Skrypnyk on July 7, 1933. Just how serious the situation within Soviet Ukrainian literature became as a result of the deaths of Khvyl'ovyi and Skrypnyk can be seen from Kulyk's speech in July, 1933:

I shall not deny that the general situation in the building of national culture in the Ukraine, including literature, has become complex. It would be more accurate to say that we have now become more aware of this situation than we were previously, before the unmasking of counterrevolutionary chauvinist organizations which also tried to enroll writers for their activities. . . .

We shall simply say that in view of the events which have recently occurred in the Ukraine . . . we dearly need your help, the help of the proletarian Party cadres of Russian literature. Comrades, I hope that we shall agree here as to the concrete conditions for such assistance. I should like to mention in particular that the visit of comrades Fadeev and Chumandrin to Kiev at a very critical moment for our collective group helped us a great deal. I should also like to stress that the arrival of comrades Bezymenskii and Ilёnkov at that critical time, immediately following the suicide of Khvyl'ovyi, and their participation in the Komsomol meeting, to which some non-Party Ukrainian writers were also

25 D. Halushko, "Lytsari zrady," *Chervonyi shliakh,* No. 2–3, 1934, p. 179.
From a draft of one of Kulish's letters, preserved in the Liubchenko Papers, we learn that the Party conducted a legal investigation into the causes of Khvyl'ovyi's death. In this letter, addressed to the coroner, Kushars'kyi, of the Kharkov District Procurator's Office, Kulish wrote that he had just read Khvyl'ovyi's preface to his selected works, written shortly before the latter's death. The preface, he claimed, revealed some of the reasons which drove Khvyl'ovyi to commit suicide. "In my earlier reports to you about the motives for Khvyl'ovyi's suicide," wrote Kulish, "I wrote that he had never complained to me or to any other of his friends about his personal position in literature (attitude of critics and critical evaluation, the striking injustice and abnormality of which was obvious to me). However, this preface reveals how painful it was for Khvyl'ovyi to keep silent about it, and how difficult he found it to continue the career of a proletarian writer, fourteen years of which some of our less careful critics irrevocably erased. My conjectures as to the motives for the inner crisis in Khvyl'ovyi must be seen in the light of this preface."

invited, has helped us a great deal, comrades, to clear the air and to raise the spirits of our young people.[26]

This was nothing less than an admission of Russian superiority and wisdom by the Chairman of the Ukrainian Orgkomitet. The "come-and-rule-us" call was issued at the most appropriate time for the ruler—that is, when his control over the Ukraine was complete and could not be challenged.

The Delay in the Formation of the Union of Soviet Writers

There is some evidence to suggest that the proposed Congress of Soviet Writers which was to usher in the Writers' Union was delayed because of the unrest in the literary life of the non-Russian republics. The *Literary Gazette* for 1933, which utters no word on the theory of national culture in a socialist state, is full of exhortations to greater solidarity between national literatures. On May 29, 1933, it gave great prominence to the agreement between the Moscow Association of Writers and the Ukrainian publishing firm LIM (Literatura i Mystetstvo) on a mutual program of translations.[27] On July 29, A. Khvylia sang the praises of Kaganovich for routing Ukrainian nationalism.[28] Finally, Kovalenko also decried nationalism in Ukrainian literature.[29]

The All-Union Orgkomitet started a great drive for a new Soviet drama. Incentives were offered to dramatists to write a play "worthy of the great epoch." In the Ukraine this drive must be viewed in connection with the final purge of Berezil'. In October, 1933, the People's Commissariat for Education issued a declaration signed by the Deputy Commissar for Education, Khvylia. It read that "the [Berezil'] theater has failed to assume a proper place in the creation of Ukrainian Soviet art. This has happened because Kurbas led the theater in the direction of Ukrainian nationalism. Kurbas . . .

[26] I. Kulyk, "Peredz̈izdna sytuatsiia," *Radians'ka literatura*, No. 5, 1933; quoted in Iaroslav Hordyns'kyi, *Literaturna krytyka pidsoviets'koï Ukraïny*, p. 54.
[27] "Podlinnoe vzaimodeistvie literatur narodov SSSR," *Literaturnaia gazeta*, May 25, 1933.
[28] A. Khvylia, "Literatura sostavnaia chast' stroitel'stva ukrainskoi sovetskoi kul'tury," *Literaturnaia gazeta*, July 29, 1933.
[29] B. Kovalenko, "Natsionalisticheskie tendentsii v ukrainskoi literature," *Krasnaia nov'*, No. 7, 1933, pp. 203–14.

has isolated his theater from the Soviet socialist reality . . . in particular he has isolated his theater from the Soviet art of the brotherly RSFSR. Theater *Berezil'* has in the past shared the attitude of VAPLITE." [30] Further, the declaration relieved Les' Kurbas of his duties as director and producer of Berezil' and appointed Krushel'nyts'kyi in his place. Only ten days later, a meeting was arranged between the purged Berezil' and some Russian producers at which Khvylia expressed the hope that it might be the beginning of "a new era in the history of the Ukrainian theater." [31]

Hirniak, a close associate of Kurbas, tells of the dramatic interview which occurred between Kurbas and Postyshev before the former's dismissal.[32] The famous producer is credited with having declared to Postyshev that the function of a theater would always be to discover falsehood and to reveal truth, and this would be also the aim of "socialist realism." Postyshev's attempts to win Kurbas by threats and blandishments failed completely. The Ukrainian producer took his calling seriously and was not prepared to betray his principles.

The use of force had, in this instance, produced the desired effect. Several members of Berezil' who stayed on were then in the course of time removed because of their past association with Kurbas, who was deprived of the title "people's artist" in December, 1933,[33] and later deported. The net result was a decline and gradual Russification (not in language but in approach) of the Ukrainian theater. In order to assuage the feelings of the Ukrainians who were profoundly disappointed with Kurbas's removal, the Drama Commission of the Orgkomitet honored two Ukrainian playwrights with high prizes at the All-Union Drama Competition. Korniichuk shared the second prize with Kirshon (the first prize was not awarded) and Kocherha was awarded the third prize.[34]

The year 1934 was greeted in Ukrainian literary life with two slogans: "Cooperation with the Russians" and "Active Interest of

[30] "Postanova narodn'oho komisariatu os'vity USRR na dopovid' teatru 'Berezil',' " *Visti,* October 8, 1933.

[31] *Visti,* October 16, 1933.

[32] Khmuryi, Dyvnych, and Blakytnyi, *V maskakh epokhy,* p. 48. For a more complete discussion of Berezil', see Iosyp Hirniak, "Birth and Death of the Modern Ukrainian Theater," *Soviet Theaters: 1917–1941,* pp. 256–338.

[33] *Visti,* December 20, 1933.

[34] "P'esy poluchivshie premii," *Literaturnaia gazeta,* April 4, 1934.

Writers in Party Policy." On New Year's Eve an important meeting took place in Kharkov between the members of the Ukrainian Orgkomitet and some Russian guests, Iudin, Selivanovskii, and Bezymenskii. In a report presented to them Mykytenko "paid special attention to the struggle which had been conducted during the previous year against the counterrevolutionary elements in the Ukraine." [35]

It is interesting to note the reappearance of Selivanovskii, who was one of the most active agents of VOAPP in the Ukraine. His bitter denunciations of Khvyl'ovyi must have earned him this assignment.

Writers were encouraged to devote more of their time to the study of the recent resolutions of the Party and to seek in them further inspiration for their works. Thus we read that "the Kiev writers spent three days discussing the resolutions of the November Plenum of the CP(B)U." [36] The meeting provided ample opportunity for the expression of self-criticism. Some fellow travelers made impassioned recantations (among them, Pluzhnyk), but there were also some exceptions. Thus, for instance, Kosynka, another member of the former Lanka, refused to abase himself. [37]

Unavailing Repentance

The difficulty for a persecuted Soviet writer in reconciling his artistic integrity with the constant demands for confession before the Party may be seen from three explanatory statements by Kulish, preserved in the Liubchenko papers. The first of them, dated April 24, 1929, is addressed to the Chief Repertoire Committee of the People's Commissariat of Education, and is concerned with the defense of Kulish's comedy *Myna Mazailo*. Its tone is bold and aggressive with no trace of guilt or self-reproach.

Having selected for the comedy *Myna Mazailo* the theme of Ukrainization and philistinism, I directed my attention first of all to the crystal-clear ideological content of the play, and secondly, to the careful analysis

[35] "Brigada vsesoiuznogo orgkomiteta v Kharkove," *Literaturnaia gazeta*, January 11, 1934.
[36] P. K. and O. R., "Za tvorchu realizatsiiu ukhval lystopadovoho plenumu TsK i TsKK KP(b)U," *Zhyttia i revoliutsiia*, No. 1, 1934, p. 163.
[37] *Ibid.*, p. 176.

of every word and idea. On completion of the comedy (which I read before a meeting of writers, members of the Party, who considered it an artistically accomplished and ideologically useful play) I sent one copy of it to the chairman of the Repertoire Committee, and the other to the chairman of the Agitation and Propaganda Section of the Central Committee of the CP(B)U, comrade Khvylia, requesting each to give an authoritative political criticism of the play. After minor suggestions, the chairman of the Repertoire Committee permitted and recommended the play for performance at all state theaters. . . .

After March 20, the play was put on by the Shevchenko Theater in Dniepropetrovs'k (the press reviews were very favorable). The Kiev critics regarded the play as my greatest achievement and as a triumph of Soviet Ukrainian drama.

After all this, in the central organs of the Party, *Komunist* and *Visti*, the deputy editor and the responsible editor have performed an act of political execution (the articles of Kost' Kotko and E. K.). They have branded my comedy as of doubtful value ideologically, and almost anti-Soviet, setting the public against it, and the Komsomol against the author and also against the best theater in the Ukr.SSR—Berezil'.

I feel confident that the Repertoire Committee places a higher value upon the opinion of writers, critics, and spectators than on the two articles mentioned above. However, wounds, inflicted by this political execution, are deep and smarting, and I am therefore bringing the matter to the attention of the Repertoire Committee and the Agitation and Propaganda Section of the Central Committee of the CP(B)U.

Two years later (January, 1931) Kulish, defending himself against another attack, spoke a different language. His self-assurance and defiance were gone. In an attempt to explain his "errors," which he now meekly admitted, he embarked on the highly dangerous task of reexamining and analyzing his own earlier works. This time he attempted to "explain" his play *The People's Malakhii*. He admitted that the first version of the play (1928) lacked "ideological clarity," and that this was the result of his own "dualism, which influenced my consciousness, my feelings, and my whole philosophy. This dualism was also reflected in the literary form of the play, its style, composition, and characters." This, after being typed, must have seemed inadequate to Kulish or to someone who was asked to read this confession, for in longhand in the margin we find this sentence added: "the play was the expression of Ukrainian nationalist deviation against the Party." Obviously this was the kind of admission that was required. There may be personal or ideological motives in a work of art, but in a recantation it was the political reason which was important.

In the next paragraph of this "letter to the editor," Kulish analyzed the reasons for his "dualism." He blamed it on the NEP, his failure to see the positive achievements of the Revolution, and his own tendency to be in the opposition. "This oppositionist vagueness," he wrote, "which could not offer a clear political concept, permeated the first version of the play." Characteristically enough, again on the margin we read the following addition or substitution for this sentence: "Trotskyism plus Ukrainian nationalism—simply counterrevolutionary demands." Obviously the latter explanation, perhaps suggested to Kulish by someone else, was more acceptable to the Party. In his way Kulish was forced to "frame" himself as a "Ukrainian nationalist," hoping for atonement from those who were bent on his destruction. Behind every "nationalist" confession of a Ukrainian writer there were probably similar reasons.

On June 14, 1934, Kulish was expelled from the Party, as the author of "plays with a clear nationalist tendency, directed against the Party." A few days later Kulish wrote a "Declaration to the Dzerzhinsk District Committee in Charge of the Purge of the Party," appealing against this decision. This document, full of self-condemnation, is a plea for mercy. Yet even complete spiritual prostration before the Party and his assurance that he was then busy writing a new play which would show "the growth of the new socialist man" were of no help to Kulish. The comedy of recantation had, in most cases, no bearing on the fate of those who were earmarked for "liquidation." In 1934 Kulish was arrested and deported, never to reappear in the Ukraine.

Tightening the Noose

In January, 1934, a Party Cell (*Partoseredok*) was formed within the Ukrainian Orgkomitet. Its purpose was to "raise the level of Party work among the writers and to bring it closer to the widest circles of non-Party writers." [38] Mykytenko, Levitina, and Zorin

[38] "Utvoreno partoseredok radians'kykh pys'mennykiv," *Chervonyi shliakh*, No. 1, 1934, p. 196.

were appointed to head this official cell of Party propaganda among the writers.

In order to find still better excuses to tighten its control and to extend its influence over Ukrainian literary life, the Party uncovered counterrevolutionary plots in which Ukrainian writers were allegedly implicated. The purges which Postyshev was at that time conducting in the Ukraine took a heavy toll of writers and intellectuals. No accounts of the numbers involved were published and our estimate of the losses suffered by Ukrainian literature during 1932–34 will be given in the final chapter of this study and will be based on eyewitness accounts and a survey of Ukrainian literary periodicals in which names of many regular contributors ceased to appear.

There are, however, some few direct testimonies, recorded in the Soviet Ukrainian press, of the liquidation of writers. Thus in an English language article written in 1934, I. Kulyk stated:

As a result of the aid extended to the Ukraine by the Central Committee of the Communist Party of the Soviet Union and above all by Stalin, the agents of the imperialist interventionists were defeated, the nationalists were unmasked, and the kulak ideologists and their hangers-on were practically ousted from the field of Ukrainian Soviet literature. . . . Gone was the glory of those erstwhile "stars" whose fame had been artificially inflated by the nationalists: the kulak jester Ostap Vyshnia, the untalented scribbler O. Dos'vitnyi, Pylypenko, O. Slisarenko, and their like.[39]

The four writers mentioned here as "practically ousted from the field of Ukrainian literature" were all distinguished, though belonging in the past to different literary organizations. The most startling fall was that of Pylypenko, the former leader of Pluh and a confirmed enemy of Khvyl'ovyi. He, Slisarenko, and Dos'vitnyi never reappeared again; Vyshnia survived the storm and today contributes to *Krokodil* and to the Ukrainian press.

Writing at the end of 1933, D. Halushko lists the following writers among the traitors: "Khvyl'ovyi, Dos'vitnyi, Pylypenko, Irchan, Gzhyts'kyi, Zahoruiko, Tkachuk, and many other fascist writers and critics (Richyts'kyi, Desniak, Berezyns'kyi), the whole gang of the literary critics from the All-Ukrainian Academy of Sciences and the Shevchenko Institute." [40]

The intensity of the fury of the Russian exterminators is evidenced by the decision taken at the Third Plenum of the All-Union Orgkomitet concerning Vyshnia and Khvyl'ovyi. The *Literary Gazette* printed this short announcement:

The Third All-Union Plenum of the Organizing Committee of the Union of Soviet Writers of the USSR has excluded from the staff of the All-Union Organizing Committee Ukrainian writers O. Vyshnia and the recently deceased M. Khvyl'ovyi, exposed as participants in counterrevolutionary nationalist organizations in the Ukraine.

The Plenum has elected the secretaries of the Ukrainian Organizing Committee, comrades Kyrylenko, Kopylenko, and the head of the Kiev organization of Soviet Writers, comrade Ivan Le, to the staff of the All-Union Organizing Committee of the Union of Soviet Writers.[41]

Even among the frequently bizarre practices of Soviet terrorism this is a unique instance of the expulsion of a dead writer from an official organization.

It must be remembered that charges of belonging to counterrevolutionary organizations were synonymous with high treason, for which the mildest punishment was long-term deportation. In June, 1934, three other Ukrainian writers were added to the list of "counterrevolutionaries." They were, according to I. Gans,[42] Ialovyi, Desniak, and Irchan. A milder charge was leveled against Epik.

In this atmosphere of terror and inquisition the Orgkomitet continued its work in the Ukraine. The interest betrayed by the Orgkomitet in Ukrainian literature was never purely academic. It became identical with direct interference not only with Ukrainian writers and their organizations but also with belles-lettres, the Ukrainian literary language, and Ukrainian classics.

A special commission of the Orgkomitet for the study of Ukrainian literature convened under the chairmanship of the Russian Stetskii (chief of the propaganda section of the Party). In March, 1934, two Russian writers, Gladkov and Bezymenskii, delivered

[40] D. Halushko, "Lytsari zrady," *Chervonyi shliakh*, No. 2–3, 1934, p. 180.
[41] "S"ezd pisatelei 25 iiunia," *Literaturnaia gazeta*, March 14, 1934.
[42] I. Gans, "Pisateli-kommunisty na proverke," *Literaturnaia gazeta*, June 14, 1934.

under its auspices lectures on Ukrainian literature which were followed by a discussion in which both Russian and Ukrainian writers took part. In his closing address Stetskii expressed the hope that such conferences should in future have a mutual character. "Today," he said, "we have listened to criticism of Ukrainian literature by Russian writers." Next time, he hoped, it would be the Ukrainians who would criticize Russian literature.[43] The *Literary Gazette* does not mention any further meetings of this commission.

Just how insistent and blatant were the Party demands on the writers becomes clear from a circular letter which the publishers of the literary magazine *Radians'ka literatura* sent in 1933 to Ukrainian writers. A copy of it has been preserved in the unpublished papers of A. Liubchenko. It is addressed to him and it reads:

The first issue of the almanac *Radians'ka literatura* will appear before the Congress of the Soviet Writers of the Ukraine.

In view of the fact that the Congress will be held after the November Plenum of the Central Committee of the CP(B)U, after the 17th Party Congress and the 12th Congress of the CP(B)U, the material to be published in the almanac must reflect those historic changes of world-wide significance which have occurred in the life of the Soviet Union and which, in turn, have influenced the condition of capitalist countries. The luxuriant blossoming of the Soviet literature of the Union and, in particular, of Soviet Ukrainian literature must be marked in the first issue of the almanac by the best works of the foremost phalanx of Soviet Ukrainian writers.

We should present our report to the Congress of the Union of Soviet Writers of the Ukraine, which will be held on the second anniversary of the resolution of the Central Committee of the CPSU on the reorganization of literary organizations, issued on April 23, 1932, in the form of best examples of creative work by Soviet Ukrainian writers.

The artistic content of the almanac should reflect the most significant moments of one of the following issues:

1. The Communist Party as the organizer and guide of socialist construction.

2. The uncovering of Ukrainian nationalism and the unmasking of its counterrevolutionary aims, and the growth of Ukrainian Soviet socialist culture.

3. The growth of socialist industry and the reconstruction of the agricultural economy.

4. Display of the USSR as the fortress of the international proletariat

43 "Novye knigi pisatelei Ukrainy," *Literaturnaia gazeta,* March 14, 1934.

and the growth of the revolutionary movement in capitalist countries.

5. The reeducation of the toilers in the process of socialist construction.

This, schematically, is the range of subjects which will constitute the contents of the almanac. We are sure that you have some suitable themes in your creative plans and we invite you to participate in the first issue of the almanac. We hope to receive from you suitable material. . . .

Director of the Publishing House:

[AGUF]

Chief Editor:

[M. NOVYTS'KYI]

Parallel with the drive against nationalism in Ukrainian literature, the Party was conducting a campaign against nationalism in the Ukrainian language. One of the charges against the group of scholars accused together with Professor Iefremov of forming the "Union for the Liberation of the Ukraine" was that they had harmfully attempted to separate the Ukrainian language from the Russian and to introduce nationalistic terminology into Ukrainian language. We recall that a few years later the same accusation was made by Khvylia against Skrypnyk. In 1933–34 the purges of the Ukrainian Academy of Sciences affected chiefly the Institute of Ukrainian Language. Its distinguished members and associates, Holoskevych, Hantsov, Kurylo, and several other well-known linguists (Smerechyns'kyi, Syniavs'kyi, and Sulyma), were removed from their teaching posts and deported. In 1931 the historical-philological section of the Ukrainian Academy was dissolved [44] and an Institute of Linguistics headed by Naum Kaganovich was created to replace it in part. N. Kaganovich and A. Khvylia became the greatest authorities on the Ukrainian language.

Denying the existence of any positive values in the researches and publications of the Ukrainian linguists of the last decade, the Party charged them with the following crimes:

Ukrainian nationalists contributed artificial and invented terms to Ukrainian scientific terminology, thus separating Ukrainian scientific terminology from the scientific terminology commonly used in the Soviet Union and in the Soviet Ukraine. . . .

Ukrainian nationalists destroyed those words in the Ukrainian lan-

[44] *Proletars'ka pravda,* No. 270–271, 1931.

guage which were also common to the Russian language in order to separate Soviet Ukrainian culture from the Soviet Russian culture which is an achievement of the proletarian revolution and socialist construction and is immensely important to the proletariat of the entire world.[45]

The linguistic policy of the Party in the Ukraine at that time lies outside the scope of this study. However, some of its aspects were concerned with literature. In an article, "The Language of Ukrainian Literature," we find this mention of N. Kaganovich's lecture on the language of Korniichuk:

Comrade N. Kaganovich in his lecture on the language of the *Defeat of the Squadron* pointed out that Korniichuk has succeeded in the difficult task of showing the linguistic characteristics of the representatives of different social groups appearing in the play. Comrade Korniichuk's parody of the language of Ukrainian nationalists was especially subtle. Further, comrade Kulyk pointed out how an erroneous distribution of language characteristics leads to serious artistic and political mistakes.[46]

In another article, "Notes on Language," N. Kaganovich states that "national linguists directed their efforts toward the 'Europeanization' of the literary language by artificial borrowings from Polish or German. The same path was followed by the nationalist writers." [47]

As in all other languages, there is a considerable difference between the language of the Ukrainian town and the Ukrainian village. There is little doubt that Russian influences in vocabulary and terminology were particularly strong in Ukrainian towns which, after the abandonment of the Ukrainization policy in 1932, were once more becoming Russified. It is enough to recall the fact that the proletariat of the Ukraine was in 1934 only 53 percent Ukrainian to realize how strong Russian linguistic influences must have been in the Ukraine. Moreover, Zatons'kyi, the People's Commissar for Education, did point out that the "Russian minority was of special value." [48]

The Party's drive against "nationalisms" in the Ukrainian lan-

---

[45] "Iz rezoliutsiï na dopovid' tov. Khvyli pro stan na movnomu fronti," *Visti*, June 30, 1933; also cf. Iurii Sherekh, "Pryntsypy i etapy bolshevyts'koï movnoï polityky na Ukraïni, II," *Suchasna Ukraïna*, July 13, 1952.

[46] "Iazyk ukrainskoi khudozhestvennoi literatury," *Literaturnaia gazeta*, April 16, 1934.

[47] N. Kaganovich, "Zametki o iazyke," *Literaturnaia gazeta*, June 14, 1934.

[48] *Komunist*, No. 208, August 23, 1933.

guage was therefore an attempt to sever the contact between Ukrainian literature and the peasantry and to bring it closer to the proletariat in the Ukraine. Not only were the cities regarded as better repositories of the Ukrainian language, but by 1933 they had become centers of Stalin's power, outposts of his new empire. The term "proletarian literature" lost its earlier connotation, and came to mean literature imbued with the ideology of Stalin's era. When one reads the works of Mykytenko, who was regarded in the early thirties as the model "proletarian" writer, one realizes that his pieces of Stalinist propaganda are written in a language full of Russianisms, no doubt reflecting the intellectual climate and the speech of Ukrainian towns during the reign of Postyshev.

The Soviet attitude to the Ukrainian language thus assumed a different aspect. As in the early 1920s the official policy was still in favor of the full development and use of Ukrainian, but now there was one serious reservation: Ukrainian must not be separated from Russian. The practice of the Soviet state demanded that Russian slowly be superimposed on all non-Russian republics not only as the *lingua franca* of a unified state but as a solidifying influence to the advantage of Russia.

It is an interesting fact that in 1932–34 two Russian writers whose attitude to the use of Ukrainian was unfriendly came to play an important part in the literary policy toward the Ukraine. The lesser of them, Gladkov, had declared on one occasion that in his opinion it was unnecessary "to revive the pre-Petrian epoch. Why galvanize the Ukrainian language, which is already covered with dust? All this only slows down the development of socialist construction." [49]

The other was Maxim Gorky, whom Slisarenko charged, in 1927, with having written the following letter the previous year:

It seems to me that a translation of this novel into the Ukrainian dialect is also unnecessary. I am very much puzzled by the fact that people who have in front of them the same goal, not only reaffirm the difference between dialects, but also try to make a "language" out of a dialect and even oppress those Great Russians who have found themselves as a minority in the area of the respective dialect. [50]

[49] Quoted from B. Antonenko-Davydovych, "Voskresinnia Shel'menka," *Zhyttia i revoliutsiia*, No. 2, 1929, p. 95.
[50] "Nashe s'ohodni," *Vaplite*, No. 3, 1927, p. 137.

The publication of this letter stirred heated controversy and the matter was not forgotten as late as 1934, when Gorky was chosen to perform the function of patron saint of the Union of Soviet Writers. The *Literary Gazette* published in that year a letter from Gorky to Kulyk in which Gorky refuted Slisarenko's charge that he was hostile to the Ukrainian language without denying that he wrote the letter of May, 1926. Gorky wrote to Kulyk:

Your letter reminded me of the "incident" between me and Slisarenko who accused me of a bias toward imperialism, [a thought] evoked in him by my letter in which I, somewhat hurt by Slisarenko's fiery letter, declared something like this: I hold that a single language is imperative for the mutual understanding and unity of mankind, all the same whatever language it be, English, Ukrainian, or Mordvinian, etc. To be sure even now I regard a single language as inevitable in the future, but I did reply to Slisarenko vigorously. For this reason I gave my explanations before Ukrainian writers in 1928 in the Blakytnyi Home. My sympathies toward Ukrainian nationality [*narodnost'*] sprang up as early as [18]91 when I wandered across the Ukraine, and became stronger in [18]97–98 when I lived in the Poltava *gubernia*.[51]

The editorial comment goes on to say: "Further, Alexei Maximovich [Gorky] describes how in 1915 he prepared for publication a Ukrainian Symposium and ends: 'Were I an imperialist—why should I busy myself with the preparation of symposia which were to show the presence of original cultures in the nationalities oppressed by the imperialism of the Romanovs and Co.' "

Gorky's reply was read by Kulyk during the First Congress of the Soviet Writers in the Ukraine in June, 1934. It was no doubt regarded as a conditional retreat from the position of 1926—when Gorky had described the Ukrainian language as a "dialect." The demands of socialist construction reduced the importance of the non-Russian peoples to the status of mere "singular cultures in nationalities."

The classics of nineteenth-century Ukrainian literature did not escape the Party's vigilance. Some of them were printed only rarely, others appeared in "selected editions." In the purges of Ukrainian

51 "A. M. Gorky i ukrainskaia literatura: pis'mo t. Kuliku," *Literaturnaia gazeta,* June 22, 1934.

For a detailed review of the incident which occurred following Gorky's letter to Slisarenko, see O. Doroshkevych, "Maksym Gorky ta ukraïns'ka literatura," *Zhyttia i revoliutsiia,* No. 10, 1932, p. 94.

scholars and literary historians frequent accusations were made against those who had allegedly given Shevchenko's works nationalistic interpretations. A well-known Marxist, Andrew Richyts'kyi, was charged with tendentious interpretation when he explained Shevchenko's reference to George Washington in the poem *Iurodyvyi* (The Fool) as follows: "Washington—first President of the United States. Until 1783 North America belonged to England." "Richyts'kyi," the charge read, insinuated by this footnote "that Shevchenko fought for separation of the Ukraine from Russia, just as Washington fought for separation of the United States from Britain." [52]

In 1934 the Party decided to issue special "Theses" on Shevchenko which set forth a dogma on how to interpret this poet's works.[53] This act of thought control was accompanied, however, by a generous although ironic gesture. In Kharkov a grandiose monument to Shevchenko was unveiled in 1934 by Postyshev.

The First All-Ukrainian Congress of Soviet Writers (June, 1934), a Prologue to the First Congress of Soviet Writers

The last postponement of the long-awaited Congress of Soviet Writers occurred in June, 1934, and once more resulted from a certain amount of unrest in republican literatures. It was decided to hold the congresses of writers in the Ukraine, Belorussia, Armenia, and Turkmenistan, where last rehearsals were to be made before the final show.

On June 14, 1934, Mykytenko published an article in the *Literary Gazette* entitled "Put'k soiuzu" (The Path to the Union).[54] Here, for the first time, he gave complete figures on the enrollment of writers into the Writers' Union in the Ukraine. He wrote that up to June 4, 500 applications for membership were received. Of these, 334 were considered by the Orgkomitet. Of the 334 only 120 were accepted into the Union; 73 of them were Ukrainian, 22 Jewish, 19 Russian, 4 Moldavian, and 1 Greek.

[52] *Komunist*, No. 59, March 11, 1934.
[53] "Tezy viddilu kul'tury i propagandy TsK KP(b)U do 120-richchia z dnia narodzhennia Shevchenka," *Chervonyi shliakh*, No. 2–3, 1934, pp. 5–12.
[54] I. Mykytenko, "Put' k soiuzu," *Literaturnaia gazeta*, June 14, 1934.

In explanation of this Mykytenko offered the following argument. Many applicants were turned down simply because of lack of qualifications. Others were refused admission since their works "do not by their ideological content answer the needs of Soviet literature." He went on:

In this small group there are some well-known masters, but in their previous works they placed their talents at the service of the kulaks and Ukrainian counterrevolutionary nationalists and have not even now shown such symptoms of artistic change as would prove that they are ready to serve fully with their art the interests of the Party, the Soviet government, and the workers of the great socialist fatherland —the USSR.[55]

It is very difficult to explain the small total of applications (500). In 1928 Leites and Iashek listed over nine hundred writers in the Ukraine.[56] After the campaign for the "shock workers of the pen" during the Five-Year Plan there should have been at least a thousand eligible to join the Writers' Union. It is true, of course, that the enrollment increased considerably in 1934 and 1935, but the situation in June, 1934, as described by Mykytenko, clearly indicated not only the extent of the purges but also the pressure which the Party placed on writers to make absolute loyalty a prerequisite to joining the Union.

When the First All-Ukrainian Congress of Soviet Writers finally convened in Kharkov, on June 20, 1934, it was greeted by Postyshev [57] and addressed by the Secretary of the CP(B)U, Popov,[58] and the representative of the All-Union Communist Party, Stetskii. Other Party speakers were Kosior [59] and Panas Liubchenko.[60] The

[55] *Ibid.*

[56] A. Leites and M. Iashek, *Desiat' rokiv ukraïns'koï literatury (1917–1927)*, Tom I, bio-bibliohrafichnyi. Literature in the Ukraine was shunned as an occupation after the 1932 reforms and purges. This is obvious from a cursory comparison of the name index in the above book by Leites and Iashek with a later similar publication, *Slovnyk ukraïns'koï literatury* by L. Khinkulov. Khinkulov lists only 253 writers in the Ukraine in 1949, and only 51 of these were listed by Leites and Iashek as writing in 1928.

[57] P. Postyshev, "Pershomu vseukraïns'komu zïzdovi radians'kykh pys'mennykiv," *Visti*, June 21, 1934.

[58] "Na pershomu zïzdi radians'kykh pys'mennykiv Ukraïny; promova sekretaria TsK KP(b)U t. M. M. Popova," *Visti*, June 21, 1934.

[59] "Radians'ku literaturu na riven' zavdan' pobudovy bezklasovoho sotsialistychnoho suspil'stva: promova tov. S. V. Kosiora na vseukraïns'komu zïzdi radians'kykh pys'mennykiv 22 chervnia 1934," *Visti*, June 28, 1934.

[60] "Promova tov. P. P. Liubchenka na pershomu vseukraïns'komu zïzdi radians'kykh pys'mennykiv," *Visti*, July 9, 1934.

Congress lasted until July when its final session was held in the new capital of the Soviet Ukraine—Kiev.

The keynote of all speeches was increased loyalty to the Party and its leader, Stalin. The harangues against Ukrainian nationalism [61] merged with fervid declarations of devotion to the Party and pleas for a closer union between Ukrainian and Russian literatures. The resolution of the Congress which embodies its character reads:

We know that Ukrainian Soviet literature owes its recent achievements to the direct and constant leadership of the CP (B)U headed by comrades Kosior and Postyshev.[62]

The following writers were elected to the new body deputed to direct Ukrainian literature: Gorodskoi, Hofstein, Kyrylenko, Kovalenko, Kopylenko, Korniichuk, Kotsiuba, Kulyk, Mykytenko, Milev, Panch, Pervomais'kyi, Smolych, Tychyna, Usenko, Fefer, and Shchupak.[63] In place of the missing Liubchenko there were some newcomers from the proletarian ranks (e.g., Usenko) and an ex-fellow traveler, Smolych.

Of special interest to the historian of Soviet Ukrainian literature is Popov's first open attack on Blakytnyi, the recognized "father" of Ukrainian proletarian literature, who had died in 1925. "We cannot separate Blakytnyi the politician," said Popov, "from Blakytnyi the writer. We cannot forget that comrade Stalin in June, 1926, branded an attempt to tear the Ukraine away from Russia. Blakytnyi in his 'theses' of 1920 took such a line." [64]

The revision of Soviet Ukrainian literary history, begun here by the Secretary of the CP (B)U, Popov, was continued by Kulyk in his speech before the First Congress of Soviet Writers which convened on August 17, 1934. The Ukrainian delegation to the Congress was composed of 22 Ukrainians, 1 Russian, 17 Jews, 1 Moldavian, and 1 Belorussian.[65] The head of the Ukrainian delegation, Kulyk, declared that

61 In his speech, Stetskii stressed that "we have felt the smell of gun powder in the recent struggle against the nationalists who wanted to betray our fatherland, to betray the Soviet Union, to betray the Soviet Ukraine" ("Znamia sovetskoi literatury: rech' na pervom vseukrainskom s"ezde sovetskikh pisatelei," *Literaturnaia gazeta*, June 22, 1934).

62 "Vidozva pershoho vseukraïns'koho zïzdu radians'kykh pys'mennykiv," *Visti*, August 17, 1934.

63 A. Krol', "Vseukrainskii s"ezd pisatelei," *Literaturnaia gazeta*, June 26, 1934.

64 Popov, "Zadachi ukrainskoi literatury," *Literaturnaia gazeta*, June 26, 1934.

65 *Pervyi vsesoiuznyi s"ezd sovetskikh pisatelei, 1934, Stenograficheskii otchët*, p. 708.

The creation of Ukrainian proletarian literature is a process which was completed not in separation but under the direct leadership of the Party in the struggle for the dictatorship of the proletariat, for the construction of a classless socialist society. Proletarian literature has developed in the Ukraine in an organic bond with the proletarian literature of Russia under the leadership of the united Bolshevik Party.[66]

He did not forget to give thanks to the Party for its guidance in recent years.

In this connection we are very much obliged for the help which the All-Union Orgkomitet has given us. . . . In the last year we have seen how the All-Union Orgkomitet really led the separate branches of Soviet literatures in different republics.[67]

The Congress of Soviet Writers, which finally approved the Constitution of the Union of Soviet Writers establishing "socialist realism" as the principle of artistic creation, was the high-water mark of adulation of the Communist Party by the representatives of non-Russian literatures. In the resolution on the literatures of the national republics we read:

Under the leadership of the heroic All-Union Communist Party headed by comrade Stalin and with daily help from the Party, the writers of all peoples of the USSR have come to their first congress as a collective body, ideologically, creatively, and organizationally united around the Party and the Soviet government.[68]

Now the whole choir sang in simple unison.

[66] *Ibid.*, p. 44.   [67] *Ibid.*   [68] *Ibid.*, p. 290.

[X]

RETROSPECT AND EPILOGUE

During the fifteen years following the Revolution literature in the Soviet Ukraine ran a turbulent course which was determined on the one hand by the changes in the controls exercised by the Party and on the other by the extent and the nature of the resistance to Communist regimentation. It remains to assess and interpret the most essential features of this development in the light of the historical evidence which has been presented in the foregoing chapters.

The early semi-autonomy of the Ukrainian SSR was of paramount importance. It arose as a result of the national revolution in the Ukraine and of the war of liberation which the Ukrainians waged in 1917–19, and it lasted uneasily during the NEP period as a temporary concession by the Soviet Russian rulers to the Ukrainian demands for "home rule." Nurtured by the ancient tradition of an independent Cossack Ukraine and powerfully reinvigorated by the national revival in culture, literature, and political thought during the nineteenth century, the Ukrainians emerged during the Revolution as a modern nation with a determination to form a state. Frustrated in their ultimate goal, they nevertheless secured at first a large measure of independence within the Soviet state. The impact of the national strength was so overwhelming that it looked as if the Ukrainian Communists would be able to control the destinies of their country. At least so it seemed to them, and therefore their disappointment was the more bitter and their downfall the greater when with the consolidation of Soviet power in Moscow in the late twenties, they were one by one cast out and condemned by the Party.

There is no reason to think that their hopes of creating an indigenous Ukrainian culture had any support in the policy of the Party. On the contrary, all available evidence seems to point to the fact that the ethnic and cultural freedom of the non-Russian nationalities in the Soviet state was conceded to them at the end of the civil war (1920) only on the specific condition that they must unite under the leadership of the most powerful member of the Soviet Union—Russia. The historians may continue to differ as to whether the old prerevolutionary concept of the "peoples of Russia" was actually displaced by the new formula of the "union of Soviet peoples," or whether the difference between them was only a terminological one. What is significant, however, is the fact that in the period of this illusory freedom there occurred a brief but unmistakably national spiritual revival in Ukrainian literary and cultural life as a whole. Moreover, this national renaissance was so full-bodied and resonant that it became a serious threat to the Communist Party and its centralist concept of the Soviet state and it had to be destroyed as a mortal menace. It not only produced fearless and popular defenders of Ukrainian autonomy like Blakytnyi, Shums'kyi, Skrypnyk, Khvyl'ovyi, and Kurbas, but inspired outstanding works of modern Ukrainian literature by the poets Zerov, Ryl's'kyi, Tychyna, and Bazhan, by the novelists Ianovs'kyi, Khvyl'ovyi, and Pidmohyl'nyi, and by the playwright Kulish. It also helped to produce new and original esthetic theories and to replenish the cultural and literary void left by the ravages of the Revolution and the Civil War. The Ukrainian literary and cultural renaissance of the 1920s therefore stands in the closest relation to the Ukrainian national revolution of 1917–18. It reflects the spirit of national and social liberation rather than of Marxist or proletarian consciousness. It reveals the growing conflict between the national and the Communist concepts of culture, and finally, during the stage of its· destruction, shows a determined stand by Ukrainian writers in particular in the losing battle against the "second revolution" of the early 1930s.

The conflict, it may be said, was the inevitable outcome of the relationship between Kharkov and Moscow, formed in 1919, based on the fallacy of conditional and circumscribed cultural freedom and granted to the former by the latter under the pressure of historical circumstances. While many Ukrainian writers nourished illusions about the success of a literature "national in form and socialist in content," as patterned in Moscow, they cannot be blamed for the ultimate perversion of this impracticable goal into an instrument of Soviet Russian cultural imperialism. On the contrary, they were the first to detect its true character and to fight it, defending that betrayed ideal and the conception of individual and national art which makes artistic freedom indivisible.

Beginning with the literary organization Hart, led by the Borot'bist Blakytnyi, the Ukrainian proletarian writers who had previously scorned the Russian Proletcult chose an independent path in literary creation and literary affairs. They rejected persistent attempts on the part of the Russian proletarian organizations to merge with them. Firmly convinced of the high quality of their own native resources, they not only refused to be guided by their Russian colleagues (except for the formal acceptance of the theory of proletarian literature) but attempted, with some success, to seize the initiative in propaganda and independently to contact Ukrainian literary groups in the Western Ukraine, the United States, and Canada. Simultaneously with Hart, other literary organizations were extremely active and productive either in intellectual and scholarly circles (the Neoclassicists, Lanka, the Futurists) or among the peasants (Pluh).

In 1925, taking advantage of the temporary leniency following the Party resolution on literature, the newly created VAPLITE attempted to carry on the struggle for the unfettered development of Ukrainian literature further than Hart. Its leader Khvyl'ovyi provoked a wide debate on the basic issues of literary theory and practice—the Literary Discussion—which soon reached considerable proportions in extent as well as in depth. While Zerov advocated the return to the sources of Western European literature and to classical literature, Khvyl'ovyi called on Ukrainan writers to turn to Western Europe, to set an example to the peoples of the East, and not to be in any way dependent on Moscow. The severe censure of Stalin and the Party failed to halt Khvyl'ovyi's campaign. Expelled from VAPLITE, after a personal recantation, he continued to organize the resistance to the growing interference of Moscow in Ukrainian cultural life. In the magazine *Literary Fair* (1929–30) and in the literary organization Prolitfront (1930–31) Khvyl'ovyi, convinced that the ideals of the Revolution had been betrayed, remained an outspoken critic of the Party's intention to stifle the free development of national literatures and cultures in the Soviet Union. Until the last moment of his fight against the Party Khvyl'ovyi was supported by many outstanding writers and artists of that time, among whom were the dramatist Mykola Kulish and the producer Les' Kurbas. The foremost Soviet Ukrainian painters of the day, Boichuk, Sedliar, Padalka; Oleksander Dovzhenko, the film producer of European fame; and the economist Volobuiev were all inspired by Khvyl'ovyi to seek a new and revolutionary Ukrainian art. They and their numerous associates represented a vigorous culture, born out of the actual self-determination of nations, created freely on the ruins of the Russian Empire—the "dungeon of the peoples."

Khvyl'ovyi's defeat marked not only the end of a courageous stand on the part of Ukrainian literature and culture against the dictatorial policy of the Party, but also the end of an era. The prolonged and defiant Ukrainian opposition to Party controls, which had manifested itself with such determination in the decade 1924–34, left behind it lasting traces in the cultural and political history of the Soviet Ukraine in the years to come. The Ukrainian branch of the Communist Party had, by abetting the literary deviations, exposed itself to a severe purge which extinguished the foremost light of the Ukrainian Communist movement, Mykola Skrypnyk. For the first time in the history of the second-largest Soviet republic, the Soviet Ukraine, the local Party organs lost the confidence of the Central Committee. They were therefore put under the command of a special emissary of the Central Committee, Pavel Postyshev, who exercised the powers of a despot. That in his drive "to sear with a red-hot iron" Ukrainian bourgeois nationalism Postyshev turned primarily against what was left of the indigenous national tradition in Ukrainian literature reveals how dangerous this Ukrainian intransigency was to the Soviet regime.

While it is impossible to give an exact estimate of the number of writers, scholars, and intellectuals who fell victim to the purges during Postyshev's reign in the Ukraine, the approximate extent of the persecution of the writers can be indicated. The list of losses has been compiled on the basis of such data as (1) documentary evidence in the Soviet press; (2) the date when writers' names disappeared from all periodicals, books, and literary magazines; (3) reference to individual writers who were punished in the works of their friends and associates who left the Soviet Ukraine after 1941. The following Ukrainian writers in the period 1930–38 were referred to as "traitors" or "enemies of the people" in Soviet publications and were subsequently silenced: Antonenko-Davydovych, Budiak, Desniak, Dos'vitnyi, Drai-Khmara, Epik, Fylypovych, Gzhyts'kyi, Ialovyi, Iohansen, Irchan, Ivchenko, Khvyl'ovyi, Kotsiuba, Kovalenko, Krushel'nyts'kyi, Kulish, Kulyk, Kyrylenko, Mykytenko, Os'machka, Pidmohyl'nyi, Pluzhnyk, Valerian Polishchuk, Pylypenko, Semenko, Shkurupii, Slisarenko, Staryts'ka-Cherniakhivs'ka, Tkachuk, Vrazhlyvyi, Vyshnia, Zahoruiko, Zahul, Zerov. With the exception of Zahoruiko, Tkachuk, and Budiak, all the remaining thirty-two were established writers, some of them leading figures of the day.

From later, unofficial sources we learn some details of the circumstances under which writers in this group were purged.[1] On March 28, 1935, Pluzhnyk wrote a letter from prison to his wife, which ended with these words: "I am writing to you while the sun is shining outside, and I can hardly prevent myself from crying out—how beautiful is life, how wonderful is the future of a man who has a right to have a future. I kiss you, my own, and please remember the date of this letter as the date of the most beautiful of my days." [2] Many more personal testimonies of this kind may still be discovered in the private letters of relatives of these writers. Official accounts of the deportations and executions are scarce.

On December 18, 1934, *Visti* printed the verdict of the Supreme Court in Kiev, condemning twenty-eight persons to death by execution, among them four well-known writers: Kosynka, Vlyz'ko, Fal'kivs'kyi, and Burevii.[3]

Among the literary critics purged during the same period were Iefremov, V. Boiko, Lebid', Ovcharov, Iurynets', Muzychka, Shamrai, Doroshkevych, Richyts'kyi, Nikovs'kyi, and Berezyns'kyi.

[1] H. K-ko, "Lyst Ievhena Pluzhnyka v den' vyroku," *Nashi dni*, No. 11, November, 1943.
[2] *Ibid.*
[3] "Vyrok viiskovoï kolehiï naivyshchoho sudu RSR v Kyievi v spravakh terorystyv-bilohvardeitsiv," *Visti*, December 18, 1934. For additional denunciations of writers see: M. Aguf, "Burzhuaznye agenty razoblacheny," *Literaturnaia gazeta*, June 14, 1934; "Zakonchena chistka partiinoi organizatsii pisatelei Kharkova," *Literaturnaia gazeta*, July 6, 1934.

On the basis of a close survey of Soviet Ukrainian periodicals
(1932–37) and supported by the testimony of Ukrainian refugees,[4]
it is possible to state that in addition to names listed previously, the
following writers of second rank with published works to their
credit were hamstrung or handcuffed: Atamaniuk, Bahrianyi,
Bedzyk, Bobyns'kyi, Borziak, Bozhko, Brasiuk, Buzko, Bykovets',
Chechvians'kyi, Chepurnyi, Chernov, Chuprynka, Chyhyryn, Dolengo, Dukyn, Gadzins'kyi, Gedz, Halushko, Hasko, Horban', Hor-
dienko, Hromiv, Hrudyna, Iakovenko, Iaroshenko, Ivanov, Kapel-
horods'kyi, Kichura, Kokhans'kyi, Kolomiiets', Koliada, Kosia-
chenko, Kozoriz, Lan, Lebedynets', Lebid', Lisovyi, Mykola
Liubchenko, Malyts'kyi, Mandzhos, Marfievych, Mohylians'ka,
Mohylians'kyi, Mynko, Mysyk, Orlivna, Paniv, Piontek, Klym
Polishchuk, Savchenko, Shevchenko, Shtanhei, Shymans'kyi, Ste-
povyi, Svidzins'kyi, Tas', Tulub, Voronyi, Vukhnal', Zoria, Zhy-
galko.

These lists, incomplete as they are, speak for themselves. Their
length is the best testimony to the extent of the resistance among
Ukrainian writers to the Stalinist cultural policy. Very few writers
who had at one time been under arrest were able to resume writing
and were readmitted to the loyalists after expiating their sins.
Among them were Ostap Vyshnia, Maksym Ryl's'kyi, and Volodymyr Sosiura. By their willingness to glorify Stalin and Stalin's works
they showed, at least outwardly, a definite change of heart. Force
reduced them to subjection; it failed, however, to conquer more
than one hundred others who had to be destroyed.

Very revealing of the vicissitudes of fortune which befell Ukrainian writers after 1934 is the fate of those who themselves at first
were the instruments of Party control and its chief inquisitors.
Postyshev's principal lieutenants in the Ukrainian branch of the
Soviet Writers' Union during its formation and the first year of its
existence were Kulyk, Kovalenko, and Mykytenko. In April, 1935,

4 See: S. Kokot, "Dolia ukraïns'kykh pys'mennykiv pid bol'shevykamy," *Krakivs'ki
visti,* October 27, 28, 29, 1943; H. Kostiuk, "Ukraïns'ki pys'mennyky ta vcheni u bol'-
shevyts'kykh tyurmakh i taborakh: spohady ta zustrichi," *Krakivs'ki visti,* November
13, 14, 16, 17, 1943; S. Pidhainyi, *Ukraïns'ka inteligentsiia na Solovkakh: spohady
1939–41;* Ivan Bahrianyi, "Pro svobodu slova, sovisty i presy za zaliznoiu kurtynoiu,"
Ukraïns'ki visti, No. 33–34, Easter, 1952; Iar Slavutych, "Iak Moskva nyshchyla i
nyshchyt' ukraïns'kykh pys'mennykiv," *Svoboda,* Sunday Edition, November 2, 1952.

Kulyk, who was the president of the Ukrainian Writers' Union, was removed from his post and A. H. Senchenko was appointed in his place.[5] Postyshev, who had delivered the principal address at this plenary session of the Ukrainian Writers' Union, declared that a writer should be "the protagonist of the most advanced ideals of humanity which are epitomized by our Party led by the great Stalin." [6] With the elimination of Kulyk, what was already notorious as the *dyktatura enkiv* (the dictatorship of the *Enkos*) became an established fact. Yet two years later, when Postyshev lost the confidence of the Central Committee, the triumvirate of Mykytenko, Kovalenko, and A. Senchenko came to a sudden and tragic end. All three of them, as well as such trusted literary Party stalwarts as Shchupak and Koriak, were condemned as "nationalists," "Trotskyites," and "enemies of the people." [7] Their disappearance coincided with the liquidation of Leopol'd Averbakh and other former Rappists in Russia. Having fulfilled their function, the purgers were themselves purged on charges of "Ukrainian nationalism," a general misnomer for all types of nonconformity.

Thus the purging of nationalist deviations went on claiming ever new victims. It never ceased, and most recently (1951) it has laid the Party stigma on that talented lyric poet Volodymyr Sosiura for writing the poem "Love the Ukraine." [8] Today, however, it is no longer as necessary for the Party to use stark terror as it was in the thirties. The opposition once crushed cannot revive under the watchful eye of the Writers' Union and the all-embracing Soviet thought control. Most deviators can hope for mercy after due recantation. The present state of subjection of Ukrainian literature to the dictates of the Party has only been achieved after the decimation of Ukrainian writers and intelligentsia in the earlier period. It was achieved at a cost so high that not even some of the most devout Ukrainian Communists were prepared to pay it. It was conceived and directed chiefly by non-Ukrainians (Stalin, Postyshev, Kaganovich, Kosior) and was followed by the disappearance of the top

[5] *Literaturna hazeta*, 1935, No. 19. A. H. Senchenko is not to be confused with the writer I. Senchenko.

[6] P. Postyshev, *Puti ukrainskoi sovetskoi literatury*, p. 29.

[7] Iaroslav Hordyns'kyi, *Literaturna krytyka pidsoviets'koï Ukraïny*, p. 55.

[8] See: "Reds in Ukraine Scored by Pravda," New York *Times*, July 3, 1951; Albert Parry, "Russia's Latest Witch Hunt," New York *Herald Tribune*, October 17, 1951.

Ukrainian Communists (Chubar, P. Liubchenko, Zatons'kyi, Khvylia), who assisted in the liquidation of opposition in Ukrainian literature and all of whom fell into disgrace before 1938.

The period of this "thwarted renaissance" in Ukrainian literature, therefore, provides an insight into the history of Soviet controls of literature and culture in the non-Russian republics. It reveals how, having found it impossible to achieve harmony and unity in culture on an all-Union scale, the central Communist government in Moscow resorted to violent means in order to stop the decentralizing forces, one of the most vigorous of them being Ukrainian literature. In stamping out the "enemies of the people" among Ukrainian writers and in imposing strict control of the ideological content of literature, the Communist rulers, anxious to build a monolithic Soviet state, had to use the methods and policies of political and cultural imperialism. For not only had the spontaneous development of Ukrainian literature been arrested and its tendencies suppressed, but they were then replaced by concepts imported from Soviet Russia. The Soviet theory of art as "socialist in content and national in form" came to read "Soviet (Russian) in content and only national in language," and since 1939, in English translations (published in the Soviet Union) of Ukrainian writers (e.g., Honchar), no mention is made of their Ukrainian origin.

The national content of Soviet Ukrainian literature has not been eliminated in order to be replaced by a socialist content. This could only have happened at that stage of social development when, as Lenin hoped, the national barriers would exist no more, at the point of the advance of a supranational, be it socialist or Communist, culture. Instead, a spontaneous growth of a national (although mainly proletarian) culture has been forcibly checked only to give way to another, Russian culture, carefully disguised in Ukrainian form and language. In the course of time this disguise was abandoned and the superiority of Russian culture and literature was openly admitted. In 1939 L. Pidhainyi wrote: "Ukrainian literature developed under the beneficent influence of the liberating ideas of the great Russian literature." [9] After the end of World War II, which according to Stalin's victory speech of May, 1945, was won chiefly by the "Russian people, the most prominent nation of all

9 *Literaturnaia entsiklopediia,* XI, 576.

nations constituting the Soviet Union," [10] the dogma of Russian superiority became firmly established. "Russian literature," wrote Piksanov in 1946, "is not only a great national literature; it is a pantheon of all the national literatures of the Soviet Union." [11] Finally, in 1949, Korniichuk surpassed all previous declarations of loyalty by obsequiously admitting that "Ukrainian literature followed in the footsteps of Russian literature. That the Ukrainian people were the first to follow in the footsteps of the Russian people is for us a source of the utmost national pride." [12]

Tragic as was its end, the brief period of the post-revolutionary flowering of Soviet Ukrainian literature and literary theory was of lasting value and permanent significance in the history of Ukrainian literature. It provided the long-awaited opportunity to use the Ukrainian language in literature to the fullest extent and to enrich and perfect it as never before. At the same time Ukrainian writers ceased to represent the intelligentsia alone; they now came from all strata of society and so at long last literature became the expression and the means of communication of the peasant, the worker, and the intellectual, despite the Soviet policy of aiming at the lowest rather than the highest level among the reading public. No longer was there a gap between the semi-illiterate mass and the educated class. Ukrainian literature also gained in depth and breadth by this process of democratization. Its range of genres, themes, and ideas as well as of literary talent increased tremendously. Even more important was the fact that gradually Ukrainian literature gained a definite sense of direction, which was in favor of an independent search for esthetic values in the Western European tradition and culture. The calls "away from Moscow" and "to the sources" were not merely political or cultural slogans. They were arrived at after a painfully long experience of dependence on Russian culture and in spite, or perhaps because, of repeated attempts by the Party to give a pro-Moscow orientation to Ukrainian literature, chiefly through the "proletarian" groups. The literary production of the twenties showed that the precepts of an independent cultural approach could be successfully applied in practice. The Ukrainian

[10] J. Stalin, *O velikoi otechestvennoi voine*, p. 196.
[11] N. Piksanov, *Gorkii i natsional'nye literatury*, p. 227.
[12] A. Korneychuk, "Ukrainian Literature Today," *Soviet Literature*, No. 3, 1949, p. 149.

writers, it must be remembered, were persecuted mainly not because of the pamphlets and articles in which they voiced their views, but largely because their novels, poems, and plays were imbued with an ideology hostile not so much to Communism as to the Communist policy in the Ukraine. It would be wrong to assume that these works were nationalistic or hostile to Communism as such. Soviet Ukrainian writers did not, as is sometimes claimed by émigré critics, use Communism merely as a cloak for their nationalism. Most of them, including Khvyl'ovyi, were Communists by conviction, but they were Ukrainians first and Communists second. In their evolution as writers and thinkers they became aware of the sterility of the Communist cultural policy. By 1934 those of them who had realized the full implications of their spiritual awakening were either dead or deported, while others lived to celebrate the dawn of "socialist realism."

Today, twenty years after the breakup of the Ukrainian literary renaissance, it is possible to state with definite certainty that it has remained alive in the "subconsciousness" of the people in the Soviet Ukraine and may yet prove to be an explosive force for another century. The facts were suppressed but they are not unknown, the ideas were besmirched and exorcised but they are still alive, if dormant in the intellectual and literary strata. This assertion is based on two facts: (1) the continual, though milder, purges and denunciations of "bourgeois nationalism" in the Soviet Ukraine; (2) the sizeable and significant exodus of Soviet Ukrainian writers, critics, and scholars during the time of the German occupation of the Ukraine (1941–44). The first fact is well known and does not need corroboration. The second is of greater interest and significance.

In November, 1941, when the German armies entered Kharkov, Arkadii Liubchenko, an ex-member of Khvyl'ovyi's VAPLITE, one of the few who had survived the purges and who had also succeeded in avoiding the forced evacuation of Ukrainian writers to Ufa prior to Kharkov's fall, made the following entry in his diary:

The Ukraine is rising from the dead. Amid the ruins of war, from fires and ashes she rises like the Phoenix.
Almost half of Kharkov is burnt down by the Bolsheviks. I saw it all. What have we lived through in the last month! And a lot remains ahead of us: hunger, cold, suffering, and blood. . . . But my people having

passed through that horrible blast furnace will learn of a happier life.
No matter what may come the Ukraine, having chosen twenty-five
years ago the path of her own statehood, has not lost her state despite
the storms, the tortures, the persecutions, and the exploitations, and
now a new period of her affirmation is at hand.

Away from Moscow; do you hear, Mykola? If only you were here
right now, if only you were with us![13]

That this declaration was sincere and that it represented a considerable section of Ukrainian public opinion may be seen by the
sizeable exodus of Ukrainian scholars and writers who voluntarily
left the Ukraine with the retreating German armies never to return
to the USSR. The importance of the literature (documents, memoirs, belles-lettres, poetry) of the Ukrainian "displaced persons"
and its relevance for the evaluation of Soviet literary history and
of the intellectual atmosphere have been sadly neglected.

In this study an attempt has been made to use some of the sources
available in the form of published but inaccessible materials, and
to utilize personal accounts and recently published studies of Soviet
Ukrainian literature by refugees from the Soviet Ukraine. A signal
discovery was the material contained in the unpublished papers of
Arkadii Liubchenko. A thorough study of this material, which
would demand several years of intensive research, will complement
the present study by making available the inner history of Ukrainian literary life in the late 1920s and the early 1930s. Such a study
merits a separate volume. The material from Liubchenko's unpublished papers used here has been carefully checked and scru-
tinized. It has been an invaluable aid in illustrating the various
aspects of literary events discussed in this study.

The conclusion suggested by a cursory inquiry into D.P. sources
and supported by some direct historical and some indirect, circum-
stantial evidence is that the literary resurgence in the Soviet
Ukraine during 1917–34 helped to sustain an anti-Communist and
anti-Moscow opposition within that country until 1941. It is moreover possible to think that such an opposition exists today. We
learn from Liubchenko's diary that among the Ukrainian writers
who wanted to join him in German-occupied Kharkov and to escape from Soviet rule were some (whose names, for obvious rea-

13 A. Liubchenko, *Shchodennyk*, p. 7.

sons, he does not reveal) who had received high government deco-rations and who are now manufacturing propaganda under orders from above.

How can this conclusion be reconciled with the theory, some-times offered, that in the Soviet Union "controls become convic-tions," a theory supported by what seems to be equally valid his-torical evidence? Perhaps these different conclusions are not after all conflicting. The truth may be that sometimes controls become convictions and sometimes they do not.

In the history of Soviet Ukrainian literature, in particular for each of the writers who has seemed able to accept controls (Tych-yna, Ryl's'kyi, Bazhan, Panch, Ianovs'kyi, Holovko, Vyshnia, Korniichuk, Le, Malyshko), it is possible to point to one who did not accept them (Khvyl'ovyi, Kulish, Pidmohyl'nyi, Zerov, Pluz-hnyk, Antonenko-Davydovych, Vlyz'ko, Burevii, Slisarenko, Dos'-vitnyi). And if among the latter group (in talent alone certainly the equal of the first) there may have been some whose heresies were not essentially anti-Communist in spirit, so among the first group there may be many opportunists and quietists. Those Soviet Ukrai-nian writers who, like Liubchenko, Os'machka, Bahrianyi, Hu-menna, and Domontovych, came over to the West in 1941 bear witness to the unconquerable spirit of Ukrainian literature.

Although it may be true that the ideological content of the Ukrainian literature which was condemned and suppressed by the Soviets was intensely national, this does not mean that it was an expression of what some modern historians would term with some scorn "ethnic, nationalistic narcissism." In their strivings the Ukrainian writers followed the inevitable path of development of a young nation asserting itself, sometimes exuberantly, after a stir-ring national and social revolution. Yet at the same time they themselves were aware of the limitations of ethnic sources, and they searched for links with Western European culture. "When we take our course on Western European art," wrote Khvyl'ovyi, "it is not with the purpose of hitching our art to a new rear carriage, but with the intention of rescuing it from the stuffy atmosphere of retarda-tion." [14]

At this point, having pursued literary developments in the

[14] M. Khvyl'ovyi, "Apolohety pysaryzmu," *Kul'tura i pobut,* March 28, 1926.

Ukraine chiefly from the viewpoint of power politics, we may ask ourselves what was the significance of this renaissance in purely literary terms? Did the so-called national problem obscure and cloud the vision of Ukrainian writers to the extent that their works may be studied only as documentary evidence of a political struggle?

Fortunately, this is not so. In spite of Soviet attempts (not entirely unsuccessful) to precondition literary creation and to stamp it with the mold of time and circumstance, much of what was written in the Ukraine has lasting merit. Essentially, the "national problem" in Ukrainian literature is but one aspect of the more fundamental issue of individual freedom and the creative quest. A detailed study of Soviet Ukrainian literature would reveal in many works the promise of an original and timeless quality. Not only did it exhibit a great variety of talent, richness of forms and ideas, and a search for new modes of expression. This literature sometimes rang with a force which, although rooted in native tradition, was universal in its intent. However, the conditions under which this literature developed have failed to create a climate in which writers could function as individuals and unfold a truly great art. In their attempt to emancipate themselves as individual artists and to become the bearers of a nascent national literature, the Soviet Ukrainian writers were inspired by their revolutionary national credo, their own brand of Marxism, and their vision of man. They were halted by the rising demands of the Party to conform to the Soviet cultural policy. Only the future will show whether their failure has had a lasting effect on Ukrainian literature.

[XI]

REAPPRAISAL

From Khrushchev's "Thaw" to Brezhnev's "Stagnation"

Literary Politics in the Soviet Ukraine came out in 1956, the year in which Nikita Khrushchev, speaking at the Twentieth Party Congress, attacked Stalin for his crimes against the Soviet state and people. The speech, although delivered at a closed session, had a profound effect on Soviet life and particularly on the non-Russian nationalities. Khrushchev was the first Soviet leader to reveal Stalin's genocidal policies in the Ukraine. Having mentioned the Ukrainian purges, Khrushchev declared that "the Ukrainians avoided meeting this fate [total deportation] only because there were too many of them and there was no place to which to deport them. Otherwise, he would have deported them also."[1] His disclosure of the injustices that the Soviet nationalities suffered under Stalin led to an attempt to reassess Stalin's policies and to revive Leninist ideas. The return to Leninism meant first of all publicizing Lenin's unfavorable views of tsarist Russia as a "dungeon of peoples" and his support for the self-determination and cultural autonomy of the non-Russian Soviet nationalities. New documents were published in *Voprosy istorii* (Problems of History) showing strong disagreement between Lenin and Stalin on the nationality question in general and on the formation of the Soviet Union in particular.[2] Practitioners of the Stalinist dogma found themselves threatened by a strong wave of public opinion in the Ukraine and elsewhere advocating a return to Leninist principles.

---

[1] Nikita S. Khrushchev, *The 'Secret' Speech* (Nottingham, 1976), p. 58.
[2] H. S. Akopian, "Perepiska V. I. Lenina i S. G. Shaumiana po natsional'nomu voprosu," *Voprosy istorii,* 1956, VIII; V. V. Penkovskaia, "Rol' Lenina v obrazovanii SSSR," *Voprosy istorii,* 1956, III.

At the same time, however, Khrushchev advocated the old centralist policies. Perhaps he thought that any liberalization of the nationalities policy would seriously weaken the Party and government. In any case, in 1958 he introduced the new school reform which seriously affected the non-Russian nationalities. Up to that time all Soviet schools had had two required subjects: the local national language and Russian. The 1958 reform left the decision about the teaching of a national language up to the parents. As a result, many non-Russian schools dropped the national language as a required subject and in fact replaced it with Russian. This showed that parents often considered Russian to be the only language necessary for their children, a sure fact of de facto Russification. Strong protests were raised in the Ukraine by some intellectuals, but to no avail. Thirty years later this issue reemerged in the discussion on national linguistic rights. Khrushchev also made it clear that the Soviet Union was not up for dissolution. Speaking at the Twenty-second Party Congress in 1961 he said:

The building of full scale communism is at the same time a new stage in the sphere of national relations in the Soviet Union. . . . The population in the different republics is becoming more and more mixed. . . . All this strengthens the ties between the peoples and nationalities of our country. . . . We do not put any limits on the development of national languages. But that development must not lead to the underlining of national differences; on the contrary, it must lead to a closer relationship between peoples. . . . The rapprochement (*sblizhenie*) of peoples and the social unity of our country are growing. This national unity (*iedinstvo natsii*) will progress as the building of communism goes forward.[3]

Despite Khrushchev's assurance, made in the same speech, that "even after the basis for communism is built it would be too early to declare a merger (*sliianie*) of nations," the tenor of his pronouncement was surely in favor of such a merger.[4] The difference between *sblizhenie and sliianie* is only a matter of degree.

It is against the backdrop of Khrushchev's nationality policy that further developments in the Ukraine must be seen. Obviously this was not the time to reassert Ukrainian national identity, yet the

3 *XXII s'ezd kommunisticheskoi partii sovetskogo soiuza; stenograficheskii otchet* (Moscow, 1962), pp. 215–17.
4 *Ibid.*, p. 217.

rehabilitation of writers after 1956 certainly helped reawaken the national memory. After all, many of the republished writers had been involved in the national reawakening in the 1920s. Among them was Mykola Kulish, the well-known dramatist and former president of VAPLITE. In 1960 a selection of his plays appeared in Kiev with a long introduction by Ie. Starynkevych. The selection omitted Kulish's three best plays—*The People's Malakhii, Sonata Pathetique,* and *Myna Mazailo.* The reasons for the omission are evident in this passage from the preface.

In some works of the second half of the 1920s there is obvious a harmful tendency to slander Soviet reality. . . . This harmful tendency, complicated by serious bourgeois-nationalist deviations, has dictated the distorted portrayal of reality in Kulish's play *The People's Malakhii* (1927) whose genre he defined as "tragic". . . . Kulish is also quite wrong in the portrayal of the national question in the comedy *Myna Mazailo* (1928–29), where he counterposes Ukrainian culture to Russian. . . . The reasons for these serious ideological deviations and creative attempts of the dramatist lay in his inability, for a time, to resist the harmful influence of the militant bourgeois nationalist M. Khvyl'ovyi.[5]

New editions of Kulish's plays in 1968 and 1969 included *Sonata Pathetique* and had less censorious prefaces. Not until 1970, with the publication of a scholarly monograph on Kulish by N. Kuziakina, did a complete survey of his works begin to emerge. Yet Kulish's admirers had to wait until 1989 to see his *Myna Mazailo* republished.[6]

Similarly, the rehabilitation of Mykola Zerov, the leading Neo-classicist, was a long, drawn-out process. In 1960 a volume of his selected poems was printed in an edition of 8,000 copies. In a warm introduction, fellow Neo-classicist Maksym Ryl's'kyi defended the Neo-classicist school of poetry:

Without defending everything said and created by Ukrainian Neo-classicists, among them the works of Zerov, I must, however, firmly declare that in their struggle against Futurism and other Formalist tends, in their call to honour literary tradition, in their love of the Greek and Roman classics, as well as Heredia, Leconte de Lisle, Pushkin, Mickie-

---

5 Ie. Starynkevych, "Dramaturhichna tvorchist' Mykoly Kulisha," M. Kulish, *Pesy* (Kiev, 1960), pp. XVII–XVIII.
6 N. Kuziakina, *Pesy Mykoly Kulisha,* Kiev, 1970.

wicz, Shevchenko and Franko, there was, without question, a healthy kernel.[7]

Ryl's'kyi defended Zerov as someone "who was a poet. I have already said that he loved strict structures. But does this constitute an unforgivable sin?"[8] Zerov—the literary historian and critic—still awaits rehabilitation today.

Another prominent poet, Ievhen Pluzhnyk, was selectively republished in 1966. In a fifty-page introduction Leonid Novychenko deplored Pluzhnyk's isolation and skepticism. He wrote that the poet suffered from "two complexes: first, an unstable and painful psychological position—the result of isolation—[and secondly] the unconquered remnants of social passivity and civic 'uninvolvement'."[9] Novychenko was trying to "explain" Pluzhnyk's poetry as a reflection of the NEP (New Economic Policy) era.

Despite cautionary and apologetic introductions to books by the rehabilitated writers, much was accomplished in bringing into the light some of the prominent forgotten writers of the 1920s. Among them were Hryhorii Kosynka, Dmytro Zahul, Volodymyr Gzhyts'-kyi, Ostap Vyshnia, Serhii Pylypenko, Geo Shkurupii, Oles' Dos'vit-nyi, and Hryhorii Epik. Among those who were not rehabilitated were Mykhailo Semenko, Mykola Khvyl'ovyi, and Valeriian Pid-mohyl'nyi.

All this happened during a gradual relaxation of Party controls over literature. During the Khrushchev regime Soviet Russian writers were split into two camps—conservatives and liberals—and despite official insistence that all literature should follow the precept of "socialist realism" and *partiinost* (Party spirit), many writers and critics, among them Alexander Solzhenitsyn, were following a different path.[10] In the Ukraine the 1957 publication of the lyrical autobiography *Zacharovana Desna* (The Enchanted Desna) by Oleksander Dovzhenko, a leading name in the 1920s and a former *Vaplitian,* began to push back the limits of "socialist real-

[7] M. Ryl's'kyi, "Mykola Zerov—poet i perekladach," M. Zerov, *Vybrane* (Kiev, 1966), p. 7.

[8] *Ibid.*, p. 13.

[9] L. Novychenko, "Po toi bik spokoiu," Ie. Pluzhnyk, *Vybrani poezii* (Kiev, 1966), p. 10.

[10] See Deming Brown, *Soviet Russian Literature Since Stalin* (Cambridge, 1979), pp. 4–10.

ism." In the 1960s many young Ukrainian poets challenged the literary dogmas. Among them was Vasyl Symonenko (1935–63), a poet committed to social and national problems, many of whose poems circulated clandestinely. A group of young poets, referred to as *shestydesiatnyky* (the sixtiers), became very popular with readers. It included Ivan Drach (b. 1936) , Mykola Vinhranovs'kyi (b. 1936), Lina Kostenko (b. 1930), and Vitalii Korotych (b. 1936), who, in the distant future, was to become a leading Soviet journalist. It has been argued that this group received vital stimulus for their works from the republished poems of the 1920s. At about the same time Ukrainian dissidents began to publish in underground *samvydav* (samizdats). Among them was Ivan Dziuba, the author of *Internatsionalizm chy rusyfikatsiia* (Internationalism or Russification, 1968) , who later recanted and was pardoned after a brief imprisonment. In the chapter devoted to the abolition of "Ukrainization" Dziuba dealt with the purges of writers and intellectuals in the 1930s. His call was for a return to Lenin's nationality policy. Other dissidents were the essayist Valentyn Moroz, the poet Ihor Kalynets', and the prose writer Mykhailo Osadchyi. Echoes of the 1920s were clearly evident in their works.

An event of great literary importance was the publication in 1967–71 of the *Istoriia ukrains'koi literatury* (History of Ukrainian Literature) in eight volumes. Volume 6 (1970) dealt with literature between 1917 and 1932, the "period of struggle for the victory of socialism." In spite of the usual jargon about class struggle and the war on "bourgeois nationalism" the volume does contain a great deal of factual information about the writers who later perished in the purges. Seventeen whole pages are devoted to the works of Khvyl'ovyi, yet little is said about the decimation of the writers. This period in literature, we learn, "was complicated by the circumstances of the personality cult which seriously affected the development of literature."[11] A different type of literary history of the 1920s was contained in the three volumes of memoirs by a prominent writer, Iurii Smolych: *Rozpovid' pro nespokii* (A Story of Restlessness, 1968); *Rozpovid' pro nespokii tryvaie* (A Story of Restlessness Continues, 1969); and *Rozpovidi pro nespokii nemaie kintsia* (A Story of Restlessness Has No End, 1972) . Like the popu-

11 *Istoriia ukrains'koi literatury* (Kiev, 1970), VI, p. 15.

lar Russian memoirs of Iliia Ehrenburg, Smolych's work helped re-create the atmosphere of the earlier period. Smolych devoted separate chapters to the purged writers Kulish, Iohansen, Vyshnia, Irchan, Slisarenko, Dos'vitnyi, Pidmohyl'nyi, and Svidzins'kyi, but he also wrote at length about VAPLITE and other disbanded literary groups. His novelistic style omits any direct mention of the purges, but many of the writers are recalled as fine and sensitive human beings. No statistics are offered, but the book replenishes the memory of a forbidden era.

What was given with one hand, enlivening recollection of the short-lived revival, was taken away by another, preaching the new dogma of "multinational Soviet literature." As if to exorcise the earlier period, much was made of Russia's "elder brotherhood" as the cornerstone of Soviet literary history. Mykhailo Pryhodii, an expert in reinterpreting the past (when mentioning Khvyl'ovyi he puts the word communist in quotation marks) published two treatises showing the "drawing together" of Russian and Ukrainian literatures.[12] The independent development of Ukrainian literature, a dream of the leading writers in the 1920s, was not to be.

In 1972, with the fall of the Ukrainian Communist Party chief, Petro Shelest, there came a new wave of arrests of Ukrainian dissidents. This time Sverstiuk, Chubai, and Stus joined those previously arrested. The period of "stagnation" was, once more, a euphemism. Recent articles in *Literaturna Ukraina* described it as follows:

The problems of publication, documentation and work themes were discussed at the beginning of the past decade superficially, from the conservative point of view. Fast journalism was regarded as the last word in literary creation; artistically valuable works were pushed onto the back burner and their authors were subjected to abuse. Ready-made, clearly defined optimism was propagated everywhere by administrative measures. Every sign of civic courage, if it managed to get into the pages of literary publications, was treated as "subversion." Several fine works by O. Honchar, H. Tiutiunnyk, Ie. Hutsalo and V. Drozd were suppressed. Rarely printed were M. Vinhranovs'kyi and I. Zhylenko; Valerii Shevchuk, Lina Kostenko, M. Vorobiov were silent. . . . It was a time of great social demagoguery and deafening solemn rheto-

12 M. Pryhodii, *Dialektyka zblyzhennia literatur* (Kiev, 1970); *Vsesoiuzna konsolidatsiia literatur* (Kiev, 1972).

ric, which paralyzed many living forces, killed many altruistic strivings. Writers were visibly broken, getting used to the instructions not to write as they felt but as they ought to feel, with ready-made models and recommended cliches. No mention was made of V. Symonenko, Ie. Pluzhnyk, V. Ellan-Blakytnyi, M. Zerov, V. Svidzins'kyi, B. I. Antonych. It was recommended that several words in the Ukrainian language not be used, although they were to be found in Shevchenko and Lesia Ukrainka.[13]

A year later the same writer wrote even more harshly:

Gross administrative interference in the literary process, artificial restrictions placed on the freedom to create, the ruthless meddling of a
whole army of officials into purely literary matters during the period
of stagnation led poets to be cautious, afraid of the man with an at-
tache case, ready to conform to the milieu. Those who could not or
would not conform were left alone with thoughts of their own professional inadequacy.[14]

The Brezhnev regime did not resort to the stark terror used by Stalin, but stifled literature nonetheless. Such opposition as there was came from silent non-cooperation and from the dissent move-
ment. The nature of this opposition reflected, to some extent, the problems encountered by writers in the 1920s. Then, as now, some writers tried to escape into a personal and apolitical world (in the 1920s, Pluzhnyk, Zerov, and Pidmohyl'nyi; in the 1970s, exemplars were the poets Chubai and, in part, Kalynets and Stus). On the other hand, like some of the writers of the earlier period (Khvyl'-
ovyi, Kulish, Ianovs'kyi), their successors in the seventies (Symo-
nenko, Kostenko) devoted themselves to national, even political, themes. The politicization of literature through the enforcement of "socialist realism" thus evoked a twofold response.

In the West the 1960s and 1970s saw unflagging interest in the literature of the 1920s and 1930s, expressed above all in the repub-
lication in the United States, Canada, and Western Europe of banned or forgotten works of that period. The five-volume edition of the works of Mykola Khvyl'ovyi[15] and the editions of Zerov[16] and Pluzhnyk,[17] to mention only the most important, belong here.

13 A. Makarov, "A chomu b ne sprobuvaty," *Literaturna Ukraina,* May 21, 1987.
14 A. Makarov, "Pisni pokhmurykh dniv," *Literaturna Ukraina,* May 19, 1988.
15 Mykola Khvyl'ovyi, *Tvory v piatiokh tomakh* (New York-Toronto, 1978–86).
16 Mykola Zerov, *Sonnetarium* (Munich, 1948); *Catalepton* (Philadelphia, 1951); *Corollarium* (Munich, 1958).
17 Ievhen Pluzhnyk, *Try zbirky* (Munich, 1979).

Some English translations of Khvyl'ovyi,[18] Kulish,[19] and Pidmohyl'nyi[20] were also published. Last, but not least, mention should
be made of some Ph.D. dissertations at American and Canadian
universities—the literary discussion of 1925–28,[21] Khvyl'ovyi,[22] and
Pidmohyl'nyi.[23] These contributions enhanced the knowledge of
the forgotten period.

The Coming of Glasnost

Radical changes in the life and culture of the Soviet Ukraine
came only in the wake of the new regime of Mikhail Gorbachev,
especially his policy of glasnost. As part of this policy he declared
and reiterated several times that there must not be any "blank
spaces" in Soviet history. "Openness, as was stated at the January
[1987] plenary session of the CPSU Central Committee, is a necessary condition for the process of democratization of our society and
one of the most important guarantees of the irreversibility of the
changes that have begun."[24] In the same speech Gorbachev acknowledged that "Soviet nationalities have developed their own
intelligentsias. They are studying the roots of their origins, and
sometimes this leads to the worship of history and everything connected with it, not just the progressive elements. . . . The only
correct approach here is the Leninist nationalities policy, the Leninist spirit. . . ."[25]

Yet while proclaiming "openness" and freedom to delve into national histories, Gorbachev was sounding a note of caution. "Openness," he declared in another speech, "does not mean the under-

18 Mykola Khvylovy, *Stories from the Ukraine* (New York, 1960); *The Cultural
Renaissance in Ukraine; Polemical Pamphlets* (Edmonton, 1986).

19 Mykola Kulish, *Sonata Pathetique* (Littleton, 1975).

20 Valerian Pidmohylny, *A Little Touch of Drama* (Littleton, 1972).

21 M. Shkandrij, "The Literary Discussion in the Soviet Ukraine, 1925–28," unpublished Ph.D. dissertation, University of Toronto, 1980.

22 D. Ferguson, "Lyricism in the Early Creative Prose of Mykola Khvylovy," unpublished Ph.D. dissertation, University of Toronto, 1976; for an original study of
Khvyl'ovyi's links with the anthroposophy of Rudolf Steiner, see L. Pliouchtch, "Le
mystère de l'anthroposophie ukrainienne," *Triades,* XXXVI (1989), p. 3.

23 M. Tarnawsky, "Valerijan Pidmohylnyj, Guy de Maupassant and the Magic of
the Night," unpublished Ph.D. dissertation, Harvard University, 1986.

24 M. Gorbachev, *Pravda,* February 14, 1987, here quoted from the *Current Digest
of the Soviet Press,* XXXIX, No. 7 (1987), p. 6.

25 *Ibid.,* p. 7.

mining of socialism and our socialist values."[26] Obviously, interpretations of national history could clash, in his opinion, with "socialist values." An even clearer picture of how Gorbachev viewed
the history of the 1920s and 1930s was provided by him in "October and Restructuring" in *Pravda* on November 3, 1987:

The period after Lenin—the 1920s and 1930s—occupies a special place
in the history of the Soviet state. Fundamental social changes were
carried out, there was a sharp and many-levelled struggle. Industrialization, collectivization, the cultural revolution, the strengthening of the
multinational state . . . all these things took place during this period.
For decades we have returned to this time again and again. . . . This
was an exploit of historic scope and historic significance. . . . And if
today we look at our history with a sometimes critical eye, it is only because we want to get a better and fuller picture of paths to the future.
It is necessary to assess the past with a sense of historical responsibility
and on the basis of historical truth. . . . [It is necessary] because these
years are at the center of many years of debate, both in our country and
abroad, a debate in which, in addition to the search for the truth, attempts are frequently made to discredit socialism as a new social system, as a realistic alternative to capitalism.[27]

It is clear from the above that Gorbachev does not advocate a
revisionist view of the 1920s–30s. Not once does he mention Stalin
or Stalinism. Although he encourages a search for truth he is ada-
mant that this period was an "exploit of historic scope."

The Ukrainian intellectuals in 1987 saw it very differently. The
1930s particularly were being viewed as a period of martyrdom for
the Ukrainian intelligentsia and peasantry. As for Stalin, they saw
in him the embodiment of all evil. Still, in 1984, shortly before his
death, the veteran inmate of the GULAG, Borys Antonenko-
Davydovych, released an account of Stalin's meeting with the
Ukrainian writers in 1929. In the first edition of my book this episode was mentioned briefly (p. 144). Now, fifty-five years later,
Antonenko-Davydovych, who was present at the meeting in 1929,
has made his account public in *samvydav*. He described how, at the
meeting with Stalin and Kaganovich, Stalin, in defining the difference between a nation and a nationality, declared that Ukrainians were not a nation. Told by a Ukrainian writer that there was

---

[26] M. Gorbachev, *Izvestiia*, July 16, 1987; here quoted from the *Current Digest of
the Soviet Press*, XXXIX, No. 28 (1987), p. 6.
[27] Here quoted from the *Current Digest of the Soviet Press*, XXXIX, No. 44
(1987), pp. 4–5.

one Ukrainian literary language in both Western and Eastern Ukraine, the West being represented by such writers as Franko, Shashkevych, and Fedkovych, Stalin asked mockingly: "Tell me, is this Shashko, Fed'ko, Franko translated into Ukrainian?"[28] Then someone asked why, in the Ukraine, only Ukrainian bourgeois nationalists and not Russian chauvinists were being arrested and tried. Stalin brushed this aside, asking for concrete examples of Russian chauvinism (no one dared to name any). When asked why Ukrainians living just outside the Soviet Ukraine were not joined with their brethren, Stalin answered: "We must not offend the Russians." Finally, to wind up the interview, Kaganovich asked an inane rhetorical question—"Do the Ukrainian girls still sing?"— and the meeting came to an end. The Ukrainian writers, who included Tychyna, Khvyl'ovyi, and Pidmohyl'nyi, were disgusted both with Stalin's answers and with his flippant tone. Now, in the 1980s, this story has gained wide circulation among those who held Stalin responsible for many heinous crimes in the Ukraine.

The Congress of Soviet Ukrainian writers which met in Kiev in June 1986 devoted much of its time to the discussion of language, the bureaucratization of literature, censorship, and ecology. Pleas were heard for the republication of writers of the 1920s. Still under the impact of the Chernobyl tragedy, most speakers showed concern about the state of the environment and about the Ukrainian language, which was fast disappearing from schools and public life. Khrushchev's law allowing parents to choose the language of instruction for their children no longer held, since many cities, having no Ukrainian schools, could offer no choice. The Ukrainian literary magazine *Prapor* (Banner), published in Kharkov, began printing a series of debates on the "dialectics between the national and the international in life and literature,"[29] with frequent reference to the 1920s. This debate continued from 1987 to 1989 and grew more and more open. The eminently readable newspaper *Literaturna Ukraina* (Literary Ukraine) announced on June 4, 1987, that it would devote some space in each issue to the "forgotten heritage." The first item was a tribute to Mykola Zerov by

28 B. Antonenko-Davydovych, "Spohad pro pryiom Stalinom ukrains'koi delegatsii 1929 roku," *Suchasnist'*, Nos. 7–8, 1984, p. 10.

29 "Dialektyka natsional'noho ta internatsional'noho v zhytti i literaturi," *Prapor*, Nos. 7–11, 1987; Nos. 1–3 and 5–12, 1988; Nos. 1–4, 1989. For continuation see "Cherez pravdu zhyttia do istynnoi kul'tury," *Prapor*, No. 8, 1989.

Borys Ten on June 18, 1987. In April 1988 the paper published an article by Mykola Zhulyns'kyi on Mykola Khvyl'ovyi which signalled the rehabilitation of this major figure. It was followed by very revealing articles on VAPLITE by Natalia Kuziakina[30] and by an article on Mykhailo Semenko by Halyna Chernysh.[31] Many more "forgotten" figures were brought to light in subsequent issues—too many to be listed here. Literary journals were not to be outdone in publishing the banned works of the 1920s. The magazine *Kyiv* (Kiev) printed Volodymyr Sosiura's long poem "Mazepa," first written in 1928 and rewritten in 1959–60. It may be viewed as Sosiura's attempt to reinterpret the famous Hetman. In the same issue of *Kyiv* Iurii Barabash wrote a daring interpretation of Mazepa as being "governed by love of his native country as well as love of power."[32] The same magazine published Sosiura's novel *Tretia rota* (the name of the author's native village) first written in 1926 and continued in 1942 and 1959. Sosiura described the free artistic milieu of *Hart* and his open admiration of Khvyl'ovyi. "After Ialovyi's arrest," he wrote, "a shot from a Browning was heard, when Mykola Khvyl'ovyi blew out his magnificent brain, spattering blood on the walls of his room where he worked, I swear, only out of love for his people."[33]

Apart from Khvylovyi, another major writer, Valeriian Pidmohyl'nyi, untouched by the rehabilitations of the 1960s, was recovered. Several of his short stories were republished in 1988. The February 1988 issue of the journal *Vitchyzna* (Fatherland) contained his novella *Povist' bez nazvy* (A Tale Without a Title). The same issue of *Vitchyzna* printed a selection of Pidmohyl'nyi's letters to his wife from exile. Both are a signal contribution to our knowledge of Pidmohyl'nyi. His letters, chiefly concerned with his work, contain a very revealing expression of what came to be known in the West as "the Stockholm syndrome" (love of one's captors). Writing to his wife from a concentration camp in 1936, Pidmohyl'nyi confesses that "I have seen now that in my life I

30 Natalia Kuziakina, "Mykola Kulish v 'Harti,' Urbino i VAPLITE," *Literaturna Ukraina*, February 4, 11, 25, and March 3, 1988.
31 H. Chernysh, "Ne obmynaite Semenka," *Literaturna Ukraina*, September 18, 1988.
32 Iurii Barabash, "Ivan Mazepa—shche odna literaturna versiia," *Kyiv*, No. 12, 1988, p. 145.
33 V. Sosiura, "Tretia rota," *Kyiv*, Nos. 1–2, 1988, p. 103.

was wrong, and life has never been as beautiful as it is now. . . .
My occupation now is reading, above all Marxism-Leninism, the
history of socialism."[34] The year 1989 was even kinder to Pidmohyl'nyi. His great novel *Misto* (The City) was republished in
an edition of 30,000 copies. In the preface the prominent prose
writer Valerii Shevchuk characterized the author of *Misto* as a
"psychological writer whose chief artistic task is the analysis of the
human psyche."[35] Another publication, like Pidmohyl'nyi's letters,
was the release of Zerov's letters from the GULAG.[36] They are a
sad account of Zerov's attempts to continue his translations. It is
expected that more material of a similar nature will soon appear
in print. Khvyl'ovyi's letters to Zerov make fascinating reading.[37]
Excerpts from Tychyna's diaries from 1921–22 were published in
Dnipro.[38] An open discussion of Tychyna's years under the Stalinist regime (he, like Ryl's'kyi and Bazhan, accepted Party controls)
was started by Stanislav Tel'niuk. He wrote: "Writers and artists
such as Tychyna, Ryl's'kyi, Bazhan, Sosiura and others experienced
moral torture and also had to write 'Long live Stalin.' Sometimes
they even believed in the greatness, wisdom and farsighted genius
of Stalin and his henchmen. This was not unreality but the terrible reality of these times."[39] An important republication was
of Pluzhnyk's poetry with a long and disappointing introduction
by Leonid Cherevatenko, who rejects the notion that Pluzhnyk was
a skeptic and attempts, unsuccessfully, to portray him as an almost
engagé writer.[40] A very different view of Pluzhnyk, the alienated
artist, was provided by Volodymyr Bazylevs'kyi.[41] Finally, Mykola
Kulish's brilliant comedy *Myna Mazailo* was published in *Vitchyzna*, No. 1, 1989.

A new history of Soviet Ukrainian literature appeared in 1988
as the second volume of a History of Ukrainian Literature. The

34 *Vitchyzna*, No. 2, 1988, p. 103.
35 V. Shevchuk, "U sviti prozy Valeriiana Pidmohyl'noho," V. Pidmohyl'nyi, *Misto*, (Kiev, 1989), p. 4.
36 "Z lystuvannia M. K. Zerova," *Radians'ke literaturoznavsto*, Nos. 1 and 4, 1988.
37 "Vidrodzennia maibutnioho; Lysty M. Khvyl'ovoho do M. Zerova," *Radians'ke literaturoznavstvo*, Nos. 7 and 8, 1989.
38 P. Tychyna, "Shchodennyk," *Dnipro*, No. 2, 1988. See also S. Tel'niuk, *Pavlo Tychyna; Iz shchodennykovykh zapysiv* (Kiev, 1981).
39 S. Tel'niuk, "Narodovi ie chym pohordytysia," *Literaturna Ukraina*, October 6, 1988.
40 L. Cherevatenko, "Vse chym dusha bolila," Ie. Pluzhnyk, *Poezii* (Kiev, 1988).
41 V. Bazylevs'kyi, "Ievhen Pluzhnyk," *Literaturna Ukraina*, November 10, 1988.

pages dealing with the 1920s and 1830s (pp. 22–110) are on the whole accurate, but with less stress on Party controls and the purges. The volume defends "socialist realism" and accuses Western "bourgeois" scholars of maintaining that control was imposed from above. It contains a short and mild paragraph about the purges:

Great difficulties arose in the literature of that period caused by the complicated internal and external circumstances of the time and particularly by the negative influence of Stalin's personality cult on the development of art. Many prominent writers (Vyshnia, Kulish, Mykytenko, Irchan, Kulyk, Pylypenko, Kosynka, Slisarenko, Pluzhnyk, Vlyz'ko et al.) as a result of a violation of Soviet legality, were in the latter part of the 1930s purged for no reason and this has complicated the atmosphere of creative life.[42]

The ink was barely dry on the second volume when furious attacks were launched against it. It was pointed out that this history was still a product of the "era of stagnation" and the Academy of Sciences demanded that a new volume be published reflecting the devastation of literature during the 1920s and 1930s.[43]

A Reevaluation of the Literature of the 1920s and 1930s

The rediscovery of this literature has begun during the present era of glasnost and is likely to continue on a much larger scale. Plans have been announced for the republication of multivolume editions of the works of Khvyl'ovyi, Zerov, Pidmohyl'nyi, Kulish, Antonenko-Davydovych, and many other banned or hitherto only partially rehabilitated writers. There is general agreement today that the past heritage of Ukrainian literature must be restored, although accompanied by new interpretative introductions. Soviet readers are still not trusted to make up their own minds about what they read. The new introductions will, no doubt, tell of the fate of the writers, but will they truly cast light on their works? It remains to be seen.

The rehabilitation of the charismatic leader of VAPLITE, Mykola Khvyl'ovyi, deserves special mention. In several articles his

---

42 *Istoriia ukrains'koi literatury v dvokh tomakh*, II (Kiev, 1988), p. 47.
43 V. Donchyk, "Radians'ke literaturoznavstvo prahne suspil'noho rozholosu," *Literaturna Ukraina*, September 28, 1989.

suicide in 1933 has been described as an act of defiance. A suicide note, which rather pathetically proclaimed that he died a true communist, was produced in order to include him in the fold of the true Leninists. A long search was conducted to recover the second part of his novel *Val'dshnepy* (The Woodcocks) and the seditious pamphlet *Ukraina chy Malorosiia* (Ukraine or Little Russia). Finally, perhaps the most fitting tribute was paid to him by the young writers who issued an almanac called *Literaturnyi iarmarok* (A Literary Fair) in emulation of his famous magazine of 1928–30.

In the meantime, on a much deeper level, attempts are being made to reevaluate the bright as well as the tragic aspects of the 1920–30 period and to draw lessons for a new understanding of Ukrainian culture. First of all the magnitude and the significance of the purge of writers in the 1930s are being discussed. One author has suggested that

the genocide of 1933 and 1937 in Eastern Ukraine was, indeed, terrible in its consequences because not only did it deform historical memory, not only did it destroy the healthiest link with the national life, but it affected the genetic code of the nation. Thoughtless and untested acts in the sphere of international relations [between the Ukraine and Russia] have decidedly altered the traditional structure of both national mores and the national psyche.[44]

Genocide here refers primarily to the manmade famine of 1933 in which 7 million peasants are said to have perished, but the decimation of the Ukrainian intelligentsia in the 1930s is now seen as part of this genocide. It has begun to figure prominently on the long list of grievances which the Ukrainians in an era of glasnost are ready to submit to public scrutiny. No wonder, therefore, that one of the questions they have been trying to answer is just how many writers were destroyed during the national holocaust of the 1930s. Unexpected help in estimating the losses came from a Russian source. In 1988 a Russian researcher, Eduard Bel'tov, published the results of his study of the purges of all Soviet writers. Among them, "almost 500" came from the Ukraine.[45] Bel'tov's staggering figure seems a little inflated to me, as in 1988 I also

44 V. Medvid', "A se vin sam," *Literaturna Ukraina*, June 22, 1989.

45 E. Bel'tov, "Eto nuzhno ne mertvym—zhivym," *Knizhnoe obozrenie* June 17, 1988; see also V. Panchenko, "Ne zabuty b pro korin' problemy," *Literaturna Ukraina*, July 25, 1988.

published my study of the literary purges.[46] Working with limited sources, with no access to Soviet archives, I arrived at a total of 254 writers who were victims of repression. Later, in 1989, Mykola Zhulyns'kyi gave the total approximate figure as 300.[47] But even if the total is less than Bel'tov's 500, the losses are staggering. Further painstaking research is needed to arrive at an accurate conclusion. There is little doubt as to the absurdity of the official charges against individual writers. The writers included both fellow travelers and communists, those showing a great deal and others with little promise, some for and some against the Party policy. In the final analysis, they were destroyed because they were Ukrainian intellectuals. Now they have become martyrs.

As soon as the enormity of Stalin's crimes was established, a great deal was published in various journals documenting individual cases. For reasons of space these cannot be listed here. A journal that paid special attention to this field was *Zhovten'* (October), published in L'viv. It printed several factual reports as well as Roman Ivanychuk's novel *Bo viina viinoiu* (This Is War, *Zhovten'*, Nos. 7–8, 1989), which contains a rare novelistic treatment of the tragedy of Mykola Khvyl'ovyi and his friends (in the chapter "The Story of Nina Krauze").[48] Very occasionally, scholarly books have attempted to reassess the literature of the 1920s and 1930s (for example, Iu. Kovaliv's *Romantychna styl'ova techiia v ukrains'kii radians'kii poezii 20–30-kh rokiv* [Romantic Stylistic Currents in Soviet Ukrainian Poetry of the 1920s–30s, Kiev, 1988]).

At the end of 1987 an important conference took place, dedicated entirely to the literature of the 1920s and 1930s. It was convened in December 1987 at the initiative of the Writers' Union and the Academy of Sciences and included both writers and scholars among the participants. It was a landmark among scholarly deliberations in the Ukraine and deserves close scrutiny.[49]

[46] G. S. N. Luckyj, *Keeping a Record; Literary Purges in Soviet Ukraine (1930s); A Bio-Bibliography* (Edmonton, 1988).

[47] M. Zhulyns'kyi "Iz falanhy vybuvaly naikrashchi," *Suchasnist'*, No. 10, 1989, p. 32.

[48] E.g. M. Horbach, "Ukrainizatsiia; zlet i trahediia," *Zhovten'*, No. 2, 1989; P. Arsenych, "Vy zhertvoiu vpaly," *Zhovten'*, Nos. 5 and 6, 1989.

[49] The first report appeared in "Pravo na vdiachnu pamiat," *Literaturna Ukraina*, January 21, 1988. A more detailed account is in "Perebudova i literaturna nauka; pro vyvchennia i vydannia ukrains'koi radians'koi literatury 20–30-kh rokiv," *Radians'ke literaturoznavstvo*, No. 5, 1988. Here the second report will be used.

The first speaker was Mykola Zhulyns'kyi, deputy director of the Shevchenko Institute of Literature of the Academy of Sciences. He declared that

As long as we are not certain that VAPLITE and Mykola Khvyl'ovyi, "Literary-Scientific Herald" and Chuprynka, VUSPP and Serhii Pylypenko, Hnat Mykhailychenko and Mykhailo Ivchenko, Andrii Khvylia and Volodymyr Koriak, Panfuturism and the Neoclasicists, Aspanfut, and the "Young Muse" with all their positive and negative qualities belong to the history of Ukrainian literature we cannot, with confidence, speak of a national literary process and of the place of Soviet Ukrainian literature in a panunion and world context. This does not mean that we must close our eyes to ideological mistakes.[50]

He pleaded for additional "deeper and systematic" study of the period, admitted that all those writers who were destroyed were "groundlessly excluded" from literature, and called for the preparation of a complete bibliography of the period. Above all, he demanded that new "canonic" texts of all the forgotten writers be established.

The next speaker, writer Dmytro Pavlychko, made this interesting observation:

The pessimistic books by V. Pidmohyl'nyi and Ie. Pluzhnyk, as well as the many works of that period written in a minor key (e.g. the mood of "Blind Minstrels" by M. Bazhan or V. Mysyk's "Horizon Blackens in the South")—are symptoms of the uncertainty and disappointment brought about by Stalin's dictatorial policy. . . . Ukrainian literature, in the early 1930s and even before, sensed the danger of Stalinism.[51]

Critic Anatolii Pohribnyi spoke of the need to understand the priority of universal human values over class values. He was also worried that new editions of banned writers would be printed in small editions and cited as an example a recent publication of Valeriian Polishchuk in 1,500 copies.

Critic Petro Kononenko wondered how a new history of Ukrainian literature could be written in the complete absence of philosophical and aesthetic works. In other words, much more is needed than the mere republication of the literature.

The writer Ivan Drach was conscious that the 1920s were a time of "decisive events in the Ukraine: the being or non-being of the

50 *Radians'ke literaturoznavstvo,* No. 5, 1988, p. 8.
51 *Ibid.,* p. 13.

Ukrainian people. . . . We wish, somehow, to go back to those years, to the tragic truth of that era."[52] Oddly enough, as a good communist, Drach felt that work on the 1920s and 1930s should be directed by the Institute of the History of the Party, including the Central Committee.

Leonid Boiko illustrated his argument for the rehabilitation of the writers of the thirties by concentrating on the unjust treatment of Borys Antonenko-Davydovych. Literary historian Mykhailo Iatsenko returned to the question of supporting disciplines needed in the preparation of a new history of literature. "Where, in our universities," he asked, "do we teach the history of Ukrainian art, the history of Ukrainian culture, where, apart from the faculty of history, is the history of the Ukraine taught? Our student, the future specialist [in literature] does not have the foggiest idea about these."[53]

A note of caution and disagreement with earlier speakers was sounded by Iurii Kovaliv, who saw a danger in creating "a coordinating council," perhaps a "new administrative bloc." He was interested in using other means (*inshi khody*). So not everybody agreed with the idea of a central administrative approach to the problem.

Vitalii Donchyk was pessimistic—"we have not yet done anything." He hoped for a new Marxist approach to the problem.

At last, the eminent critic Leonid Novychenko had this to say: "We all know only very inadequately the literary developments of the 1920s–30s, especially about the part which until now has been hidden, like the legendary Atlantis, under water. Hence we still use half-century-old stereotypes. . . ."[54] He then turned to Lenin for assistance in approaching the forgotten era. He called for a careful analysis of all the past phenomena—"the contradictory nature of that era," especially of the "literary discussion of 1925–28." He upbraided Khvyl'ovyi for issuing the call "away from Moscow"—which, in Novychenko's opinion, was and is a mistake. Yet he admitted that Khvyl'ovyi's concept of "psychological Europe" is applicable to Ukrainian literature notwithstanding its close ties to Russian literature. Like other speakers before him,

52 *Ibid.*, p. 19.
53 *Ibid.*, p. 23.
54 *Ibid.*, p. 25.

Novychenko would like to see the preparation of "A History of Ukrainian Culture" in three volumes to give a wider context for literary studies.

The conference issued the following "resolutions":

The scholarly council of the Shevchenko Institute of Literature of the Academy of Sciences of the Ukrainian SSR and the presidium of the executive of the Writers' Union of the Ukraine having discussed at a joint meeting the problems of scholarly study, propaganda, and publication of the literary heritage of writers of the 1920s and 1930s, have produced a program of action for scholars and writers for the coming years.

The decisions of the 27th Party Congress and the last plenums of the Central Committee of our party have opened to specialists of all branches of the national economy and culture the paths of revolutionary restructuring, the establishment of the principles of *glasnost,* the widening of democracy, the application of a new approach to analysis of social events and phenomena. This also applies to literature and literary scholarship, particularly in rectifying historical justice as regards a series of works and their authors, the confirmation of a scientifically objective view of artistic phenomena etc. "I agree"—said the Secretary-General of the Central Committee of the CPSU M. S. Gorbachev in January 1987 at a meeting with the leader of the mass media and propaganda—"there should be no forgotten names or blank spaces in either history or literature. Otherwise it is neither history nor literature, but artificial opportunistic structures."

Soviet Ukrainian literature, born in class struggle for the victory of the ideals of October and formed according to the Leninist principles of the Party (*partiinost*) and national spirit (*narodnost*) was created by a large number of artists dedicated to the cause of socialism. Some of them were immediate participants in the socialist revolution and civil war, others entered the literary field a year or two after October. Side by side with them there were also those who gradually accepted the program of a revolutionary restructuring of life and became its literary chroniclers.

Succeeding generations are grateful to the pioneers of a new Soviet literature in the task of building socialist culture. Their successes are generally known and appreciated as their weighty contribution to the artistic life of the people, the aesthetic education of the workers.

Yet, as a result of objective and subjective causes, the literary development of the 1920s–30s has been presented by literary historians as impoverished. Many names of writers and their works were groundlessly excluded from the literary process. A large number of these names and works remains unknown to the general reader and to some literary scholars, especially the younger ones.

It is necessary, therefore, to create the concept of a genuinely complete literary process. The result of such an initiative will have not only purely scholarly but also social significance because it relates to the problems of scientific methodology and the counter-propaganda of ideological activists.

The scholarly council of the Shevchenko Institute of the Academy of Sciences of the Ukrainian SSR and the presidium of the executive of the Writers' Union of the Ukraine has decided:

1. The Shevchenko Institute of Literature should direct its scholarly efforts towards improving the existing concept of the history of Ukrainian literature and begin preparations for a new multi-volume history of Ukrainian literature.

2. To request the social sciences section of the Academy of Sciences to begin as part of its scholarly projects work on an interdisciplinary history of Ukrainian culture.

3. The Shevchenko Institute of Literature of the Academy of Sciences and the secretariat of the Writers' Union of the Ukraine should create a co-ordinating scholarly council dedicated to the study and publication of the works of Ukrainian writers who, for different reasons, have been excluded from the history of Soviet literature or were studied tendentiously and not objectively.

4. To produce, by 1995, a most complete and new edition of the works of the rehabilitated and silenced writers of the 1920s–30s (in particular, complete editions of the works of M. Zerov, M. Kulish and M. Khvyl'ovyi) adhering constantly to high ideological and aesthetic standards and principles of Marxist-Leninist methodology. The Institute of Literature should work out recommendations for the publications up to 1995 and oversee their fulfillment [of the project] and the necessary scholarly apparatus. Editions of all works should be accompanied by the necessary research apparatus, with analytical prefaces and commentaries and an analysis of the texts. Qualified literary scholars, especially those from the Shevchenko Institute of Literature, must be brought into the work on the proposed volumes.

5. To ask the State Publishing of the Ukrainian SSR to empower central and regional publishing houses of the republic to prepare plans for editions of original and translated works of authors of the 1920s–30s who were unjustly silenced.

6. For the purpose of a thorough and objective study of the literary process of the 1920s–30s to begin publication of the annual "Heritage" which would print the unknown or little known manuscripts of writers, works printed with deletions, diaries, notes, letters and other archival material.

7. To raise before the Presidium of the Academy of Sciences the question of photo-offset republication of a series of scholarly works for research purposes, like *Za 25 lit, Literaturna khrestomatiia* (For 25 Years—a Literary Anthology) by A. Lebed' and M. Ryl's'kyi, the two-

volume *Khrestomatiia novoi ukrains'koi literatury* (Anthology of New Ukrainian Literature) by M. Plevako, the collection of materials *Shliakhy rozvytku ukrains'koi proletars'koi literatury; Literaturna dyskussiia 1925–28 rr.* (The Paths of Development of Ukrainian Proletarian Literature; Literary Discussion 1925–28, 1928), the two-volume bio-bibliographical reference work by A. Leites and M. Iashek *Desiatrokiv ukrains'koi literatury; 1917–27* (Ten Years of Ukrainian Literature, 1917–27); the almanacs *Muzahet* (Musagetes, 1918), *Zshytky borot'by* (Chapbooks of Struggle, 1919), *Chervonyi vinok* (Red Wreath, 1919), *Hrono* (Cluster, 1920), *Vyr revoliutsii* (Whirlpool of Revolution, 1921), *Zhovten'* (October, 1921) *Kvartaly* (Quarterlies, 1921) as well as a series of periodicals from those years.

8. To empower the Shevchenko Institute of Literature and the Writers' Union to plan a series of literary portraits of writers, especially writers of the 1920s–30s who have not received the attention of specialist studies (Mykola Khvyl'ovyi, Mykola Zerov, O. Vlyzko, D. Buzko, H. Kosynka, Ia. Mamontov, M. Iohansen, Ie. Pluzhnyk, V. Pidmohyl'nyi, B. Antonenko-Davydovych, V. Polishchuk et al.).

9. To consider it advisable to publish an exhaustive anthology of literary and critical studies of the 1920s–30s including the speeches of prominent party and state personalities (M. Skrypnyk, V. Zatons'kyi, P. Postyshev, S. Kosior et al.) concerned with the development of Ukrainian literature and culture.

10. To publish in the series "School Library" separate volumes and anthologies of the better works of the 1920s–30s, for children and young people.

11. To recommend to the State Committee on Television and Radio to disseminate widely on television and radio the little-known works of the 1920s–30s, with the help of leading literary scholars and writers.[55]

Beneath the jargon of the resolutions hides the serious intent to restore the period from 1920 through the 1930s to its rightful place. But the rigidity and central control of all the measures proposed must also be acknowledged. Is the same machine which decades ago expunged the 1920s and 1930s to be trusted with their restoration? There seems to be no alternative. Perhaps most disturbing is the fact that the resolutions say nothing about more liberal access to the so-called *spets-fondy* (special library funds) of literary material and to the KGB archives.

Immediately after the publication of these resolutions voices were raised expressing some apprehension. Anatolii Pohribnyi used a much more graphic description of the purges than was

55 *Ibid.,* pp. 27–28.

given in the restrained language of the resolutions. "Like a deluge," he wrote, "the 'heroes' of Stalin and Kaganovich passed over our literature. We must add to this martyrology many of the names of writers of the highest calibre who violated their talents in order to fit in with Stalinist ideology."[56] He was worried that the republication work would be slow and that editions would be limited. A similar concern was expressed a few months later by the well-known dissident Vasyl' Barladianu, who, writing in an underground publication, pleaded for the mass publication of the works of the 1920s.[57] He claimed that the Ukraine, like Ireland, was in danger of losing its language. This happened in Ireland, he argued, because Irish writers stopped writing in Gaelic and wrote in English. Only mass editions of the literature of the 1920s could attract Ukrainian readers who have been gradually abandoning Ukrainian literature.

A prominent part in the discussion which followed was played by Ivan Dziuba, the former dissenter and now a leading proponent of glasnost. In January 1988 he wrote a provocative article on the "incompleteness" of Ukrainian culture.[58] He often referred in his article to the 1920s as representative of the beginning of a complete culture which was later shattered. Now he urged swift action in restoring the 1920s. "So far names have appeared, but we need books, books, books," he wrote.[59] He saw the problem of reevaluation in much more complex terms.

We stand in need of a new concept of the literary history of the 1920s–30s–40s. This problem has two aspects, each dramatic in itself. First—the restoration of everything in literature which was confiscated. Second, a sanitary investigation of those infected zones which arose in areas of mass political and ideological poisoning. . . . While [a new history of literature] is being written, literary scholars, critics and writers would perform a welcome service if they would give us their subjective versions, some alternative approaches to different periods in our literary past.[60]

[56] A. Pohribnyi, "Pro mimikriiu-pavliukiiu, zabuti imena abo bili pliamy," Literaturna Ukraina, September 15, 1988.

[57] Kafedra, No. 5, 1989.

[58] I. Dziuba, "Chy us'vidomliuiemo natsional'nu kul'turu iak tsilisnist'?" Kul'tura i zhyttia, January 24, 1988.

[59] I. Dziuba, "V oboroni liudyny i narodu," Literaturna Ukraina, June 23, 1988.

[60] Ibid.

In other words, Dziuba, like many others, was afraid that the Academy of Sciences will come up with a single "line." A pluralistic approach to reevaluation was better.

The problem of how to approach the 1920s and 1930s was again evident in a conference, convened in 1989, devoted to "socialist realism."[61] Most speakers agreed that "socialist realism' was a harmful dogma, but Novychenko tried to salvage a place for it in literary history. Today, "socialist realism" is dead as a literary theory and its death in the Ukraine was assisted by the reclamation of the literary works of the 1920s which readers have recognized as much superior. On the whole, however, Ukrainian attempts to reevaluate practices and policies of the 1930s have been timid in comparison with Russian attempts. It was in Russia, too, that attempts are now being made to form literary groups in loose association with the centrally controlled Writers' Union (for example, the group "April"). In the Ukraine very few voices were raised against that former bastion of "socialist realism"—the Writers' Union. Among them was the voice of a prominent prosewriter, Volodymyr Drozd, who was not afraid to criticize the bureaucracy of the Writers' Union.[62] A dissolution of the Writers' Union and a return to the free atmosphere of various literary groups in the 1920s seems inconceivable.

The political events of 1989 have had an impact on literature. The dismissal of the hard-line Party boss in the Ukraine, Volodymyr Shcherbyts'kyi, coincided with the formation in September 1989 of the National Movement in Ukraine for Reconstruction (*Narodnyi rukh Ukrainy za perebudovu,* known as *Rukh*), led by the writer Ivan Drach. The man who replaced Shcherbyts'kyi, Volodymyr Ivashko, "offered," according to an American correspondent, "to curb the official harassment of his republic's growing nationalist movement and to begin a period of co-operation, provided the nationalists do not advocate secession from the Soviet Union."[63] The Rukh leadership seems to have accepted this new

61 "Sotsialistychnyi realizm—poniattia teoretychne chy istorychne, *Radians'ke literaturoznavstvo,* No. 8, 1989.
62 V. Drozd, "Literaturni pytannia i literatura," *Literaturna Ukraina,* June 16, 1988.
63 Bill Keller, "For Ukraine, Softer Touch by the Party," *New York Times,* October 8, 1989.

Party line and is pursuing a course of moderation. In its program, Rukh clearly recalled "the almost total destruction of the Ukrainian national intelligentsia during the era of Stalinist repression." and pleaded for "the restoration of the lost works of literature," a clear reference to the 1920s and 1930s.[64] In a separate resolution the manifesto went on to denounce Stalinism in the strongest terms.[65]

There are striking historical parallels between 1917 and 1989. On both occasions the political leadership in the Ukraine fell into the hands of writers and intellectuals (in 1917 Hrushevs'kyi and Vynnychenko; in 1989 Drach and Iavorivs'kyi). The prestige of writers has always been high in the Ukraine and real politicians were in short supply. This analogy with 1917 raises another interesting point: Is there, in the politicization of the writers, a parallel today with the era of Khvyl'ovyi? I put this question directly to Ivan Drach in an interview in Toronto on October 19, 1989. Without hesitation, Drach replied that he and other leaders of Rukh regard themselves as successors to Khvyl'ovyi, whose portrait adorns Drach's study. The work begun in the 1920s is being continued today. Let us hope it will have a different denouement.

It seems that today the restoration of the great cultural renaissance of the 1920s and 1930s has begun in earnest. One can still have serious reservations about the methods, the extent, and the success of this restoration. The present moment of intense politicization of culture does not favor the restoration of the more private aspect of that era which, in a "complete culture," is of lasting value.

In a different sense, however, the "completeness" of Ukrainian literature has made good progress under glasnost. The drive to vindicate the literature of the 1920s and 1930s has also led to the lifting of the ban on some prominent Ukrainian writers of the nineteenth century (notably Panteleimon Kulish), as well as many émigré writers hitherto regarded as nationalists. Today their nationalism is being disregarded and they have rejoined Ukrainian literature. Those writers publishing in Ukrainian in the diaspora

---

64 "Prohrama narodnoho rukhu Ukrainy za perebudovu," *Literaturna Ukraina*, September 28, 1989.
65 "Pro stalinizm i stalinshchynu," *Literaturna Ukraina*, October 19, 1989.

(North America, Europe, Australia) have also been admitted to the fold. In this way the rehabilitation of the 1920s has led to the enrichment of the literary heritage of the Ukraine.

The ravages of Stalinism will continue to fascinate and repel any human being. A little-known writer, Stefaniia Andrusiv, speaks for many when she writes:

> Perhaps no other literature has produced so many toadying, enthusiastic and obsequious *chefs d'oeuvre*, to put it bluntly, such lies, that it is no wonder that our people have turned their backs not only on literature, as something irredeemably false, flattering and primitive, but also on the language. . . . Our terrible judgement on these carriers and servants of evil must also be a judgment on ourselves, because evil of such a magnitude, such a deep deformation of morals and psychology, could not avoid anyone. We are all victims and we are all guilty, though not in a criminal sense. . . . We must purge ourselves, at last, from the curse of Stalinism, from malice, hatred, cruelty, impatience, suspicion, slavish humility and all-pervasive fear, from stupidity, provincialism and falsity of thought and feeling.[66]

The need to reflect on the past brings to light unspeakable terrors but also the beauties of a literature which although submerged, was never quite lost. The rediscovery of this literature in the era of glasnost leads to a greater awareness of Ukrainian national identity on the eve of momentous historical changes.

[66] S. Andrusiv, "Shcho my bez materi u sviti?" *Zhovten'*, No. 9, 1989, pp. 88–89.

APPENDICES

APPENDIX A

DRAFT DECREE ON ENCOURAGING THE DEVELOPMENT

OF CULTURE OF THE UKRAINIAN PEOPLE [1]

Explanatory Note to the Decree

In the course of the development of the world revolution the Soviet government of the Ukraine has become, by force of circumstances, a source of supply for Soviet Russia and the bridge which links the latter with the outbreaks [i.e., centers] of European revolution. To strike at this bridge and destroy it is the aim of counterrevolution. Establishment of this bridge has more and more become an [urgent] necessity for the motive forces of the All-Russian [*Rossiiskaia*] Revolution.

Hence the intermittance and complexity of the development of the revolution in the Ukraine; hence its involvement by attendant factors, external forces, and blows. During the fierce reaction of the Hetmanate and the time of the mighty surge of the proletarian revolution, leadership was in the hands of external forces, in large measure alien to the basic conditions of life of the Ukrainian people and to the natural course of their revolutionary development.

This circumstance, this constant pressure of external forces, entangles manifestations of the social struggle with those of the national struggle, disproportionately aggravates the manner in which the already complex national question is raised, and gives vitality to the nationalist movement originating among the bourgeoisie and the bourgeois intelligentsia.

At the same time the proposition which conditions us to regard the Ukraine merely as a convenient ground for the development and maneuvering of the military forces of the socialist revolution, on the one hand, does not provide an opportunity to exhaust and enroll in the struggle all reserves of the local social forces and, on the other

[1] "Proiekt dekreta o sodeistvii razvitiiu kul'tury ukrainskogo naroda," in *K razresheniiu natsional'nogo voprosa* [Toward a Solution of the National Question], 2d enlarged ed., Kiev, Borot'ba, 1920, pp. 15–20. The draft was prepared in 1919 by Oleksander Shums'kyi. For permission to use this translation of the decree I am indebted to the Research Program on the USSR, the publishers of Iwan Majstrenko, *Borot'bism: A Chapter in the History of Ukrainian Communism.*

hand, impedes a formulation, in all its fullness, of the question—of limitless importance—concerning the development of the culture of the Ukrainian people.

Constrained by centuries of national and social oppression, without schools in their native language, deprived of an intelligentsia, and reduced to inertia resulting from the Russification of all state and public institutions throughout the land, the Ukrainian proletariat and peasantry are faced either with the nationalist tendencies of the bourgeois intelligentsia or with the actual domination of the Great Russian language and culture in all the vast apparatus of the Soviet government in the Ukraine.

The one threatens, through the nationalist poison, to obscure the purity of the class consciousness of the working masses; the other does not provide or create the conditions for the natural development of national forms of culture and their use as an important weapon in the struggle for international unification of the toiling masses.

Formal recognition of the equal rights of languages and cultures, a policy of neutrality [in these matters], offers no solution to these socio-political and cultural conflicts.

The century-old process of systematic and planned "Russification" [obrusitel'stvo] brought about a state of affairs in which the Ukrainian nation, once literate almost to a man [sic], by 1898 had a literate population of only 13.5 percent; the cities were transformed from centers for the crystallization of cultural attainment into coercive seats of an alien culture; the school became, as Ushinskii aptly remarked, the only place in the village where the spoken language was not understood. The entire state technical apparatus, all leaders and agents of the government for decades were trained automatically and without exception to eliminate all Ukrainian forces from administrative life. There developed a serious inertia which is reflected with rare eloquence in the figures for the ratio of the [total] population to the secondary schools in the Ukraine: Ukrainians, 77.1 percent of the population, have 121 schools; Russians, 12.6 percent of the population, have 950 schools; in other words, the quota of secondary schools for the entire native population is 10.8 percent, while the quota for the Russian population is 84.7 percent.

Text of the Decree

The victorious movement and lasting success of the Communist Revolution, which is paving the way for the construction of new social relationships and which is enrolling in this construction vast masses of the proletariat and peasantry, depend in large measure on the fullness, clarity, firmness, and sharpness of the class consciousness among these masses of revolutionary builders, on the constancy of their consciousness in the face of enormous ideological dangers resulting from the social system which is being overthrown.

The clarity and constancy of class consciousness, its depth and strength, are directly linked with the general cultural level of the working class, with the degree to which the working class, as a whole and among its individual members, is enrolled in active and independent creative work in the culture of mankind. But the growth of culture, especially at its outset, is unthinkable outside of national forms, outside the natural and free development of the national element of a given people; therefore, the paths of the Communist International lie not on the plane of disregard and oppression of national forms, particularly among backward nationalities, but in the necessity of raising their cultural development to the level of the more progressive nationalities and of merging them at the heights of international unity of all toilers.

Whoever sincerely desires the growth of consciousness and international unification of the working masses can only want and strive for the most rapid development of the national forms of culture among those peoples who, like the Ukrainian people, have been held in a state of national stagnation and oppression by the harsh rule of capitalist society.

In the extraordinarily complex circumstances of the development of the socialist revolution in the Ukraine, special attention must be devoted to projecting a true policy with regard to the development of national cultures, in order thereby to disarm those social groups who, through their native or Jesuitical guardianship of national culture, conceal social aims which are alien and hostile to the working class and who regard the development of national forms not as a road to international unification of the toilers but as a means of realizing their own imperialist desires.

On these grounds, in supplementing and elaborating upon the corresponding articles [of the Constitution] of the Provisional Workers' and Peasants' Government, the Central Executive Committee directs the People's Commissariat of Education, as the organ responsible for cultural and educational work in the Republic, systematically and in a planned manner to pursue a policy of encouraging in every way the development of Ukrainian culture in all branches of national life. It is therefore essential:

1. In education outside the schools, as the most important field of educational activity, during the trying period of the socialist revolution, to carry on systematic work in widening the limits and deepening the basis of class consciousness, utilizing for this purpose all facts and impulses flowing from the national element which is native and close to the people.

2. In social education (the preschool and school system) for the Ukrainian population in schools and other educational institutions, to carry on instruction in the native Ukrainian language.

NOTE 1. For the non-Ukrainian population schools will be founded with instruction in the language of that nationality for which the school is opened.

NOTE 2. Determination of the language of instruction in educational institutions will be made by the People's Commissariat of Education through its organs.

3. In the realization of this task, to organize on a broad basis the training of a suitable cadre of professionals [*rabotniki*] and the publication of appropriate literature and technical materials.

4. In the organization of higher institutions of learning, tirelessly to pursue the constantly growing need and demand for the suitably trained Ukrainian professional in all walks of life, the professional able with creative initiative to enter this life and enrich the spontaneous growth of national culture.

5. Into the unplanned and chaotic growth of the Ukrainian book market, to bring organization and system, which will lead to the broad development and dissemination of both original works of Ukrainian national literature and translated literature in all problems and branches of learning.

6. In the field of art, to develop, discover, and record the results of all branches of national art work in national forms, by organizing appropriate institutions and [taking] proper steps.

APPENDIX B

BLAKYTNYI'S MANIFESTO OF THE ALL-UKRAINIAN

LITERARY ACADEMY

The national rebirth of the Ukraine coincided with her social liberation. On the historical-cultural stage there appeared simultaneously a young nation and, leading it, a young advanced social class.

That is why the flowering of Ukrainian letters at the present time inevitably shows itself in proletarian literature. That is why contemporary Ukrainian October literature should, and does, enter the arena of world culture as one of the first proletarian cultures in the world, marking the path which, sooner or later, will be trodden by literatures of other nationalities.

The signs of the proletarian flowering of contemporary Ukrainian literature and art are here. Before our eyes, during the past two or three years, there has grown and continues to grow the pleiad, born in October, of prominent Ukrainian poets, novelists, and critics—Bolsheviks in spirit, masters of their craft.

It would be criminal toward proletarian Communist culture not to exploit, not to notice, the present moment, a moment of spontaneous cultural and creative upsurge of the Ukrainian masses inspired by the proletarian revolution. An opportunity must be given to this cultural movement of the Ukrainian masses to develop both widely and deeply. It is imperative to remove all obstacles, whether psychological or physical, from the path of this development. First of all, the literary sector of Ukrainian proletarian literature, the most important ideological front, must be strengthened and supported. The Ukrainian October literature must be led out into the broad, all-Union, and European arena. Now, in the interests of both the Ukrainian and the Russian proletariat, the time has come to end the period of self-limitation of Ukrainian culture.

In Europe, and particularly in Russia, not only do the wide circles of proletarian society not know Ukrainian culture, but they have, instead, a distorted, crude, coarsely jocose idea of it. In Russia, where the oppression of the old ruling culture of the nobility and the bourgeoisie is especially perceptible, where an ideological irresolution still reigns in the field of the embryonic proletarian literature, the experiments, tendencies, and successes of Ukrainian October proletarian culture are of special importance.

The Literary Academy intends to acquaint the Union republics and the proletarian circles of the West with the achievements of Ukrainian literature.

The Literary Academy intends to establish contact between Ukrainian proletarian literature and the proletarian literatures of other nationalities, and to encourage the reciprocal exchange of creative and cultural experience.

The Literary Academy intends to awaken the activity of the Ukrainian masses in the field of literature and to organize this activity in the proletarian Communist spirit and in the highest contemporary style.

The Literary Academy intends to apply the principles of Leninism to the field of literary and artistic policy.

The Literary Academy accepts the pronouncement of comrade Trotsky, "the methods of art are not the same as those of Marxism," as meaning that art demands a subtler, deeper, and tactically finer—in Lenin's interpretation—application of the methods of Marxism, and aims at the further development and application of these methods.

The Literary Academy strictly adheres to the class principle in the field of culture. It regards as one of the tasks of contemporary Ukrainian literature the strengthening of the union between village and town, between the peasant and the proletarian intelligentsia, and the expression of this union under the ideological leadership of the proletariat.

The Literary Academy intends to organize cells of Ukrainian proletarian literature in Western Europe and America.

The Literary Academy takes the initiative in organizing similar academies in the federal Soviet republics.

Long live the proletarian renaissance in Ukrainian literature! Long live Ukrainian proletarian culture! Long live the International of proletarian culture!

APPENDIX C

RESOLUTION OF THE POLITBUREAU

OF THE CENTRAL COMMITTEE OF THE CP(B)U

ON UKRAINIAN LITERARY GROUPINGS, 1925

I. *On Hart*

The Politbureau reaffirms that no single existing literary organization, including Hart, can claim that it alone represents the Party in the field of literature, or holds a monopoly in applying the Party line in this field.

At the same time, however, the Politbureau of the Central Committee regards as harmful the agitation against Hart alleging that it is a nationalist organization, hostile to the Party, and so forth. Notwithstanding some errors which were shown in the inadequate enrollment of the proletarian writers, especially from among the workers' correspondents, and in some castelike exclusiveness, the Politbureau of the Central Committee recognizes that Hart, during the entire period of its existence, has accomplished a great deal in uniting around the Party and Soviet government the most active and talented representatives of contemporary Ukrainian literature and poetry. To a certain extent, Hart has unified the Ukrainian front of proletarian writers against the bourgeois nationalist ideology. The Congress of Hart acknowledged the defects of the organization and passed resolutions which should remedy them.

II. *On Pluh*

The existing organization of peasant writers, Pluh, is carrying on a great and responsible work which the Party must support, on condition that the local groups of Pluh do not assume a mass character and do not merge with the organizations of the village correspondents. The workers' and village correspondents are, as was pointed out in the resolutions of the 13th Congress, only reserves, from which, through the work of literary organizations, proletarian and peasant writers should be recruited. Pluh should remain the organization of peasant

writers. Local centers of Pluh must be created only where there are
Party organizations to direct their work. The Central Committee calls
on the Party organizations to take this task upon themselves and on
no account to allow the local centers of Pluh to be severed from the
Party.

III. *On Fellow Travelers*

Fellow travelers in the Ukraine (Lanka, a group of writers centered
around the journal *Life and Revolution*) who accept the platform of
the Soviet government should be treated according to the directive on
fellow travelers issued by the All-Union Party.

IV. *On Literary Criticism*

The Central Committee deems it necessary to organize serious Marxian criticism and a bibliography which would disclose defects and deviations which are present in an equal degree among the writers of
Hart and other literary groupings. Such criticism, while aiding talented
Soviet writers, should at the same time point out their errors, which
occur because the Soviet writers do not always understand correctly the
Soviet policy, and should also direct them toward the liquidation of
bourgeois and nationalist transplantations.

APPENDIX D

POLICY OF THE PARTY CONCERNING UKRAINIAN LITERATURE;

RESOLUTIONS OF THE POLITBUREAU OF THE

CENTRAL COMMITTEE OF THE CP(B)U, 1927

1. Accepting as a basis the resolution on literature of the Central Committee of the All-Union Communist Party of June, 1925, the Central Committee of the CP(B)U considers that:

The building of socialism in our land, which predicates the creation of a Soviet Ukrainian culture, gives special prominence to the creation and development of Ukrainian literature. While it is a powerful instrument in the cultural advancement of the masses of workers and peasants, in manifesting the building of a new socialist culture, Ukrainian literature at the same time becomes one of the most important means of strengthening the union of the working class with the peasantry, a weapon of the proletariat in its direction of the entire Ukrainian cultural development. Therefore, the proletariat is faced with the task of actively participating in this field and, above all, of gaining wide knowledge of Ukrainian literary art, as well as of organizing proletarian thought connected with this problem (the dissemination of Ukrainian books among the workers, in the trade union and other libraries; the study of this literature in workers' clubs, in Party committees, in the Komsomol; literary debates and the holding of "evenings" with the participation of the workers; etc.).

Ukrainian literature should be provided with a proletarian environment which would influence it and thus direct it socially, while bringing out new literary talent from among the workers.

2. In directing the work, aimed at the heightening of the social and artistic qualities of literary art, the Party combats all counterrevolutionary, bourgeois-liberal, and similar tendencies in literature. At the same time, however, the Party is in favor of free competition between different groupings and trends in this field. "While supporting materially and morally the proletarian and proletarian-peasant literature, aiding fellow travelers and other writers, the Party cannot give a

monopoly to any single group, even the most proletarian, as to its ideological content, since this would mean the end of proletarian literature" (from the Resolution of the Central Committee of the CPSU, of June, 1925).

Therefore, no single literary group existing in the Ukraine can claim a monopoly or priority.

3. The artistic quest of Ukrainian writers who accept the platform of the proletarian revolution is conducted in the realm defined by the June plenum of the Central Committee of the CP(B)U, which proclaims that in the building of socialist culture a struggle for its ideological purity continues against the hostile forces of the bourgeoisie.

As to the path of Ukrainian literature:

The Party stands for an independent development of Ukrainian culture for an expression of all creative forces displayed by the Ukrainian people. The Party supports the wide use by the Ukrainian socialist culture of all the treasures of world culture. It is in favor of a definite break with the traditions of provincial narrowness, in favor of the creation of new cultural values worthy of a great class. However, in the Party's view, this cannot be done by contrasting Ukrainian culture with the cultures of other nations, but through brotherly cooperation between the working and toiling masses of all nationalities in the raising of an international culture to which the Ukrainian working class will be able to contribute its share. (The June Plenum of the Central Committee of the CP[B]U.)

The creation of a young Ukrainian proletarian literature can be advanced only along the path of its own betterment, by the revelation of new artistic values, by enrichment with the cultural heritage of mankind as a whole. However, Ukrainian proletarian writers must approach all the sources of bourgeois literature armed with sharp Marxian weapons in order not to fall into the snare of a hostile ideology.

4. The creation of a genuine Ukrainian proletarian literature can take place only on the basis of a constant connection with the masses of the workers and peasants, a manifestation of artistic qualities characteristic of the proletariat, and a continual mutual influence between the writers and the masses.

The turning away of individuals from this basis, the severance of contacts with it, self-adulation and exclusiveness, even if carried on under the slogan of "qualifications," would lead to social and artistic decay.

5. One of the means by which literature preserves its ties with the masses is the use of artistic images characteristic of the working class or peasantry. This must not, on any account, lead to literary backwardness, that is, to the rejection of the achievements of world literature and to the vulgarization of the work itself. The slogan of the fight

against parochialism is correct when it protests against parochial narrow-mindedness and the influence on literature of the backward kulaks; it is, however, unconditionally false and harmful when it ignores entirely literary material characteristic of the peasantry.

The task consists in leading the growing cadres of the peasant writers on to the path of proletarian ideology, without depriving them of those artistic images which are characteristic of the peasantry, and which form a necessary precondition of influencing the peasantry. (The Resolution of the Central Committee of the CPSU.)

6. In order to fulfill the task of the proletariat, which is the transformation of all social life, Ukrainian literature, sharing the platform of the proletarian revolution, must comprehend and express, in artistic transformation, all aspects of social life. All kinds of limited concentration of art, in the narrow circle of village life, or standing aloof from the entire proletarian complexity of the life of the workers, or else, on the contrary, an absolute detachment from the life of the toilers, or an escape from life in general—into mysticism, exoticism, decadence, or individualist self-analysis—impair the forces of the proletariat and its creativeness. Decadence, which may be seen in certain provinces of literature, leads to a lack of proper perspective and deprives literature of its active influence in socialist construction.

All the above phenomena decrease the social value of a literary work and at the same time become bridges over which foreign influences of class elements hostile to the proletarian construction pass into our literature.

7. Recently, the bourgeois elements in literature have manifested themselves not only in the "ideological work, designed to satisfy the demands of the growing Ukrainian bourgeoisie" (Resolution of the June plenum of the CP[B]U), but also abroad, among Ukrainian writers of the fascist and nationalist camp, where began, in union with fascist Poland, a literary campaign against the socialist Ukraine. (For example, the novel *Vbyvstvo* by Mohylians'kyi and other works.) Such anti-proletarian tendencies manifested themselves in the works of Ukrainian bourgeois litterateurs of the type of the Neoclassicists. They were not met by any opposition; on the contrary, some fellow travelers and VAPLITE, headed by Khvyl'ovyi and his group, supported them.

8. All this demands that Ukrainian proletarian writers most clearly define the social significance of their works, that they most definitely rid themselves of all bourgeois influences, and most attentively approach the task set for them by the Party—of struggle against the antiproletarian and counterrevolutionary elements, of combating the ideology of the new bourgeoisie, encouraged in literature by the fellow travelers of the "Change of Landmarks" group, while at the same time "viewing patiently the ideological thought of different social elements

and constantly helping to use this inevitably wide range of forms in the process of comradely collaboration with the cultural forces of Communism" (Resolution of the Central Committee of the CPSU).

9. These tasks will be fulfilled only when the Party shall muster sufficient cadres of Ukrainian Marxist criticism. Ukrainian Marxist criticism should set as its goal an approach to every work of literature from the class and social point of view and should note the artistic accomplishments of a work regardless of the school to which it belongs. (Molodniak, Pluh, Ukrlef, VAPLITE, the Neoclassicists, Khvyl'ovyi's group, Mars, etc.) While aiding the discovery and development of fresh literary talent, especially from the proletariat, Marxian criticism should help, in a comradely fashion, individual writers and literary groups which have committed errors, deviated from the proletarian path, and have been in danger of succumbing to nationalism, to realize that they have an obligation to recognize and to confess their errors and to amend them in their further practical literary work.

Criticism should expose the divergencies in the camp of the fellow traveler writers, combat bourgeois manifestations, recognizing those who gravitate to proletarian literature, and thus enroll those fellow travelers who are closest to us in the socialist construction.

10. Ideological differences as to literary forms among groups which continue to sustain the tasks of socialist culture must not assume the form of enmity; they should be manifested on the unifying ground of proletarian solidarity, which sets before all literary groups the task of their union in an All-Ukrainian Federation of Associations of Proletarian Writers, which should also embrace the literary groups of the national minorities in the Ukraine (Jewish group and Russian group— with its journal *Red Word,* etc.).

11. In view of the fact that a large number of Ukrainian workers and toilers abroad live in a state of cultural austerity, and that many Western Ukrainian writers (from Poland, Czechoslovakia, and Rumania) are now residing in the Soviet Ukraine, an association of Western Ukrainian revolutionary writers should be created.

12. The unity required by the creation of socialist culture, which faces the toilers of every Soviet republic, demands an even greater unity in cultural work of all the peoples of the USSR.

The association of proletarian writers of the Ukraine should enter into friendly relations with similar writers' associations in Russia, Belorussia, Georgia, and all other Union and autonomous Soviet republics. This would lead to their union into an All-Union Alliance of Literary Federations of all Peoples of the USSR on the principles of proletarian internationalism, while combating any national opposition or pretensions at hegemony, as well as attempts to belittle the independent cultural creation of each people. This work should be carried on in a friendly manner for the common mutual influence of literature on socialist construction.

13. In order to fulfill these tasks, it is necessary to use and support all measures to widen the contacts of Ukrainian writers with the writers of other peoples of the USSR (increasing translations into Ukrainian of works by writers of other nationalities of the USSR, as well as foreign exchange of visits between the writers of Ukraine, Russia, Belorussia, Georgia, and other Soviet republics; obligatory participation of Ukrainian writers in various literary delegations from the USSR abroad, which have a Pan-Union character; etc.).

The Central Committee asks all Party and Soviet organs to give moral and material aid to Ukrainian writers and their organizations.

The Central Committee instructs the Commissar of Education to take concrete steps toward the improvement of the status of the revolutionary writers of the Ukraine (author's rights, standard of living, health services, publications).

14. The Politbureau of the Central Committee of the CP(B)U instructs the Press Department to take concrete steps toward the implementation of the above resolutions and to take prompt action to see that they are carried out.

APPENDIX E

THESES ON THE RESULTS OF UKRAINIZATION; PASSED BY THE

PLENUM OF THE CENTRAL COMMITTEE OF THE CP(B)U

IN JUNE, 1927

[EXTRACTS]

X

At the present time we observe an ideological struggle among Ukrainian literary groups, like the Neoclassicists and the higher intelligentsia, which is designed to satisfy the demands of the growing Ukrainian bourgeoisie. One feature common to all these circles is the desire to direct the economic development along capitalist lines, to direct a course toward relations with bourgeois Europe, opposing the interests of the Ukraine to the interests of other Soviet republics.

Such views have found some sympathy in declarations by some members of our Party who have fallen under an alien influence and have again put forward the watchword of the "struggle of two cultures," and who request that the Party give its unreserved support to Ukrainian culture, as opposed to Russian culture, and who quite forget the clear advice of Lenin on this matter:

When one speaks of the proletariat, then the opposition of the Ukrainian culture as a whole to the Great Russian culture as a whole means a shameful betrayal of the proletariat in favor of bourgeois nationalism. If a Ukrainian Marxist is possessed by a quite natural hatred for his Great Russian oppressors, and if he transfers even a small part of this hatred, be it only a feeling of alienation, to the cause of the Great Russian proletariat, then this Marxist will fall into the mire of bourgeois nationalism. (Lenin, "The National Bugbear of Assimilation," *Sochineniia*, Vol. XIX.)

The watchwords of orientation toward Europe, "Away from Moscow," and so forth, which have appeared in the press, are significant symptoms of this, although so far they have dealt with the problems of culture and literature.

Such watchwords can only be banners for the Ukrainian petite bourgeoisie, which grows on the soil of the NEP, and for which the rebirth of a nation means its bourgeois restoration toward capitalist Europe and separation from the fortress of the international revolution, the capital of the USSR, Moscow.

To this bourgeois path of development we oppose our proletarian path. The Party stands for an independent development of Ukrainian culture, for an expression of all creative forces displayed by the Ukrainian people. The Party supports the wide use by the Ukrainian culture of all the treasures of world culture. It is in favor of a definite break with the traditions of provincial narrowness, in favor of the creation of new cultural values worthy of a great class. However, in the Party's view, this cannot be done by contrasting Ukrainian culture with the cultures of other nations, but through brotherly cooperation between the working and toiling masses of all nationalities in the raising of an international culture to which the Ukrainian working class will be able to contribute its share.

XI

In the struggle against Ukrainian chauvinism, which grows more intense in city and village alike, the Party must not put the brakes on Ukrainization, but continue it decisively, directing it not only on the surface but also in depth, mercilessly combating the Great Russian chauvinism which largely creates the basis for an awakening of Ukrainian chauvinism among the masses.

The Party must educate all its members, among them also these Ukrainian comrades who joined it during the revolution and the adolescent youth, in the spirit of a Leninist understanding of the nationality policy, leading the struggle against national deviations within the Party.

Taking into account the complexity of the execution of the nationality policy in the Ukraine, especially Ukrainization, the Central Committee requests all those comrades who have practical suggestions to send them to the Central Committee, and it directs the local Party organizations to pay special attention to these suggestions and petitions, thus removing the estrangement which was noticeable in certain cases.

APPENDIX F

RESOLUTIONS OF VAPLITE

Concerning the Congress of Proletarian Writers
(adopted by the General Meeting, January 25, 1927)

Having considered the fact that: 1) the Organizing Committee which was responsible for convening the Congress of Proletarian Writers has by its more than scornful treatment of VAPLITE prevented the latter from participating in the congress; 2) has not invited a representative from VAPLITE and has made no attempt to discuss with VAPLITE even formally the idea of the congress; 3) finally, requesting us to take part in the opening of the congress, has sent us one (1) ticket, in a consultative (!) capacity, together with an ultimatum to clarify the attitude of VAPLITE to the congress before 6 P.M., it has been decided not to take part in the congress and to ask the Presidium to reply to the ultimatum in accordance with this resolution.

Concerning the Bulletin of the Organizing Committee for the Convention of the Congress of Proletarian Writers
(adopted by the Presidium of VAPLITE, January 23, 1927)

This is like a contest of fishwives who out-swore and out-cursed the whole village.

It was decided not to reply.

Concerning the Attitude of VAPLITE to the New Literary Organization
(adopted by the Presidium on February 15, 1927)

Our attitude will depend on how far the above-named union proves, by its ideological and creative work, that it has earned the honorable name it has assumed.

Resolutions of VAPLITE on Ideological Questions
(adopted by the General Meeting, February 19, 1927)

To print in the next issue of VAPLITE the following explanation:
1) The aim of VAPLITE—to participate, along with the brotherly literatures of the USSR, in the creation of socialist culture. In order to

maintain this contact, all attempts to exclude or to maneuver Ukrainian October literature into a position hostile to the literatures of other peoples of the USSR will be combated.

2) VAPLITE categorically rejects the theory of the struggle of two cultures.

Leninism forms the philosophic basis of VAPLITE's activity. As often as necessary, technical literary devices are borrowed by VAPLITE from those bourgeois, highly developed cultures which have the greatest organic structure. These are then used as a means of forging weapons for revolutionary art.

3) Guided by the resolutions of the June Plenum of the Central Committee of the CP(B)U, VAPLITE accepts, as it always has, the formulation of these resolutions in regard to the Neoclassicists.

4) VAPLITE puts into perspective the concept of "mass work," distorted by "pious literary arch-priests." The writer's contribution to the masses is in his works, not in literary soirees and the enlightment of a handful of spectators instead of tens of thousands of readers.

Concerning Comrades Dos'vitnyi, Khvyl'ovyi, and Ialovyi
(adopted by the General Meeting, January 28, 1927)

During the Literary Discussion, comrades Dos'vitnyi, Khvyl'ovyi, and Ialovyi arrived at some faulty conclusions which assumed the significance of ideological deviations.

At the same time, the above-named comrades, being members of the Presidium and the Auditing Board of VAPLITE, failed to submit debatable issues in advance to the forum of the entire organization (with the exception of the issue of the Neoclassicists). Having control over the publishing affairs of VAPLITE, they published in the first issue of VAPLITE Dos'vitnyi's article on the Neoclassicists without taking account of the reservations and contrary opinions expressed at the general meeting.

In the course of time it became clear that these comrades had not given up their tendency to pursue a separate policy which led to their rupture with VAPLITE.

Although these comrades confessed their errors in a letter of December 1, 1926, no agreement was reached between them and VAPLITE either on the final conclusions of the Literary Discussion or on the path of development of proletarian literature in the Ukraine. It was resolved, therefore, to expel comrades Dos'vitnyi, Khvyl'ovyi, and Ialovyi from the membership of VAPLITE.

APPENDIX G

1. The Central Committee ascertains that, as a result of the considerable successes of Socialist construction, literature and art have, in the past few years, exhibited a considerable growth, both in quality and quantity.

Some years ago, when literature was still under the strong influence of certain alien elements, which were particularly flourishing in the first years of NEP, and when the ranks of proletarian literature were still comparatively feeble, the Party helped, by every means in its power, the creation of special proletarian organizations in the sphere of literature and art, with a view to strengthening the position of proletarian writers and art workers.

Now that the rank and file of proletarian literature has had time to grow and establish itself, and that new writers and artists have come forward from factories, mills, and collective farms, the framework of the existing proletarian literary-artistic organizations (VOAPP, RAPP, RAPM, etc.) is becoming too confined and impedes the serious development of artistic creation. There is thus the danger that these organizations might be turned into a means of cultivating hermetic groupings and alienating considerable groups of writers and artists, sympathizing with the aims of socialist construction, from contemporary political problems.

Hence the necessity for a corresponding reconstruction of the literary-artistic organizations and for the extension of the basis of their work.

Therefore the Central Committee resolves:

(1) To liquidate the association of proletarian writers (VOAPP, RAPP);

(2) To unite all writers upholding the Soviet power and striving to

participate in socialist construction into a single Union of Soviet Writers with a Communist faction therein;

(3) To promote a similar change in the sphere of other forms of art;

(4) To entrust the Organizing Bureau with the working out of practical measures for the application of this resolution.

APPENDIX H

A Summary of the Most Immediate Tasks in the

Fulfillment of the National Policy

in the Ukraine, 1933

[EXTRACTS]

5

Directing the Theoretical Front

The work on the theoretical front (history, philosophy, political economy, agricultural problems) demands the most urgent attention of all Party organizations. On this front we have witnessed an utterly insufficient struggle against bourgeois nationalist contraband (the theory that the Ukrainian nation had no bourgeoisie), against the embellishing of the activities of the bourgeois idealist philosophy, and against harmful theories in the field of rural economy. Work on the theoretical front in all sectors must be raised to a Bolshevik level. It is imperative that the publication of the basic works of Marx, Engels, Lenin, and Stalin in the Ukrainian language should be completed as soon as possible.

Directing the Front of Literature and the Arts

The Party must achieve an effective day-to-day Bolshevik guidance of the literary and artistic fronts. During the considerable growth of Soviet Ukrainian literature and the cadres of writers there was clearly shown the bourgeois-nationalist elements and their agents in the ranks of the Party. Nationalist ideas were expounded for several years by the management of the Berezil' Theater. This management and the literary group VAPLITE created by Shums'kyi and supported by Skrypnyk conducted a policy of forcible separation of the entire Ukrainian literature, art, and culture from the proletarian culture of the Russian working class; it steered a course toward the bourgeois capitalist West.

The Party is now faced with the task of intensifying the campaign against these nationalist tendencies hostile to the proletarian revolution and of welding the cultural contacts between Soviet Ukrainian literature and art and the literature and art of other peoples of the Soviet Union, and with the strengthening of the brotherly union, of preparing the cadres of Ukrainian writers, and of expanding and improving editions of works of literature in the Ukrainian language.

APPENDIX I

LIST OF LEADING COMMUNIST OFFICIALS IN THE UKRAINE

BLAKYTNYI, VASYL' M. (pseudonym of Ellans'kyi), b. 1895. Before the Revolution he was active in the youth movement; after 1917 he was one of the leaders of the Borot'bists. Elected to the Central Committee of the CP(B)U in 1920, Blakytnyi was also editor of the *Visti Vseukraïns'koho Tsentral'noho Vykonavchoho Komitetu*. He died in 1925 of a heart ailment.

CHUBAR, VLAS IA., b. 1891, an old Bolshevik. In 1922 Chubar became a member of the Central Committee of the CPSU and in 1923 Chairman of the Council of the People's Commissars in the Ukraine. From 1935–38 Chubar was a member of the Politbureau of the CPSU. Disappeared in the purge of 1938.

HRYN'KO, HRYHORII F., b. 1890, a Borot'bist who later occupied a very high post in the Soviet Union. In 1923 he was Commissar of Education in the Ukraine; from 1926–29 he held the office of Deputy Chairman of State Planning Commission of the USSR. In 1930 Hryn'ko became the Commissar of Finance of the USSR. Executed in 1938.

KAGANOVICH, LAZAR M., b. 1893, was secretary general of the CP(B)U from 1925 to 1928. He is the only survivor from among those Communists who held high offices in the Ukraine in the 1920s.

KHVYLIA, ANDRII, b. 1898, a Borot'bist who rose to power with the help of Kaganovich. In 1926–28 Khvylia was in charge of the Press Section and later the Cultural Propaganda Section of the Central Committee of the CP(B)U. In 1933 he became Deputy Commissar of Education of the Soviet Ukraine. Arrested in 1937, Khvylia disappeared soon afterwards.

KOSIOR, STANISLAV V., b. 1899, an old Bolshevik. In 1919 Kosior became secretary of the Central Committee of the CP(B)U; from 1925–28 he was secretary of the Central Committee of the CPSU. In 1928 he was appointed secretary of the Central Committee of the CP(B)U. Disappeared in the late thirties.

LEBID', DMITRI Z., b. 1893. In 1920 Lebid' was secretary of the Central Committee of the CP(B)U; after 1926 worked in Russia.

LIUBCHENKO, PANAS P., b. 1895, a Borot'bist; in the twenties he held several important posts in the Soviet Ukrainian government. In 1933 he became Chairman of the Council of the People's Commissars in the Ukraine. Elected candidate to the Central Committee of the CPSU in 1934. Committed suicide in 1937.

PETROVS'KYI, HRYHORII I., b. 1877, an old Bolshevik. Represented the Bolshevik faction in the Fourth Duma. In 1919 Petrovs'kyi became Chairman of the Ukrainian CEC; after 1921 he was a member of the Central Committee of the CPSU. Disappeared during the "Iezhov period."

POSTYSHEV, PAVEL P., b. 1888, an old Bolshevik. In 1930 Postyshev became secretary of the City Committee of the CPSU in Moscow. In 1933 he was sent to the Ukraine with special powers to supervise the economic and cultural life of that country. Postyshev fell into disfavor and was recalled from his post in 1937. He died in 1939.

RAKOVSKII, KHRISTIAN, b. 1873, an old Bolshevik, active before the Revolution in the Balkans. In 1919 Rakovskii was made Chairman of the Council of the People's Commissars in the Ukraine. In 1923 he was appointed Soviet envoy to Great Britain and later (1925–27) to France. Accused of being a Trotskyite, Rakovskii was expelled from the Party by the Fifteenth Party Congress (1927).

SHUMS'KYI, OLEKSANDER IA., a Borot'bist; he was the Commissar of Education in the Ukraine (1925–27). Accused of nationalist deviation, Shums'kyi was transferred to Leningrad and later disappeared.

SKRYPNYK, MYKOLA O. (1872–1933), an old Bolshevik, active in the revolutionary movement since 1901. After the Revolution Skrypnyk held many responsible posts in the Ukraine (he was, in succession, Commissar of Labor, Commerce and Industry, Foreign Affairs, Interior Affairs, Justice). In 1926 he was appointed Commissar of Education; in 1927 he became Chairman of the Soviet of the Nationalities of the USSR; and in the same year he was elected a member of the Central Committee of the CPSU. Skrypnyk committed suicide in 1933.

ZATONS'KYI, VOLODYMYR P., b. 1888, an old Bolshevik, member of the Central Committee of the CP(B)U, replaced Skrypnyk in 1933 as Commissar of Education. Disappeared in the late thirties.

BIBLIOGRAPHY

SPECIAL TERMS

AND ABBREVIATIONS

Berezil'	A Ukrainian theater in Kharkov, directed by Les' Kurbas
CC	Central Committee
CCC	Central Control Commission
CEC	Central Executive Committee
Central Rada	Ukrainian democratic government during the Revolution
CP(B)U	Communist Party (Bolsheviks) of the Ukraine
CPSU	Communist Party of the Soviet Union
CPWU	Communist Party of the Western Ukraine
DVU	Ukrainian State Publishing House
FORPU	Federation of Associations of Revolutionary Writers of the Ukraine
Hart	Literary organization of proletarian writers
KPZU	See CPWU
Lanka	Literary organization of Ukrainian fellow travelers
Molodniak	Literary organization of young writers, chiefly members of the Komsomol
Orgkomitet	Organizing Committee
Pluh	Literary organization of peasant writers
RAPP	Russian Association of Proletarian Writers
RCP(B)	Russian Communist Party (Bolsheviks)
RKP(b)	See RCP(B)
SD's	Social Democratic Party
SR's	Socialist Revolutionary Party
SVU	Union for the Liberation of the Ukraine
TsK	See CC
UKP	Ukrainian Communist Party
VAPLITE	The Free Academy of Proletarian Literature
VAPP	All-Russian Association of Proletarian Writers
VKP(b)	See CPSU
VOAPP	The All-Union Alliance of Organizations of Proletarian Writers
VUAPP	The All-Ukrainian Association of Proletarian Writers
VUSPP	The All-Ukrainian Union of Proletarian Writers
VUTsVK	The All-Ukrainian Central Executive Committee

BIBLIOGRAPHY

I. LIUBCHENKO PAPERS

These papers, at present in a house formerly occupied by the St. Nicholas Monastery, Grimsby, Ontario, Canada, were entrusted to the care of the Most Reverend Archbishop Mstyslav after Liubchenko's death, in 1945. The following materials have been used in this study:

"Do chleniv 'Vaplite' " (To Members of VAPLITE) [Mykytenko's letter to VAPLITE].

"Do holovrepertkomu NKO; kopiia APO TsK KP(b)U" (To the Chief Repertory Committee of the People's Commissariat for Education; Copy to the Agitation and Propaganda Section of the CC CP(B)U) [Kulish's letter].

"Do komfraktsiï 'Vaplite' " (To the Communist Faction of VAPLITE) [Khvylia's letter to VAPLITE].

"Do viddilu presy" (To the Press Section) [Kulish's letter to the Press Section of the CP(B)U].

"Komunistychna partiia (b-v) Ukraïny; tsentral'nyi komitet; tsilkom taiemno; vytiah 69 zasidannia S-tu TsK KP(b)U vid 14, III, 1927" (The Communist Party [Bolsheviks] of the Ukraine; Central Committee; Top Secret; Excerpt from the 69th Meeting of the Secretariat of the CC CP(B)U on March 14, 1927).

"Literaturnyi shchodennyk" (A Literary Diary).

"Manifest vseukrainskoi literaturnoi akademii" (Manifesto of the All-Ukrainian Literary Academy).

"Oblik chleniv Vil'noï Akademiï Proletars'koï Literatury" (Register of Members of the Free Academy of Proletarian Literature).

"Otkrytoe pis'mo M. Gorkomu" (An Open Letter to M. Gorky).

"Postanovy 'Vaplite' " (Resolutions of VAPLITE).

"Protokol narady pys'mennykiv m. Kharkova vid 14 zhovtnia 1925 roku" (Minutes of the Conference of Kharkov Writers on October 14, 1925).

"Protokol orhanizatsiinoho zasidannia hrupy pys'mennykiv proletars'-

koï literatury 20 lystopada 1925" (Minutes of the Constituent Meeting of a Group of Proletarian Writers on November 20, 1925).
"Rezoliutsiia zahal'nykh zboriv Vil'noï Akademiï Proletars'koï Literatury 'Vaplite' 14 sichnia 1928 roku" (Resolution of the General Meeting of the Free Academy of Proletarian Literature VAPLITE on January 14, 1928).
"Zapysky-zapytannia pidchas podorozhi do Artemivshchyny ta Dnipropetrovs'ka hrupy Khvyl'ovyi, Kulish, Vyshnia, Ianovs'kyi, Liubchenko, berezen' 1929" (Notes and Questions during the Visit to Artemivsk and Dniepropetrovsk of the Group: Khvyl'ovyi, Kulish, Vyshnia, Ianovs'kyi, and Liubchenko, March, 1929).

The following untitled materials were also used: Kulish diary (1928); Minutes of VAPLITE's meetings held on November 20, 1920, January 23, 25, 28, 1927, February 15, 1927, March 12, 26, 1927, April 21, 1927, November 9, 1927, January 12, 1928; Minutes of Hart's meetings held on November 1, 18, 1923, December 28, 1923, and January 10, 1924.

Some personal letters written by Khvyl'ovyi, Kulish, Ianovs'kyi, Dniprovs'kyi, and Liubchenko have been edited by the present author and published under the title *Holubi dylizhansy: Lystuvannia Vaplitian* (The Sky-Blue Diligences: Correspondence of the Vaplitians), New York, Slovo, 1955. Some materials relating to Mykola Kulish have been included in the volume of his works (*Tvory*, New York, Ukrains'ka vil'na akademiia nauk v SShA, 1955).

II. Party Pronouncements and Resolutions

Biuleten' V-oi vseukrainskoi konferentsii KP(b)U (The Bulletin of the Fifth All-Ukrainian Conference of the CP[B]U), November 22, 1920.
Budivnytstvo radians'koï Ukraïny—Zbirnyk (Organization of the Soviet Ukraine: A Compendium). 2 parts, Kharkov, 1929.
Deviatyi s"ezd RKP(b): Protokoly (The Ninth Congress of the RCP [B]: Proceedings). Moscow, 1934.
Istoriia KP(b)U v materialakh i dokumentakh; vypusk druhyi (History of the CP[B]U: Materials and Documents: Second Series). n.p. Partvydav TsK KP(b)U, 1934.
"Iz rezoliutsii na dopovid' tov. Khvyli pro stan na movnomu fronti (From the Resolution on the Report by Comrade Khvylia about the Situation on the Linguistic Front), *Visti*, June 30, 1933.
Kaganovich, L. "Ukrainizatsiia partiï i borot'ba z ukhylamy" (The Ukrainization of the Party and the Struggle against the Deviations), *Visti*, November 27, 1927.
Kosior, S. "Itogi khlebozagotovok i zadachi KP(b)U v bor'be za podniatie sel'skogo khozaistva Ukrainy" (Results of the Grain Deliveries and the Tasks of the CP[B]U in the Struggle for the Improvement of Agriculture in the Ukraine), *Pravda*, February 15, 1933.

—— "Literaturni spravy" (Literary Affairs), *Prolitfront*, No. 4, 1930, pp. 5–8.

—— "Pidsumky i naiblyzhchi zavdannia natsional'noï polityky na Ukraïni" (Results and Immediate Tasks of the National Policy in the Ukraine), *Chervonyi shliakh*, No. 8–9, 1930, pp. 205–44.

—— "Politychnyi zvit TsK KP(b)U" (Political Report of the CP[B]U), *Visti*, June 17, 1930.

—— "Radians'ku literaturu na riven' zavdan' pobudovy bezklasovoho sotsialistychnoho suspil'stva" (Soviet Literature to Be Equal to the Tasks of a Classless Socialist Society), *Visti*, June 28, 1934.

—— "Za rishuche perevedennia lenins'koï natsional'noï polityky: za bil'shovyts'ku borot'bu proty natsionalistychnykh ukhyliv" (For a Determined Application of Leninist National Policy: For a Bolshevik Struggle against Nationalist Deviations), *Visti*, July 23, 1933.

Liubchenko, Panas. "Pro deiaki pomylky na teoretychnomu fronti" (About Some Errors on the Theoretical Front), *Visti*, July 6, 1933.

—— "Promova na pershomu vseukrains'komu zïzdi radians'kykh pys'-mennykiv" (Address at the First All-Ukrainian Congress of Soviet Writers), *Visti*, July 9, 1934.

—— "Stari teoriï i novi pomylky" (Old Theories and New Errors), *Zhyttia i revoliutsiia*, No. 12, 1926, pp. 75–88.

"Mystets'ki konkursy do X rokovyn zhovtnevoï revoliutsiï" (Art Competitions on the Tenth Anniversary of the October Revolution), *Visti*, March 18, 1927.

"O perestroike literaturno-khudozhestvennykh organizatsii" (On the Reconstruction of the Literary and Artistic Organizations), *Pravda*, April 24, 1932.

Ot XVI konferentsii do XVI s"ezda VKP(b) (From the Sixteenth Conference to the Sixteenth Congress of the All-Union Communist Party [Bolsheviks]). Moscow, Partizdat, 1932.

"Perestroika literaturnykh organizatsii" (The Reconstruction of Literary Organizations), *Literaturnaia gazeta*, June 5, 1932.

Pervyi s"ezd KP(b)U: Statti i protokoly s"ezda (The First Congress of the CP[B]U: Articles and Proceedings of the Congress). Kharkov, Gosudarstvennoe izdadel'stvo Ukrainy, 1923.

"Pidsumky i naiblyzhchi zavdannia provedennia natsional'noï polityky na Ukraïni: Rezoliutsiia obiednanoho plenumu TsK i TsKK KP (b)U na dopovid' tov. Kosiora, ukhvalena 22 lystopada 1933 roku" (Results and Immediate Tasks of the National Policy in the Ukraine. Resolution of the Joint Plenary Session of the CC and the CCC of the CP[B]U on the Report by Comrade Kosior, Adopted November 22, 1933), *Chervonyi shliakh*, No. 8–9, 1933, pp. 261–72.

Popov, M. "Na pershomu zïzdi radians'kykh pys'mennykiv Ukraïny" (On the First Congress of Soviet Writers of the Ukraine), *Visti*, June 21, 1934.

—— "Pro natsional'ni ukhyly v lavakh ukraïns'koï partorhanizatsiï i pro zavdannia borot'by z nymy" (On Nationalist Deviations within the Ranks of the Ukrainian Party Organization and the Task of Fighting against Them), *Visti*, July 12, 1933.

—— "Zadachi ukrainskoi literatury" (The Tasks of Ukrainian Literature), *Literaturnaia gazeta*, June 28, 1934.

"Postanova biura kom. fraktsiï VUSPPu v spravi konsolidatsiinykh zboriv kharkivs'koï orhanizatsiï VUSPPu" (Resolution of the Bureau of the Communist Faction of VUSPP concerning the Meeting of Consolidation of the Kharkov VUSPP Organization), *Chervonyi shliakh*, No. 5, 1931, pp. 112–13.

"Postanova narodn'oho komisariatu os'vity USRR na dopovid' teatru 'Berezil' 5 zhovtnia 1933 roku" (Resolution of the People's Commissariat of Education of the Ukrainian SSR on the Report by the Berezil' Theater on October 5, 1933), *Visti*, October 8, 1933.

"Postanova TsK KP(b)U pro zhurnal 'Chervonyi perets' " (Resolution of the CC CP[B]U on the Journal "Red Pepper"), *Literatura i mystetstvo*, October 20, 1929.

Postyshev, Pavel. "Itogi 1933 sel'sko-khozaistvennogo goda i ocherednye zadachi KP(b)U" (Results of the 1933 Year in Agriculture and the Next Tasks of the CP[B]U), *Pravda*, November 24, 1933.

—— "Mobilizuem massy na svoevremennuiu postavku zerna gosudarstvu" (We Are Mobilizing the Masses for a Timely Delivery of Grain to the State), *Pravda*, June 22, 1933.

—— "Osobennosti klassovoi bor'by na nyneshnem etape sotsialisticheskogo nastupleniia" (The Peculiarities of the Class Struggle at the Present Stage of Socialist Advance), *Pravda*, July 3, 1933.

—— "Pershomu vseukraïns'komu zïzdovi radians'kykh pys'mennykiv" (To the First All-Ukrainian Congress of Soviet Writers), *Visti*, June 21, 1934.

—— Puti ukrainskoi sovetskoi literatury. Rech na plenume pravleniia soiuza sovetskikh pisatelei Ukrainy (Paths of Ukrainian Soviet Literature. Speech at the Plenary Session of the Board of the Soviet Writers' Union in the Ukraine). n.p. Partizdat TsK VKP(b), 1935.

—— "Radians'ka Ukraïna na novomu pidnesenni: Politychnyi zvit TsK KP(b)U zïzdovi KP(b)U" (The Soviet Ukraine in a New Upswing. Political Report of the CC CP[B]U to the Congress of the CP[B]U), *Visti*, January 24, 1934.

—— "Radians'ka Ukraïna—nepokhytnyi vorpost velykoho SRSR" (Soviet Ukraine—Bastion of the Great USSR), *Chervonyi shliakh*, No. 8–9, pp. 245–60.

—— "Sovetskaia Ukraina na novom pod"ëme: Politicheskii otchët TsK KP(b)U na XII s"ezde KP(b)U" (The Soviet Ukraine in a New Upswing. Political Report of the CC CP[B]U at the Twelfth Congress of the CP[B]U), *Pravda*, January 24, 1934.

"Pro natsional'ni ukhyly va lavakh ukraïns'koï partorhanizatsiï i pro zavdannia borot'by z nymy: Rezoliutsiia kharkivs'koho mis'koho partaktyvu na dopovid' tov. M. M. Popova 9 lypnia 1933 roku" (On Nationalist Deviations in the Ranks of the Ukrainian Party Organization and on the Tasks of Fighting Them: Resolution of the Kharkov City Party *Aktiv* on the Report on Comrade M. M. Popov on July 9, 1933), *Visti*, July 11, 1933.

Rakovskii, Kh. "Beznadezhnoe delo" (A Hopeless Affair), *Izvestiia VTsIKS*, January 3, 1919.

Reshenia partii o pechati (Decisions of the Party concerning Printing). Moscow, Politizdat pri RKP(b), 1941.

"Rezoliutsiia po dokladu t. Skrypnyka 'Pro zavdannia kul'turnoho budivnytstva na Ukraïni' " (Resolution Following the Report of Comrade Skrypnyk on "The Tasks of Cultural Organization in the Ukraine"), *Visti*, December 4, 1927.

"Rezoliutsiï obiednanoho plenumu TsK i TsKK KP (b)U" (Resolutions of the Joint Plenary Session of the CC and CCC CP[B]U), *Chervonyi shliakh*, No. 8–9, 1933, pp. 267–68.

"Rivnopravnym braters'kym spivrobitnytstvom bude zbudovano mizhnarodniu sotsialistychnu kul'turu: Rezoliutsiia narady pry APPV TsK VKP(b) v pytanni pro zviazok ukrains'koï i rus'koï literatury" (Equal and Brotherly Collaboration Will Create an International Socialist Culture: Resolution by the Conference of the Section of Political Agitation and Propaganda of the CC CPSU[b] concerning the Problem of Liaison between Ukrainian and Russian Literature), *Visti*, May 23, 1929.

XVI s"ezd vsesoiuznoi kommunisticheskoi partii (b): Stenograficheskii otchët (The Sixteenth Congress of the All-Union Communist Party [Bolsheviks]: Stenographic Report). Moscow, Partizdat, 1930.

Skrypnyk, Mykola. Dzherela ta prychyny rozlamu v KPZU (Sources and Reasons of the Split in the CPWU). Kharkov, Derzhavne vydavnytstvo Ukraïny, 1928.

—— "Itogi literaturnoi diskussii" (The Results of the Literary Discussion), *Bol'shevik Ukrainy*, Vol. I. 1926.

—— Nasha literaturna diisnist' (Our Literary Reality). Kharkov, Derzhavne vydavnytstvo Ukraïny, 1928.

—— Novi liniï v natsional'no-kul'turnomu budivnytstvi (New Tendencies in the National and Cultural Organization). Kharkov, Derzhavne vydavnytstvo Ukraïny, 1928.

—— "Perebuduvatysia po spravzhniomu" (For a Genuine Reconstruction), *Chervonyi shliakh*, No. 5–6, 1932, pp. 103–9.

—— Pereznaky tvorchoho terenu (Changing Marks in the Creative Field). Kharkov, Derzhavne vydavnytstvo Ukraïny, 1930.

—— Stan ta perspektyvy kul'turnoho budivnytstva na Ukraïni (The

Status and Future Prospects of Cultural Organization in the Ukraine). Kharkov, Derzhavne vydavnytstvo Ukraïny, 1929.
—— Statti i promovy (Articles and Speeches). 5 vols. Kharkov, Derzhavne vydavnytstvo Ukraïny, 1930–31.
—— "Z kraïny nepivs'koï v kraïnu sotsialistychnu" (From a NEP County to a Socialist Country), *Chervonyi shliakh*, No. 9, 1930, pp. 70–79.
Stalin, J. V. Political Report of the Central Committee to the Sixteenth Congress of the CPSU (B). Moscow, Foreign Languages Publishing House, 1951.
Stenograficheskii otchët X s"ezdu RKP (b) (The Stenographic Report of the Tenth Congress of the RCP[B]). Petersburg, 1921.
Stenohrafichnyi zvit plenumu TsK i TsKK KP(b)U (The Stenographic Report of the Plenary Session of the CC CP[B]U). June 1–6, 1926.
Stetskii, A. I. "Znamia sovetskoi literatury: Rech' na pervom vseukrainskom s"ezde sovetskikh pisatelei" (The Banner of Soviet Literature: Speech at the First All-Ukrainian Congress of Soviet Writers), *Literaturnaia gazeta*, June 22, 1934.
"Tezy do dokladu tov. Skrypnyka na X-mu zïzdi KP(b)U 'Pro zavdannia kul'turnoho budivnytstva' " (Theses on the Report by Comrade Skrypnyk at the Tenth Congress of the CP[B]U on "The Tasks of Cultural Organization"), *Visti*, November 1, 1927.
"Tezy viddilu kul'tury i propagandy TsK KP(b)U do 120 richchya z dnia narodzhennia Shevchenka" (Theses of the Section of Culture and Propaganda of the CC CP[B]U on the 120th Anniversary of the Birth of Taras Shevchenko), *Chervonyi shliakh*, No. 2–3, 1934, pp. 5–12.
Tsentral'nyi ispolnitel'nyi komitet 3 sozyva, 2 sessiia: Stenograficheskii otchët (Central Executive Committee Third Convocation, Second Session: Stenographic Report). Moscow, Izdanie TsIK Soiuza SSR, 1926.
"Ukrainizatsiia Partiï i borot'ba z ukhylamy" (The Ukrainization of the Party and the Struggle against the Deviations), *Visti*, November 27, 1927.
"Utvoreno partoseredok radians'kykh pys'mennykiv" (A Party Cell of Soviet Writers Has Been Created), *Chervonyi shliakh*, No. 1, 1934, p. 196.
VKP (b) v rezoliutsiiakh i resheniiakh s"ezdov, konferentsii i plenumov TsK (CPSU[B] in the Resolutions and Decisions of Congresses, Conferences, and Plenary Sessions of the CC). Part 2. n.p. Partizdat, 1936.
Vsesoiuznaia kommunisticheskaia partiia (b) v rezoliutsiiakh eë s"ezdov i konferentsii (The All-Union Communist Party [Bolsheviks] in the Resolutions of Its Congresses and Conferences). 3d ed. Moscow-Leningrad, 1927.

"Vyrok viiskovoï kolehiï naivyshchoho sudu RSR v Kyievi v spravakh terorystiv-bilohvardeitsiv" (The Sentence of the Military Board of the Supreme Court of the Soviet Socialist Republic in Kiev concerning Terrorists–White–Guardists), *Visti*, December 18, 1934.

"Zakonchena chistka partiinoi organizatsii pisatelei Kharkova" (The Purge of the Party Organization of the Kharkov Writers Has Been Completed), *Literaturnaia gazeta*, July 6, 1934.

Zatons'kyi, V. P. Natsional'no-kul'turne budivnytstvo i borot'ba proty natsionalizmu: Dopovid' ta zakliuchne slovo na sichnevii sessiï VUAN (National-Cultural Building and the Struggle against Nationalism: Report and Concluding Remarks at the January Session of the All-Ukrainian Academy of Sciences). Kiev, 1934.

III. Other Printed Materials

"A bit' po val'dshnepam vsëtaki nuzhno" (And Yet the Woodsnipes Must Be Shot Down), *Na literaturnom postu*, No. 5, 1928, pp. 3–5.

"A. M. Gorkii i ukrainskaia literatura: pis'mo t. Kuliku" (A. M. Gorky and Ukrainian Literature: A Letter to Comrade Kulyk), *Literaturnaia gazeta*, June 22, 1933.

Aguf, M. "Burzhuaznye agenty razoblacheny" (The Bourgeois Agents Unmasked), *Literaturnaia gazeta*, June 14, 1934.

Akhmatov, L. "Literatura i SVU" (Literature and the Union for the Liberation of the Ukraine), *Literaturnyi arkhiv*, I–II (1930), 108–24.

Allen, William E. D. The Ukraine. Cambridge, England, Cambridge University Press, 1941.

Antonenko Davydovych, B. "Voskresinnia Shel'menka" (The Resurrection of Shel'menko), *Zhyttia i revoliutsiia*, No. 2, 1929, pp. 89–96.

Averbakh, Leopol'd. "Boiovi zavdannia proletars'koï literatury URSR" (The Fighting Tasks of Proletarian Literature in the Ukrainian SSR), *Krytyka*, No. 9, 1931, pp. 17–36.

—— "O sovremennoi literature" (On Contemporary Literature), *Na literaturnom postu*, No. 11–12, June, 1928, pp. 5–19.

—— "Proletarian Literature and the Peoples of the Soviet Union: For Hegemony of Proletarian Literature," *Literature of the World Revolution*, V (1931), 93–125.

—— "Trevoga a ne samodovol'stvo" (Alarm Not Complacency), *Na literaturnom postu*, No. 18, June, 1931, pp. 1–11.

—— "Zadachi literaturnoi politiki" (The Tasks of Literary Policy), *Pravda*, August 28, 1930.

Bahrianyi, Ivan. "Pro svobodu slova i presy za zaliznoiu zaslonoiu" (On Freedom of Speech and Press behind the Iron Curtain), *Ukraïns'ki visti* (Ulm), No. 33–34, Easter, 1952.

Beloff, Max. The Foreign Policy of Soviet Russia. Vol. I. Oxford, Oxford University Press, 1949.

Blakytnyi, V. Ellan. "Komunistychna partiia Ukraïny i ïï zmitsnennia" (The Communist Party of the Ukraine and Its Strengthening), *Kommunist*, November 17, 19, 1920.

—— "Pytannia shcho stoït' na poriadku dennomu" (The Question on the Agenda), *Literatura, nauka, mystetstvo*, September 21, 1924.

Bloom, Solomon F. The World of Nations: A Study of the National Implications in the Works of Karl Marx. New York, Columbia University Press, 1941.

Borev, B. Natsional'ne pytannia: Kurs natsional'noho pytannia dlia komvyshiv ta radpartshkil (The National Question: A Course on the National Question for the Communist Higher Schools and Party Schools). Kharkov, Derzhavne vydavnytstvo Proletar, 1931.

Borshchak, Il'ko. "Dvi zustrichi" (Two Meetings), *Ukraïna* (Paris), No. 4, 1950, pp. 253–57.

—— "L'Ukraine sous le régime soviétique (1918–1952)," *Bulletin de l'Association d'Études et d'Informations Politiques Internationales BEIPI*. Supplement du No. 73, September, 1952.

"Brigada vsesoiuznogo orgkomiteta v Kharkove" (Brigade of the All-Union Organizing Committee in Kharkov), *Literaturnaia gazeta*, January 11, 1934.

Brown, Edward J. The Proletarian Episode in Russian Literature: 1928–1932. New York, Columbia University Press, 1953.

—— "The Russian Association of Proletarian Writers: 1928–32." Unpublished doctoral dissertation, Columbia University, 1950.

Carr, Edward Hallett. The Bolshevik Revolution: 1917–1923. Vol I. New York, Macmillan, 1951.

Chamberlin, William Henry. The Ukraine: A Submerged Nation. New York, Macmillan, 1951.

Chepurniuk, A. "Poeziia vyshukanykh katastrof idealistychnoï filoso-fiï" (The Poetry of Invented Catastrophes of Idealist Philosophy), *Chervonyi shliakh*, No. 1, 1934, pp. 176–86.

"Dekliaratsiia vseukraïns'koï federatsiï revoliutsiinykh radians'kykh pys'mennykiv" (Declaration of the All-Ukrainian Federation of Revolutionary Soviet Writers), *Prolitfront*, No. 1, 1930, pp. 260–64.

"Dekliaratsiia v spravi bloku mizh VUSPPom, VUSKKom (Nova Generatsiia) i VUARKom" (Declaration concerning the Block between VUSPP, VUSKK [The New Generation], and VUARK), *Visti*, November 5, 1929.

"Do chytacha" (To the Reader), *Prolitfront*, No. 1, April, 1930, pp. 5–6.

"Do robitnykiv udarnykiv Ukraïny" (To the Shock Workers of the Ukraine), *Krytyka*, No. 11, 1930, pp. 155–56.

Doroshenko, V., and P. Zlenko. "Vydavnytstva" (Publishing), in Entsyklopediia ukraïnoznavstva. Munich, Molode zhyttia, 1949. Vol III, pp. 972–81.

Doroshkevych, O. "Maksym Gorkyi ta ukraïns'ka literatura" (Maxim

Gorky and Ukrainian Literature), *Zhyttia i revoliutsiia*, No. 10, 1932, pp. 86–95.

—— Pidruchnyk istoriï ukraïns'koï literatury (A Handbook of the History of Ukrainian Literature). 3d ed. Kharkov, Knyhospilka, 1927.

Dos'vitnyi, O. "Do rozvytku pys'mennyts'kykh syl" (The Development of Literary Forces), *Vaplite, zoshyt pershyi*, 1926, pp. 5–17.

Dovhan', Kost'. "Iak my vykonuiemo boiovu dyrektyvu partiï" (How Are We Fulfilling the Fighting Directive of the Party), *Krytyka*, No. 11–12, 1931, pp. 3–12.

—— "Z pryvodu odniieï dekliaratsiï" (On the Occasion of a Declaration), *Krytyka*, No. 3, 1930, pp. 20–27.

Drai-Khmara, M. "Lyst to redaktsiï" (A Letter to the Editor), *Literaturnyi iarmarok*, No. 4, 1929, p. 172.

Eastman, Max. Artists in Uniform: A Study of Literature and Bureaucratism. New York, Alfred A. Knopf, 1934.

Freeman, Joseph, Joshua Kunitz, and Louis Lozowick. Voices of October: Art and Literature in Soviet Russia. New York, Vanguard Press, 1930.

Gans, I. "Pisateli-komunisty na proverke" (A Screening of Communist Writers), *Literaturnaia gazeta*, June 14, 1934.

H. "Pidsumky zïzdu obiednanykh hartovans'kykh orhanizatsii" (Results of the Congress of United Hart Organizations), *Kul'tura i pobut*, March 20, 1925.

Halushko, D. "Lytsari zrady" (Knights of Treason), *Chervonyi shliakh*, No. 2–3, 1934, pp. 177–201.

Han, O. Tragediia Mykoly Khvyl'ovoho. n.p. Prometei, n.d.

Harkins, William E. "Slavic Formalist Theories in Literary Scholarship," *Word*, VII, No. 2 (August, 1951), 177–86.

Hirchak, Ie. F. Na dva fronta v bor'be s natsionalizmom (The Struggle against Nationalism on Two Fronts). Moscow-Leningrad, Gosizdat, 1930.

—— Shumskizm i rozlam v KPZU (Shumskism and the Split in the CPWU). Kharkov, Derzhavne vydavnytstvo Ukraïny, 1928.

Hirniak, Iosyp. "Birth and Death of the Modern Ukrainian Theater," in Soviet Theaters: 1917–41. New York, Research Program on the USSR, 1954, pp. 256–338.

—— "Mystets'ke obiednannia 'Berezil' " (The Artistic Association Berezil'), *Kyïv*, No. 3, 1952, pp. 159–66.

Hlobenko, M. "Nainovisha doba: Literatura" (The Latest Period: Literature), in Entsyklopediia ukraïnoznavstva. Munich, Molode zhyttia, 1949. Vol. II, pp. 775–85.

—— "Twenty-five Years of Ukrainian Literature in the USSR," *Slavonic and East European Review*, XXXIII, No. 80 (December, 1954), 1–16.

Holubenko, Petro. Vaplite. n.p. Orlyk, 1948.
Hordyns'kyi, Iaroslav. Literaturna krytyka pidsoviets'koï Ukraïny (Literary Criticism in the Soviet Ukraine). Ukraïns'ka Mohylians'ko-Mazepyns'ka Akademiia Nauk, L'vov, 1939.
"Hotuvannia do pershoho vseukraïns'koho zïzdu radians'kykh pys'-mennykiv" (Preparation for the First All-Ukrainian Congress of Soviet Writers), Visti, May 17, 1933.
Hrudyna, D. "Dekliaratsii i manifesty: Pro shliakhy Berezolia" (Declarations and Manifestoes: The Paths of Berezil'), Krytyka, No. 2, 1931, pp. 92–108.
Hrushevsky, Michael. A History of Ukraine. New Haven, Yale University Press, 1941.
Hryshko, Vasyl' (ed.). Volodymyr Sosiura: zasudzhene i zaboronene (Volodymyr Sosiura: Condemned and Banned Poems). New York, 1952.
Iakovenko, H. "Pro krytykiv i krytyku v literaturi" (On Critics and Criticism in Literature), Kul'tura i pobut, No. 17, April 30, 1925.
Iakubovs'kyi. "Piatnadtsiat' " (Fifteen), Zhyttia i revoliutsiia, No. 11–12, 1932, pp. 49–82.
Ianovs'kyi, Iurii. Chotyry shabli (Four Sabres). Prague, Kolos, 1941.
Iavors'kyi, M. "K istorii KP(b)U" (To the History of the CP[B]U), in Oktiabr'skaia revoliutsiia i pervoe piatiletie (The October Revolution: The First Five Years). Kharkov, Gosudarstvennoe izdatel'stvo Ukrainy, 1922, pp. 93–130.
—— Korotka istoriia Ukraïny (A Short History of the Ukraine). Kharkov, Derzhavne vydavnytstvo Ukraïny, 1927.
"Iazyk ukrainskoi khudozhestvennoi literatury" (The Language of Ukrainian Belles-Lettres, Literaturnaia gazeta, April 16, 1934.
"Iednannia radians'kykh kul'tur" (Unity of Soviet Cultures), Khronika, Chervonyi shliakh, No. 3, 1929, pp. 144–46.
Iefremov, Serhii. Istoriia ukraïns'koho pys'menstva (A History of Ukrainian Literature). 4th ed. Vol. II. Kiev-Leipzig, Ukraïns'ka nakladnia, 1923.
Islamei. "Ieshche ob ukrainskom shovinizme" (More about Ukrainian Chauvinism), Zhizn' iskusstva, June 15, 1926.
Iudin, P. "Protiv izvrashchenii Leninskogo ucheniia o kul'turnoi revoliutsii" (Against Distortion of Lenin's Teaching on the Cultural Revolution), Pravda, April 23, 1932.
Iuzovskii, Iu. "Pateticheskaia sonata: p'esa Kulisha v Kamernom teatre" (Sonata Pathetique: Kulish's Play in the Kamerny Theater), Literaturnaia gazeta, January 4, 1932.
"K politicheskim itogam vsesoiuznogo s''ezda" (Political Conclusions of the All-Union Congress), Na literaturnom postu, No. 10, 1928, pp. 1–5.

Kachaniuk, M. "Materialy do istoriï futuryzmu na radians'kii Ukraïni" (Materials for the History of Futurism in the Soviet Ukraine), *Literaturnyi arkhiv*, I–II (1930), 186–92; III–IV (1930), 312–18.

Kaganovich, N. "Zametki o iazyke" (Notes on Language), *Literaturnaia gazeta*, June 14, 1934.

Kerzhentsev, P. "Deiaki pytannia literaturnoï polityky" (Some Questions of Literary Politics), *Chervonyi shliakh*, No. 9, 1930, pp. 80–93.

Khinkulov, L. Slovnyk ukraïns'koï literatury (A Dictionary of Ukrainian Literature). Kharkov, 1949.

Khmuryi, V. Iu. Dyvnych and Ie. Blakytnyi. V maskakh epokhy (The Masks of an Era). n.p. 1948.

Khrystïuk, Pavlo. "Rozpechenym perom" (With a Scorching Pen), *Vaplite*, No. 5, 1927, pp. 194–203.

Khvylia, Andrii. Iasnoiu dorohoiu (Along a Bright Path). Kharkov, Derzhavne vydavnytstvo Ukraïny, 1927.

—— "Literatura sostavnaia chast' stroitel'stva ukrainskoi sovetskoi kul'tury" (Literature—a Component Part in the Building of Soviet Ukrainian Culture), *Literaturnaia gazeta*, July 29, 1933.

—— Pro nashi literaturni spravy (About Our Literary Affairs). Kharkov, Proletarii, 1926.

—— "Stan na movnomu fronti" (The Situation on the Linguistic Front), *Visti*, June 30, 1933.

—— Vid ukhylu v prirvu (From Deviation to Schism). Kharkov, Derzhavne vydavnytstvo Ukraïny, 1928.

Khvyl'ovyi, Mykola. "Apolohety pysaryzmu: do problemy kul'turnoï revoliutsii" (The Apologians of Scribbling: On the Problem of Cultural Revolution), *Kul'tura i pobut*, February 28, March 7, 14, 21, 28, 1926.

—— "Do knyhy sto trydsiat' druhoï" (Preface to the Book 132), *Literaturnyi iarmarok*, No. 2, 1929, pp. 1–9.

—— Dumky proty techiï (Thought against the Current). Kharkov, Derzhavne vydavnytstvo Ukraïny, 1926.

—— Kamo hriadeshy (Whither Are You Going?). Kharkov, Knyhospilka, 1925.

—— "Krychushche bozhyshche" (The Lamenting Deity), *Komunist*, January 27, 1930.

—— "Odvertyi lyst do Volodymyra Koriaka" (An Open Letter to Volodymyr Koriak), *Vaplite*, No. 5, 1927, pp. 158–73.

—— "Sotsiolohichnyi ekvivalent triokh krytychnykh ohliadiv" (The Sociological Equivalent of Three Critical Views), *Vaplite*, No. 1, 1927, pp. 80–101.

—— Tvory (Works). Vol. I. Kharkov, Derzhavne vydavnytstvo Ukraïny, 1927.

—— "Val'dshnepy" (The Woodsnipes), *Vaplite*, No. 5, 1927, pp. 5–69.

—— "Za konsolidatsiiu" (Toward a Consolidation), *Chervonyi shliakh*, No. 4, 1939, pp. 88–91.

Klen, Iurii. Spohady pro neokliasykiv (Reminiscences about the Neo-classicists). Munich, Ukraïns'ka vydavnycha spilka, 1947.

K-ko, H. "Lyst Ievhena Pluzhnyka v den' vyroku" (Letter of Eugene Pluzhnyk Written on the Day of Verdict), *Nashi dni*, No. 11, November, 1943.

Knorin, W. (ed.). Communist Party of the Soviet Union: A Short History. Moscow, Leningrad, Cooperative Publishing Society of Foreign Workers in the USSR, 1935.

"Ko vsem chlenam RAPP" (To All Members of RAPP), *Na literaturnom postu*, No. 13–14, 1930, pp. 1–8.

Kokot, S. "Dolia ukraïns'kykh pys'mennykiv pid bol'shevykamy" (The Fate of Ukrainian Writers under Bolshevik Rule), *Krakivs'ki visti*, October 27, 28, 29, 1943.

Kolarz, Walter. Russia and Her Colonies. London, George Philip, 1952.

Koriak, Volodymyr. Borot'ba za Shevchenka (The Struggle for Shevchenko). Kharkov, 1925.

—— "Khudozhnia literatura na suchasnomu etapi sotsialistychnoho budivnytstva" (Literature in the Present Phase of Socialist Construction), *Chervonyi shliakh*, No. 5, 1931, pp. 69–77; No. 6, 1931, pp. 83–88.

—— Narys istoriï ukraïns'koï literatury: Burzhuazne pys'menstvo (An Outline of the History of Ukrainian Literature: The Bourgeois Literature). Kharkov, 1929.

—— Orhanizatsiia zhovtnevoï literatury (The Organization of the October Literature). Kharkov, Derzhavne vydavnytstvo Ukraïny, 1925.

—— "Z literaturnoho zhyttia" (Literary Life), *Kul'tura* (L'vov), No. 3–4, 1927, pp. 106–12.

Korneychuk, A. "Ukrainian Literature Today," *Soviet Literature*, No. 3, 1949, pp. 145–55.

Kostiuk, H. "Stalinskaia chistka Ukrainy" (The Stalinist Purge of the Ukraine). Unpublished manuscript, New York, Research Program on the USSR, 1953.

—— "Ukraïns'ki pys'mennyky ta vcheni u bol'shevyts'kykh tiurmakh i taborakh: Spohady ta zustrichi" (Ukrainian Writers and Scholars in Bolshevik Prisons and Camps: Reminiscences and Meetings), *Krakivs'ki visti*, November 13, 14, 16, 17, 1943.

Kotsiuba, H. "Teatr Berezil' " (The Berezil' Theater), *Kul'tura i pobut*, No. 13, April 2, 1927.

Kovalenko, B. "Cherhovi zavdannia perebudovy roboty VOAPPu" (The Next Tasks in the Reconstruction of VOAPP's Work), *Zhyttia i revoliutsiia*, No. 1, 1932, pp. 99–108.

—— "Natsionalisticheskie tendentsii v ukrainskoi literature" (Nationalist Tendencies in Ukrainian Literature), *Krasnaia nov'*, No. 7, 1933, pp. 203–14.

—— "Ukrainskaia literatura pered novimy zadachami" (Ukrainian Literature Before the New Tasks), *Na literaturnom postu*, No. 30, 1931, pp. 2–6.

—— "Vsesoiuznyi smotr proletarskoi literatury: Itogi plenuma VOAPP" (The All-Union Survey of Proletarian Literature: Conclusions of the Plenum of VOAPP), *Na literaturnom postu*, No. 17, 1931, pp. 1–3.

—— "Za vsesoiuznoe napostovstvo" (For All-Union On Guardism), *Na literaturnom postu*, No. 1, 1939, pp. 6–9.

Krol', A. "Vseukrainskii s"ezd pisatelei" (The All-Ukrainian Congress of Writers), *Literaturnaia gazeta*, June 26, 1934.

Kulish, Mykola. "Krytyka chy prokurors'kyi dopyt" (Criticism or Interrogation by a Procurator), *Vaplite*, No. 5, 1927, pp. 146–57.

—— Tvory (Works). New York, Ukraïns'ka vil'na akademiia nauk v SShS, 1955.

Kulyk, Ivan. Ohliad revoliutsiï na Ukraïni (A Survey of the Revolution in the Ukraine). Vol. I. Kharkov, Vseukraïns'ke derzhavne vydavnytstvo, 1921.

—— "Peredz̈izdna sytuatsiia" (The Situation before the Congress), *Radians'ka literatura*, No. 5, 1933.

—— "Pidsumky i perspektyvy" (Resumes and Perspectives), *Chervonyi shliakh*, No. 4, 1933, pp. 92–100.

—— "Razvernutym frontom" (In an Expanded Front Line), *Literaturnaia gazeta*, February 11, 1933.

—— "Ukrainian Soviet Literature," *Literature of the Peoples of the USSR, Voks Almanac*, No. 7–8, 1934, pp. 53–59.

—— "Za bol'shevistskuiu bditel'nost' " (For Bolshevik Vigilance), *Literaturnaia gazeta*, April 23, 1933.

Kurbas, Les'. "Shliakhy 'Berezolia' " (The Paths of Berezil'), *Vaplite*, No. 3, 1927, pp. 141–65.

Kyryliuk, Ie. "Leninove vchennia pro dva shliakhy kapitalistychnoho rozvytku v zastosovanni do istoriï ukraïns'koï literatury" (Lenin's Teaching about Two Paths of Capitalist Development in Application to the History of Ukrainian Literature), *Zhyttia i revoliutsiia*, No. 10, 1933, pp. 76–84.

Lakyza, I. "Na literaturnomu fronti" (On the Literary Front), *Literaturnyi arkhiv*, III (1939), 3–15.

Lawrynenko, Jurij. Ukrainian Communism and Soviet Russian Policy toward the Ukraine: An Annotated Bibliography, 1917–1953. New York, Research Program on the USSR, 1953.

Leites, A., and M. Iashek. Desiat' rokiv ukraïns'koï literatury: 1917–1927 (Ten Years of Ukrainian Literature: 1917–1927). 2 vols. Instytut Tarasa Shevchenka, Kharkov, Derzhavne vydavnytstvo Ukraïny, 1928.

Lenin, V. I. Sochineniia (Works). 3d ed. Moscow, Gosudarstvennoe izdatel'stvo, Partizdat, 1930–35.

Lenin, V. I., and J. V. Stalin. O bor'be za ustanovlenie sovetskoi vlasti na Ukraine (On the Struggle for the Establishment of Soviet Government in the Ukraine). Kiev, Partizdat TsK KP(b)U, 1938.

Levada, O. "Notatky pro tvorchist' Mykoly Bazhana" (Notes on the Creative Art of Mykola Bazhan), Radians'ka literatura, No. 7, 1933.

"Literatura i iskusstvo: Vtoroi plenum orgkomiteta SSP SSSR" (Literature and Art: Second Plenum of the Organizing Committee of the Soviet Writers' Union of the USSR), Novyi mir, No. 2, 1933, pp. 248–67.

Literaturnaia entsiklopediia (The Literary Encyclopaedia). Moscow, Gosizdat, 1929–39.

Liubchenko, Arkadii. "Ioho taiemnytsia" (His Secret), Nashi dni, No. 5, 1943, pp. 4–5, 10–12.

"Lyst III: O. Kopylenko do Hr. Epika" (Letter III: O Kopylenko to Hr. Epik), Literaturnyi iarmarok, No. 7, 1930, pp. 101–6.

Majstrenko, Iwan. Borot'bism: A Chapter in the History of Ukrainian Communism. New York, Research Program on the USSR, 1954.

Manning, Clarence A. Ukraine under the Soviets. New York, Bookman Associates, 1953.

Maslov, S. I., and Ie. P. Kyryliuk. Narys istorii ukrains'koi literatury (A Survey of the History of Ukrainian Literature). Kiev, Vydavnytstvo Akademii Nauk URSR, 1945.

Miiakovs'kyi, Volodymyr. "Zoloti zerniatka: Pamiati M. O. Drai-Khmary" (The Golden Seed: In Memory of M. O. Drai-Khmara), Nashi dni, No. 11, 1943, pp. 4–5.

Mykytenko, Ivan. "Put' k soiuzu" (The Path to Union), Literaturnaia gazeta, June 14, 1934.

—— Za hegemoniiu proletars'koi literatury (For the Hegemony of Proletarian Literature). n.p. 1930.

"Na pervom vsesoiuznom s"ezde proletarskikh pisatelei" (At the First All-Union Congress of Proletarian Writers), Khronika, Na literaturnom postu, No. 10, 1928, pp. 74–80; No. 11–12, 1928, pp. 118–24.

"Na pidhotovlenomu grunti" (On Prepared Ground), Literatura, nauka, mystetstvo, August 10, 1924.

"Nashe siohodni" (Our Today), Vaplite, No. 3, 1927, pp. 131–40.

"Novye knigi pisatelei Ukrainy" (New Books by Ukrainian Writers), Literaturnaia gazeta, March 14, 1934.

Novyts'kyi, Mykola. Na iarmarku (At the Fair). Kharkov, Hart, 1930.

Nusinov, I. "Natsional'naia literatura" (National Literature) in Literaturnaia entsiklopediia, VII (1934), 627–41.

Nykolyshyn, S. Kul'turna polityka bol'shevykiv i ukrains'kyi kul'turnyi protses (The Cultural Policy of the Bolsheviks and the Ukrainian Cultural Development). n.p. 1947.

—— "Natsionalizm u literaturi SUZ" (Nationalism in the Literature of the Eastern Ukraine), in Na sluzhbi natsiï (In the Service of the Nation). Paris, 1938, pp. 107–40.

"O literature narodov SSSR" (Literature of the Peoples of the USSR), Oktiabr', No. 10, 1925, pp. 3–5.

"O poputnichestve i soiuznichestve" (The Fellow Travelers and Unionism), Na literaturnom postu, No. 26, 1931, pp. 1–6.

Ocherk istorii ukrainskoi sovetskoi literatury (An Outline of the History of Ukrainian Soviet Literature). Moscow, Izdatel'stvo Akademii Nauk SSSR, 1954.

Odarchenko, Petro. "Soviet Interpretation of Shevchenko," Unpublished manuscript, New York, Research Program on the USSR, 1954.

"Otsinka roboty 'Hartu' i 'Pluha' " (Appraisal of the Work of "Hart" and "Pluh"), Literatura, nauka, mystetstvo, September 14, 1924.

P. K. and O. R. "Za tvorchu realizatsiiu ukhval lystopadovoho plenumu Tsk i TsKK KP(b)U" (For Creative Realization of the Resolutions of the November Plenum of the CC and CCC of the CP[B]U), Zhyttia i revoliutsiia, No. 1, 1934, pp. 163–77.

Page, Stanley. "Lenin and Self-Determination," The Slavonic and East European Review, XXVIII, No. 71 (April, 1950), 342–58.

Pap, Michael. "Soviet Difficulties in the Ukraine," The Review of Politics, No. 2, April, 1952, pp. 204–32.

"Pered vsesoiuznym s"ezdom proletarskikh pisatelei" (Before the All-Union Congress of Proletarian Writers), Oktiabr', No. 4, 1928, pp. 209–16.

"Pershyi vsesoiuznyi z'izd radians'kykh pys'mennykiv" (The First All-Union Congress of Soviet Writers), Visti, March 30, 1933.

Pershyi vseukraïns'kyi z'izd proletars'kykh pys'mennykiv: Stenohrafichnyi zvit (The First All-Ukrainian Congress of Proletarian Writers: Stenographic Report). Kharkov, Derzhavne vydavnytstvo Ukraïny, 1927.

Pervyi vsesoiuznyi s"ezd sovetskikh pisatelei, 1934: Stenograficheski otchët (The First All-Union Congress of Soviet Writers, 1934: Stenographic Report). Moscow, Gosizdat, 1934.

"P'esy poluchivshie premii" (Plays Receiving Awards), Literaturnaia gazeta, April 4, 1934.

"Pid haslom literaturnoho internatsionalu" (Under the Slogan of the Literary International), Literaturnyi arkhiv, IV–V (1931), 129–47.

Pidhainyi, L. "Ukrainskaia sovetskaia literatura" (Ukrainian Soviet Literature) in Literaturnaia entsiklopediia, XI (1939), 576–88.

Pidhainyi, S. Ukraïns'ka inteligentsiia na Solovkakh: spohady 1939–41 (Ukrainian Intellectuals on the Solovky). Neu Ulm, Prometei, 1947.

"Pidsumky pershoho plenumu Orgkomitetu Spilky Radians'kykh Pys'-mennykiv SRSR ta zavdannia radians'koï literatury USRR" (Summary of the First Plenum of the Organizing Committee of the Soviet

Writers' Union of the USSR and the Tasks of Soviet Literature), *Visti*, January 26, 1933.

Piksanov, N. Gorkii i natsionalnye literatury (Gorky and the National Literatures). Moscow, Ogiz, 1946.

Pipes, Richard. The Formation of the Soviet Union: Communism and Nationalism, 1917–1923. Cambridge, Harvard University Press, 1954.

"Pis'mo tov. Stalina i zadachi VOAPP" (Stalin's Letter and the Tasks of VOAPP), *Na literaturnom postu*, No. 35–36, 1931, pp. 1–3.

"Platforma vseukrainskoi assotsiatsii proletarskikh pisatelei" (The Platform of the All-Ukrainian Association of Proletarian Writers), *Kommunist*, February 28, 1924.

"Podlinnoe vzaimodeistvie literatur narodov SSSR" (Genuine Collaboration between the Literatures of the Peoples of the USSR), *Literaturnaia gazeta*, May 25, 1933.

Popov, M. Narys istorii KP(b)U (An Outline of the History of the CP[B]U). 2d ed. Kharkov, Vydavnytstvo Proletarii, 1929.

Pors'kyi, Volodymyr. "Lebedynyi spiv" (Swan Song), *Kyïv*, No. 1, 1951, pp. 27–39.

"Pro vydavnychu robotu" (On Editorial Work), *Krytyka*, No. 9, 1931, pp. 3–10.

"Pro zavdannia perebudovy VUSPPu" (On the Tasks of VUSPP's Reconstruction), *Zhyttia i revoliutsiia*, No. 1, 1932, pp. 130–33.

"Proloh do knyhy sto sorok druhoï" (Prologue to Book 142), *Literaturnyi iarmarok*, No. 12, 1930.

Pylypenko, Serhii. "Nashi hrikhy" (Our Sins), *Pluzhanyn*, No. 4–5, 1925.

"Pys'mennyky Ukraïny vitaiut' istorychnu postanovu TsK VKP(b)" (Ukrainian Writers Greet the Historic Resolution of the CC CPSU), *Visti*, May 11, 1932.

Radkey, Oliver H. The Election to the Russian Constituent Assembly of 1917. Cambridge, Harvard University Press, 1950.

Radzykevych, Volodymyr. Ukraïns'ka literatura XX stolittia (Ukrainian Literature of the Twentieth Century). Philadelphia, Ameryka, 1952.

Ravich-Cherkasskii, M. Istoriia kommunisticheskoi partii (b-ov) Ukrainy (The History of the Communist Party [Bolsheviks] of the Ukraine). Kharkov, Gosudarstvennoe izdatel'stvo Ukrainy, 1923.

Reshetar, John S., Jr. "National Deviation in the Soviet Union," *The American Slavic and East European Review*, No. 2, April 1953, pp. 162–74.

—— The Ukrainian Revolution. Princeton, Princeton University Press, 1952.

"Retsydyvy vchorashnioho" (Setbacks of Yesterday), *Hart*, No. 2–3, 1927, pp. 74–84.

Revuts'kyi, Valeriian. "Mykola Kulish," *Novi dni,* No. 14, 1951, pp. 13–18.

Reznikov, B. H. Vasil'kovski, I. Ierukhimovich, I. Bogovoi, and A. Nazarov. "Neudavshaiasia patetika (P'esa 'Pateticheskaia sonata' N. Kulisha v Kamernom teatre)" (Unsuccessful Pathetics: The Play "Sonata Pathetique" by M. Kulish in the Kamerny Theater), *Pravda,* February 9, 1932.

"Rezoliutsiia zahal'nykh zboriv 'Prolitfrontu' v spravi konsolidatsiï syl proletars'koi literatury vid 19 sichnia 1931 roku" (Resolution of the General Meeting of the "Prolitfront." Held on January 19, 1931, concerning the Consolidation of the Forces of Proletarian Literature), *Prolitfront,* No. 7–8, 1930, pp. 321–26.

Rodov, S. "Pos'le vsesoiuznoi konferentsii proletarskikh pisatelei" (After the All-Union Conference of Proletarian Writers), *Oktiabr',* No. 2, 1925, pp. 120–31.

Rulin, Peter. "Das ukrainische Theater in den Revolutionsjahren," Kulturchronik, *Slavische Rundschau,* No. 8, 1929, pp. 709–12.

"Samoopredelenie ili shovinizm" (Self-Determination or Chauvinism), *Zhizn' iskusstva,* No. 14, April 6, 1926.

Savchenko, Fedir. Zaborona ukraïnstva 1876 r. (The Ban on Publishing in Ukrainian in 1876). Kharkov-Kiev, 1930.

Selivanovskii, A. "Na pochatkovi novoho etapu" (At the Beginning of a New Phase), *Krytyka,* No. 10, 1930, pp. 12–20.

———— "V bor'be protiv shovinizma" (In the Struggle against Chauvinism), *Na literaturnom postu,* No. 4, 1927, pp. 41–46.

———— "Za iedinstvo natsional'nykh otriadov proletarskoi literatury" (For a Union of National Detachments of Proletarian Literature), *Na literaturnom postu,* No. 5, 1928, pp. 33–38.

Semenko, Mykhail', Geo Shkurupii, and Mykola Bazhan. Zustrich na perekhresnii stantsiï: Rozmova triokh (Meeting at the Crossroads: A Conversation of a Trio). Kiev, Bumerang, 1927.

Senchenko, I. "Iz zapysok" (Notes), *Vaplite,* No. 1, 1927, pp. 3–11.

———— "V parkakh zblidlykh fantazii" (In the Parks of Pale Phantasies), *Prolitfront,* No. 2, 1930, pp. 177–210.

Shchupak, Samiilo. Borot'ba za metodolohiiu (A Struggle for Methodology). n.p. n.d.

———— "Literaturnyi front na Ukraine" (The Literary Front in the Ukraine), *Na literaturnom postu,* No. 18, 1931, pp. 12–16.

———— "Literaturnyi front na Ukraïni" (The Literary Front in the Ukraine), *Zhyttia i revoliutsiia,* No. 5–6, 1931, pp. 105–17.

Sherekh, Iurii (Shevelov, G.). "Edvard Strikha: The History of a Literary Mystification," *The American Slavic and East European Review,* XIV, No. 1 (February, 1955), 93–107.

———— "Khvyl'ovyi bez polityky" (Khvyl'ovyi without Politics), *Novi dni,* No. 40, 1953, pp. 2–6.

—— "Kolir nestrymnykh palakhtin': 'Vertep' Arkadiia Liubchenka" (The Colour of Irresistible Flames: "The Puppet Show" by Arkadii Liubchenko), *MUR,* I, 147–74. n.p. Prometei, 1946.

—— "Poeziia Mykoly Zerova" (The Poetry of Mykola Zerov), *Khors,* I (1946), 112–30.

—— "Pryntsypy i etapy bol'shevyts'koï movnoï polityky na Ukraïni" (Principles and Stages of the Bolshevik Linguistic Policy in the Ukraine), *Suchasna Ukraïna,* June 29, July 13, 1952.

—— "Trends in Ukrainian Literature under the Soviets," *The Ukrainian Quarterly,* No. 2, 1948, pp. 151–67.

Shliakhy rozvytku suchasnoï literatury: Dysput 24 travnia 1925 (The Paths of Development of Contemporary Literature: Debate on May 24, 1925). Kiev, Derzhavne vydavnytstvo Ukraïny, 1925.

"Shliakhy rozvytku ukraïns'koho teatru" (The Paths of Development of Ukrainian Theater), *Literatura i mystetstvo,* June 22, 1929.

Simmons, Ernest J. An Outline of Modern Russian Literature (1880–1940). Ithaca, Cornell University Press, 1944.

Slavutych, Iar. "Iak Moskva nyshchyla i nyshchyt' ukraïns'kykh pys'-mennykiv" (How Moscow Destroyed and Is Destroying Ukrainian Writers), *Svoboda,* Sunday Edition, November 2, 1952.

Slisarenko, Oleksa. "V borot'bi za proletars'ku estetyku" (In the Struggle for Proletarian Aesthetics), *Vaplite, zoshyt pershyi,* 1926, pp. 18–24.

Slonim, Marc. Modern Russian Literature. New York, Oxford University Press, 1953.

"Slovo partii skazano" (The Party's Word Has Been Spoken), *Oktiabr',* No. 7, 1925, pp. 3–7.

Sovetskaia literatura na novom etape: Stenogramma pervogo plenuma orgkomiteta soiuza sovetskikh pisatelei (29 oktiabria—3 noiabria 1932) (Soviet Literature in a New Stage: Stenographic Report of the First Plenum of the Organizing Committee of the Soviet Writers' Union Held from October 29 to November 3, 1932). Moscow, Sovetskaia literatura, 1933.

"Sprava 'Spilky Vyzvolennia Ukraïny' " (The Case of the Union for the Liberation of the Ukraine), *Visti,* March 23, 1930.

"Statut Vil'noï Akademiï Proletars'koï Literatury VAPLITE" (The Constitution of the Free Academy of Proletarian Literature), *Vaplite, zoshyt pershyi,* 1926, pp. 94–96.

Stavskii. "Litsom k tvorchestvu" (Facing the Creative Arts), *Pravda,* December 23, 1931.

Stepniak, M. "Ohliad potochnoï virshovanoï poezii" (A Survey of Current Poetry in Verse), *Hart,* No. 5, 1929.

Strikha, Edvard. Parodezy, Zozendropiia, avtoekzekutsiia (Parodezy, Zozendropiia, Autoexecution). New York, Slovo, 1955.

Struve, Gleb. Soviet Russian Literature: 1917–1950. Norman, University of Oklahoma Press, 1951.

Sutyrin, V. "Napostovskii dnevnik: O zadachakh VOAPPa" (An On Guardist Diary: The Tasks of VOAPP), Na literaturnom postu, No. 1, 1929, pp. 7–12.

Tarnovs'kyi, M. "Pionery ukraïns'koï zhovtnevoï literatury" (The Pioneers of Ukrainian October Literature), in Vpered, Calendar, New York, 1928, pp. 70–85.

Turkalo, Kost'. "Sorok piat' " (Forty-five), Novi dni, November, December, 1952; January, February, March, April, May, 1953.

Tychyna, Pavlo. "Lyst do redaktsiï" (A Letter to the Editor), Komunist, November 3, 1927.

"U pisatelei" (With the Writers), Literaturnaia gazeta, December 23, 1932.

"Uhody mizh orhanizatsiiamy 'Hart' i AsKK (Komunkul't)" (Agreements between the Organizations "Hart" and AsKK [Komunkul't]), Visti, April 5, 1925.

Ukrainets, I. "O 'Pateticheskoi sonate' Kulisha" (About the Sonata Pathetique by Kulish), Pravda, March 4, 1932.

V. P. "Mykola Zerov: Kamena, poeziï" (Mykola Zerov: Camena, Poems), in Ukraïns'kyi zasiv, No. 4, 1943, pp. 144–50.

"V radi spryiannia teatrovi 'Berezil' " (In the Council for Promotion of the Berezil' Theater), Visti, March 23, 1927.

Vedmits'kyi, O. "Literaturnyi front: 1919–1931" (The Literary Front: 1919–1931), Literaturnyi arkhiv, IV–V (1931), 104–28.

"Vseukraïns'ka federatsiia revoliutsiinykh radians'kykh pys'mennykiv oholoshuie sebe mobilizovanoiu" (The All-Ukrainian Federation of Revolutionary Soviet Writers Declares Itself Mobilized), Literatura i mystetstvo, September 14, 1930.

"VUSPP, 'Molodniak' i 'Nova Generatsiia' pryimaiut' zaklyk kharkivs'koho komsomola" (VUSPP, "Molodniak" and "New Generation" Accept the Challenge of the Kharkov Komsomol), Visti, March 4, 1930.

"Za bol'shevistskuiu konsolidatsiiu sil proletarskoi literatury" (For a Bolshevik Consolidation of the Forces of Proletarian Literature), Na literaturnom postu, No. 23–24, 1930, pp. 69–71.

"Za hegemoniiu proletars'koï literatury: Pidsumky pershoho poshyrenoho plenumu VUSPPu" (Toward the Hegemony of Proletarian Literature: Summary of the First Expanded Plenum of VUSPP), Visti, May 27, 1930.

"Za internatsional'nuiu solidarnost' " (For International Solidarity), Na literaturnom postu, No. 3, 1929, pp. 1–4.

Zelinskii, Korneli. "Otkrytoe pis'mo ukrainskim konstruktivistam-spiralistam po povodu sbornika 'Avangard 3' " (An Open Letter to

Ukrainian Constructivists-Spiralists concerning the Compendium Avant-garde 3), *Literaturnaia gazeta,* November 18, 1929.
Zerov, Mykola. Do dzherel (To the Sources). Kiev, Slovo, 1926.
—— Do dzherel (To the Sources). 2d ed., enlarged. Crakow–L'vov, Ukraïns'ke vydavnytstvo, 1943.
—— "Nashi literaturoznavtsi i polemisty" (Our Literary Scholars and Polemicists), *Chervonyi shliakh,* No. 4, 1926, pp. 151–78.
—— Nove ukraïns'ke pys'menstvo (New Ukrainian Literature). Kiev, Slovo, 1924.
Zhukova, Varvara. "Fashyzm i futuryzm" (Fascism and Futurism), *Prolitfront,* No. 3, 1930, pp. 205–28.

IV. FILES OF PERIODICALS AND NEWSPAPERS CONSULTED

American Slavic and East European Review, 1948–55.
Arka, 1948.
Chervonyi shliakh, 1923–34.
Hart, 1929–31.
Krasnaia nov', 1928–32.
Krytyka (later: Za markso-lenins'ku krytyku), 1929–31.
Kul'tura i pobut, 1925–28.
Kyïv, 1950–54.
Literatura, nauka, mystetstvo, 1924.
Literaturnaia gazeta, 1929–34.
Literaturno-naukovyi vistnyk, 1929–30.
Literaturnyi arkhiv, 1930–31.
Literaturnyi iarmarok, 1929–30.
MUR, 1946.
Na literaturnom postu, 1928–32.
Nashi dni, 1942–43.
Novi dni, 1952–55.
Oktiabr', 1924–30.
Visti VUTsVK, 1919–34.

A BIBLIOGRAPHICAL NOTE

Documentation for the last chapter has come chiefly from the Soviet Ukrainian press and periodicals. The weekly *Literaturna Ukraina* (Literary Ukraine) is in the forefront of glasnost. Reminiscent in format of the Russian *Literaturnaia gazeta* (Literary Gazette), it favors the national front, Rukh. Three of the periodicals are from Kiev: *Vitchyzna* (Fatherland), *Dnipro* (Dnieper), and *Kyiv* (Kiev), which compete in publishing material from the 1920s and 1930s with the Kharkov journal *Prapor* (Banner) and the monthly *Zhovten'* (October) appearing in Lviv. It is interesting to note that the monthly of the Academy of Sciences *Radians'ke literaturoznavstvo* (Soviet Literary Scholarship) and *Zhovten'* (October) will, from January 1990, appear under new titles, the former as *Slovo i chas* (Word and Time) and the latter as *Dzvin* (The Bell). In both cases any Soviet connotations have been dropped.

INDEX

INDEX

Academists, *see* Neoclassicists
Academy of Sciences, members purged, 191
Acmeism, 32
Across the Ukrainian Land (Antonenko-Davydovych), 118
Ad Fontes (Zerov), excerpt, 100
Adventures of Don José Pereira, The (Iohansen), 152
Against the Golden Gods (Kosynka), 116
Age of Electricity, The (Khvyl'ovyi), 112
Agriculture, mass collectivization of, 137, 188; lagging and dislocations in harvesting crops, 189; failure to fulfill plan, 190; cause of breakdown in production, 195
Aguf, 223
All-Russian Association of Proletarian Writers, *see* VAPP
All-Russian Communist Party, resolution of Central Committee, 264-65
All-Russian Union of Writers (VSP), 140
All-Ukrainian Academy of Sciences, literary critics from, listed among traitors, 221
All-Ukrainian Association of Proletarian Writers, *see* VUAPP
All-Ukrainian Association of Revolutionary Cinematographers (VUARK), 148
All-Ukrainian Association of the Marx and Lenin Institutes (VUAMLIN), 191
All-Ukrainian Center of Proletarian Writers, 58
All-Ukrainian Center of Revolutionary Literature, controversy arising out of creation of, 57
All-Ukrainian Central Committees, held unnecessary, 63
All-Ukrainian Congress, 6
All-Ukrainian Congress of Proletarian Writers, 73

All-Ukrainian Congress of Soviets, 7
All-Ukrainian Congress of Soviet Writers, First: 227-30
All-Ukrainian Congress of Writers, 205
All-Ukrainian Drama Committee, The, 130
All-Ukrainian Federation of Literary Organizations, proposed, 78; favored by Skrypnyk, 80
All-Ukrainian Literary Academy, Blakytnyi's manifesto of, 251-52
All-Ukrainian Literary Committee (Vseukrlitkom), 37, 38
All-Ukrainian Union of Proletarian Writers, *see* VUSPP
All-Ukrainian Union of the Workers of Communist Culture (VUSKK), 148
All-Union Alliance of Associations of Proletarian Writers, *see* VOAPP
All-Union Alliance of Literary Federations of All Peoples of the USSR, 78
All-Union Drama Competition, 216
All-Union Orgkomitet, *see* Orgkomitet
All-Union Party, policy, 52; resolution concerning Ukrainian literary groupings, 57; directive on fellow travelers, 58; Agitation and Propaganda Section, 140; conference at Press and Propaganda Section of Central Committee, 144; Sixteenth Congress and fate of proletarian literature, 159-67; key men in hierarchy, 192; radical change in literary development brought about by, 207; high-water mark of adulation, 230; *see also* CP(B)U; CPSU; CPWU; Party, Communist; RCP(B)
—— Central Committee: resolution on non-interference with literary affairs, 103; resolution on cultural work in Ukrainian villages, 158
America, branch of Hart founded in, 55;

330   INDEX

Irchan, Myroslav (*Continued*)
   Ukraïna, 162; elected to Orgkomitet,
   204; listed among traitors, 220, 221;
   purged, 235
I Shall Tell for All (Vlyz'ko), 126
"Istoriia zakordonnoho pashportu" (Vlyz'-
   ko), 127
Iudin, P., 217; article on RAPP, 203
Iura, H., 130
Iurodyvyi (Shevchenko), 227
Iurynets', V., 97, 135; expelled from Party
   and Academy of Sciences, 191; purged,
   235
Ivan Ivanovych (Khvyl'ovyi), 115, 152
Ivaniv-Mezhenko, Iurii, 30, 39
Ivanov, Vsevolod, 204, 236
Ivchenko, Mykhailo, 110, 118, 135; forced
   to leave the Ukraine, 119; in under-
   ground organization, 154 f.; cross-ex-
   amination of, 155; purged, 235
Izvestiia, 45, 204

Jeanne, the Soldier (Shkurupii), 127
Jewish Bund, 8
Jimmy Higgins (Sinclair), 129

Kaganovich, Lazar, 68n, 79, 87; Stalin's
   letter to, with excerpt, 66 ff.; discussion
   with Ukrainian writers, 144; voices will
   of Party to subdue peasants, 189; pro-
   nouncements regarded as revelations of
   supreme wisdom, 201; praised for rout-
   ing Ukrainian nationalism, 215; decimation of Ukrainian intelligentsia and
   writers, 237; record, 268
Kaganovich, Naum, authority on Ukrainian language, 223; quoted, 224
Kaledin, General, 7
Kamena (Zerov), 125
Kamenev, 79; opposed by Stalin, 199
Kamernyi Theater, Moscow, 132
Kamo hriadeshy (Khvyl'ovyi), excerpt, 94
Kapel'horods'kyi, P., 42, 236
Kerzhentsev, P., 161
Kharkivs'kyi proletarii, 73
Kharkov, *de facto* capital of Soviet
   Ukraine, 39; prose and poetry by shock
   workers of factory, 158; district com-
   mittee meeting, 190; conflict resulting
   from relationship between Moscow and,
   232; almost half burned down by Bol-
   sheviks, 240n
Kharkov-Katerynoslav group, 10
Khlebnikov, V., 33

Kholui, 74
Khortytsia island, 117
Khrystiuk, Pavlo, 83, 84, 191
Khulii Khuryna (Kulish), 130
Khvylia, Andrii, 59, 71, 73, 75, 76, 86, 117;
   appraisal of *The Woodsnipes*, 83; participant in Literary Discussion, 93,
   102 ff.; denunciation of bourgeois intelligentsia, 102; watchdog of Party's
   supremacy, 103; delegate to Moscow,
   144; declaration re Berezil', 215; accusation against Skrypnyk, 223; authority
   on Ukrainian language, 223; assisted in
   liquidation of opposition: fell into disgrace, 238; record, 268
"Khvyl'ovism," 79, 157
Khvyl'ovyi, Mykola (pseud. of M. Fitilov),
   37, 39, 60, 61, 62, 64, 73, 78, 136, 164,
   204; quoted, 48, 88, 153; dramatic role:
   program for VAPLITE, 62; rise and
   decline, 65-74; political role within the
   CP(B)U, 65 ff.; new conception of
   Ukrainian Communist culture, 65; demand that proletariat in Ukraine be
   de-Russified, 67; Shums'kyi's opinion
   of, 69; public recantation, 70; expulsion
   from VAPLITE, 71, 72, 263; measures
   taken to defeat, 74; bitter attack on, 79;
   fired artistic and intellectual life with
   enthusiasm, 82; a contributor to *Vaplite*, 82; novel published in *Vaplite*
   condemned, 83 f.; not barred from *Vaplite*, 84; in Europe, 87; recantation and
   return, 88; battle against Party control,
   92 ff.; challenge by, provoked Literary
   Discussion, 92; participant in Literary
   Discussion, 93-100; declaration of literary faith: admiration for Europe, 94;
   purpose in organizing VAPLITE, 96;
   anti-Moscow views, 97 f.; foundation for
   cultural theory, 99; accord between
   Zerov and, 101; warned against falling
   into mire of nationalism, 103; Skrypnyk's analysis of position of, 105 f.;
   Hirchak on errors of, 106 f.; impression
   after article by, 109; plea for a pro-
   Western orientation of literature: support among debaters, 110; writings, 112,
   152; romanticism which permeated
   earlier works, 115; work of followers for
   cause of Revolution, 119; delegate to
   Moscow, 144; fight against Party, 156,
   233; final capitulation of, and his
   group, 165; accepted as member of

Symbolists (Muzahet), 30, 33, 37, 40, 43
Synia dalechin' (Ryl's'kyi), 124
Syniavs'kyi, O., deported, 223
Syni etiudy (Khvyl'ovyi), 112
Syrtsov, 163

Tairov, A., 132
Tak zahynuv Huska (Kulish), 130
Taran, F., 73
Taras Triasylo (Sosiura), 123
Tas', D., 236
"Tasks of Cultural Construction in the
   Ukraine" (Skrypnyk), 80
Teachers, shortage of, in Soviet Ukraine,
   186
"Teatral'nyi lyst" (Kurbas), 30
Tempering, see Hart
Tereshchenko, M., 30, 38, 135, 204
Terminology, changed, 208
Textbooks, Ukrainian: used in higher
   education, 184
Theater, 50, 128 f., 149; performances in
   Little Russian dialect forbidden, 25n;
   Russification, 216; task of, 150; see also
   Berezil'
There Were Three of Us (Dos'vitnyi), 119
"Theses on the New Proletarian Art"
   (Mykhailychenko), 38
Theses on the Results of Ukrainization
   (issued by CP[B]U), 69
"Third Revolution, The" (Pidmohyl'-
   nyi), 117
Thirteenth Spring, The (Ryl's'kyi), 124
Thought control, Soviet, 237
Thoughts against the Current (Khvyl-
   ovyi), excerpt, 62
"Three Musketeers, The," 72
Through Storm and Snow (Ryl's'kyi), 124
Thus Perished Huska (Kulish), 130
Thy Name is Woman (Liubchenko), 120
Tibullus, Zerov's translation of, 125
Tikhonov, N., 204
Tkachenko, M., 15
Tkachuk, I., listed among traitors, 220;
   purged, 235
Tolstoi, Alexei, 212
Tomskii, opposed by Stalin, 199
To the Contemporaries (Os'machka), 126
"To the sources," slogan, 239
To the Sources (Zerov), excerpt, 100
"To the Workers and Peasants of the
   Ukraine" (Lenin), 17
Trade union, Shums'kyi dissatisfied with
   behavior of elite in, 68n; fear that

Writers' Union would function as a
   writers', 212
Trains Go to Berlin (Vlyz'ko), 127
Transitional period, "contradiction" of,
   180
Translators, 135
Travels of a Man in a Cap (Iohansen),
   120
"Tretia revoliutsiia" (Pidmohyl'nyi), 117
Trotsky, 79; ideology, 66; struggle be-
   tween Stalin and, 66, 199; on methods
   of art, 252
"Trotskyite" views of Rappists, 170
Trynadtsiata vesna (Ryl's'kyi), 124
Tsarist administration, see under Russia
Tulub, Z., 236
Turians'kyi, O., 80
Turkmenistan, national tendencies, 162;
   Congress of Soviet Writers held in, 227
"Tvaryna" (Slisarenko), 120
"Tvorchist' individuuma i kolektyv"
   (Ivaniv-Mezhenko), 30
Tvory (Pidmohyl'nyi), 117
Tychyna, Pavlo, 30, 38, 48, 61, 73, 91, 124,
   204, 206, 229; "poet of the Ukrainian
   Revolution": pantheistic philosophy,
   121 f.; joined VAPLITE on side of
   literature of resistance, 122; renounced
   past associations, joined the Party, 122;
   accepted as member of VUSPP, 165;
   inspired by national renaissance, 232;
   accepted controls, 242
Tytarenko, 129

Udarniki, see Shock brigades
Udarnyi Kharkov, 158
Udary molota i sertsia (Blakytnyi), 127
Ukapists (UKP), 15, 21; cultural policy:
   writers active among, 22; won over to
   Bolshevik camp, 186
"Ukapisty," see Ukrainian Communist
   Party
UKP, see Ukapists
"Ukraïna chy Malorosiia" (Khvyl'ovyi),
   98
Ukraine, changes in Soviet regime, 3;
   Revolution of 1917, 5-22; a war for na-
   tional liberation, 5; two revolutions:
   the national and the proletarian, 6;
   autonomy for, demanded by Rada, 6;
   all power passed into hands of the
   Rada: proclaimed a separate Ukrai-
   nian People's Republic, 6; Communist

government proclaimed a Soviet Republic, 7; recognized as a separate state under German occupation, 7; national government restored: the Direktoriia, 8; Bolsheviks masters of, 8 ff.; autonomy supported by Lenin, 9n; Communists in, 10-14; proclaimed a Soviet Republic, 11; Soviet disregard for rights of language and culture, 12; failure of Communist uprising in, 13; new policy of Lenin and Bolsheviks, 15 ff.; end of second period of Communist government, 15; full independence of, acknowledged, 16, 17, 20; fictitious character of the "Independent Soviet Ukraine," 20; Moscow's decision to allow "Ukrainization" of, 44; inclined to imitate her masters, 62; nationalist witch hunt, 72; criticism of, in *The Woodsnipes*, 83; fears aroused by anti-Ukrainian sentiment in Russia, 90; ideological crisis within political and cultural life, 93; best able to pass on the true heritage of Communism, 96; ideological divergencies, 106; national policy demanded a clear answer, 107; concern about results and pace of Soviet Ukrainization policy, 107; special significance of the First Five-Year Plan, 137; important part of USSR's industrial potential, 137; most rebellious country in USSR, 137; Moscow's lieutenants in, and their problems, 147-57; importance of Sixteenth Congress of Party to, 160; chosen by Party as proving ground for activities of the International Bureau of Proletarian Literature, 162; expatriate Galicians in, 164; chief testing ground for nurture of national culture, 174; debacle in, 183-202; drastic change in, 188; crucial part in building of Stalin's new empire, 189; "Postyshev reign of terror," 190 ff.; dilemma caused by policy of discrimination, 206; struggle against counterrevolutionary elements in, 183, 217; Congress of Soviet Writers held in, 227; early semi-autonomy of Ukrainian SSR, 231; emerged during Revolution as a modern nation determined to form a state, 231; literary and cultural renaissance reflects spirit of national and social liberation, 232; rising like the Phoenix from ashes, 240n; result of

Russian domination of institutions, language, and culture, 248; cultural and creative upsurge of the masses, 251; summary of most immediate tasks in fulfillment of national policy, 266-67; list of leading Communist officials in, 268-69

"Ukraine or Little Russia" (Khvyl'ovyi), 98

Ukrainets, I. (pseud.), 133

Ukrainian Academy of Sciences, 28, 33, 135; purges: section dissolved, 223

Ukrainian Communist Party (Ukraïns'ka Komunistychna Partiia), 15; see also Ukapists

Ukrainian Constituent Assembly, 7

Ukrainian Home, 30

Ukrainian Institute of Marxism and Leninism, 174

Ukrainian Military Organization, 191, 199

Ukrainian National Army, 15

Ukrainian National Revival, 25; finest symbol of, 27

Ukrainian People's Republic (Ukraïns'ka Narodnia Respublika), proclaimed by Rada, 6; reinstated, 14; government forced to abandon Kiev, 15

Ukrainian Politbureau, Skrypnyk's name sullied by members of, 193

Ukrainian-Russian relations, see Russian-Ukrainian relations

Ukrainians, persecutions under Polish rule, 162; in non-Ukrainian territories of USSR condemned to a slow Russification, 193

Ukrainian Social Democratic Party, split: Left wing merged with Borot'ba, 15

Ukrainian Socialist Revolutionary Party, split into two groups, 14; see also Borot'ba

Ukrainian SSR, early semi-autonomy, 231

Ukrainian State Theater, 28

Ukrainian Symposium, prepared by Gorky, 226

Ukrainian Trade Unions (VURPS), 158

Ukrainization, last concession to Ukrainian nationalism, 44; as propaganda, 45; attacks on, 91; theses on results of, passed by Plenum of Central Committee of the CP(B)U, 260-61; see also Nationalism, Ukrainian

Ukraïnka, Lesia, 27

Ukraïns'ka khata, 30, 82

348   INDEX

Weeds (Holovko), 120
Western Europe, orientation toward culture of, 112-20, 135, 142
"Western Ukraine," Galician writers' group, 47
Where the Roads Meet (Ryl's'kyi), 124
Whirlpool of the Revolution, 32
White Armies, mass terror as a weapon against, 13
Whither Are You Going? (Khvyl'ovyi), excerpt, 94
Wind from the Ukraine, The (Tychyna), 121
Windows, 163
Winter of 1930, The (Shkurupii), 127
Without Ground (Epik), 119
Wolf, Friedrich, 132n
Wolfe, Bertram D., 18, 20
Woodsnipes, The (Khvyl'ovyi), 83, 115; errors in, admitted, 88
Workers' clubs, 107
Working Forces, The (Ivchenko), 119
Working masses, international education of, 180; socialist nations strengthened and guided by, 181; growth of consciousness and international unification, 249
Works (Pidmohyl'nyi), 117
Workshop of the Revolutionary Word, The (MARS), 81
World revolution, 247
Writers, subsidy for travels of, 73; section of Jewish, in Prolitfront, 157; Western European leftist, 162; Party's demand to utilize old, 205; Party expulsion of a dead writer from an official organization, 221
—— Ukrainian: "nonproletarian" groups, 29-34; literary organizations Pluh (*q.v.*) and Hart (*q.v.*), 46-52; mass organization of peasant writers, 46; proletarian writers play a prominent part in literary life, 53; failure of attempt to attract, to VUAPP, 55; conferences of proletarian, 57; Pluh (*q.v.*) an organization of peasant writers, 57; anti-proletarian tendencies reflected in the work of bourgeois, 77; organization for Western Ukrainian, envisaged by Party, 78; proletarian, commanded to rid themselves of bourgeois influences, 78; charge against, a club to strike down all Soviet opponents, 89; young, must learn from European sources, 92; dull prod-

ucts of proletarian writers, 110; anti-Moscow feelings, 111; destroyed by purges, 135; First Congress of Proletarian Writers, 140; conferences with Russian writers and Party leaders, 144; delegation to Moscow, 144 ff.; program, 145; persecution of, 156; Sovietophile groups of, in Galicia, 163; Soviet policy toward, in Galicia and Western Europe: financial assistance to non-Communist, 164; end of organized resistance to Party, 165; interest in theory of culture national in form and socialist in content, 200; left defenseless, 213; Postyshev's purges took heavy toll of, 220; listed among traitors, 220; insistent and blatant demands of Party on, 222; prologue to First Congress of Soviet Writers, 227-30; in Writers' Union (*see* Union of Soviet Writers), 227 ff.; decimation of, 231-43; stand in battle against the "second revolution," 232; called on to avoid dependence on Moscow, 233; hamstrung or handcuffed, 236; came from all strata of society, 239; reason for persecution, 240; left the Ukraine with retreating German armies, 241; inspired by their own brand of Marxism, 243; organization of young writers (*see* Molodniak); *see also* Literature
Writers' Union, *see* Union of Soviet Writers

"Young Muse, The," 30
Young Theater, reformist work, 129
Youth (Khvyl'ovyi), 112
Youth (Molodniak), 76, 81, 154, 157
Yugoslav Communist Party, 14

Zaboi, 76
Zahoruiko, P., listed among traitors, 220; purged, 235
Zahul, Dmytro (I. Maidan, pseud.), 30, 31, 38, 135; symbolist poet, 122; deported, 123; purged, 235
Zakhar Vovhura (Gzhyts'kyi), 118
Zakhidnia Ukraïna, 134, 159, 162, 163
Zakut (Kulish), 133
Zalyvchyi, Andrii, 38, 127
Zan'kovets'ka, 128
Zaporosheni syliuety (Antonenko-Davydovych), 118
Zatons'kyi, Volodymyr P., 68n, 73, 75, 189,

SUPPLEMENTARY INDEX

ABOUT THE AUTHOR

Professor Luckyj is Professor Emeritus, Slavic Languages and Literatures at the University of Toronto, and one of the world's foremost authorities on the history and literature of the Ukraine.